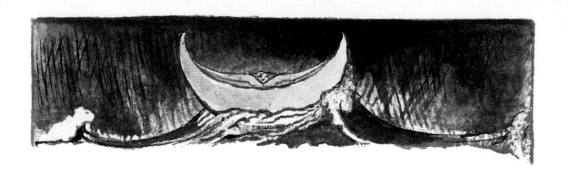

A New Waste Land

Timeship Earth at Nillennium

Michael Horovitz

New Departures

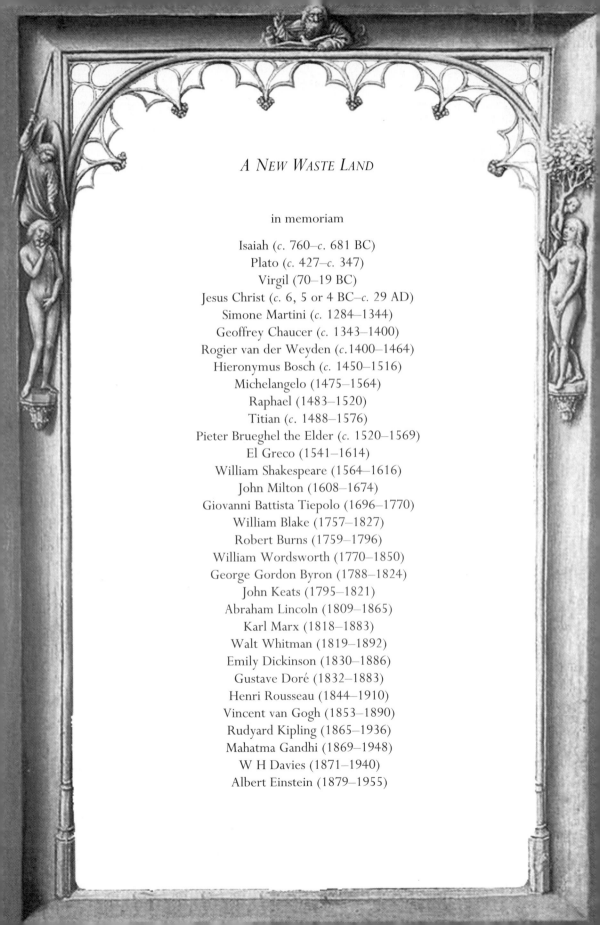

A NEW WASTE LAND

in memoriam

Isaiah (*c.* 760–*c.* 681 BC)
Plato (*c.* 427–*c.* 347)
Virgil (70–19 BC)
Jesus Christ (*c.* 6, 5 or 4 BC–*c.* 29 AD)
Simone Martini (*c.* 1284–1344)
Geoffrey Chaucer (*c.* 1343–1400)
Rogier van der Weyden (*c.*1400–1464)
Hieronymus Bosch (*c.* 1450–1516)
Michelangelo (1475–1564)
Raphael (1483–1520)
Titian (*c.* 1488–1576)
Pieter Brueghel the Elder (*c.* 1520–1569)
El Greco (1541–1614)
William Shakespeare (1564–1616)
John Milton (1608–1674)
Giovanni Battista Tiepolo (1696–1770)
William Blake (1757–1827)
Robert Burns (1759–1796)
William Wordsworth (1770–1850)
George Gordon Byron (1788–1824)
John Keats (1795–1821)
Abraham Lincoln (1809–1865)
Karl Marx (1818–1883)
Walt Whitman (1819–1892)
Emily Dickinson (1830–1886)
Gustave Doré (1832–1883)
Henri Rousseau (1844–1910)
Vincent van Gogh (1853–1890)
Rudyard Kipling (1865–1936)
Mahatma Gandhi (1869–1948)
W H Davies (1871–1940)
Albert Einstein (1879–1955)

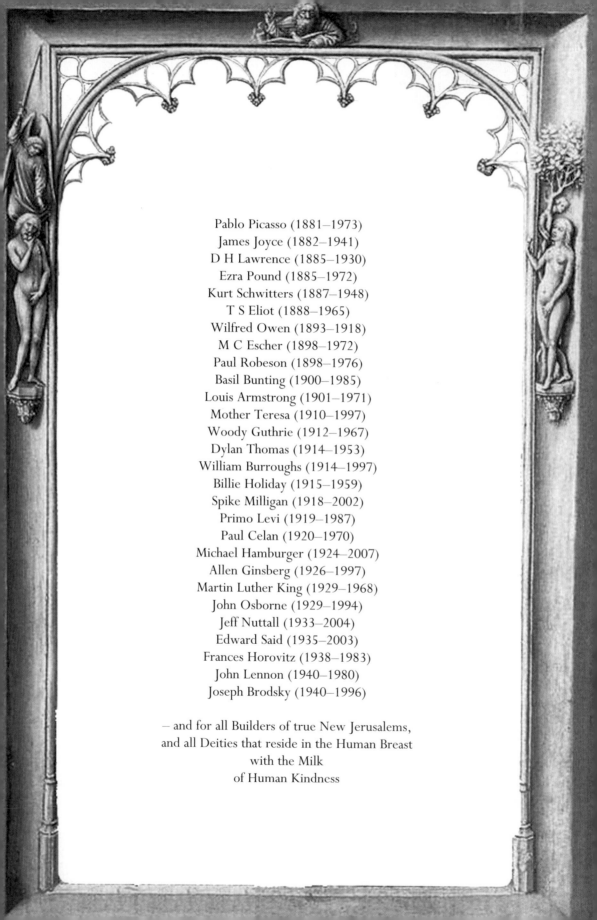

Pablo Picasso (1881–1973)
James Joyce (1882–1941)
D H Lawrence (1885–1930)
Ezra Pound (1885–1972)
Kurt Schwitters (1887–1948)
T S Eliot (1888–1965)
Wilfred Owen (1893–1918)
M C Escher (1898–1972)
Paul Robeson (1898–1976)
Basil Bunting (1900–1985)
Louis Armstrong (1901–1971)
Mother Teresa (1910–1997)
Woody Guthrie (1912–1967)
Dylan Thomas (1914–1953)
William Burroughs (1914–1997)
Billie Holiday (1915–1959)
Spike Milligan (1918–2002)
Primo Levi (1919–1987)
Paul Celan (1920–1970)
Michael Hamburger (1924–2007)
Allen Ginsberg (1926–1997)
Martin Luther King (1929–1968)
John Osborne (1929–1994)
Jeff Nuttall (1933–2004)
Edward Said (1935–2003)
Frances Horovitz (1938–1983)
John Lennon (1940–1980)
Joseph Brodsky (1940–1996)

– and for all Builders of true New Jerusalems,
and all Deities that reside in the Human Breast
with the Milk
of Human Kindness

A New Waste Land

Timeship Earth at Nillennium

by Michael Horovitz

New Departures #27-30

Published in 2007 by New Departures
PO Box 9819, London, W11 2GQ, UK

info@poetryolympics.com
www.poetryolympics.com

Designed by Michael Horovitz and Joe Paice

Front cover: Bikini Atoll Nuclear Bomb Test, 1954 (Corbis)
Back cover: Guantánamo Bay Prison, 2002 (US Navy)
Front flap: Author Photograph by David Trainer, 2000

A CIP catalogue record for this book is available from the British Library.

ISBN 1-902689-18-5   978-0-902689-18-3

Contents

A New Waste Land

There is a General Index to this book on the New Departures/Poetry Olympics website: www.poetryolympics.com

Foreword

J'Accuse . . . the UK's leading War'n'Weapons Broker at Killennium (1997-2007):

Who needs ugly rumours, when ugly facts speak for themselves? Here are just a few, culled from just two years of arms deals and warfare wheels engineered under Tony Blair.

In October 2001 he sermonised that *"The state of Africa is a scar on the conscience of the world"*, and vowed to heal it – notwithstanding the fact that over the previous year, his government had licensed arms sales to Africa netting between 126 and 130 million pounds.

In July 2002 Blair got a spokesman to denounce the Israeli-Palestinian *"cycle of violence which has scarred the region"*, just two weeks after his government had announced new guidelines which actively fuelled the violence by allowing British companies to export components to the US for incorporation into Israeli F-16 jets. According to Jack Straw, stopping the supply of the parts would have had "serious implications" for US-UK defence relations. Presumably Jackboots didn't stop to think about the serious implications, worldwide, of further US-UK support for Israel's occupation of the West Bank and Gaza Strip.

With weapon sales manager Blair having ardently engaged – and finally, in September 2003, succeeded – in flogging 66 new Hawk jets to India as it teetered on the brink of nuclear war with Pakistan, the outlook for a cessation of international hostilities was not rosy. Nor was the outlook for the poor of the Indian subcontinent: the deal cost them one billion pounds – all of 1000% the amount of aid Britain was sending them each year.

As if this wasn't two-faced enough, Saint Tone continued to piously implore the international community to help reverse the military build-up in Kashmir, whilst at the same time providing the means for its detonation. Blair's government had just licensed the selling of no less than 64 million pounds' worth of arms to India, and of another six million pounds' worth to Pakistan the year before.

Such arrogance and double standards were similarly glaring in the spring of 2003 when Blair, visibly grovelling under George Dubbya's thumb, insisted that an all-out invasion of Iraq must go ahead at all costs. He played every trick in the New Labour whiplash reserves that might coerce and/or bamboozle Parliament and the people of Britain – over two million of whom had expressed their total opposition to this illegal pre-emptive war with orderly, but unmistakeably outraged demonstrations, marches and peace rallies throughout the country on Saturday 15 February '03.

The omniscient Blair had *"absolutely no doubt at all that . . . [Saddam] was a threat"*, in possession of Weapons of Mass Destruction which could lay the UK to waste at 45 minutes' notice. The only problem with this was to sell it to the world. As the United Nations, Hans Blix, Clare Short, Robin Cook, David Kelly, Baha Mousa and others discovered to their various costs, no perversion of PR-techniques or control systems was out of bounds, if it might contribute to the achievement of this nefarious end.

Our People's Padre's oft-vaunted sincerity and "passionate beliefs" regarding his militant arms trading/warfaring tendencies were and remain irrelevant. Do we really need or want more wars to be fought on the basis of one person's "strong and barely controllable emotion", as the OED defines "passion"? Saddam Hussein, Milosevic, bin Laden, the Taleban, Mugabe, Ahmadinejad et al have said and done the most terrible things with all too much sincerity and passion. What is required is an open and accountable scrutiny of the facts – a process that seems to have been anathema to the Blairite creed.

My hope with this book is that the mistakes that have resulted in so much more premature loss of life than more temperate transatlantic leaders might have led to over the past decade or two can, at the very least, be seen as examples of how not to proceed in the future.

Many Britons dreamed, and some assumed, that the new government elected in May 1997 would seize its golden opportunity to foster and cement genuinely radical change.

Sadly, New Labour has done nothing at all – after a decade in (at first) mega-mandated power – to improve upon the self-serving status quo deplored by Samuel Taylor Coleridge in his *Fears in Solitude* of 20 April 1798, musing on the causes and effects of profiteering, oppression and sanctioned violence in the England of his day:

> "... We have offended, Oh! my countrymen!
> We have offended very grievously,
> And been most tyrannous. From east to west
> A groan of accusation pierces Heaven!
> The wretched plead against us; multitudes
> Countless and vehement, the sons of God,
> Our brethren! Like a cloud that travels on,
> Steamed up from ... swamps of pestilence.
> Even so, my countrymen! have we gone forth
> And borne to different tribes slavery and pangs.
> And, deadlier far, our vices, whose deep taint
> With slow perdition murders the whole man,
> His body and his soul! Meanwhile, at home,
> All individual dignity and power
> Engulfed in Courts, Committees, Institutions,
> Associations and Societies,
> A vain, speech-mouthing, speech-reporting Guild,
> One Benefit-Club for mutual flattery,
> We have drunk up, demure as at a grace,
> Pollutions from the brimming cup of wealth;
> Contemptuous of all honourable rule,
> Yet bartering freedom and the poor man's life
> For gold, as at a market! ..."

New Labour has been sham Labour. Let it choke on its own obsolescent exhaust fumes.

Let the post-military body politic grow, and deepest green transnational commitments redeem our planet's woes.

Long live the creative visions and common causes of all humankind.

Long live our mutual reawakening to one another's potential for decency and fellow feeling.

Even unto yours, Gorge Bash and Tory Blur, and those who succeed you in office, and your counterparts in parallel (or possibly still more corrupt) régimes elsewhere.

As Bob Dylan sang: "... don't hate nothing at all/ Except hatred".

Long live the navigators and passengers in every berth of timeship earth.

Long life, dear reader, to you.

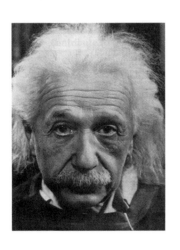

". . . they shall beat their swords into plowshares, and their spears into pruning-hooks: nation shall not lift up sword against nation, neither shall they learn war any more."

> — Isaiah (2,4), c. 747–700 BC

"The penalty that good people pay for failing to participate in public affairs is to be governed by others worse than themselves."

> — Plato, *The Republic*, c. 380 BC

"Mother is putting my new secondhand clothes in order. She prays now, she says, that I may learn in my own life . . . what the heart is and what it feels. Amen. So be it. Welcome, O life! I go to encounter . . . the reality of experience and to forge in the smithy of my soul the uncreated conscience of my race."

> — James Joyce, *A Portrait of the Artist as a Young Man*, 1914

"My subject is War, and the pity of War. The Poetry is in the pity . . ."

> — Wilfred Owen, Preface to *Poems*, 1918

". . . What is that sound high in the air
Murmur of maternal lamentation
Who are those hooded hordes swarming
Over endless plains, stumbling in cracked earth
Ringed by the flat horizon only
What is the city over the mountains
Cracks and reforms and bursts in the violet air
Falling towers
Jerusalem Athens Alexandria
Vienna London . . ."

> — T S Eliot, *The Waste Land*, 1922

When asked by an interviewer in the early 1930s what he thought of Western civilisation, Mahatma Gandhi replied:

"I think it would be a good idea."

"Science without religion is lame: religion without science is blind."

— Albert Einstein, 1940

"What sphinx of cement and aluminum bashed open their skulls
and ate up their brains and imagination?
Moloch! . . . . . . unobtainable dollars! Children screaming
under the stairways! Boys sobbing in armies! Old men
weeping in the parks! . . . Moloch the vast stone of War!
Moloch the stunned governments!
Moloch whose mind is pure machinery! Moloch whose blood is
running money! Moloch whose fingers are ten armies!
Moloch whose breast is a cannibal dynamo! Moloch whose
ear is a smoking tomb!
Moloch whose eyes are a thousand blind windows! . . . Moloch
whose factories dream and croak in the fog! Moloch whose
smokestacks and antennae crown the cities!
Moloch whose love is endless oil and stone! Moloch whose soul
is electricity and banks! . . . Moloch whose fate is a cloud
of sexless hydrogen!"

— Allen Ginsberg, *Howl*, 1955

"If the big bang does come, and we all get killed off . . . It'll
just be for the Brave New nothing-very-much-thank-you . . ."

— John Osborne, *Look Back in Anger*, 1956

When asked the effect of the Beatles on Britain, John Lennon said in 1970:

> "The people who are in control and the class system and the whole bourgeois scene are the same . . . We've grown up a little, all of us, and we are a bit freer and all that, but it's the same game. Nothing's *really* changed. They're doing exactly the same things – selling arms . . . people are living in poverty with rats crawling over them. The same bastards are in control . . . They hyped the kids and the generation."

> ". . . What are poems for? They are to console us
> with their own gift, which is like perfect pitch.
> Let us commit that to our dust. What
> ought a poem to be? Answer, *a sad*
> *and angry consolation.*"

>   – Geoffrey Hill, *The Triumph of Love*, 1999

> "Loud,
>   heap miseries upon us
>   yet entwine our arts
>   with laughters low!"

>   – James Joyce, *Finnegans Wake*, 1926–1939

> ". . . These fragments I have shored against my ruins . . ."

>   – T S Eliot, *The Waste Land*, 1922

I. *Prologue:*
The Burial
of the Living

I. *Prologue: The Burial of the Living*

  May seemed the kindest month, breeding
roses out of the dying land.
That first May day in '97
was surely signaling
our long-benighted country's
new beginning.

  After all our yesterdays'
false dawns,
sheer bliss was it in that May
to be alive in Britain
– and to see
           piercèd to the roots
           the entire
           sour shower
of sharks and hawks and toads
who'd shat on us relentlessly
for eighteen years
               – bliss to see
them in their turn, so much
terminal lost deposit
               flushed overnight
               to the sewers

  – and in their stead to lift
our spirits, minds and voice
united with the 417
candidates of our choice
in Parliament,
pledged to carry through
the practical resurrection of
human society
                – Albion awake again,
                pledged to respect
                all its people
                from the bottom up.

  That surely was
the very heaven
         so long yearned for

     – so hard worked and fought for
  and eventually
won.

We thought, at last
grim time past
       so long embossed
       at such sere cost
will be redeemed
by this concerted riff –
          time present into
          good time future,
          open accountability
          of plain dealing and fair do's.

The May landslide
exposed long buried
democratic vistas

– piled windfalls
of sungold apples
ripe and sweet
and free for all
to feast on
under trees
in all the orchards
that for eighteen years
had festered, fruitless

    [– save as nest-egg reserves
    for corporate profits
    walled in and policed,
    safe and untouchable
    as the Houses of Thatcher's
      Parliament decrees, for
      survival of the richest
      maximum security-
      portcullised against
    all access
        for the dispossessed]

But now
           – our souls exulted –
we drank the uncontaminated air
tingling with intimations
of immanent recovery
     – joined – hand in hand
as at the outset of a quest
for peaks of human aspiration
seldom scaled save on the wings
of great literature and drama,
music and art.

     Our hearts sang as we revelled
in comradeship
             – no Utopian mirage
but in the air for all to share
as Robert Burns's red red rose
of love that's newly sprung
     – tender, pure, passionate

– our flag of promise,
scent of hope,
emblem of the earthen
             beauty that is truth.

I had a dream . . .
it felt as real
as sunlight after fog

. . . the living shades
of John Milton and Blake,
Rabbie Burns and Byron,
young Wordsworth and Coleridge
and still younger Keats and Shelley
were beaming at that hour
in Westminster

. . . heart in heart
with Whitman, Wilfred Owen,
Gandhi and Paul Robeson,
Woody Guthrie and George Orwell,
Joan Littlewood and Martin Luther King

. . . their fervent communality
on the march again with ours
for a new future,

voted into power.

With Labour in office again

           we felt free

                            – Well

                              for a month

– or three . . .

. . . or seven —

Then the summer sky

darkened and shrank

— its way-marking starscape dimmed

then   v a n i s h e d

as ugly threats rained down:

— accusations and petty cuts
hassled and slashed at just those
hapless citizens boxed and strung and bundled
hard by rubbish in tight corners,
cowed against crumbling walls.

Where beds of roses had beckoned
punishing thorns closed in
and tore at the most vulnerable throats

— unwaged parents,
the handicapped and wheelchair-strapped,
underpaid nurses and teachers,
unestablished artists and writers,
beginning musicians,
skint students

— just those
whose circumstances, talents and vocations
most need support — if they're to revive, swing out
and enhance the public good.

— New Labour switched
from bleeding-heart voter-hugging
up until the landslide
to claimant-mugging

— not quite overnight
but creepily, insidiously
week by week
and day by dastard day

. . . so that the underclasses —
     powerless
     defenceless
     demoralised

were made yet more alien
— failed before they could even start:
     harassed
     panicked
     made to feel guilty

by a government department
that pretended to care
about "Social Security"

                     — though the people it rejected
                     were mostly penniless, friendless,
                     desperately ill

                            — no direction home
                     beyond Cardboard City ghettos
                     disused doorways
                     back alley waste pipes
                     of the Great God Commerce

                                  (freshly rebranded
                                  'wealth creation')

— as if to say,
          since it was ever thus
("It's the rich
what gets the gravy,
It's the poor
what gets the blame")
              — thus must it
                   ever be.

In 1996, in Singapore
Tony Blair said that
        ". . . economics
should be geared to
all our people,
not a privileged few"

                — and on the new dawn
                of Labour's triumph
                2 May '97
                the new leader
                declared it
                        ". . . now, today,
                The People's Party"

                                        But after that
                                sunrise high
                                general erection
                                thrill subsided
                                        — what beyond cold comings
                                        and short change
                                        did most people,
                                                        humble people
                                        actually have of it?

Six months on
    the rebirth of community
was aborted
    – red roses of commitment
a faint whiff of ashes
as the New Westmonsters
             binned
    every claim on public money
    that risked curbing the greedy
       to salvage the needy

                 . . . the healing balm of social justice
       – redistribution, equality
    were shelved,
         'Old Labour' ideals
erased from the lickspittle-purring
so-called Centre Left Agenda
         – Socialism excommunicated,
    an airbrushed currency,
              disused bucket –

leaving even less welfare
          than the cold comfort sediment
          we'd been force-fed for years
          on Her Maggie-sty's iron-thatched
          Flintstone farm.

The corporate breasts
of public service
stayed exactly as dry
as the Tory-scaled eye
had
            – untouched and untouchable
high in the macho turrets
of Government 'Think Tanks'

later rebranded
                        'Focus Groups'

– gee, thanks

                        . . . whilst the free milk
                        of human kindness

                                                that brazen education hacker
                                                (prentice union sacker)
                                                Thatcher snatched
                                                from huddled classrooms
                                                and drab playgrounds of the poor

                        briefly restored

                        was
                                as abruptly

                        snatched away again

                                                to remain

                                                        a distantly

                                                                fading

                                                silver-topped memory

                                                of the governors

                                                                with bottle

                                                of yore.

Down

    down

        down

we were bludgeoned
through the deepening gloom
of top-dog-eats-underdog chances
unleashed and rampant

            – rebranded 'The Free
            Market economy'

                     (. . . but
            What's free about it
            if you've no capital
            to start with?)

– and our kids

on

    down

        . . . with

            – What wondrous new
            millennial vision?

                    – What prospect beyond
                  the random website chances
                      of money-slots, repeated
                      CV shots
                                  – at conforming enough
                                (or missing out)
                for the government-acceptable careers
                  and Job Securities on offer?

                          – Not a lot

                              beyond
                      makeshift permutations
                    of a few plastic carrots

                  like staggered payrise
              measly pension, labyrinthine
            tax and insurance schemes . . .

— What use the hard-sold addictive routines
of junk shopping, comfort eating, trash telly

    leaving innermost hungers
    for reparation
    or reunion
    or sex
          unassuaged

               in the empty-bed disco
               of porn-brokered dreams

— that only hasten
          senile stumbles

  from switch-off

      to fadeaway

— where longed-for retirement
  dissolves

     to hospital

        — or as often

    to hospital waiting-list blues

with pills and booze on acrid
    smoke-punctured breath

          — old folks buffeted,
         baited and hooked
       on cost-cutting policy guidelines pulled
        on a once thriving health service
          gutted and culled —
         carved up and auctioned

               to Finance Initiative death?

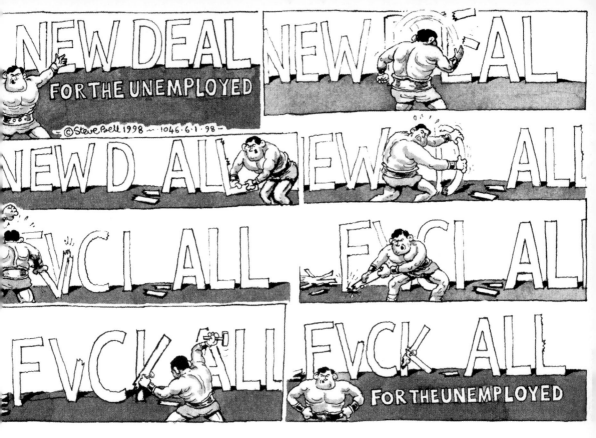

     – Uninspiring end zone . . . notwithstanding
PR sweet-talk – Third Ways and New Deals

     – like Lotto's vision of riches
          via numbers-game wheels

     – like mega-funded times out
                        ("for all the family")
          in vacuous theme tents

     – like staying snug
               plugged in
                     to the opiate pitch
     to keep switching channels, video, dvd
     and sink square-eyed, dreaming . . .
                            '*H*'*m*
                       that could be Me'

                      on so-called Reality
                      (=banality) TV

– imaginations numbed in the race
     to keep up with the *latest* latest
     smash hits and fashions

     – our just desert rations
                     set by hardnosed pap-chefs
                             in Big Brother Marketspace

— they're so *elegant*, so in*tell*igent
— oh so *digit*ally fine-tuned to mask
the machinery of meaningless

                        or murderous

    job-for-life fabrication

— palmed off as that

           smooth-orisoned
           talismanic
                ". . .*Window*
              of *Opportunity*"

        — the ". . . *welfare*
                    to work
                        for all . . . "

        — Think about it:
                  you too
    can fulfil your creativity
    with a Rewarding Job
    in advertising
    or lung cancer

      — or make a comfortable killing
    in the army
    or (lots cushier)
                in the arms trade

      — why, you might get as rich
    as BAe Systems

               or Marlboro Maggie

               or Bernie Ecclestone

   — Birmingham's Roman Catholic Cathedral

     — even as rich as the Church of England . . .

    — A prospect of millions
           of lifelong treadmills
motored by a monolithic
         state-rigged seesaw
    exacting drudgery
      for every payment,
    dumb allegiance
      for each enticement
    of escapist rewards

    programmed by philistine
      committees that cook
    the mind-blinding neon
      New Domesday Book

  of randomly space-filling
         Unadventures
  in a glumly time-serving
         Underland

    — the wonderless
     bottomless
      pit

    of enslavement
     to mill banks
    embedded in shit.

It's as D H Lawrence wrote
seventy years ago, in

'All that we have is Life' —

> "*All that we have, while we live, is life;
> and if you don't live during your life, you are a piece of dung.*
>
> *And work is life, and life is lived in work
> unless you're a wage-slave.
> While a wage-slave works, he leaves life aside
> and stands there a piece of dung.*
>
> *Men should refuse to be lifelessly at work.
> Men should refuse to be heaps of wage-earning dung.
> Men should refuse to work at all, as wage-slaves.
> Men should demand to work for themselves, of themselves,
>   and put their life in it.
> For if a man has no life in his work, he is mostly a heap of dung.*"

As packaged dung
                whizzes along
today's lifeless conveyor belts

    tomorrow's waste
                congeals

– and it feels ever more
        as though
                only *Hype*
springs diurnal
                . . . and nocturnal

            with no gods
            except money
            and destruction
            in sight
                    to save us   ". . . *victorious,*
                            happy and glorious . . ."

            – with mechanised
            brute power only

                        long
                            to rain

                                over us

– a festering smog
        of disinformation
fed with McDonald's
        all over the nation

as ordained via salesmen
        groomed to grandstand
by corporations of the Biggest
        Big Money gland

                – retailed over
                and over
                by their gutless lackeys

                all over this promised
                                once and future
                    (still could be) pleasant
                                    green land

– land the more wasted
the more they rebrand
their lies and greed

                      as if planned
from an honest concern
for a brave new Britain

– a "Humane Coalition"

– for any truly creative
worldwide order

                                – as if *not*

                                      for this fat Pharaohs' story
spun out to bury
Labour's pure-hearted lifeblood,
human rights eisteddfod

                                              – as if not
for the comforts and cruelty
of Philistia's vainglory

wallowing in the spoils
of its universal deal-broker vision
(– *vision!*)

for the fabled New Millennium.

As lust for profit
breeds blight and plague
across country and town,
  state contracts with carnage
  click legal on-line –

. . . with no new lease of life
held out by the latest
landlords and captains
   for tied tenants
                  or galley slaves
                  whipped out of mind
– dumb as donkeys
denied grazing

      – yet labouring
                  to keep
      earth's timeship afloat

      – despite their masters' scorn
      for renavigation
                  bar the occasional
                     vote-catching ruse
                  of drawing up bogus
                     new maps for survival

                  – but no concern
                  to move on from
                        upgrading the military
                  as the only safeguard
                        for peace and security

– for the sake of *'Defence'* and *'The Economy'*, they say
and bray *'for dear life'* about so-called *'tough choices'*

      while sticking to the same old commercial deceiving
      better guns, *'smarter'* bombs, evangelical poses
            – with only the same old flags unfurled
            of the same infinitely fruitless old world
            smash and grab ways of strife,
                  deathly job-stunted lives

. . . No sign of real new beginnings
in store for this planet

only more self-seeking and war

for nothing more than
the governing shares
of consumerist garbage

. . . no recourse to spiritual values,
just triumphal propaganda and sick-making pap

spread about in fake tribute to Christ's rebel rap

. . . while His essential teachings
are buried alive
by chameleon ad-men,
money-changers and warlords

– our rulers

at Nillennium

all over these

their sold-out

and bombed out

nothing new wastelands.

II.

"Growth",
they are shouting,
"Growth" –

II. *"Growth", they are shouting, "Growth" —*

On 4th October '94
the Labour Party's faithful core
gathered in Blackpool
                    — a grim dark pool
    of exiles in despair
after fifteen years of Tory rule
— yearning for something
                        — *any*thing
                    to cheer

    — and thrilled to hear
its new Foreman, Comrade Blair
                                declare
that he proposed

                    ". . . to build
        . . . a thriving community
        . . . secure in social justice,
        confident in political change;
        a land in which our children
        can bring up their children
        with a future to look forward to . . ."

    On 10th December '97
Britain's single parents
                        chilled to hear

from the selfsame so-called Right Hon
    by then
            Prime Minister Blair

(through the PA cover
of his so-called Right Hon
Social Security Ministress
and Minister for Women,
Harriet Harman)

                — the maxi-stressful news
                that their right to choose
        to spend more time
        bringing up their broods

                        was to be axed

39

– and yet, this same so-called Social
Welfare Minister-to-be, when asked
before the '97 election:
 " . . . Would you cut
   lone parents' benefit?"
      had replied,
       on the record:
               "Of course not."

– And this same so-called Leader
      (despite his supposed
      new commitment
      to leading the Nation
      as well as the Party)
                  declined
      to limousine his arse
to grace the debate
               – or rather, farce
in Parliament, at which Harman was left
(– left!)
      to rubber-stamp the bill
ordained by Her Master
               – expressly
to cut loners' benefit
               and clinch their big chill.

   A quite different but, for Tony Boy, unmissable
party gig At Home
               – being photographed
               schmoozing pop stars, luvvies,
               rich cronies and backers
took precedence

     (– "Of course.")

   But many whose hard graft,
dedication and beliefs
had moved him to prime office
– and into that Home –
were wondering *Why?*

               And wonder still.

– If Tony truly wanted *"social justice"*
for *"all* our people",
                    he could so easily have cut, instead
those lavish binges for his favoured glitterati
– *"a privileged few"*
                    who can (and do)
                    get stuffed and sloshed
                    wherever they fancy
                    anyway, any day.

– If Tony truly wanted social change
it would have been so easy to arrange
        a slap-up meal and champers with Cherie
for a party of single parents and their kids
        at Number Ten that night
along with a quorum
        of London's homeless and jobless,
        hungry and unwell

            – it could so easily have been
            a genuine social security forum
            homing in on the breadline range
            for genuine political change

– whilst he got moving on the job
he wooed us to elect him for

                                – to fight
their case for a better deal, not worse

on the shop floor of his own workplace
– his supposed parent-friendly
        consultation House
        of democratic Commons

        – especially given that
        only three years before
        he'd vowed
                    *". . . to build
                    . . . a thriving community
                    . . . a land in which our children
                    can bring up their children
                    with a future to look forward to . . ."*

So much for
             courage –
so much for
             honesty –
so much for
             trust –
so much for
             the security
             of social justice –
so much for
             the confidence
             in political change.

    It's as though this composite
would-be right-on
Blair-Harman mission
with all its undercover
blah-blah man's coercion
had been cynically planned
as an early exercise
in cutback-toting

    to see just how blandly
    *wrong*ly, *dis*honourably
                        and far to the right
                        of the Tory story
    so-called Labour Ministers
    could get away with promoting
    inhumanity and oppression

– bringing home
New blue Labour's
brazen imperious
on-message to women:

                    its plastic-souled bossmen
                    appoint plasticine-doll groupies

                    for the unquestioning servility
                    of their mouthpiece ministrations.

When Harman's usefulness as fall girl
for New Labour's discouragement
of parenting by parents
had run its course
                    without the ghost of a Fabian
                    scruple of remorse

Blair replaced her as Minister
with A(nother) Darling
                    – who continued
spouting on autocue
                    – never doubting
                    the same macho unfeeling
                    dough-for-jobs-only ceiling.

                    What such leading men most need
                    could be a course in how to weed
                    their own garden

                    how to plant
                    and beg pardon

                    – a course
                                    in standing back
                        to face fact
                        and think more clearly

                        before they act

                                        – a course

                                            in compassion
                                            imagination
                                            spirituality
                                            fellow feeling

— a course in which
an early exercise might be
picking up this leaf
of earth mother wit
from the single parent
and poet
      Jeni Couzyn:

'The Message' —

"The message of the men is linear.
Like rapid pines they swarm upwards
jostling for space
mutilating their roots in the race
sowing a shade so deep
within their conquered space
little else can grow

and growth, they are shouting, growth.

But the message of the women is love

. . . It is the luminous shining
under the greasy substance
opaque stickiness of pain and grief
greyness of wanting, heaviness of getting.

. . . It is the circle of light we carry
at the centre of our bodies
knowing, and forgetting
see with our eyes in visionary radiance
when we give birth
and lose and discover again
season after season
because we are orchard."

III.

A Little Kite Music

III. *A Little Kite Music*

All over London late for work
underslept worry-frayed faces
clench and sweat,
                    drip dream-dregs
in and out
of sardine-tin tubeholes, hurriedly
grimace into mirrors.
                        Hands
dab, adjust hair
make-up, clothing, chit-chat
to changing weather,
manoeuvre newsprint, shift
shopping, pounce
at better perches.
        Some speculate
on what might lie inside
their fellow travellers' façades,
on what they might be like
in bed.
        Not thrumming headsets
nor dregs of dawnstrained DayGlo orange
sustain body or soul through the cut-throat scrum
to more than passively blunder aboard
whatever buses capriciously zoom by
    — or pause momentarily
    or stay for long shop talks
                        then scarper like tadpoles
    — others that look sleepy will suddenly charge off
    like Dogs of The Wild Hunt
        whilst others again, though stationary
        — driverless even — throb and judder fitfully
                    as if retreading parlous junctures
                    from that morning's journeys done
                    or gearing up to forestall
                                even worse to come.

You'd think greasy tomato, oozing
bacon, egg and chip-bread fry-ups
still sloshing around catarrh-queasy gulletshafts
athwart the remorselessly closing ranks
of His-and-Hers' clattering armour
of elbow-stabbing breast-gunnels
of baggage bulging with old age
missed boat failed hope
nursed fear in thrall to
daily darkening
lonesome road rage
might leaven with their furtive eructations
of pungent softness
the arduous schlepp
for at least a few co-mangled commuters
jostled along the nerve-racked edgeworn
Edgware Road-to-Oxford Street traffic jams,
to a secret moment, or five,
of hard-won peace of mind

– but more likely only Gods know,
only noosed whelps sense
anything remotely nice about
the usual dog-tired
diesel fume fart-winded
h a l f - h o u r
s t a n d s t i l l

at merciless strident *parp*-harangued
marmoreally impervious
– unspreadable
Marmalade Arch, Capital
Interchange Dungheap
– monumental hubs
of endlessly spreading
repetitious daily grind.

– What's in a job
if clocking in, and out
on the dot
(– or out
before the dot, if poss . . .)
just for the money
is all?

Whereas
— as Lawrence saw it, in his poem

'Work' —

"There is no point in work
unless it pre-occupies you as well as occupies you.
When you are only occupied, you are an empty shell.
A man needs to be independent at his work, so that he can put his
    own self into it.

When a man puts his own self into his work
he is living, not merely working.
When men wove with their hands and their soul's attention the
    cloth they wore,
they lived themselves forth, like a tree putting out woven leaves
and it made them happy, and the woven cloth of their hands
came from them living like leaves from the tree of their life
and clothed them with living leaves . . ."

Somewhere
– not here,
                nowhere near
the partisan bellowing, sheep-herd braying
                        (– this degrades sheep)
of Prime Minister's Question Time

                – but over there
        in the museum
                        without walls
                        that's always open
                        for whoever calls
        sing other creatures
        hard at work
        and soft at play
        in un-
                employments
        that convey
        the free mind's eye

– like this poem
my dear departed
ever present
muse and mentor
Frances Horovitz wrote
in the late 1960s:

                        'London Summer' –

                                        "high flying
                                        tattered flags
                                        of blue and white
                                        a Tiepolo sky
                                        over London streets

                                        and we –
                                        summer kites
                                        borne gently down
                                        to the warm pavements
                                        at peace –
                                        stretched frail and luminous
                                        by the passionate freedom of the air"

              – living leaves
          indeed, weaving on
             through the loom
       of that same lightsome air
           where – young, in love
      we used to walk
          round the park
      – talk and walk
         round and round
      the Round Pond

– where,
        above the bandstand
you can still, if you will
soon hear
         somewhere there
a mellifluous
           parliament
   of birds

               and, in fair weather
              often see, if you look

                           – the fluttering
             lilt of
                a little kite

                       hang-gliding
                       by a thread

spooled out

       from the hands
       of a capering child

— blue and white
kite borne aloft
by twitches and tugs
and air currents
zig-zagging
unpredictable
             spontaneous

  — playful kite
swirls efflorescent
tendrils
       of bassoon
flute and oboe trills

             veining
             like the moon's
             lucencies
                 the night

in slow motion
white
          lightning

  — like a lark

               soaring

exploring

        the blue and white

                   sky

little kite
       climbs high

undeterred

       by passing clouds

— melodises

nether brawls
over washing up, car keys
taken-for-grantedness,
arriving late
and drunk
at parents' meeting,
         the lost
            sink plunger

rarely if ever
mentioned in opera,
mimed in ballet
where we're all a*greed*

                    (– aren't we, in our lust
                    for the best of life
                    held in common, there
                    on stage?)

– art is

    light – is awareness

bassoon lines
            veining
    oboe notes
              creaming
flute flights
        feathering

    the inner city
daydream, night sky

              – making their sound
                      only

    – while summer kites

    in flight by day, or parked
                away at night
    make no sound*bite*

– but they do make

           a little

              kite

                  music

    for all that

        it does nothing

for the enter-
     prize
       culture.

Waterfowl undeterred
by the little boats floating
round the Round Pond
                              spatter
their babble of birdage

                              – to be
   disparaged by other beaks
that waft toploftical
from the nearby trees
in a colloquy as subtly
bounteous as the medley
of perfumes that breeze
from the sunken garden
across from the Orangery
at the edge of the park
hard by Kensington
                    Palace Gardens,
with its embassy ballrooms
where parleys of instruments
float their night musics
light, deft and airy

– and maybe sometimes
as electricly sexy
as the primitive
earth-mother yawp
of Les Paul's, and his wife
Mary Ford's
                    oomphatic
overdubbed
                    multitrack

         orgasm

                    that fused the fine frenzy
                    of their rocketing ascent
                    of 'How High The Moon'
                    recorded for fun
                    back in '51

– but nary as high
as this sun at noon
that spreads its beams
in a cosmic smile
that warms tendril,
bassoon

       – and the genial Goon
    Spike Milligan's tree
    of gnome and fairy
    spreading wonderment
    as of flocculent heartbuds

– heart curled in heart

breaths

     – rising
falling

     – beating
as one within our nest
within the tree
from there to bear
fruit perennial

        – to spread our feathers
      and bare our breasts
    and roam the skies
and give thanks

      in love
    that transforms all,
   outshining every
dark night's terrors

— trees of life

in whom we take

so much nourishment

refuge and

pleasure

spell out your secrets

without end

fluttering

your tender

leaf caress

that lifts

our spirit-

toetips

to dance

on up

higher

and

that little bit

deepe

away

up and

up

in

to synchronicity

of summer sounds

of ducks and water

games and laughter

with farther sight

at bird's eye height

twirling –

shimmering

spiralling   up

                                                            umpteen feet

                                            upon feet

                    – borne aloft

          – skipping feet
    and hands

    of children
and parents

              – spirits raised

                              as high
                              as their kites

              in mid-air

scudding –

    eddying –

              floating –

                              buoyed by the ripples
                              of light winds
                                                  that whiffle

                              the ever-changing – yet
                                    perfectly patterned

                                          formation dance

                                                  kaleid
                                                      O
                                                  scope

                              of wingbeats whirring

                    – soughing and singing

          – effortlessly choreographed

    by the Hyde Park ensemble

of feathered friends

    – fellow travellers all

– till eventually (with luck)

abseiled

back

`easy

and graceful   as heron

cascading

downstream

to haven

(with luck)   nowhere near

the unthinking
yah-boos and catcalls   (– this
                                        degrades cats)

of world leaders
routinely   enmeshed
in their routinely
world-shattering   Work

        – on whose outcome
                    the hopes
                    of their people
                    (among others)
                            are pinned

                                    – then binned

        lottery tickets

                in the wind

Katyr... hoped was safety. 'There was a white flag on our car, flying from a wooden stick,' she said. 'Then two planes came and they hit us and my dad and mum were sitting in front of us and my brother and me were sitting in the back seat. Then we were blown up. I fell to the mud in the ground.'

Taisa winced as her aunt, Tabarik Zaumajeva, swabbed the burnt skin around her eye. The aunt said: 'At night she is scared to close her eyes. She told me that she was afraid the whole picture would come back.'

The worst is that Taisa's aunt cannot bring herself to tell the little girl she is the only survivor... the ... people ... don't ... we tell ... be abl... already ... eyes at n... woke 10 t... calm her do...

Katyr Yu... Grozny, was ... untouched on ... February. But ... fallen and Chec... had fled Russia... Some of them pass... Katyr Yurt. There i... that two Russian ... were kidnapp... night. Or ... Februa...

Put... expec... when ... – ha... hum... Che... hav... ers... eig... me... ou... K... g...

...urnt ...t and ...t leg ...knee ...s and ...t she ...hap- ...Man- ...her ...chool ...thers, ...wha...

Taisa lies, terribly burnt, on the hospital bed where her aunt has not dared to tell her all her family is dead. A village woman, left, who escaped the massacre. And, right, Rizvan Vakhaev inside his ruined home, where two vacuum bombs killed 18 people.
Photographs by John Sweeney

RUSSIA
CHECHNYA
RUSSIA
Grozny
KATYR YURT
DAGESTAN

...vil... ...oop... ...ler... ...ry ... ...A...

...satal... ...hit by ...r was so t... ...ve the wor... cellar. You ... ...vacuum bo... whoosh". We ... cellar and th... next to us ... destroyed. If ... the apartm... trance, snipe... hit arms and... and her moth... the road and...

...le ...and ...and his ...ities for 'Russia are ones that we share'
Robin Cook on Vladimir Putin

lotto

IT'S A LOTTO ROLLOVER ON WEDS
ESTIMATED £9 MILLION JACKPOT
166-01328422-22593

01 02 03 04 42 44 L.D

WED 15 JUN 05
FOR 01 WED DRAW

270 RET NO. 415232 £ 1.00
166-01328422-22593
FILL BOX TO VOID

...mainly ...ren – the ...make more ...ildren, said ...headed west ...the town of Achoi

— countless lives reduced

        to job market

             investment statistics

  — wilfully disinherited

        from the peaceable kingdoms

— mortgaged away

      from the heavens on earth

           nightly bestowed

      — daily explored

    on byways and skyways
    by far-sighted free spirits

    like DHL — or Van Gogh

    — or the early beat Super-Tramp
  W H Davies

    in *'Leisure'*:

> *"What is this life if, full of care,*
> *We have no time to stand and stare.*
>
> *No time to stand beneath the boughs*
> *And stare as long as sheep or cows.*
>
> *No time to see, when woods we pass,*
> *Where squirrels hide their nuts in grass.*
>
> *No time to see, in broad daylight,*
> *Streams full of stars, like skies at night . . .*
>
> *. . . A poor life this if, full of care,*
> *We have no time to stand and stare."*

              — Somewhere else
          there is always
          music, somewhere

                    stillness

          — sometimes
          something near

                silence.

IV.

Is there Life beyond the Gravy?

IV. *Is there Life beyond the Gravy?*

. . . . But this dank hungover mid-December jingle-jungle morning I — neither Lawrence or Davies, nor Eliot's all-seeing Tiresias — only like many another last night's blind drunk now queasy-arsed ex-New Labour voter, am late for work, heavy head-cold coming, choked with indigestible government policies, clutching with at least 50 other filthy-tempered wage-slaves to the cage-bar hand-rails of a so-called 'Golden Arrow' single-decker cattle-truck-type ex-airport bus that lurches sickeningly through convoluted crater-scarred roadwork-blockaded streets — till

. . . . a long-drawn-out wait, somewhere between Harrow Road and Kilburn

— I need to get to Camden Town, but we're stuck for no apparent reason in the shadow of a looming derelict tower block. The cadaverous young female driver's just sitting in the cab varnishing her nails. Britpop sizzles at irregular intervals from her leaky headphones.

When I chime in with a horde of other passengers who start moaning at her, puh-*leeze* to get going, she shouts "THAT'S IT"

— and leaves the bus. I worm to the rear in low dudgeon and sprawl a clumsy entrée amidst the stinky gaggle of gluesniff-gasping bums who've taken over the back seats alcove. Despite their stoned scatological invective, random retchings and flailing bottles, my exasperation subsides into a cosy doze

. . . . . . but the very moment I'm about to ease into the inner sanctum of my dream (continuous orgasm, gushingly reciprocated by the ultimate Immortal Beloved sex-bomb on the mossy riverbank of a tropical paradise garden where all creatures lie down at ease with one another and get up to no bad)

— I'm awoken by a hectic grinding of gears in a blizzard of *fuüüms-bø-wo-rö-thé-tZeh*

— *ooorrgh* . . . . The bus heaves off again at last, with a surly middle-aged burly male at the wheel

— but he's done a U-turn, I slowly apprehend, for the bus is racketing back in the *wrong* direction: in another ten minutes or so we'll be at the World's End in King's Road, Chelsea.

I also find that I can't get up — the ceiling keeps getting lower and lower and I'm forced, like Alice in the White Rabbit's upstairs room, to lie flatter and flatter on the floor — gradually realising there are no other passengers

. . . . gradually realising this must be my coffin.

Everything starts blacking out, except one question faintly flickering

. . . . *Will the world to come be any better?*

V.

This little island went to Market

V. *This little island went to Market*

At the 1994 Labour Party Conference
Tony Blair promised the disenchanted

". . . *A New Politics:*
a politics of courage,
honesty and trust."

William Blake
            — courageous, honest and trustworthy
            prophet of a new Jerusalem
            in England's green and re-formed land —
believed that

". . . *Where any view of Money exists*
Art cannot be carried on

. . . but War only."

T S Eliot, architect of the would-be classic
Faber and Faber poetry canon,
wrote, in his *Choruses from 'The Rock'*:

". . . *All men are ready to invest their money*
But most expect dividends.
I say to you: Make perfect your will.
I say: take no thought of the harvest,
But only of proper sowing."

High aspirations
fulfilled by Blake
and Eliot

— and too few others
in living memory.

Editorial Flabberghast

Posy Simmonds

SIC TRANSIT → GLORIA

Art is long   Shelf-life is short

ARS LONGA → VITA BREVIS

The rock of artistic aspirations today
– publishing, broadcasting, prizegiving,
so-called critical standardising –
looms immalleably fixed
– defined, motivated and controlled
by a transatlantic Dunciad
of accountants, profiteers, expert packagers
of compromise and cliché, payolas and lies.

Every day
        so-called culture supplements
of the so-called quality press
churn out their sterile dairy-rounds
    of received opinions
– a closed circuit of spurious captions
to the marketing of each product
through its datelined shelf-life

as though art were no more durable
than last week's butter or golf

– as though culture were a freemasonry
of scholars of current trends
chained to uniformity
in a huddle of links
endlessly reminding
each other of themselves

        – and of the rigidly circumscribed
        nature and number
        of churns or holes
        by which achievement
        can be measured and placed,
        savoured, bought into, understood . . .

Behold:
          "The Poetry SuperLeague"
— waxing fabber and fabber
and ever more fab

— floating sales of glory
with whatever flash hyperbole
or quick-sell story
might serve to aggrandise the stable,
or nudge a Name
a few points higher up the table

— thus . . . *"The best* Irish poet
since Yeats" (Famous Seamus)

or . . . *"The best* letters ever
since Keats" (Growser Larkin)
or . . . . . .

     Not that Larkin or Heaney, Yeats
and Keats, aren't fine writers, but that
such parasitic sales talk only disconnects
the singularity of each, diluting inspiration
into computer-blanded flab

— the commonplace obsolescent mess
of blurby gunk considered Viable
by our catchall world trade nillennium

                              — *'Viable'!*

                         Oh yes,
          about as helpfully viable as that congealed
               but tenaciously adhesive wodge
                 of tasteless spat-out chewing-gum
          your shoe or skirt or trouser-seat latch on to
          stuck on the tube at rush hour.

— *Of course*:
what this or that hired smoothie of the day plugs

        must be
        The Best

because — it seems to go
without saying — he's read
(well, virtually)   *every*thing

— which is to say
he's not really read
    anything.

 — Squint at this puff-inflated stock exchange, and note
from yesterday's paper scraps aswirl
in the shifting winds of place-your-bets bookmaking,
        how
   . . . hard on the hooves
of one hotly tipped runner (Heathcote Williams)
     — backed, almost reasonably
     for sounding
      ". . . *like*
   . . . *Alexander Pope on speed*",
and of another galloping
     major courser (James Fenton)
       — brand-labelled,
       just plausibly:

      ". . . *a new Auden*"
 . . . strutted forth
     the likes of
schlock-publishing mogul Felix Dennis
— millionaire at 30
 — born-again Poet at 55
  — and after just two years
  at the teats of the Muse
   — self-appointed and multi-plugged as:

   ". . . *The New Kipling* . . ."

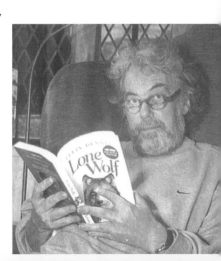

— or the likes of one
Murray Lachlan Young
   bullet-pointed by ad-men
   for instantly marshalled
   sharp-shooting stardom
      in consequence of being
      young-ish, pretty-ish
and — extra brownie-joint —

"*. . . A graduate of*
*   the World's First*
Media Performance
*   Degree Course*"

— fancy-frock-coated,
wing-collared, raffishly permed

         — ergo:

"*. . . The New Byron*".

      But that's not enough
   — he also had to be paraded as:

"*. . . The 1990s' Oscar Wilde*"

   . . . and
            as if to set
   the ultimate jewel
   in this matchless crown
   of historic credentials,
   even as
            — er:

"*. . . Shakespeare on Acid*",
                        yet

— Not merely *like* Shakespeare
   but — *gadzooks!*

      — the definitive Incarnation . . .

The World's Media
　　is One jealous Moloch.

His Performance Degree decrees
nillennium's Global Supersale
　　Delivery disease

　　　　— via
Hot Ancestry Categoritis
　　Him spread
His Tropic of Hypertitis

— to disgorge Him voracious pot belly
all over nonstop　　　website and telly

　　— *Log on*, Him wink　　— *join the fame plan*
why don'cha

　　　　　　— surf Him, snort Him

　　and in passing, chew
the fool's gold-fatted calf, lap up
the sacred milch cow's fetid barf.

In this celebrity forebear-claimants' fiddle
and froth of quick turnover rout
*Every*one must get Dumbed Down
from the Bard on out.

　　Moral: would-be poets
　　— stay off the acid.

VI.

Art is Long

What does Tony Blair want to replace and what does the fish need?

(See page 413)

The Present Tense

I am

I am Colin Hodd. I'm hot, the next big thing.....so I'm told.

I am Colin Hodd. I am indeed the next big thing!

SIC TRANSIT → GLORIA

You are

..a literary colossus.!

Yes, Colin..and I want to shake your hand!

He is

..a bit of a flash in the pan, Colin Hodd

over rated

You mean unreadable

He isn't

..quite the draw he was

Know where the toilets are?

We are

We are sorry, we don't seem to have those titles in stock..we could order them for you...what's his first name, again?

Colin..Colin Hodd.

BOULDER BOOKS

You are ?

Colin Hodd

'Oh. Think my mum used to like your books

They are...

...collectors' items now, Colin Hodd's books — mind you, only for the dust jackets.....

..they're designed by Mario Zolo — very sought after... in good condition, like this, they fetch a tidy sum . . .

HAY-ON-WYE BOOKSELLERS
BOOKSELLERS

Art is long *Shelf-life is short*

ARS LONGA → VITA BREVIS

Making Hay Conjugations

Posy Simmonds

VI. *Art is Long*

The overblown hypeings
of Felix Dennis and Lachlan Young
were only brief scene-stealing rashes
    – but they still yield revealing flashes
on the murk pitched at art- and word-lights
by thousands of ponced-up promotions
of pretend-'leading' pseuds and gobshites
    which have ground their mills
ever more slyly – slithy-tovily – since . . .

        the declining health of the years
        ex-P M/conductor Ted Heath's
           tusk-padded shoulders
             milled and hove
        up and down, back and forth
        when he guffawed at signings
        on his whistle-stop book tours
           like a premier conductor
            sweatily conducting
    the flagging sails of a pooped out yacht

– unto the manufactured schmooze
    of 'prestige' lecture suck-ins
selling deadly humbug'n'cover-up brokers
    like Henry Kissinjure,
    Bill-the-Thrill Clinton
    or Cherie la Bouche
as obscenely price-tagged 'culture heroes'

        . . . Puff and Blow, Orchestrate,
    conduct, swagger, blaze the trail
    image makeovers, razzle-dazzle
    have been putting the shine,
    the biz and the spin
    on the ever more neon
    names of the games
    for yonks *ad nauseam* – priming
    this PR-zeitgeist's
    cornball accolade
    of state-registered Fame
    Academy courses

    – and of prentice bards groomed
to win PR-sired flimflam,
    flashbulb and TV heat
like so many photo-
            genetically cloned
    investments in saleable
pretend-pedigree – would-be poetry
      – whirlgig-roistered . . . racehorse meat

. . . Investments priming the grounds
for Felix D and his ilk
to milk newsprint, clog airwaves
and crown themselves Kings
of Parnassus
                            astride the mounds
                of their wretchedly cloth-eared and
                    — *Poop-poop!* — so fat Toadish
            off-rhyme rabble-rousing rasp-tentacled sounds

. . . much as
Murray Lachlan's
Cash-in Young
productions of '97
                        had gilded pell-mell
                        a relentless hard sell
                        of corny jingles
                                    — sheer slop
                    posing as poetry
        — to cop
    for precisely the style
                            of widespread Goforit
                            media idolatry
        that the sanitised crap-can
        of Brit market forces
        had pitched around language
since it firmed up its money-mouthed
    brain-twisting
                    preda-
                            tory spam
        with her Barrenness
                        of Granite Ham
        back in '79.

The Sitwells sat ill with Doc Leavis
for boosting

> ". . . *the history*
> *of publicity, rather than*
> *that of poetry"*

                       – but at least
      inside their façades
      of fey eccentricity
each of them made
from artistic necessity
a body of work that still breathes.

    Whereas Dennis's bluster
    rich wine-pumped
    with fake lustre
               and young Lachlan's
               'Get Me
                    – aren't I cute!'
               fancy bell-bottomed farts

were exactly as Wicked
                  (that's to say as thick
                  and brash and quick)
as moshed with the tawdry
                   PR trick
New Labour required from
         (and dumped on) the arts

                      (that's to say –

                      the familiar philistine shtick
                      of getting loadsamoney
                      so very gladly

                      for doing very little
                      very badly).

Felix D's versified *'Rules of Success'*
may be whizz for big biz
   – but their pretension
   to poetico-
     moral largesse
falls flat on its face
    – a fraudulent mess:
. . . the lines confide that –

    ". . . The First Rule of success in making coin
    Is: 'Buy it Cheap and Sell It to a Fool'.
    But keep close watch for new fools to enjoin:
    For most of us – there is no Second Rule."

Corporation bosses
drily ruling out losses
    can hardly speak
    for "*most* of us"

  – any more than half decent writing
    will seek to profit
      by deceiving
        presumed fools into believing
        it's worth a huge lot
        – when it plainly
           is not.

    . . . And while Dennis's would-be
antique – nay, antic – so-called
'Craft' of Twenty01
is no well-wrought
barrel of fun:
    "Speak not to me of Craft as Art untaught,
    What need the trowel to curtsey
    to the brush?
    A walk within an old cathedral's hush
    is worth all the Picassos
    ever bought"

  – Rudyard K's unstrained praise
for *'The Craftsman'*, though writ
a century before, yet displays myriad
cadenced light chords more – telling how:
    ". . . with a thin third finger marrying
    Drop to wine-drop domed on the table,
    Shakespeare opened his heart till the sunrise
        Entered to hear him.
    London waked and he, imperturbable,
    Passed from waking to hurry after shadows . . .
    Busied upon shows of no earthly importance?
        Yes, but he knew it!"

In 1814, aged 26
Byron wrote:

"She walks in beauty, like the night
Of cloudless climes and starry skies;
And all that's best of dark and bright
Meet in her aspect and her eyes:
Thus mellow'd to that tender light
Which heaven to gaudy day denies . . ."

In 1997, the 28 year-old so-called
'New Byron' wrote:

". . . Tell me not now of whom I might be
I shall take dreams over earthward-bound cares
Speak to me not then my angel
I know I will love you upon my deep dreams
I'll see you glow bright no trace of a seam
Leave now whilst you can lest the wind does change . . ."

Murray L's gooey, transient topics –

('MTV Party', 'Designer Labels'
'Simply *Every*one's Taking Cocaine',
'I'm Being Followed
By The Rolling Stones . . .')

in the lamest of rhythms –

(". . . there in a haze of *eau de toilette*
She casually lit two international-length cigarettes
And said: *'Luxury goods, luxury goods,*
I've had my eye on luxury goods' . . .")

may have won him a record
record company advance

– considered as poetry

they oafishly
lurch
instead of dance.

Yet
      — "Poet lands £1 million contract"
fan-fared Murray's press corps
                                to fabricate
                                and stir

a flurry of front page
banner headline
                re-runs
— serving swirl upon swirl
of Mega-Moolah bedazzled
                        sales machine curry

— meaning:
              media fixing lands
a palpable hit
for the creeping currency
of well-marketed shit

                     — for twisting wordsounds
                            through the pipelines
                  of industrial waste

                    to programme and spread
                  GMTV-corporate
                    degradation of taste —

slamming gaudy myths
down the gee whizz-
                  bling brutalised ear

    — as that
            ". . . Poetry had
                    a terrific year."

In 1804 Blake warned —

". . . Suffer not the fashionable Fools
to depress your powers
by the prices they pretend to give
for contemptible works,
or the expensive advertising boasts
that they make of such works . . ."

— If poetry is a craft,
                    an art
and healing spirit
                    well repped by the inimitable
                    George Gordon Byron, Kipling, Oscar Wilde

                    and by all-time Oscar-winning
                    multi-medic trouper undefiled
                    Will Shakspeare — grandmaster builder
                                        of the unfettered globe

— then tacky poo-bags of doggerel
getting pushed round the networks
as hard as cocaine
                    or The Rolling Stones
                    or pop music TV
                    get pushed

far from made '97
a good year
for the growth
                    of any true
                                poets' tree.

1997 was in fact
a bad, sad year for poetry

because so many true voices
of feeling
died:

     — Kathy Acker;
Jon Silkin;
     Shake Keane;
Jill Neville;
     Edwin Brock;
Laurie Lee;
     William Burroughs

     — each of them
irreplaceable.

But death cannot
undo their works.

*". . . The only riches,
the great souls . . ."*

— wrote D H Lawrence, after reading
Walt Whitman.

In April '97
Blake's grandchild, Whitman's heir
Allen Ginsberg died

after seventy years of questing
naked truth.

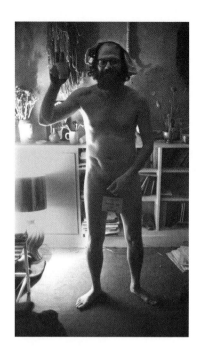

Early on
he embraced the bonhomie
of Whitman's *'Song of the Open Road'*:

"*. . . Camerado, I give you my hand!*
I give you my love more precise than money,
I give you myself before preaching or law . . ."

Early on his lifelong buddy
Burroughs warned how

"*. . . Selling*
gets to be more
of a habit
than using . . ."

Early on, in *'Death to Van Gogh's Ear!'*,
Ginsberg lamented the way

"*. . . Money has reckoned the soul of America*
. . . Money! Money! Money! shrieking mad celestial
Money of illusion! Money made of nothing, starvation, suicide!
Money of failure! Money of death!
Money against Eternity!"

In June 1965
             (fifteen years before money
             had just as thoroughly gutted
             the souls of Britain and Europe)
Ginsberg wrote *'Who Be Kind To'*,
an orgasmic psalm for humanity

                        – which he declaimed
                        cajoling and caressing
                        eight thousand celebrants
                        of the historic *'Wholly Communion
                        Poetry Incarnation'*
                        at London's Royal Albert Hall.

The poem ends –

             "Tonite let's all make love in London
                        as if it were 2001 the years
                        of thrilling god –
             And be kind to the poor soul that cries in
                        a crack of the pavement because he
                        has no body –
             Our prayers to the ghosts and demons, the
                        lackloves of Capitols & Congresses
                        who make sadistic noises
                        on the radio –
             Statue destroyers & tank captains, unhappy
                        murderers in Mekong & Congo,
             That a new kind of man has come to his bliss
                        to end the cold war he has borne
                        against his own kind flesh
                        since the days of the snake."

Making love is better
than making money
because there can never be
too much real love

                    — whereas the pursuit of money
                    and its power
                    corrupts, setting humans
                    at each other's throats

                                    — till

". . . *Art cannot be carried on*

               but War only."

VII.

Gland

of

Hype's

Vainglory

VII. *Gland of Hype's Vainglory*

Like a clapped-out whore in a clap ward
like a junkie without a fix
– like the USSR and Tiananmen Square
the EnterPrize Culture will run out of tricks.

But meanwhile
get your kicks
on Big Blather's

pic 'n' mix

– and Lo
– View Halloo
Demon Bratwurst!
– indisputably the best
postmodernist rock'n'roll model spearhead
of the Goldspivs' Collage head-butting school
of Virtual New Vandalism
('. . . Dead beasts are Cool')
since Ifor'n'I Slaughter Whaleflesh
won the Sky TV Gold-Shower Spunk Dish
for running a mock turtle soup chef
through
to the Saatchi punk slag and bone yards

in the same year (1990) that Maggie
loveless Goddess of Money and War
with socialism pulped
to glop through her maw,
got the loveless notice
to quit her throne
– and saw
in the sudden cold
what an unfunny
new (not so wonderful)
world this can be

– but her long overdue removal
did not set us free.

So we looked to thee, T B –
leading New Labour God
that spunneth forth such a squeaky-clean
        prosperous future
                        (for some)

– ye gilt-edged gods! how it glistered
with Big Names of Showbiz and Pop,
media moguls, celebs

                        . . . a few slimy chancers,
    legal fiddlers, shameless sharks

    and more than a few
                        Big Business bosses

– but, er . . .
                mainly
the
        . . . uh –
        . . . Great and the Wise,

nay –
        The Best

– all agrovel
at your behest

        – for thou wertst to be
right gladsomely
and –

                                zill –
                trill –   ienn
            bill-   umpt
        mill-   uously
        multi-   pompa-

        Domed thereafter

– for what?

        For that
. . . thou shreddedst state welfare
from those most in need

. . . for that they may Switch,
                you did say
(for "– at the *end* of the day
all shall have pay" . . .)
           and Buy In –
                to the hallowed overworlds
                of museums and high art,
                of specialist healthcare whenever it's called for,
                of offshore trusts . . .

                        of high times
                        in your Dome

                . . . of ever higher
                    education
                        for all

              – for an ever higher
                  class of fees
                    if you please
                    you did say . . .

Yes Minister, of course
with ample time over
– no sweat, no stress –

        for working mums
        and single dads
        and working widows
        and, erm
            – *literally*
              . . . *every*one
            to share

      in
        our great British heritage

        of survival of the toffest

– meaning . . .
      everyone
      contracted
      to Pay-As-You-Earn

– and those who've no money
and want to learn
will get loans to help
with their fees
            you did say
   – plus new schemes for trainees
   to help the bees knees
   of agile youngsters
   to roust on spin fare,
   to straddle the peaks
   of Job Markets
                – of Corporations
                of The World, even
(loans they'll have
to learn to repay
as a matter of par
for their course,
you did say)

. . . while others

er, well

           . . . fall by the way

– that's life,
you did say

– but even they

can, *um*

        – get . . . some,

                er –

       . . . Cultural training

in . . . just how to Access,
          sample and relish

far and away,
      you did say,
         um – you know –
   the best ever
      (though lumpen
      Lottery-buttressed)
          state of the Arts

                meaning, mainly
        the (so-called)
           Arts of the States

– meaning daftly expensive
hi-tech gadgets
that nobody needs,
custom-built fads
Super-Sponsored
for the idle prestige
supposedly reflected
from the overblown halo
of a Dome of Domes

. . . where there could have been space
for walkways and homes
and the organic creative
arts of Albion in place

there
            – where

you *could* once again
build anew without pain

– if only Government and business
stop inflating them*selves*

    – invest in good earth,
    dig deep down
                    and delve
    to the polluted bottom
      of the toxic bog
      well sussed by Mogg

– *then* might regeneration
rescue for real
                    this stagnant cesspit
                    of our overblown nation

– *then* might more than a trace
of Greenwich pastures
                            grow green again

  – with clean air to breathe again

fresh flowers and produce,
    sky and water seen plain.

So,
      pray show us just what
                    and where
Tony Blair,
        were the radical
". . . *New Politics*" you proposed

– that new land so many
voted you and yours in for
to plant with your vaunted

                  ". . . politics of courage,
                  honesty and trust"?

      We did put our trust
                in your proper sowing:

HURRY UP WITH IT PLEASE, *IT'S TIME*

– it really is

    high time
          ". . . *to make a difference*"

as your inane Domespeak
slogan had it

      – but where on earth
      is any improving difference?

    – Just how did New Labour's
long gestated emergence
from incubation
deliver us
      one newly hatched ant's
              fore-footstep on

      from compromise-addled
Old Tory?

HOMEWORK

Where Nye Bevan, John Smith
and countless true Labour workers
fought
       – and still fight –
for nationwide health,

                  you
– Tory Blair
         – arselicked and spun
more like Thatcher,

               avid
for privatised wealth.

We'd had eighteen years
of government oppression

— seen the pleasant land
of mother nature's given
bounty of nourishment
                    — derided, written off
                    as 'not cost-effective'

                    — therefore

    cheapo tower
    blocked over

            and out.

        We'd watched — with hands tied
to the indifferent On-Off switch —
                        the pitiless extinction
                        of Britain's last tribes
                            that mined
                        the salt of the earth

— watched the common grounds and culture,
hearth and home of generations
laid waste to

            shredded heat

            in fell sacrifice

            to placate the jealous gods
            of 'market realism'

                        — gods of Philistia, mining
                        the so-called
                                    multinational
                        so-called community

                        of Big Money Rules.

111

And after those long years
manacled
      in thrall to Mammon

the biggest Difference
Labour's apostles
of National Newness
claimed to be making
to our so-called
         artistic horizons
lay in the promotion
of astronomical spending
on a monumental
(unironically)
      Disneyfied folly
conceived by the Tories
to squat on Greenwich

– with less outward grace
or inner necessity
than the mythic New Clothes
tailor-made for the arrogant
Emperor of empty
designer pomp

      – at just the same time
      as the Kubla Khans
          puffing
      themselves up with pride
      for launching this,
         told us

      there was no money for thousands
      of deep-rooted, widely cherished
      (and far less costly)
      arts in progress
         to survive.

As in Eliot's
                    and in Thatcher's
dehumanised countries
these would-be New
Millennium Managers
contrived only

      to "*. . . connect
      Nothing with nothing*"

      in their New Waste Land:

this England

      – rebranded

      New Domesday World.

**DISNEY GIVES
MANDY DOME IDEA**

VIII.

How Astutely
Faulty Towers . . .

. . . Corrupt Absolutely

VIII. *How Astutely*
Faulty Towers . . .
. . . Corrupt Absolutely

In London town did Kubla Tone
a stately treasure-dome decree
all New Brits' home from home
to be.
　　　　— Trust me, quoth he,
just wait and see:
　　　　　　　this Dome will Deliver
. . . our nation's rebirth:
　　　　　　　　　nothing less than

". . . *the greatest*
　　　　　　day out
on Earth . . ."

　　— What, greater than Day One
of the original Creation?

　　— Than the very first
Christmas?

　　　　— Greater than The Second
　　　　Coming, yet?

— And were all the days after
Dome's day is done
to be denied all hope
of such greatness again?

　　　　　　Size isn't everything
　　　　　　and small can be beautiful

　　　　　　but these reruns of hype's vainglory
　　　　　　　　　　　　sucked

　　　　　　like a con-man staking his claim
　　　　　　at a burgher without a brain.

Saint Tony proclaimed
that the Dome in its Whizzdom
would make Britain

                nothing less than

". . . *The envy*
        of the world . . ."

    – But hold on, Brit Poppa:

if we really wanted
to wish Our Lord
a Happy Anniversary,

would not a *Healing*
of the grapplement of nations
have been the gift
He'd much prefer?

          The arousing of world envy
          figures nowhere in His creed.

And *if* Jesus *had* been invited
to choose between, say
France's celebration
of His projected reformation
of our fallen civilisation,
    and Dome's opportunistic, triumphalist
        commodity range inflation,
    flaunting fake Annunciations
        of a single year
            of the nation's
market-driven speculations
        about the following year or three's
            most modish exploitations

– He'd hardly have come whooping
like wildfire across the water
to this un-green
    braggart-bullish
    Antichrist-motored
    newspeak-metallic
    Non-Memorial

           would He

– when He could walk freely, peaceably
with all the others walking freely, peaceably
    – unimportuned for entrance fees
    or sponsorship, or endorsements –
along the meridian line
from Dunkirk to the Pyrenees

where a row of fir trees
twelve hundred
           kilometres long
was planted in His honour

    – which the people pay nothing to enjoy;

    – which was assured of immeasurably longer, richer
        life expectancy
            than coyly
            disposable Dome;

    – which cost its creators
        a tiny smidgen
            of the irreparable
                crock of Dome's
                obscene greed?

In the gospel
according to Saint Prater
Tonyminder
        (as was – till December '98
        – Labour's Saviour
        of New Fangles Incarnate)
on TV
      – it was
          ". . . going to be
      . . . ENORMOUSLY Successful".

Dome Templar Mandy Mouse
found only one note to play
in trumpeting his Temple
      – crowing over and over
      with the nagging insistence
      of a maniacal martinet
      how
          "– en*or*mously BIG,
            and en*or*mously Suc*CESS*ful"
      it was going to be,
      our brand new, *BEST*
      and BIGGEST EVER
      Monument.

      – Successful, he implied, *not*
because of any intrinsic
moral
        or aesthetic qualities

                – Successful only because
                SO much lovely lucre was well bonded
                in multiple-entry ensuring
                it would succeed in luring
                millions
                      and millions
                            and millions more pounds

                from sponsors to pay to install it

                    – with a view to succeed
                  in luring as many
                          millions
                                and millions
              of punters
                  to pay
                      to visit it

. . . meaning

— the cash flow of Dome
would *surely* ping and gibber
and tinkle resoundingly

— stacking up, feeding back
a music most dear
to the New Labour ear

. . . So:
      "Time to make a difference"

only meant
         Time to gerralorralolly
*shar*pish

      — whilst other countries
turned green

      — meant the meaner
      than ever
           con-
             tin-
         u-
           ation

    of the same
        heartless mean time

conturbations imposed
by the same soulless brand
    of clenched ironhand
    prime profit gland-
        fixated
Blue Meanie bosses

    as of yesteryear's money-plagued land

   – So: raising,
holding on to
     and multiplying
gilt ingots
  remained this

      not so brave
      not so new
      not so Labour priesthood's
           New Jerusalem

   – And the Nillennium Dome
        its shrill-fêted
        dross-plated
        tinpot-
           inflated
             would-be
               fabled bower

           – mega-doomed
              Babel Tower.

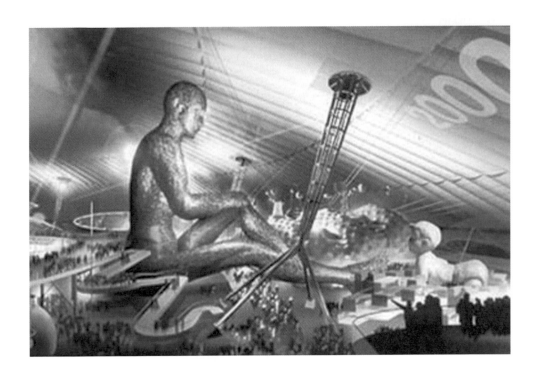

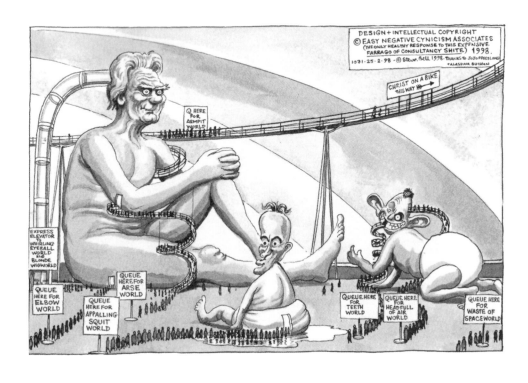

THE BEST OF BRITAIN... *Peter Brookes* 25 ii 98

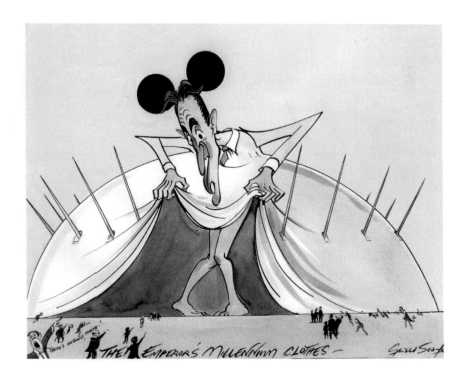

THE EMPEROR'S MILLENNIUM CLOTHES — *Gerald Scarfe*

        Yet — despite such debasements
of language and good faith and meaning,
let's take courage and strength
from other musics —

                        common loneliness transformed
in plain-speaking folksong

— in harmonies of comradeship
        that disown competition
        and lies
        and dead ends of selling

but replenish the springs
that bring benign paths to light again

— paths that prove
                        enduring routes forward

— ways paved and imbued
with prophecies and ideals,
art-works and prayers
        and poems
                and visions

                        embraced by the gathering
                        resistance movement
of unprogrammed people
in every country
who want to live
        — and to help
        their fellows to live

        — inspired by the teachings
        of Buddha
        and Christ
        and Blake

                        and the indestructible good sense
                        of Luther King's dream
                                of keeping faith
                                with the realities
                                        of equality
                                        and freedom
                                        and justice

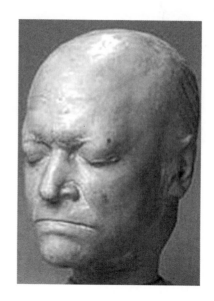

– sustained by down-to-earth anthems
like this one, adapted
from Woody Guthrie
by Billy Bragg:

> "This land is your land, this land is my land
> From the coast of Cornwall to the Scottish Highland,
> From the sacred forests to the Holy Islands,
>   This land was made for you and me . . . "

– Adapting both Woody and Billy
let's recognise

it's not only U S and U K
– not just 'us and them'
(let alone 'Us *versus* Them')

– but this whole earth the homeland
that's made for

(and nourished
– or destroyed by)

you and me

with room for every
she and he.

Let's recognise
with John Lennon

           (who, remember
           like Jesus and Karl Marx,
           thought it only reasonable to

             ". . . Imagine
                       all the people
             Sharing all the world . . . ")

that
    ". . . We are all Christ
    and we are all Hitler"

           – somewhere . . .

           – Or not?

Belsen Concentration Camp, 8/5/1945

Alright then, not

— if such notions
could be taken
               to deny
the witness borne
by Holocaust survivors

— Primo Levi,
Paul Celan's *'Totenfuge'*,

the *'Shoah'* of Claude Lanzmann

— each flashlit attestation
                      a memorial

to the unaccounted millions more

who weren't allowed to be

                themselves

— whose voice and histories
snuffed in the death camps

                  will never be heard.

Humiliation of an elderly Jew beside the bodies of his comrades. This photograph was taken by a Nazi soldier and sent home to show how 'the final solution' was being put into effect.

Humiliation (six decades later) of unidentified political prisoners in Guantánamo Bay, Cuba, at the hands of US Military.

But let's agree
with Lennon that

"... *We want Christ to win*"

— Meaning the Christ who
as Blake understood him

"was all Virtue
and . . . taught that God
forbade all contention
for Worldly prosperity"

— meaning the Christ
who whipped the money-changers
out of the Temple

— overturned their tables,
poured away their profits

and pronounced them Thieves.

IX.

Touchstones for Babylon

IX. *Touchstones for Babylon*

Blake's deathless light
of pure spirit
stands guard
day and night

– tyger-lamb
burning bright

to keep our sights clear
of bullshit and blight:

> ". . . *set your foreheads*
> *against the ignorant hirelings!*
> *For we have hirelings in the Camp, the Court*
> *& the University, who would, if they could,*
> *for ever depress Mental & prolong*
> *Corporeal War . . ."*

Once elected,
the New Labour government
immediately cut a further
                    three million pounds
from the public
subsidies for arts.

Yet it automatically continued
        – this self-styled socially progressive
frozen-blooded firm
of unnatural-death promoters –
to sponsor the mass production
        of ever more lethal weapons
        to be sold at knockdown prices
        to any creeps who might want them,
                            worldwide
from the earnings
of each British taxpayer
                – to the tune
                    of a cool
                            two *hundred* million
                            pounds each year

    – to what end?

        – To perpetuate
    the self-riven state
    pastor Virgil bemoaned
    twenty years before Christ:

                        ". . . Round here it's upside-down: atrocity
                    Instead of righteousness; so many wars
                    Spread all over earth, so multiple
                    The faces of wrong-doing; the peaceful plough
                    Abandoned, farmers violently evicted,
                    The untended fields despoiled to waste land,
                    Curved pruning-hooks, estranged from vines,
                    Battered into the rigidness of swords

                    . . . and neighbouring
                    Cities scrap their peace accords and fight
                    And the murderous war-god ravens everywhere."

Two thousand years
and hundreds of pointless
                        wars later
Bob Dylan
(among millions
of others)
            sang it
                    again
and again:

>   ". . . *While money doesn't talk, it swears*
>   *Obscenity, who really cares*
>   *Propaganda, all is phony . . ."*

– Or not quite all:

not Dylan himself

– nor what his spiritual
great aunt Emily
Dickinson knew –

>   ". . . *The Poets light but Lamps –*
>   *Themselves – go out –*
>   *The Wicks they stimulate –*
>   *If vital Light*
>
>   *Inhere as do the Suns –*
>   *Each Age a Lens*
>   *Disseminating their*
>   *Circumference –"*

          Dickinson and Blake
       – so perennially unique –
     yank our smugly
     made-up minds
                    awake

       – well-springs to revive us
     from the drought and alienation
   at the bed of Blair's stagnant
   New Babble-on Nation

   with its uniform
                  "life styles"
          freshly ground from the mills
          of "The Culture of Enterprise"

                           – meaning:
                         cultureless compromise

       – with the business-deal ethic

       – with Moloch and Murdoch

       – with all the Megabuck-spinning
                              brainwash that bleaches
                              (". . . purer than pure"?)
           at astral soft-soap admin level

          – suspect crops;
                       suspect food;
                           suspect chemicals

             – to be cleared
          of fears and suspicions
          by publicly funded
          'researches' controlled by
          'Corporate Welfare' commissions . . .

                              the big lies of
                              (". . . whiter than white"!)

             – mass brainwash that launders
          arms and bomb distribution
          and cleans up mass profits
          from murder and pollution.

This was no solid ground
or clean air
Labour Leader Blair
for the *"thriving and confident"*
   land of the future
   you said
   you so wanted
   to build

– It felt a lot closer, damn it,
to the *"fascist regime"*
the Sex Pistols fired at
in *'God Save the Queen'*:

> *". . . It made you a moron*
> *– a potential H-Bomb*

. . . There is no future
in England's dream."

Were you ever listening for real
                     would-be Big Daddy Blair?

– Such a wow with your women that most of them feared
To call you to task – feared even to ask
"Hey, what about Me . . . ?"

Here's shame on you, so high-handedly
Raising up like a drawbridge the charge
For access to transport, education and health
Just so's the wealthy could pile up more wealth.

Here's three loud boos for the hype and schmooze,
For your superposh mega-dosh parties
And your smoothed-out lengths of old Tory rope
That kept the helpless hung out with less and less hope

– Told:
        "Lone parents, new mothers,
        Sickos, disabled –
        On your bikes, get straight
        Back to work, all's well"

                . . . Save for those who aren't
              – left to rot in hell.

Here's mud in your eye for making us cry
As we tried to bite with good cheer
On the sound of the same cruel cop-outs
We'd had for too many a year.

What a howling, animal-degrading shame
the high-flown armchair-driven hardball game
shot your rating up from Bambi deer

to Bombardier Extraordinaire

— whilst retaining just one trace
of your *'Smart Boy Wanted'* face
that had us polling in the Isles

— those flashing teeth, those gnashing smiles . . .

It's as though
    — Bomb-blagging SuperStag
you'd learned nothing to declare

    — for yourself
    or 'your' people —

from the pitfalls and pratfalls
and cop-outs of history.

BUDDIES

Having watched you crawling
for acceptance by America
as Second Top Nation
   – or rather
         51st State

I'd rather think
of myself and my friends
as citizens of Blakeland
than Britons
        mate.

Third Way's pop-tosh muzak
may have jollied along
the fleeting fancies
of media-sloshed throngs

— though it led nowhere clear

save
        — awash with dosh
    — to get itself
                re-elected my dear.

But the trustworthy ways are still here,
flanked by long-standing touchstones

     – lit by the plenitude
     of long-burning Wicks

    for us to rekindle

        and renew

           their
           "*. . . vital Light . . .*

                   Disseminating their
                   Circumference —"

. . . Fire of Lorca's *duende*,
and Dylan Thomas's *hwyl*,
Robeson's *'Old Man River'* rolling
'The Weary Blues' of Langston Hughes

   . . . age-gold voices

— Solomon, Sappho
— Bessie Smith, Leadbelly
   recall and replenish
the impassioned stream
of ageless folk forms

   . . . indelible ache
of *'Black and Blue'*
played and sung
by Louis Armstrong
red-hot and true

— choked stab of Billie Holiday
intoning how (even now)

   "*. . . Southern trees*
   bear a strange fruit,
   Blood on the leaves
   and blood at the root . . ."

   . . . Joseph Brodsky's implacable chant,
Ginsberg's inner gospel
in *'Kaddish'* and *'Howl'*

                  — revive the roots
               that clutch
                  . . . stir deep rhythms
               in the blood.

Sometimes however
race memory's blood-calls
can obscure the most glaring
evils and horrors

"A man lives in the house
he plays with the serpents

. . . he writes when dusk falls to Germany
your golden hair Margarete

. . . he whistles his pack out
he whistles his Jews out
in earth has them dig for a grave
he commands us strike up for the dance . . . "

— bestial *fatwas*

— murderous jihads

— unabating genocides

– the routine savagery
of '. . . *ethnic cleansing* . . .'

– routine denial
of asylum
to refugees
and victims of torture

". . . your ashen hair Shulamith
we dig a grave in the breezes
there one lies unconfined . . . "

– routinely inflicted
more often than not
with some version
of God on call

". . . a man lives in the house
your golden hair Margarete
your ashen hair Shulamith
he plays with the serpents"

Poetry that would bring together
local dialects
              and global tribes
needs to bury old hatreds

– tune into the music
of shared ancestry

yet open up, fine tune
the shared destinies to come

              – futures that never figure
              in the career-move jostling
              of trumped up front-runners

              or their marketeers' pratings
              of supersonic sales and ratings.

". . . The age demanded an image
of its accelerated grimace"

observed the crazed purist
– vile ranter – Ezra Pound

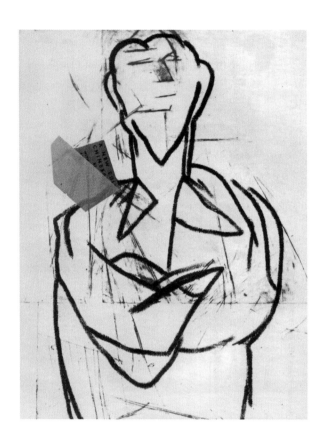

– and forbore to provide it.

Instead, came to see
– and sometimes, to show – that

". . . To have gathered from the air a live tradition
or from a fine old eye the unconquered flame
This is not vanity . . ."

So Bob Dylan gathered
from his adopted namesake

– and from Allen Ginsberg
(who'd learned from Pound and Buddha
to pull down *his* vanity)

ways to compose
and chant
defiant
prophetic lines –

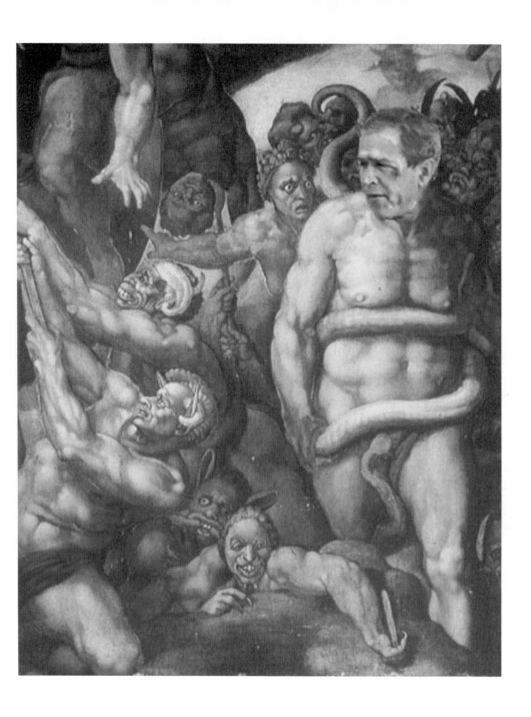

"While preachers preach of evil fates
Teachers teach that knowledge waits

   . . . even the president of the United States
Sometimes must have
To stand naked . . ."

"As some warn victory, some downfall
Private reasons great or small
Can be seen in the eyes of those that call
To make all that should be killed to crawl
While others say don't hate nothing at all
Except hatred."

". . . Disillusioned words like bullets bark
As human gods aim for their mark
        . . . It's easy to see
        without looking too far
Not much
Is really sacred."

In *'Little Planet Blues'*
the Japanese poet
Kazuko Shiraishi
reflects on how —

". . . *Killers get high on*
     the God of Science
     & cheer the big Arms Race on
Kicking the globe in the head and
     puncturing its skin

Earth looks like it won't recover,
     too many humans watching TV . . .

". . . *Will anyone witness our little*
     Noah's Ark planet drown
     in the Universe?

Only if they're able to dig up a
     Time Capsule named the Future . . . "

In Hindu tradition
             "Shanti"
– the Sanskrit word with whose repetition
Eliot ended his *Waste Land* –
                              is a mantra
                              questing
                              meditative truth.

Eliot's note says
     "The Peace which passeth understanding"
     is "our equivalent to this word".

     Om . . .

"Shantih shantih shantih . . . "

— Yet furthermore

". . . Loud sing Goddam!"

       — For at the end of twenty centuries
of avowedly Christian values,
a basic keeping of peace
still looks to go on passing
beyond the understanding
of the *UN*united nations
of this once fertile planet
so suicidally run to waste
by its power-crazed leaders

            — empowered to lead
by no more than the volume
of weapons and money
banked up their arses

— self-disabled from leading
their respective subjects
to anything

    but mutual destruction

by their inflexible
     uniform addiction
     to the Moneyburg Address:

". . . That this Nation,
under Arms, shall have
a new birth of Money;
and that
    government of the Money,
by the Money,
and for the Money,
shall not perish
     from the earth."

U.S. ARMS INDUSTRY DIAGRAM: HOW SON OF STAR WARS WILL WORK.

① ENEMY MISSILE LAUNCHED...

② U.K. RADAR TRACKS TRAJECTORY...

③ 'KILLER VEHICLE' INTERCEPTS...

④ GEE, THAT IS **SO** BEAUTIFUL!

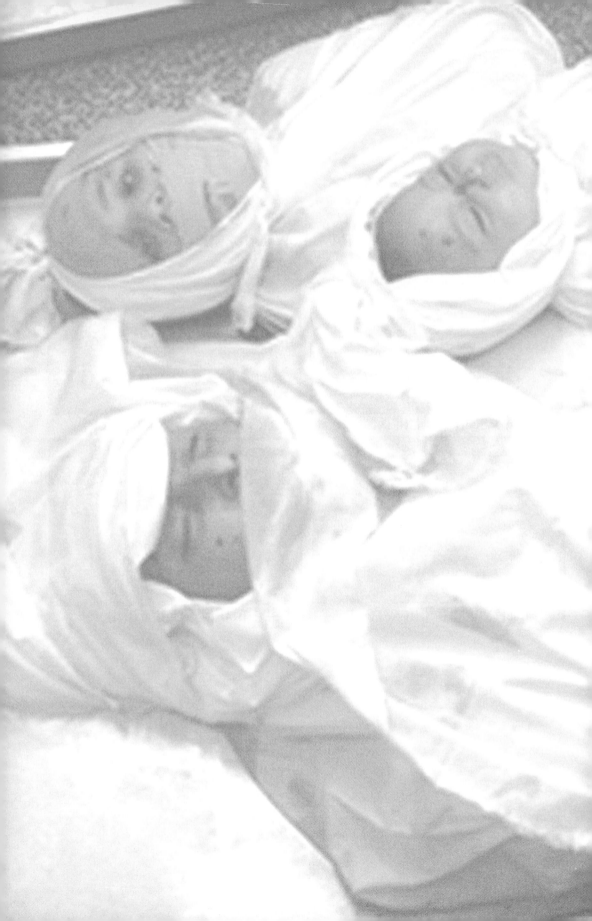

X.
Bombs Degrade Humanity

LONDON

I wander thro' each charter'd street,
Near where the charter'd Thames does flow
And mark in every face I meet
Marks of weakness, marks of woe.

In every cry of every Man,
In every Infants cry of fear,
In every voice; in every ban,
The mind-forg'd manacles I hear

How the Chimney-sweepers cry
Every blackning Church appalls,
And the hapless Soldiers sigh
Runs in blood down Palace walls

But most thro' midnight streets I hear
How the youthful Harlots curse
Blasts the new-born Infants tear
And blights with plagues the Marriage hearse

X. *Bombs Degrade Humanity*

Two hundred years ago Blake saw
"... Marks of weakness, marks of woe"
in every face he met
on every polluted Thames-bank street

. . . goods, labour, people
then as now – bought up only
to be sold for profit
over and over
– bought up and sold
                              all the way
up and down each river, chartered
pollutant pipeline and trade canal

. . . each wage-slave reflecting
the drear porn-gilt skies,
Satanic drudge-mills, wanton lies
of this time-dishonoured
nation of shopkeepers.

After the First World War, amid
The Waste Land's ". . . heap of broken images"
     Eliot saw how, on London Bridge
". . . each man fixed his eyes before his feet".

     Today's descendants of those eyes
who have the job security or means

     – or just
     the job

          . . . such as minding
          – and being minded by –
          computer screens . . .

are just as lowly fixed
– repetitively stressed
and strained, disjointed
because plugged
                    (sometimes blinded)

– cyber militia
locked deep and dull within
the warring systems
of ever more multi-programmed
supersales machines

                    – to what new chartered ends

                    O High Tech governors

                              – Mister Jobsworth's Friends?

If millennial technology
can replace sweat-of-brow enslavement,
the supergod of money can stop
                              setting the pace
      on every road and pavement

— and all those drives for "wealth and job creation"
can U-turn and park in the ample
work fulfilment and liberation
spawned by creation pure and simple.

          Western governments could do (have done)
a lot worse than think (and act)
on Blake's homespun intelligence:

      ". . . Poetry Fetter'd Fetters the Human Race.
      Nations are Destroy'd or Flourish in proportion
      as Their Poetry, Painting and Music
      are Destroy'd or Flourish . . ."

                              — except that
                              we're over forty years
                              into the *Space* Age:

                                        Nationalism has to be
                                        an anachronism

                                        — this flag or that
                                        a dead language

                                        instead of
                                        the same old
                                        death-dealing one

"NOT ONE OF US"

    — yet Britain's political leaders ape
U S notions
            of war being fun
— and show wannabe Super-Star Warriors
in Russia and China,
                North Korea and Iran,
    Israel, India, Syria, Pakistan
— possibly even, alas, Japan
how to rise from the nuclear also-rans
    — what to do to be reckoned potential
    World Cup calibre
              New-Age Guns.

    And then these same Western leaders
ring alarm bells and spout moral outrage
at the copycat reverberation

— New *UN*clear
          bomb proliferation
    — which America first set in motion

                    — and which America, with Britain in tow,
                    keeps most threatfully on hold
                      (trump card in the game)
                    for "contingency" devastation

    — which helps genocidal potential
shoot on up and become the essential
corporate nation-status credential

                  to be flashed — the prime blue-chip crest
                  at the helm
                      of the prime
                  (multi) national interest

— whilst the actual people
subsumed by the nations
    remain sand-grains in the domes

        of that
            "Class of Men"
        Blake warned us to fight

                ". . . whose whole delight
               is in Destroying . . ."

HURRY UP PLEASE,

     IT'S TIME

    . . . Closing Time

for the leading men
(playground bullies)
who fly too high
           above themselves
           and play God

— men who've made machines
  that hit and miss
their strongest hand

             and arms outstretched
              beyond clear use
            their holy trump

— leading men who keep on
misleading
        so-called servicemen
        and service women
(meaning pawns, wage-slaves
— pawned men and women

             who could otherwise be
             good, brave, loving men
             and loving women)
to be reduced, in war
to packs of hounds,
to bay for blood

     — programmed to keep
     their laser-sharpened claws
     on standby for the next
     Crusader high command

             to maim, shoot, or annihilate
             their sometime fellow
                   man and mate
    — to zap in for the kill

            in the *"nobly*
               . . . *decorous"* service
         of wars against the same
           feeling flesh,
           breathing blood
           — bare bone as blameless
                as their own.

Terror in London, 1940

Terror in Dresden, 1945

Terror in Hiroshima, 1945

Terror in Nagasaki, 1945

I feel the heartbeat
of my beloved
as my hands stroke
her sleeping breast
and belly

 . . . as I listen
to the peaceful
rhythm
of her breathing

    echoes
     of the songs
we used to sing, and dance to
run through my mind

 and mingle
with the twining cadenzas
 of early birds

" . . . Just 'cause you're black,
folks think you lack,
They laugh at you
and scorn you too
. . . All my life through
I've been so black and blue.

"How will it end?
Ain't got a friend.
My only sin
is in my skin.
What did I do
to be so black and blue?"

. . . Old blue song
quests the quiet
small hours air
for an answer

. . . moon fades
to a thumbprint

beyond the curtain
at daybreak

. . . new bird songs
shy sylvan sounds

that recall
the sweet falls

of water
    plashing
        over stones

    in the streams
        running through
            a Cotswold valley

    all through
        the summer nights

                long

                    years

                        ago

falling

   falling

        water becomes water

                over stone

— till

     radio waves
break

     imploding that idyll

with brain-dead rumbulations
of Big Bomb-bloated
techno-megalo-
        Man
           at large

               — staccato braggadocio
                 of the inescapable Voice
          of Top Doktor Amerikkka's
          "surgical"
              missile strikes

                     — inflaming terror

                         in Afghanistan

       — cremating medicine

           in Sudan

– praxis of

              (for whose sins?)

recurrent man-made thunder

– of Cruise-Aider Clint's
and Bomb-Trader Tone's

             and Bash-Blagger Dubbya's

mutual bad-habit hardened
blunderbuss cluster-

           bombardments of Iraq

THE NEO-CRUSADERS

           – day in,

           night out –

inescapable, uncontrollable
hard floods of fire

                     falling

                          falling

— bursting chemical tanks
that erupt poisoned rain

(nor any drop
to drink . . .)

— for eleven weeks
of "degrading
Serbia's infrastructure"
to rubble and dead flesh

— on 'good' days piously
written off as

" . . . *regrettable,*
but unavoidable
uh . . . collateral damage"

— as directed by Nato's
top couch potatoes

(meaning
the bombing out
of basic lifelines
for fellow humans
who've done nothing
to warrant
being sacrificed as scapegoats
to the insatiable idols
of superpower mania

— as charred fig leaves
to camouflage
one military hit man's
sexual miscellanea)

"... When will they
ever learn ... ?"

Wall Street, New York, 9/11/2001

Tavistock Square, London, 7/7/2005

– Extra time?

  – Only till
  some unrefereed
  foul-up

    beyond "conventional"
    penalty shoot-out

Nagasaki, 9/8/1945

  nukes to oblivion

  the worldwide game.

— Random scattershot
explosions implant
untold more scattershot
land, sea and air wounds
inexorably
            corroding the future

— extending the death-for-death
futilities of the past

~ Dresden

~ Hiroshima

~ Nagasaki

~ Vietnam

~ Cambodia

— the barbarous terrors
of Hitler's 1940
airblitz on London

. . . and later

his doodlebugs

— unassailably unpiloted
flametailed dive-bombs
whose despotic drone
then ———————————

suddenly

silent

plunge

scattered us   kids

from searching out
velvet-cased walnuts
amidst the damp
leafmulch
beneath the trees
in suburban Cheam

— to run   for cover

under the   high-arched

railway bridge

— with frenzied parents

teachers, neighbours

— friends and enemies alike . . .

Nillennium could be
the last chance
for "our" time

. . . to begin afresh
for real

for the race
that calls itself
human

to dump warfare
and nationblare

— and run

and together
rebuild

itself
to new futures
as one

meaningfully
new
millennium

before the last
green ground

experience

on the planet

is bomb dust

and
company

corpse ashes

unlimited . . .

all gone

XI.

U-Turn On All This
— or Die

XI. *U-Turn On All This — or Die*

What we actually have
in pseudo-millennial Britain
is a new waste land
                    over which
a cold central government darkness
            thick with the swarming farts and grafts
            of opportunism, gambling, infinite greed
                — of obligatory bar-coded consumerism
                pleated in as sternly as Thatcher's suits were
                with martial buttons and he-man padding
                    and the same unconcern
                    for the weak and disadvantaged
— is imposed, officialised
— bankroll-modelled
                    by the new Alright-Hons

— callous
and complicit as the last gang
        with planned obsolescence
        — with that casual victimisation of the powerless
            which is bound to leave worse-off than ever
            anyone who won't
                        — or can't —
                                buy into
                                profit from
                                        and spread
            this government darkness visible
            — clotted as Monsanto — thick
                        as thieves in the night
        with sycophancy, cronyism, owed favours, bribery
        — with prostitution on every level,
        with calculated deception and finagling,
        with state-scripted killer drug addiction
            — with planted questions, evasive answers,
            ballot-rigging, censorship, ruthless arm-twisting,
            industrial giantism, global market-worship,
            gung-ho chauvinism, pea-brained Hollywooden
                        conquering heroics and kneejerk violence
                — with blind eyes turned
                to detentions without trial, pornogoric charades,
                    serial beatings, rapes and torture renditions
                        in the sacrosanct name of so-called
                                        Intelligence

                                   — all
           inextricably twinned with
      abject habitual sucking up
                                   to Uncle Sam's leaden
                                   dreamless design
                                   of Mob-rule materialist
                                   world domination

— so that what we're breathing
is Washington smog
expertly packaged
in Westminster fog

   — central darkness imposed
   by crafty farter figures
   as overfed
                   and avid as the last gang
   to pile up the spoils
      of unremitting arms deals

   — callous
   and complicit as the last gang
   in stoking the death fires
      of more and more wars

   that only stoke up the death fires
      of more and more wars
   amongst the earth's far-flung inmates

      — cynical as the last gang
      in plundering and poisoning
         the wide world's
                              (once) whole
                                      eco-system.

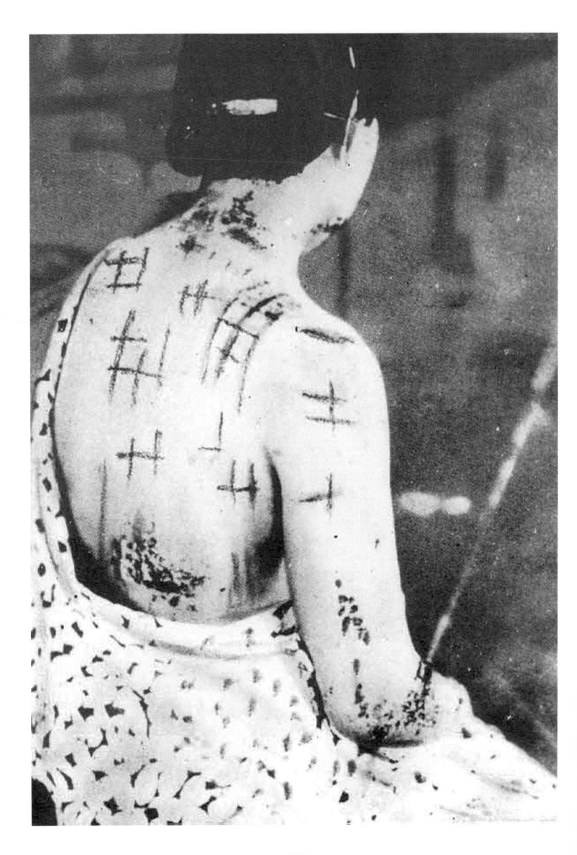

No arms race
is ever won
for good
after all

— think on the

e v e r l a s t i n g l y

l o s t   f a c e s

and bodies
of Japanese
generations —

    – belatedly think, and repent, Bomber Blur
and your confrère Gorge Bash, over there
in silly-con missile Valhalla
– toxic Tex, *try to* –   *think*

              (stop fiddling with oilmen while forests burn),

on T S Eliot's prediction
of the ultimate
         doomed waste land
your uncontrollably spiralling military glands
have ground so many ships
           of state
and statelessness   towards

   – upon which

        "*. . . the dead tree gives no shelter, the cricket no relief,*
        And the dry stone no sound of water. Only
        There is shadow under this red rock,
        (Come in under the shadow of this red rock),
        And I will show you something different from either
        Your shadow at morning striding behind you
        Or your shadow at evening rising to meet you;
        I will show you fear in a handful of dust . . ."

Is not a reverence
for life
      – for all land, sea and air
the path Jesus struck,
      Shock and Awe Basher Bush,
      Trade and War Preacher Blair?

Have you no shame?
          How could you claim
to follow Christ
when your fame has spread
so many dark days and nights
          with more dead
across so many lands, from your hands

      – famed oily blood brothers
who wrought so much hurt, loss and fright
    – dread of so many children and mothers
with your gospel of markets and self-righteous might
whose weapons ignite still more terror and plight
filling land, sea and air
with endless infection, bombs and despair?

   "Love thy neighbour
          as thyself"
  – NOT
    "An eye for an eye"

is what Jesus preached,
    Big Top Barker Bush,
          and your yapping
    Dog-collared Upsucking
          Mascot Blair.

— How can arms trading,
bomb threatening — avenging — sky-raiding

— or your rape of nature
    for agronomic, patriotic, mere opinion poll gain

— or your cock-crowings of
    'God Bless
           AMERICA'

   and
      'BRITAIN
           is Leading the world'

— or your dictatorial imperatives
   of 'any old — or new
               — WORK
                   will set us free'

   because
      'MONEY
          Conquers All'

                  — how could any of this nurture
                 a land and a future

                    to which any two lovers
                    will want to look forward

                      to adding
                     one more

                          earthling

                            at all?

. . . It has written off Britain
as just another
               arms trade stockpile

in whose nooks and crannies
                              weapons
of limitless destruction
are assembled, and stashed

                    to spread contamination
                    and fear
                    and unnatural death

                              – to make money
                              from oppression
                              and unnatural death

                    by making weapons
                          for other lands
                          to pay for

                              – making weapons
                    designed
                    to terrorise
                              – designed
                                        to murder

                    – designed to bank on
                    ever smarter
                              missiles of money

                    from their victims' total fall

— and if this craven Britain
is any part
of any common wealth

    of any worldwide
    family
     of man

as invoked
since humanity
   began

 — how can it but appal

  such children

   grandchildren

    or mutated lives

      as may contrive

     to survive

       the post-nuclear

      chemi-strafed

       bio-spangled ball?

— Rather than promote
the means to trap,
methodically mutilate
and massacre,
   why not

 — help push
world creature comforts

in the opposite
     — child friendly,
   new futurely
       direction

   — Wind down
  all those sexless
      military-industrial
        divisions

      — Why not

       out the corny sham heroics
       of presidential wheeler-dealing

       — dump sham economics

       — close off once for all
       that frantic
         fast-lane
          selling drive?

     — Work anew
    instead, to keep
       all god's children
         healthily alive

     — for *trans*global

       "community to thrive"

Politicians – get real:

    – forget
"*Leading*
        the world"

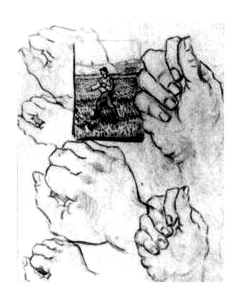

– just knuckle down

to weeding it.

Dump old greeds

    – plant new seeds

New statesmen
and – with luck –
more new stateswomen

– U-Turn

and redeem us
from the arrant lies

of the woolly bully
Wild West henchmen
oiled into office
by pseudo-legal benchmen

– those power-drugged
scar-spangled
bomblet-bangled
nothing new
American Centurions,
Britsuck Millenarians:

– Forget pseudo-Churchillian
interventions
– give up for good
on spreading terror
by brown-nosing any more
of yon Neo-Con Captains'
ill-conceived
ill-targeted
illegal
amoral
inhuman
so-called pre-emptive
strikes

Hiroshima, 1945 – c. 175,000 killed

– kill not . . .

— Cultivate gardens.

Plant afresh
from what's left
of the grass roots:

— that will help
strike up
a true new world music

— help replace
America the booty-full's
doom-booming cacophony
of empire-preserving scams.

As we have seen

. . . they that live by the Bomb
perish by the Bomb . . .

So let us
see afresh

New York, 2001 — c. 3,000 killed

. . . that we be not killed —

Nato Intervention (= Terror) in Belgrade, 1999

(Un-Press Released) Terror in New York, 2001

Shock and Awe (= Terror) in Baghdad, 2003

(Un-Press Released) Terror in Madrid, 2004

Terror in Abu Ghraib, 2003

Terror in London, 2005

This Page – A bus carrying high school and college students blown up by suicide bombing in Haifa, March 2003

Facing Page – Top: Palestinian family with the remains of their demolished home in Galilee, February 2004
Middle: (Palestinian) David and (Israeli-American) Goliath in the West Bank, 2002
Bottom: 10 year old Huda Ghalia weeps by the body of her dead father on a Gaza beach, June 2006

XII. *Epilogue:*
A New Land's Hymn
to would-be Star War Saints
like Bulls Clint, Bash and Blur

whose rigged haloes bleed

Christ's gospel to despair

A President thumbs up his pose

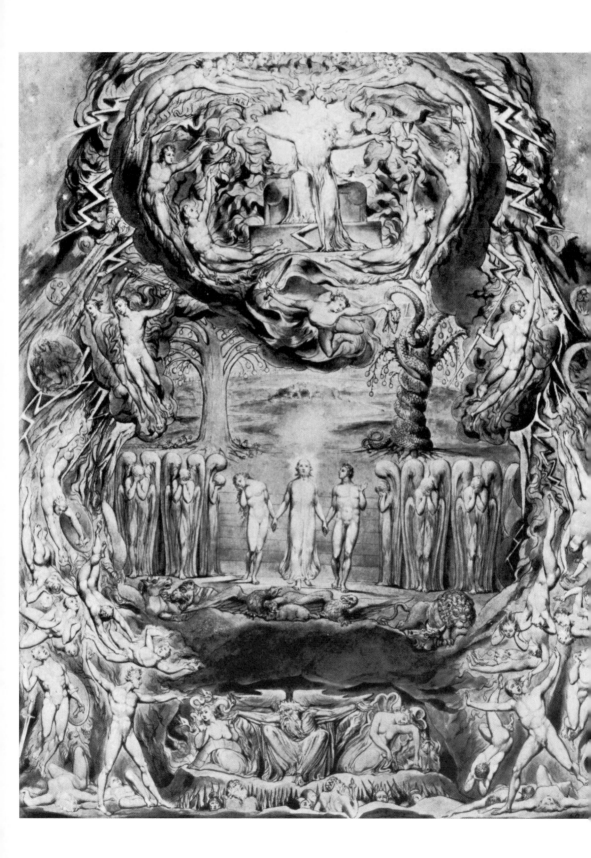

XII. *Epilogue: A New Land's Hymn to plaster saints like Tone and Gorge*

. . . . whose bombastic orgies still feed
more bloodlusts — more terror —

more god-hawking death-trade greed.

If Christ were to grace His Millennium today
He'd have bopped Bush, whipped Blair
— and shooed out of play
All the fat corporations
that swag on the nations
From every cent of their ill-gotten gains

— Yea

— His shout to World Leaders
would be pointed and plain:

"Decommission armies
and arms,
Put your trust in eco-farms.

Only interconnect
Every race, creed and sect
With the earth's rich resources

And reap the effect
Of new practical courses
For true global kinship

Through the peace-loving forces
Of equal rights
and fair
Shares for all — coexisting

In mutual human respect."

      – Wherefore,
World Leaders
               . . . soft,
think ahead

  – of how
each space age human
not prematurely dead
     will thank and value
     and bless and love
     those who heal this planet's pain
         and build our children's futures plain

     – those who'll heed the challenge of a rap
like this one
           that welled up from the lap
             of the poet Grace Nichols

in a cadence that tickles
that trustworthy touchstone,
the serious funny bone

            – spelling out
         what her daughter
         Kalera taught her
                – in *'Baby-K Rap Rhyme'* : –

"My name is Baby-K
An dis is my rhyme
Sit back folks
While I rap my mind;

Ah rocking with my homegirl,
My Mommy
Ah rocking with my homeboy,
My Daddy . . .

. . . Wish my rhyme wasn't hard
Wish my rhyme wasn't rough
But sometimes, people
You got to be tough

Cause dey pumping up de chickens
Dey stumping down de trees
Dey messing up de ozones
Dey messing up de seas
Baby-K say, stop dis —
please, please, please

    poop po-doop
      poop-poop po-doop
    poop po-doop
      poop-poop po-doop

. . . dey hotting up de globe, man
Dey hitting down de seals
Dey killing off de ellies
For dere ivories
Baby-K say, stop dis —
please, please, please

. . . Dis is my Baby-K rap
But it's a kinda plea
What kinda world
Dey going to leave fuh me?

What kinda world
Dey going to leave fuh me?

      Poop po-doop . . ."

Olé!

So
         — Hear the pleas of babies,
                              heed the birds that fly far
From those lies about change, peace and growth

    That still shadow each day
                            with munitions that scar
The whole world with pollution and death.

Should old assurances be forgot
  — Nay, banished from your mind

When arms deals thrive
                    and hospitals clot
  'Tis cruel to be kind —

Hear the cries of babies
                    and the birds on the wing
  From your lies about wrongs righting wrongs

That hot up night and day
                    with more Big Deals that pay
  Endless wages to war and bombs.

    . . . *Should old assurances be forgot*
    And long gone from your stand

  When hucksters swell
                    and paupers slue
  'Tis killing to be bland —

Sure, if Jesus Christ were alive again
His word to People's PMs would be plain:

"Halleluja Saint Tories, memento mori —
One day yous too will be down and out . . .

"Money changers ring in, underclasses rot?
Recall, Sirs, your mandate so quickly forgot

"— U-turn on all this,
　　　　　　　replace hardship and piss
With full cups of kindness yet . . ."

— Amen indeed:
　　　　— *If* you'd slash away
　　　　　　　　　Top People's greed,
Build a Britain that's really new
　　Letting each of us have what we need

— We'd give of our best, thanking you —

For a caring country, bold Ministers
　　For commitment through and through

We'll fill our cups, running over yet
　　For a brave new land, and true:

Yea —

Let's sow fresh seeds of kindness yet

In this good earth we'll renew.

— Amen indeed:

       — Slash away imperial powers,
     Big Business greed

          — and instead
Give every land's poor their due.

       Let every Muslim
           who wants to

           — live, work or breed
    with each
         agnostic, Christian or Jew.

Now Israelis and Arabs
play music together

like seeds in the pod

      of their godliest
      nature curled

           — why can't you too
          share your light,

               proud
                multi-
                national mates

               — and unite
                  all the states
                  of the world?

You preached
                    ". . . the values
                    of civilisation"

    to sponsor

    and market
                    world war.

                    Now relearn
                                    – and at long last
                    practise
                                    those values

                                    to rebuild

                                    and keep
                                                    world peace.

    . . . . For healing the nations, bold Ministers –

    For commitment through and through

    We'll take a cup of kindness yet
                                    – and launch

    Our Timeship Earth anew.

— or . . .

. . . not? –

Civilian victims of 'War' in Haifa, July 2006

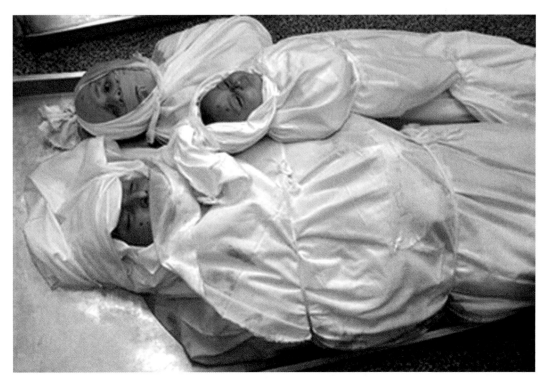

Civilian victims of 'War' in Gaza, July 2006

Civilian victims of 'War' in Qana, Lebanon, April 1996

Civilian victims of 'War' in Qana, Lebanon, July 2006

". . . . . . it's a kinda plea
What kinda world
Dey going to leave fuh me?"

"......mine in every land,
Mutual shall build Jerusalem,
Both heart in heart, and hand in hand."

"A poem is never finished . . ."

— Paul Valéry (*Littérature* 1930)

Notes to
A New Waste Land

HOUSEHOLDS WILL BE TAXED ON THE AMOUNT OF RUBBISH THEY PUT OUT

Notes to 'A New Waste Land'

Front Cover photograph of Bikini Atoll Nuclear Explosion

This photograph depicts the fiery mushroom cloud that rose into the sky after the test detonation of an 11-megaton nuclear bomb (charmlessly codenamed "Romeo") over Bikini Atoll on the 26th March 1954.

It was one of the twenty-three United States nuclear bomb tests carried out on Bikini Atoll between 1946 and 1958. The first day of March 1954 saw the first test here of a practical hydrogen bomb, codenamed "Castle Bravo". This was the largest nuclear explosion ever detonated, and created widespread radioactive contamination.

Bikini Atoll is a member of the Marshall Islands in the West Pacific Ocean, 2,000 miles south-west of Hawaii. Before the tests began, the indigenous population was relocated to the underdeveloped Rongerik Atoll.

In 1968 the US declared Bikini island habitable again, and over the subsequent years brought many Bikinians back to their homes. But in 1978 the islanders were re-evacuated when it was discovered that they had ingested the largest dose of plutonium ever monitored in any population. Strontium-90 in their bodies had reached highly dangerous levels, with women falling ill and dying during childbirth at an extraordinarily high rate.

Two-piece bikini swimsuits came into vogue just days after the first nuclear test, taking their name from the island with reference to their supposedly explosive effect. One wonders whether the abovementioned codename "Romeo" was arrived at by a similar token.

Here are some pertinent lines from *'SPAM'*, by the Hawaiian performance artist and poet Stacy Makishi: —

> ". . . *My Uncle Sam canned SPAM.*
> *Grinding meat was his daily grind.*
>
> *. . . In 1946 the Yanks dropped a series of nuclear bombs*
> *on an island in the Pacific called Bikini Atoll.*
>
> *The islanders were relocated*
> *to where there were no natural resources,*
> *but for compensation the Yanks gave them SPAM.*
>
> *My Uncle decided to change his name,*
> *while the Yanks changed his address,*
> *and renamed him and his wife, Sam and Pam.*
> *My Uncle said, "We're Sam and Pam,*
> *together we make SPAM!"*
>
> *. . . On July 10th 1968, on the bombing anniversary of Bikini Atoll,*
> *my Uncle Sam jumped into the meat grinder at SPAM.*
> *It was Sam's way of bombing them back.*
>
> *But the Yanks compensated Pam*
> *with 300 cans of SPAM*
>
> *The cans that might contain my Uncle Sam."*

The full text of this poem can be read in *'The POT! (Poetry Olympics Twenty05) Anthology'* (New Departures #36-37, 2005).

Page 2

"*. . . Jesus Christ (circa 6, 5 or 4 BC – c. 29 AD) . . .*"

Controversy continues to rage regarding this Messiah's dates. Among the most persuasive arguments, those of Dr Ethelbert William Bullinger (1837-1913) in *'The Companion Bible'* (Oxford 1921, and Kregel, Grand Rapids, Michigan, USA 1990) are meticulously researched, putting His birthdate as 29 September, 4 BC and His death as 3 April, 29 AD.

One thing which seems fairly certain is that His 2000th birthday did *not* fall between December 1999 and January 2001 . . .

Page 6

"*The state of Africa is a scar on the conscience of the world . . .*"

– first mooted by Tony Blair in his speech to the Labour Party Conference on 3 October 2001

"*. . . arms sales to Africa netting between 126 and 130 million pounds . . .*"

See the *'Strategic Export Controls, Annual Report'* of 2001, as quoted in the Campaign Against Arms Trade publication *'Arms Export Licences to Africa (1999 & 2000)'*, via *www.caat.org.uk.*

This staggering amount included sales of weaponry to Kenya and Morocco, both countries with deeply suspect human rights records. It also included sales worth £63.5m to South Africa alone, a country that had recently committed itself to arms purchases totalling almost four *billion* pounds from European companies – more than ten times the amount it set aside for the treatment and prevention of AIDS.

And this deal was pulled in a year when Britain's aid to South Africa totalled only thirty *million* pounds.

All these facts and figures are detailed further in the December 2001 CAAT publication *'Arms to Africa'* by Catherine Brown, Nick Gilby and Simon Kearns (*www.caat.org.uk*).

In December 2001 Blair took the extraordinary step of personally intervening in order to clinch the sale of a £28 million military air traffic control system to Tanzania, despite the fact that this country had only *eight* military aeroplanes.

The system, supplied by BAe, was in fact condemned by the World Bank as a waste of money: a far more appropriate civilian system could have been bought for one fifth of the price.

Nevertheless our PM arm-twisted the grindingly poor country into the deal, against the wishes of his own International Development Secretary, merely to safeguard 280 jobs on the Isle of Wight.

For more on this, see *'Tanzania aviation deal a waste of money'* by David Hencke, Charlotte Denny and Larry Elliott in the Guardian of 14/6/02. Also, re the sham government claims that weapons'n'war-friendly production and exports are essential for job maintenance and the economy, see the quotations from Samuel Brittan, and further reflections, on page 368 & ff. And see also other takes on this, including Clare Short's thoughts about the £28m deal, on pages 432-433.

The question of how any scars would be healed by getting Tanzania, which owed $7,238 million in debts in 2002, to waste so much more money on such a ludicrously useless item, is one to which Blair has yet to offer the Tanzanians an answer.

If our Dr Jekyll Care Blair genuinely wanted to heal Africa, he needed to stop tossing teensy scraps with one hand, whilst clawing back desperately needed finance from endangered lives with the other. He needed to actually speak, deal and behave like the *"pretty straight kind of guy"* he had captioned himself to be in the triumphalist wake of Labour's landslide election victory of 1997.

". . . Blair got . . . to denounce the Israeli-Palestinian 'cycle of violence which has scarred the region' . . ."

– from *'Eight children among F-16 strike victims'* by Mark Oliver (Guardian 23/7/2002):

"Last night's attack by F-16 warplanes on a densely populated Gaza City neighbourhood killed Salah Shehadeh, 48, a founder and top commander of Hamas's military wing, the group has now confirmed.

"The Israeli prime minister, Ariel Sharon, hailed this killing as *'a great success'*. But many voices from the international community have been aghast at the killing of the children and apparent disregard for the lives of civilians.

"The airstrike just before midnight, which obliterated a three-storey apartment block and destroyed or badly damaged several adjacent ones, came at a time when Palestinian and Israeli political leaders were discussing ways to relieve tensions in the West Bank.

"The raid appeared likely to derail those efforts as Hamas said it would take revenge. A statement from the militant group said it would leave Israeli "human remains" in every street, adding: 'This Gaza massacre will not go without a strong penalty'. . ."

– And so it went. And goes. On, and on, and on. Yet all Sharon could repeat was ". . . This operation was in my view one of our biggest successes".

– Thus spake the unchangingly heartless language of murderous Realpolitik. And thus Mark Oliver's report continued:

". . . The Israelis said they did not intend to harm civilians, and the Defence Minister, Binyamin Ben-Eliezer, issued a statement saying that '. . . the information which we had was that there were no civilians near'. However, by firing a powerful missile into a heavily populated residential neighborhood in the middle of the night, civilian casualties were a certainty.

"Shifa Hospital in Gaza City released a separate list of eleven dead that included eight children, aged between two months to 11 years, and three adults. The hospital also said that more than 100 people were wounded . . . The death toll subsequently rose, first to '. . . at least 15', and thereafter – as so often – who will ever know for sure?

"Washington's White House spokesman Ari Fleischer rejected comparisons between the missile strike and American attacks in Afghanistan that have killed hundreds of civilians: '. . . It is inaccurate to compare the two, because the United States, because of an errant bomb, a mistake in a mission, has occasionally *(sic)* engaged in military action that very regrettably included losses of innocent lives. This was a deliberate attack on the site, knowing that innocents would be lost in the consequences of the attack', he said, adding that Bush still remained a strong backer of Israel."

– Indeed. So much so, that the US – actively abetted by Blair – has constantly gone on supplying weapons to Israel, most of which have gone on (and are most likely for the foreseeable future to go on going on) being used to wound and kill Palestinians.

And this murderous supply continued unchecked at the same time as both leaders constantly said and did absolutely nothing to question Israel's more than thirty year-strong and presumably still growing stockpiles of nuclear weapons, whilst constantly turning blind eyes to Israel's obdurate failure to sign the Nuclear Non-Proliferation Treaty.

Furthermore, both leaders have kept their stocks of lethal weaponry and military forces embroiled in the wounding and killing of many thousands of Iraqi civilians. The toll of *additional* (violent) deaths there "above the level expected under pre-war conditions" between the notoriously unthought-through Bush-led invasion on 20/3/2003 and July '06 was clocked at 654,965 by the Bloomberg School of Public Health in Baltimore, published online by The Lancet in October '06.

And meanwhile Dubbya, the most powerful, most bomb-happy, and arguably least accountable living world shaker and mover of the Noughties to date, continued threatening to do the same to several other Bush-branded "axis of evil" countries – as their due for nothing demonstrably worse than, in some cases, researching into or harnessing nuclear energy.

– I too would be much happier if they did not do this. Nor any others at all. But for as long as big powers like America and Britain keep flaunting, enlarging and upgrading their nuclear arsenals and developments, how can smaller ones be blamed for reflecting that they too need to develop similar and significant counterweights?

As long as US and UK armaments of any kind are supplied to any régimes at all, the "cycles of violence" Blair pretended to bemoan are bound to go on scarring the regions occupied, coveted or cherished by such régimes.

". . . *new guidelines which actively fuelled the [Israeli-Palestinian] violence . . .*"

As Mandy Turner put it in the October 2002 CAAT publication *'Arming the Occupation: Israel and the Arms Trade'* –

> "The figures . . . indicate that UK arms exports to Israel have been pretty constant since 1994 – the change of government from Conservative to Labour in 1997 appears to have made little difference – until the quantum leap in 2001.
>
> "This was the year in which Sharon had come to power denouncing Oslo, and the al-Aqsa Intifada raged – a time of great pessimism in the peace process. The value of UK military export licences to Israel almost doubled from £12.5m in 2000 to £22.5m in 2001."

Furthermore, a Guardian report of 29/5/02 revealed that both Israeli Merkava tanks and US-made Apache helicopters, in use against Palestinian civilians in the West Bank and Gaza Strip, contained essential components made in Britain.

As oft-times before and since, our self-styled "ethical" leaders tried to evade responsibility for the end-use of weapons by shifting blame onto the intervening country. But these blood-slippery bucks cannot be so easily passed over. It became increasingly clear that New Labour's claims to be running an ethical arms policy were so much sanctimonious hot air.

"*weapon sales manager Blair . . . flogging 66 new Hawk jets to India . . . The deal cost them one billion pounds*"

– see *'BAe wins £1bn Hawk contract'* by Mark Tran (Guardian 3/9/03)

"*Blair had* 'absolutely no doubt at all that . . . [Saddam] was a threat', *in possession of Weapons of Mass Destruction which could lay the UK to waste at 45 minutes' notice . . .*"

In an MTV Forum *'Is War the Answer?'* on 6 March 2003, the Prime Minister stated:

> ". . . I've absolutely no doubt at all that if we don't deal with this issue of weapons of mass destruction, certainly he's a threat . . . When we call them weapons of mass destruction, I sometimes think it deludes the language of any real meaning."

The irony in hearing this master of delusion complaining about corruption of meaning lent another touch of sick humour to his gruesomely uncomical enterprise.

New Labour's screening, manipulation and abuse of language were central to the war-boosting project.

The BBC Radio 4 Today Programme's accusation that Intelligence reports were "sexed up" turns out, after subsequent revelations, to be irrefutable. The reports were punctiliously censored and dumbed down, with a lot of their original carefully worded and qualified structures twisted out of alignment, and their basic ascertainable facts pulled by the nose to serve the US administration's preconceived plan.

The false pretence that Iraq could launch UK-threatening Weapons of Mass Destruction strikes within 45 minutes was mentioned four times, and highlighted in Blair's Introduction, in the dossier presented to Parliament on 24 September 2002. The authors of the dossier knew that this figure referred to short-range battlefield weapons, but omitted this crucial fact from the dossier in order to wring out the maximum pretend air-raid-warning alarm bells.

Another omission deemed politic was the fact, mentioned in a draft of Blair's foreword to the dossier, but subsequently dropped, that –

> ". . . the case I made is not that Saddam could launch a nuclear attack on London or another part of the UK (he could not) . . ."

A view as balanced as this (which was subsequently revealed in the Intelligence and Security Committee's report published on 11 September 2003) would have taken most of the wind-up out of Blair's sales. So the notional threat of nuclear or other annihilation was left just tacitly hanging, the better to brainwash MPs and the public.

In point of fact Blair was explicitly told by the Joint Intelligence Committee on 10 February 2003 that there was *no* evidence that Iraq had passed on chemical or biological materials to al-Qaeda, nor that Iraqi agents intended to conduct terrorist attacks.

However, according to the ISC's report of 11/9/03, the JIC ". . . judged that *in the event of imminent régime collapse there would be a risk of transfer of such material . . .*" They further assessed that ". . . al-Qaeda and associated groups continue to represent by far the greatest terrorist threat to western interests, and *that threat would be* heightened *by military action against Iraq*".

Yet Blair kept intensely quiet about this risk in his melodramatic speech to Parliament on 18 March 2003, claiming instead that "the possibility . . . of terrorist groups in possession of weapons of mass destruction . . . *is now, in my judgement, a real and present danger to this country, to Britain, to our national security*" – and urging MPs to "*confront the . . . terrorists* who put our way of life at risk", by voting for war.

These and many similarly suspect allegations and appeals were made in the Prime Minister's Statement that opened the debate about invading Iraq, which was played out in a deeply divided House of Commons (– available from *www.number-10.gov.uk*).

As Paul Keetch, the Liberal Democrat defence spokesman pointed out (Independent, p5, 12/9/03), these were profoundly serious matters:

> ". . . The [Intelligence and Security Committee] report shows we did not go to war on the basis of intelligence, but rather on the basis of *selective use of* intelligence."

Blair ringmastered the debate to highlight the moral case for attacking Iraq as a given: he kept stumm about régime change, yet paid lip-service to the tenet that "if we do act, we should do so with a clear conscience".

– How could any avowedly moral minister seek parliamentary endorsement of a "Shock-and-Awe" programme for massive bombardment and killing of fellow humans (to be written off, as so many had been in the Balkans four years previously, as "unavoidable collateral damage"), on so wilfully distorted a prospectus, *"with a clear conscience"*?

The PM's cavalier disregard for the deaths of innocent people that were bound to result from the invasion, and for its questionable legitimacy under international law, showed him to be a moral chameleon with a conscience (if any) more sere than clear – apparently committed to little more than self-aggrandising political manipulation, with White House brown-nosing his *sine qua non*.

Many MPs swallowed or pretended to buy the dodgy dossier's insinuations. But even if one considered that Blair's determination to go along with Bush and his corporate gang's invasion of Iraq might – just might – have been based on *bona fide* strategic or moral convictions rather than dubious ulterior motives, the fact remains that he fraudulently presented the case for war as watertight.

In fact it was as ultra-selectively leaky and disinformative as the machinations of Blair's press corps thought fit for his (poodling) and George Bush's (oil-and-territory controlling) purposes.

In all probability the two Bleeders had done a deal a year or more before in which Blair had committed shoulder-to-shoulder British support for the US-led invasion no matter what. Plus, since the Parliamentary debate and vote were scheduled only 24 hours before the projected invasion, with masses of UK troops out in the Gulf at the ready, even if the Commons majority had ended up vetoing the onslaught, it could have had little effect in delaying it. A number of MPs later volunteered that this was what had restrained them from voting against. (See also pages 314-317.)

"Baha Mousa"

– see pages 341-349

"Our People's Padre's oft-vaunted sincerity and 'passionate beliefs' . . . were and remain irrelevant"

Under the heading *'Blair says: God will be my judge over Iraq War'* (Independent 4/3/2006, pp1-2), Andy McSmith reported on Blair's interview on Michael Parkinson's TV chat show ". . . echoing statements from his ally George Bush (*'God told me to invade Iraq'* . . .)". Such cop-outs from Prime Ministerial and Presidential responsibility send unedifying signals to our so-called enemy combatants and to (potential) terrorists and their trainers, against whom Bush'n'Blair's foreign policy words and actions are supposedly targeted.

Is not deferring responsibility for massive quantities of unnatural deaths and destruction to gods of any kind one of the things subscribers to (western) democracy most understandably hate?

– And the more so when we witness or experience the maiming, abusing and felling into dusty oblivion of ourselves or our fellows, families and buildings by (suicide) bombers who are doing their worst whilst stridently debasing articles of faith like *"Allah is Great"*?

Are such destroyers too not saying, ". . . *God will be my judge"* – ?

By what rationale, then, can the latter be branded categorically "evil" and hence legitimate bomb, shock and awe fodder, whilst (western) armed forces carrying out Bush'n'Blair's allegedly God-driven warfarings can not be so branded and attacked – ?

And on what grounds different from those of other pseudo-religious killers will the Gods of Bush or Blair smile the results of their coalitions of bombardments to see?

– Meaning the murders and disruptions of the lives of innumerable children, women and men at the indelibly bloodstained hands of these "our" presumed "good" missionaries?

– Not in my name (despite Michael meaning *"who is like God"* in Hebrew). Double standards, victors' justice and presumed divine rights need to be recognised for what they are: plain wrong – and therefore need to be kept down, over and out.

". . . as the OED defines 'passion' . . ."

– i e, the Concise Oxford English Dictionary, tenth edition (2001), edited by Judy Pearsall

Page 7

". . . don't hate nothing at all/ Except hatred . . ."

– from *'It's alright Ma (I'm Only Bleeding)'* by Bob Dylan

Page 9

"What is that sound high in the air . . ." and following lines

– from T S Eliot's *'The Waste Land'* (1922), V, lines 366-375

Page 10

"Science without religion is lame: religion without science is blind"

– from Albert Einstein's paper for a conference in New York, 9-11 September 1940 (Chapter 13 of *'Science, Philosophy & Religion: a Symposium'*, published by the Conference on Science, Philosophy & Religion in their relation to the Democratic Way of Life, Inc, New York 1941)

"Moloch . . . . . . unobtainable dollars . . ." and ff

– Allen Ginsberg's gloss on this (in *'Collected Poems, 1947-1980'*, Viking 1985) reads:

"Moloch or Molech, the Canaanite fire god, whose worship was marked by parents burning their children as propitiatory sacrifice. *'And thou shalt not let any of thy seed pass through the fire to Molech'* (Leviticus 18, 21)."

In an interview with M H (Jewish Chronicle Literary Supplement, 15/6/1984, pp i-ii), Ginsberg added:

"You're not supposed to sacrifice your children to this fire god . . . not meant to send them off to nuclear war. We're not supposed to send children to mechanical doom . . ."

Page 11

"The people who are in control and the class system and the whole bourgeois scene are the same . . . We've grown up a little . . . but . . . They hyped the kids and the generation"

– from Jan Wenner's interview with John Lennon in Rolling Stone (1970), published in Britain as *'Lennon Remembers'*, Penguin 1971, and then republished (the original uncensored interview, over 176 pages) in 2000 by Rolling Stone Press, NYC, and Verso Books, London

"What are poems for?" and ff

– from section CXLVIII of Geoffrey Hill's *'The Triumph of Love'*, Penguin 1999

"These fragments I have shored against my ruins . . ."

– from *'The Waste Land'*, V, line 430

Page 12

Collage of Margaret Thatcher with Mother Teresa and down-and-outs under Waterloo Arches in 1983 –

Mother Teresa visited London in 1983 and, horrified at the large numbers of homeless people sleeping on the streets, dubbed the capital "a cardboard city". She berated Mrs Thatcher for the rampant hardship and poverty on show, and extracted a promise from the Prime Minister to get a hostel for the homeless constructed in Central London.

Several hours of trawling databases and quizzing experts have not thrown up a scrap of evidence that Thatch ever fulfilled the promise. If in fact she did, I suppose I will for once have to tender apologies and respect to thon perfume-hissing fartfanged monstress.

However, the then Prime Minister's general view, as articulated for instance in the (in)famous interview with Woman's Own magazine (31/10/87), was by no manner of means looking to prioritise hostels for the homeless:

> "I think we have been through a period where too many people have been given to understand that if they have a problem, it's the government's job to cope with it. 'I have a problem, I'll get a grant'. 'I'm homeless, the government must house me'. They're casting their problem on society. And, you know, there is no such thing as society. There are individual men and women, and there are families . . ."

When she revisited the city in April 1988, Mother Teresa took journalists on walkabouts for two successive nights round the areas she had found to be so flagrantly deprived five years before, notably under Hungerford and Waterloo Bridges. She stated that, to her chagrin –

> "I believe there's much *more* suffering now, much *more* loneliness, painful loneliness of people rejected by society, who have no one to care for them.
>
> ". . . I did not know what to say, my eyes were full of tears. It hurt me so much to see our people in the terrible cold with just a bit of cardboard around them."

Thirteen years later the plight of down-and-outs had got much worse still – as witness the following excerpts from a speech by Paul Stinchcombe, then Labour MP for Wellingborough, on the second reading of the Homelessness Bill (2 July 2001: Hansard Columns 93-95):

> "Homelessness is an evil that has no place in modern society, yet like all Hon Members I have seen sights in this country, and especially in this city, that shame us all. There seems to be unanimity among the parties that that is a scourge and a cancer that we must tackle with all the weaponry that we can bring to bear . . .
>
> "Although I am now a Member of Parliament for a Northamptonshire seat, I cut my political teeth in inner London. I became a Camden councillor in 1990, at a time when, across the border in Conservative Westminster, certain councillors were talking of being cruel and nasty to the homeless – and homeless there were, many of them.
>
> "I lived at that time in Arlington Road, just down the road from Arlington House, which

was then and perhaps still is the biggest homeless persons' hostel in Europe. For one year I served on the board of management of that hostel. My council ward was the Brunswick Ward, host to the architecturally celebrated Brunswick centre. Above ground at the centre was a shopping centre, a cinema, a club and flats housing several hundred people. Below ground, however, there was a carpark housing dozens of homeless people. After a surgery one Friday evening, representatives of the local residents association took me into that carpark to see for myself that subterranean housing estate. It was a site viewing that lasted only five minutes, made physically unbearable by the stench of urine. Residents had to park their cars there, and the homeless had to sleep there.

"Down the road from my ward was Lincoln's Inn Fields, next door to the Inn of Court where I had dined with Law Lords to be called as a barrister a few years earlier. It was also home to dozens if not hundreds of homeless people. If they were not in Lincoln's Inn, they were underneath the arches of Waterloo, littering every doorway in the Strand or hanging around hopefully outside amusement arcades in Leicester Square, hoping just for a punter for their prostitution.

"Some of them were the hardened homeless, on the road for years; some may have even been exercising a freedom of choice to live that way; but many were the victims of the then Tory Government. Some were indirectly caught by the side wind of disastrous economic policies – the booms, the recessions, the mass unemployment, the negative equity, the repossessions and the widening gulf between North and South.

"The then Government's influence on the homelessness of others, especially youngsters, was even more direct. The Tories closed down short-stay accommodation in, for example, Covent Garden, but they never replaced it. They also withdrew benefits from 16 to 18 year-olds except for those in the most exceptional and extremely vulnerable circumstances, so that even youngsters fleeing from abusive homes or abusive parents could find themselves unaided and forced into homelessness by the very Government to whom they should have been looking for protection.

"The result of all of that was that, at the tail end of the Thatcher Administration, 140,000 people were homeless – 140,000 scars on the modern history of this nation. The homelessness figure peaked in 1990, since when there have been steady decreases, but the decreases have been nowhere near fast enough. Moreover, the decreases seem only very rarely to have been due to concerted Government action to tackle homelessness as a key political priority.

"During the Major Administration, when numbers fell to 116,000, the decrease was due to external factors, not to deliberate Government action. Indeed, the principal initiative of the then Government moved in entirely the wrong direction if the objective was to rid the nation of homelessness.

"When the Labour Government came to power in 1997, we inherited not only 116,000 or so homeless people but a legislative régime and a benefits system that were designed to make things tough for the homeless.

". . . The Bill is a belated response. That delay was unfortunate because the scale of the homelessness problem was huge when we assumed power and remained huge throughout the entirety of our first term. The number of households accepted as homeless and in priority need still stands at about 110,000.

"The problem is particularly acute in London. I described earlier the manifestations of homelessness as of the 1990s, but little has changed. The same manifestations are here now; the beggars and the bedraggled are still with us, on the streets, in shop doorways and in London Underground access tunnels. It is not just the rough sleepers who are still with us, or those without a roof over their head, but those whose roof is not their own but a friend's; those whose roof is not of a flat or house but of a car; those whose roof may be of a house or flat, but one that is sub-standard, overcrowded or unfit for occupation."

Another six years on – and ten into New Labour's supposed radical reforms – and it's still a case of just how little has changed for down-and-outs. Indeed, the situation has tended to get worse and worse for the many exiled by Gordon Brown's inflexibly Thatcherite zero tolerance for anyone unwilling or unable to pay their own way, or to get a good job, or take any old work that pays.

In *'St Gordon delivers the Holy Grail'* (The Times 10/11/99), Alice Miles remarked that

". . . The Chancellor is messianic about work as a passport to economic independence and self-respect. Not for him the handout or even the hand-up; *he is more likely to deliver a well-aimed kick. The Labour Chancellor is forcing people into work in a way that the Tories would have been slaughtered for.* The Working Families Tax Credit awards only those who work; it is not a benefit."

Despite the Homelessness Bill being passed by Parliament and resulting in the Homelessness Act of 2002, the numbers of homeless people in Britain have remained much the same over each succeeding year. Crisis, the organisation whose slogan is "Fighting for Hope for Homeless People", reported in its October 2006 publication *'Statistics About Homelessness'* (see *www.crisis.org.uk*) that 100,170 households in England were logged as homeless and in priority need by Local Authorities during 2005. And in its 2003 report *'How Many, How Much?'*, Crisis estimated that there were around 380,000 single homeless people in Great Britain, including those staying in hostels, B&Bs, squats, on friends' floors and in overcrowded accommodation.

So much for Gordon Brown's loudly trumpeted "National Crusade" (– see the notes to *"New Deals . . . welfare to work for all"* on pp 264-265; and also to *"J'Accuse . . . Gangmaster Brawn"* on pp400-410).

Page 15

"May seemed the kindest month . . ." and ff

– cf *'The Waste Land'*, opening lines, section I – *'The Burial of the Dead'*

". . . *united with the 417/ candidates of our choice . . .*"

This was the highest number of seats Labour had ever polled in a General Election, with a 43% share of the vote. 101 of these representatives were women, also an unprecedentedly high total. Nine MPs were Asian or Black, again quite a few more than hitherto. (But see also the notes to *"Such a wow with your women"* on pages 377-379.)

Page 17

". . . *Robert Burns's red red rose/ of love . . .*"

– cf Burns's *'Song'* of 1794:

> *"My luve is like a red, red rose,*
> *That's newly sprung in June:*
> *My luve is like the melodie,*
> *That's sweetly played in tune . . ."*

". . . *the earthen/ beauty that is truth . . .*"

– see the penultimate line of Keats's *'Ode to a Grecian Urn'* (1819):

"*Beauty is truth, truth beauty . . .*"

Pages 19-20

". . . *for a month// – or three . . . // . . . or seven –*"

Blair enjoyed a hot honeymoon period with voters – in July 1997 a Guardian/ICM Poll showed a record 80% approval rating. But this fell dramatically a few months later when a succession of grabby deals and grubby cutbacks – un-Labourlike in the extreme – staggered many who had been his ardent supporters (see p265 and ff re the Bernie Ecclestone scandal, and pages 39-47 and the notes about them on pages 275-282 re the Single Parent Benefit cut, plus those remarked on below, among others).

Page 20

" *– its way-marking starscape dimmed . . .*"

– cf Jeremiah (31, 21):

> "*Set thee up way marks,*
> *make thee guide-posts:*
> *set thine heart toward the highway,*
> *even the way by which thou wentest . . .*"

"*– unwaged parents, / the handicapped . . .*"

The hard-pressed people earmarked to be rescued in New Labour's populist electioneering rhetoric were the very ones to be ruthlessly deprived of benefits in the first flurries of departmental cost-cutting, so that the government could be seen to be trimming the Social Security budget exactly as ordained by its Tory predecessors.

To appear all fair and square, Blair took care, of course, not to present the issue in quite these terms. He spoke instead of his desire ". . . to build that decent Britain, to develop that decent society, to extend opportunity to those denied it, to make the most of the resources we have, to lift the dead hand of dependency and offer the helping hand of work for those that can, *and proper support for those who can't . . .*" (speech at the Vauxhall Recreation Centre, Luton, on 28/01/1998; though a check in May 2006 revealed that the Number 10 website no longer featured this speech. So much for freedom of information – and perhaps also for the erosion of high ideals under New Labour's self-devoted power-preservation régime).

The cutting of support for single parents, and the programme implemented to "help disabled people to get work", both announced in December '97, provoked disbelief and outrage throughout the country.

In 2006 efforts were being redoubled to impose labour market discipline by restricting access to Incapacity Benefit. Those receiving it were to be "helped back to work", or lose their income. The plan to take one million claimants off Incapacity Benefit by 2008 was one of the keystones of the government's green paper on welfare reform. The agency charged with carrying out the plan was set to be privatised.

This kind of policy review could not have been less realistic or less likely to prove effective. So far from any progress towards The Project's avowed 1997 commitments to "eradicate child poverty", and halve it by 2010, official data released in late March 2007 showed that the number of children living below the breadline in 2006 had *risen* by all of 100,000 from the previous year – amounting to 2.8 million, and rising to 3.8 million when housing costs were included.

The Government's answer (as given in the Guardian of 27/2/07) was, yet again, to "unveil a new strategy including the widening of the in-work credit scheme and . . . emphasising the importance of work as a sustainable route out of poverty for families in Britain".   But Bert Massie, chair of the Disability Rights Commission, was quoted (in *'Disgrace of child poverty con trick'*, The Times 28/2/07, p2) urging the Government ". . . to focus more on helping families with disabled children or parents, pointing out that one in three children living in poverty have at least one disabled parent . . . We are a country which can countenance individual bankers getting annual bonuses of £22 *million*, while we give a family of two parents and two children, living on benefits, £10,000 to live on for a whole year". Whatever happened to redistribution?

". . . underpaid nurses and teachers . . ."

New Labour's first Health Secretary Frank Dobson consistently maintained that there was not enough money available within the NHS to allow pay rises beyond the rate of inflation. Nurses were scandalously paid, starting in 1997 at £10,000 a year, and averaging £12,000.

Most teachers continued to be offered the same demeaning rate, despite a concerted campaign by the Department of Education to recruit more graduates into the profession. In the autumn of 1998 it was announced that, by contrast, Chris Woodhead, the Chief Inspector of Schools appointed by the previous government, and universally loathed by teachers, was to receive a pay rise of 34% (Guardian 28/9/98, p1).

In these as in most areas, an ever more pronounced feature of Blairism was the introduction of ever greater pay differentiation – golden carrots for super-teachers, super-nurses, etc, etc. The aim could only be to smash collective agreements altogether, in return for individually negotiated contracts, performance bonuses and the like – again confirming New Labour as the New Party of Inequality.

The Chancellor's determination to stick to Tory spending limits for the first three years of the administration retained a ceiling – no real increase – on the income of most public sector workers. Their situation was not improved until 2006 – to the still less-than-inspirational average of £19,000 per annum. The low pay of NHS support staff had become unsustainable, and hourly rates for the lowest-paid workers were raised from £5.16 to a still derisory £5.67.

In January 2007, a leaked Department of Health document predicted a chronic shortfall in the numbers of nurses and practitioners needed to provide patients with basic treatments. According to John Carvel's 4/1/07 Guardian report on 'NHS facing nurse shortage and glut of consultants', ". . . The department is forecasting shortages of 14,000 nurses, 1,200 GPs and 1,100 junior doctors, enough to cause serious disruption of services to patients".

This shocking dearth of lower-paid but indispensable medical workers contrasts sharply with "an unwanted surplus of 3,200 consultants" by March 2011 "which we cannot afford to employ".

The self-trumpeted "workforce strategy" also proposed reducing nurses' wages in certain regions, and deliberately using unemployment as a tool to "– create a downward pressure on wages". There's creativity for us . . .

Janet Davies, Executive Director of the Royal College of Nursing, regretted that "This confirms our worst fears that the government intends to use the pay, terms and working conditions of nurses as the means by which they dig themselves out of a hole of their own making". And Unison's deputy Head of Health, Mike Jackson, said patient care would be damaged by any attempt to cut nurses' pay: ". . . We face huge demographic challenges – 20% of our nurses are aged between 50 and 59. If we start cutting pay, it will make the job of attracting enough nurses even more difficult".

Increases in funding for public services were made after 2000, but – unfortunately for lower income citizens – these were designed to open up public provision to market forces and the private sector. In health and education this required fragmentation of the system. Autonomous health trusts were established and conditions imposed to enable the private sector to get stuck in to providing a wide range of clinical services.

Funds were provided to build new schools – but only as cranky 'Academy' schools, whose organisation will have to be influenced by the input of local business patrons. Provision for further new schools was made contingent on the involvement of faith groups or other private backers.

Building programmes were to be financed by Private Finance Initiatives which burdened public authorities with huge debts for years to come and involved the eventual reversion of the asset to the private financier. Investment in public housing was made conditional on organisational movement towards privatisation, from local authorities to housing associations and 'Arms Length Management Organisations'.

The common thread was a pervasive belief in the roles of private business and market mechanisms in core public services. That a local school or a local hospital cannot meaningfully compete with another a hundred miles away has been brushed aside. That markets inevitably generate and deepen inequalities of all kinds was ignored.

See '*Deficits are a symptom of the marketisation of the NHS*' by Colin Leys (Guardian, 26 April 2006): ". . . In a healthcare market born of ideology, not evidence, *patients come second* to the need to shed what is unprofitable."

On 1 March 2007, New Labour's long-standing militarism-over-health priorities were revealed once again, by Ministerial announcements of a contrasting pair of new pay awards.

Defence Secretary Des Browne pledged that from April '07, the 13,000 lowest-paid members of the UK's Armed Forces would be seeing their salaries jump by an "inflation-busting" 9.2%, a whole extra £100 per month – the highest pay rise in the public sector. Furthermore, another 6,000 military personnel would get a 6.2% rise. National Health Service nurses, on the other hand, would be in line for a *below*-inflation pay *cut*, albeit couched in the Government parlance as a "rise" of 1.5%" in April, with a further 1% – er, top-up, in November '07, comprising a derisory annual "increase" of a paltry 1.9%.

– And this although the rate of inflation between December 2006 and March '07 stood at 2.7-3%. Just why this country's Armed Service personnel's wages should be rising at three times the rate of inflation, while those of nurses plummet well below it, was another question that gave the lie to Commander-in-Chief Blair's pretensions to be completing a course of anything remotely radical, reforming or civilised.

A number of nurses were quoted as "angry and frustrated by this . . . slap in the face", and warned that many ". . . could be driven out of the profession", whilst the leaders of the health union Unison likened the decision to "a kick in the teeth . . . a real let-down" (London Metro, 2/3/2007).

So the Government went on shamelessly exploiting the traditional and presumed vocational good will, self-sacrifice and commitment to patients of these lowest-paid workers, in the same breath as ruthlessly enlisting potentially murderous mercenaries, by the most patently mercenary means.

Evidence the sharply divergent comments of the Defence Secretary, that his record pay rise for Armed Forces ". . . reflects my ongoing commitment to make sure they get the support and recognition they deserve" – as distinct from the shiftier brand of New Labourese from Health Secretary Patricia Hewitt on the pay rebuke to nurses: ". . . These are sensible increases, fair for staff, consistent with the Government's inflation target, and affordable for the NHS".

– "*Affordable*", doubtless; "*consistent*", sadly so; but Ms Hewitt was drafting a one-woman anti-dictionary in defining her so-called "*increases*" as "*sensible*"; and was yet again courting nationwide ridicule by terming them "*fair for staff*". Why, having mouthed such heartless garbage, did she not instantly resign her cabinet post and sign up for voluntary work as an NHS nurse, in tandem with Special Needs Literacy Classes for tale-bearers of little brains – ?

No less seriously: should the MoD – as directly responsible for so many wounded, diseased and prematurely dying humans – not have been offering to siphon funds towards pay rises for every nurse willing to continue with the pile-up of such thankless work, consequent as it is on the continuing pile-up of MoD violence across the planet? Surely it is health workers, and *not* still more armed forces, who deserve decent basic financial incentives to help out on the medical crises induced and proliferated by Bush's and Blair's so-called wars and pre-emptive strikes in Afghanistan, Iraq and elsewhere?

"*. . . unestablished artists and writers, / beginning musicians . . .*"

Many criticised New Labour for seeking to force an official work programme, seemingly on any terms, onto anyone not already in wage-earning or profit-motivated business. Of these protesters only Alan McGee, boss of Creation Records, was taken seriously by the government.

McGee argued that forced labour unrelated to individual predilection could deprive the Treasury of potential revenue from national assets in pop music. He cited the example of his protégés, the rock band Oasis, who had survived on Unemployment Benefit whilst laying the foundations of their eventually lucrative careers. This led to an adjustment of the policy, restoring some benefit – along with the right to work at and play music – to some would-be musicians, without obliging them to take on another day job.

Nothing much seems to have been claimed on behalf of many more would-be artists who are less likely to hit the big-time in their lifetimes, or less concerned to do so – though some such could a Van Gogh, or a 'mute inglorious Beatle' be. Many less hackneyed or derivative beginners make arguably better music than Oasis, but don't make the Top Forty.

A civilised society would surely want to encourage all youngsters with a talent for the arts to pursue their vocation even when the results may never become a financial asset at all, let alone a "national" one.

Various irreverent takes on New Labour's suppositions and impositions were articulated by the Britpop generation of musos and singer-songwriters, several of whom had been courted by the government, in a special edition of the New Musical Express on 14 March 1998. Its cover featured a picture of Blair with the headline: *"Ever get the feeling you've been cheated?"*

It's hard to appreciate the rationale by which potentially affluent pop musicians got benefits restored, whilst struggling poets – along with most other denominations of struggler – have gone on being pressurised by the Labour Government to get "wealth-creating" day jobs. For a few specific cases in point, see the notes on pages 401-410 regarding Nik Morgan, myself and Tom Pickard.

Britain has, after all, benefited quite as much (artistically if not financially) from at least as rich a flowering of pure and applied poetry over the last four decades, as it has from any comparable efflorescence on the part of authentic new pop talents.

At the Royal Festival Hall on 18 November 1997, Adrian Mitchell made a speech which he called *'No more beautiful begging letters'*, prior to announcing the first Paul Hamlyn Foundation Awards to Poets. Adrian pointed out that the 500 applicants for only five awards (of £15,000 each) –

". . . earned an average income from all sources of £12,000 a year – less than half the national average. Many of them can only keep writing because they are supported by a husband or a wife.

"My four fellow judges and I would like to have given £15,000 to at least 120 of the poets who applied. They all deserve it. These are people for whom poetry is a serious calling, a demanding art on which they bet their lives.

". . . Why should anyone pay poets to write? What use is poetry?

"Poetry excites and extends the imagination. It questions and explores the language of the world. It fights, it entertains, it enlightens, it makes love, it caresses, it disturbs and consoles and heals.

"Of course plenty of adults avoid poetry as the result of unfortunate encounters with this sticky stuff at school – compare and contrast the galoshes of William Wordsworth with the cowboy boots of Lord Byron . . . But primary school kids love poetry – they listen to it, learn it, recite it and write it – they know it's as natural as singing or swimming. Poetry isn't a luxury, but a necessity like music. But it takes time to write and rewrite and perfect. And time is, unfortunately, money.

"For three million pounds a year, say, we could pay one hundred poets wages of £20,000 a year to continue their true work, and also subsidise another hundred poets to the tune of £10,000 a year. Why not? We pay thousands of people to teach English Literature. Why not pay a few hundred people to create it?

"Three million pounds a year would relieve our best poets and their families of 24-hour anxiety, and of the need to write letters like this:

> '. . . I am extremely badly in debt, these debts are pressing and daily and horribly becoming more so; and it seems I cannot think of anything else at all. Surrounded by these debts, hurt and worried to despair in the middle of them, and seeing and hearing my home crumble because of them, I cannot write; they come between me and everything else I do. And, as I can't write, I can't make any money, and so my new day-by-day debts arise; and I can't see any good end to this, and I would be insane if I could . . .'

"That was the late Dylan Thomas. People sometimes sneer at Dylan's begging letters, but those who sneer have never been down there.

"Three million pounds a year. Where would it come from? The National Lottery? A tax on advertising? Flog a Trident to Switzerland? Refuse to take part in attacks on the men, women and children of Iraq? There's plenty of money about.

"Three million isn't much for some of the best poets in the world.

"It's about time for a change. In my lifetime I've seen how Hugh McDiarmid, Basil Bunting, George Barker, Dylan Thomas and many more of our finest poets lived and died in poverty. I want to read no more beautiful begging letters.

"For poetry is one of our great glories. The names shine out across the world: Shakespeare, Milton, Blake, Byron, Keats, Burns, Brontë, Clare, Rossetti, Yeats.

"Their children are among you, but most of them are struggling to survive – against neglect, illness and poverty. Are we going to help them now? Or should we wait until they've been good and dead for fifty years, before insulting them with the hypocrisy of a brass plaque in Westminster Abbey?"

"skint students . . ."

Only a few months after victimising lone parents and their children, and threatening the handicapped, the government hit on students. Traditionally and by manifesto the party which supports Education For All, New Labour nevertheless voted to halt the payment of tuition fees for British universities. In addition to paying their own living expenses, all students were henceforth to pay for the privilege of further education.

For half a century the costs of tuition had been covered by maintenance grants. These were insidiously whittled down during the Tories' eighteen years in office. Labour went one step further by abolishing grants entirely. Even the Conservatives railed at this injustice: their leader, William Hague, pointed out that "the worse-off people will be hardest hit – anyone can work that out" (Daily Telegraph p1, 5/3/98). And his predecessor, John Major, was aptly scathing: "This rubbish about tuition fees. They put me up to that twice, and I told them to fuck off" (Private Eye p5, 21/11/97).

The government tried to justify the changes by invoking the findings of the Dearing Committee, which had been set up by the previous administration to look into the issue of Higher Education funding. But Dearing had not in fact advocated the abolition of maintenance grants at any point. Nevertheless, despite mass student protests all over the country, and sustained opposition from the House of Lords, autumn 1998 newcomers were constrained to fork out, beg, borrow or steal the £1,000 per annum fees – as were those of their successors not completely discouraged or disqualified by this extortion.

On 26 May 2000, Gordon Brown fed the national press and media a strident whinge about the fact that Laura Spence, a working-class student from a Tyneside comprehensive school, was not included among the few accepted by Magdalen College, Oxford, for a degree course the following autumn. She was therefore pursuing her higher education at Harvard, the senior Ivy League campus of America, which welcomed her apparently top-notch academic qualifications with open arms. Our People's Treasurer made a slap-up meal of this allegedly élitist exclusion of the deserving poor, calling it *"an absolute scandal".*

The then President of Magdalen, Anthony Smith, replied (in, among other places, the Daily Telegraph of 25/4/01, p26: *'The lessons Labour should learn from Laura Spence')* that Brown's attack was "biased and ill-informed". Smith maintained that Spence's rejection had nothing to do with snobbery, only with the fact that she had come tenth in a competition for five places, awarded on the basis of objective assessments of each candidate's proven and demonstrably potential merits.

Brown's pompous disaffection over the matter struck many as 'a bit rich' since, as Chancellor of the Exchequer, he himself had as much power as anyone in the land to restore maintenance subsidy – and to withdraw the compulsory tuition fees and strictly returnable loans which steered innumerable droves of underfunded and underprivileged youth well away from further education in Britain.

Some American universities, on the other hand, offer generous grants to promising would-be students handicapped by insolvency. Ironically, even Harvard gave Laura Spence a scholarship of $25,000 a year for her course over there – which is roughly the same as she would have had to pay *out* for fees in dear old Blighty, under New "equal opportunities" Labour.

Anthony Smith added that ". . . very able working-class children will come forward in larger numbers only when the level of encouragement provided by family and school improves . . . So, *improve the cities and streets where children live, reduce the huge disparities of income in Britain, restore the quality of television . . . and reduce the level of social violence . . ."*

If the government was seriously concerned, it also needed to fulfil its education pledges of 1997, notably its loud-hailed commitment to bring down class sizes. The Telegraph of 25/4/2001 reported (under *'Failing the Children',* p27) that a headmaster in Norfolk was having to teach a class of 94.

In England – as distinct from Scotland, where tuition fees for higher education were scrapped completely by the newly devolved Scottish Assembly in May 1999 – the incentives have grown more and more overbearingly anti-educational since '97.

Thus Lois Rogers and Jane Mulkerrins reported on page 7 of the Sunday Times, 3 June 2001, that ". . . Young women are resorting to selling their eggs for thousands of pounds a time to childless couples as a way of paying off their student debts . . ." Rogers and Mulkerrins also revealed that, as of summer 2001, ". . . The introduction of tuition fees and the cuts in grants to pay living expenses mean that the average graduate begins the search for a job with debts of more than £10,000 ".

Five years later, The Times reported that students starting their courses in autumn 2006 would be paying an average of £33,152 for a three-year course, and ending up with an average debt of £14,779 (*'Three-year degree now costs £33,000'* by Fran Yeoman, front page, Times 15/8/06). These figures were based on the August 2006 NatWest Student Money Matters survey, which also found that " . . . Rises in the cost of university, however, are not being matched by increased earnings after graduation. Of the graduates who responded to this year's survey, the average starting salary was £13,860, down from £14,090 in 2005".

Most of this rising cost to students was due to the introduction of top-up fees. Blair had bullied through the Top-Up Fees Bill on 1 July 2004, allowing universities to charge differential fees of up to £3,000, (f)lying in the face of his unequivocal manifesto promise on 16 May 2001 that *"We will NOT introduce 'top-up' fees and have legislated to prevent them"*.

Vice-Chancellors had lobbied hard for the top-ups, arguing that one-third of the money thus raised could be ploughed back into academic salaries to ensure long-term standards of teaching and research. But despite a projected rise of 25% in funding for higher education between 2006 and 2009 from fees and other sources, university employers only offered their staff a rise of 5% over two years. This impasse led to the lecturers' strike that delayed the assessments of 2006's crop of graduating students. More details on these cop-outs can be accessed, as of February 2007, from *www.aut.org.uk/paybacktime*.

Much higher education has become increasingly dependent on income from foreign students' fees. The result tends to be that many places which would be occupied by UK students are filled by students from abroad.

Less inviting prospects for England's school-leavers – working-class or any class – are hard to imagine (though their bewilderingly bureaucratic and forever re-rejigged measures to date suggest that our ultra-frugal Treasury Controllers are well capable of confounding even this supposition).

Blair has kept hard-selling his resolve to implement the pseudo-egalitarian target of 50% of the youth population going to university. This begs yet again the constant worry about New Labour initiatives, viz: *"Quis custodiet ipsos custodes"* (– 'Who is to control the controllers?' – or, 'What authority authorises the authorities?').

– And again, begs the question as to how such a preoccupation with sheer numbers, for Big Numbers' sake, will improve the university educations being hyped so hard? As of early 2007, many financially beleaguered universities are risking the overall zeitgeist booby-trap of getting dumbed down from the pursuit of learning and higher awareness for their own sakes, into mere factories providing better job qualifications and eventual higher incomes for the students who emerge with the best degrees. That is supposed to be the result, in governmental theory.

But in practical daily experience, this has turned the Education-Education-Education formula into another unreliable insurance policy or pseudo-cultural Lotto gamble, by whose means (even on its own lamentably mercenary terms) a largeish quorum of students who may not excel at Uni or get lucky jobwise, could easily end – having signed up to ill-affordable premiums – by losing out on the lure of supposed paybacks that do not in fact happen.

Thus in *'Universities want fees to rise . . .'* (Sunday Times 11/2/07, News p13), Geraldine Hackett and Tom Baird reported that –

> "Leading universities are to press for tuition fees to be increased . . . Adrian Smith, Principal of Queen Mary, University of London said the money would not be provided by the Treasury: 'Politically, the only way universities are going to get extra funds is from charging students higher fees. We will need fees of £6,000 to £6,500 in 2010. Two years on from then, it will be £10,000' . . ."

Ivor Crewe, vice-chancellor of Essex University, said that middle-class applicants were fuelling the increases, and thereby fuelling also ". . . a different social composition, with fewer students from working-class backgrounds".

Hackett and Baird also observed that applicants were "opting increasingly . . . with an eye to career opportunities. Some universities report that arts applications are flat".

'Radical reform' became a more and more persistent New Labour mantra since Blair took over.

Most dictionaries define 'radical' to mean fundamental, innovative, progressive, curative, and relating to roots. The word 'reform' has long been used and understood to denote changes for the better.

But in the mouths of Blairites and above all, of Blair himself, this 'Radical reform' refrain was more often used to push regressive policies that privilege marketisation over access and social justice.

Such twisting of words, and shameless re-formulating of education, health, poverty relief, worker-friendly and other Labour policies that were truly radical in the abovementioned senses up until 1997, into their polar opposites, was a major (if sometimes craftily concealed) *pièce de résistance* on Blair's ongoing New Labour menu.

In his Foreword to the Schools White Paper, *'Higher Standard, Better Schools for All – More Choice for Parents and Pupils'* (published by the Department for Education & Skills, 25/10/05), the PM jabbered that –

> ". . . We must put parents in the driving seat for change in all-ability schools that retain the comprehensive principle of non-selection, but operate very differently from the traditional comprehensive. And to underpin this change, the local authority must move from being a provider of education to being its local commissioner and the champion of parent choice."

> – From "Education Education Education" to such anti-educational debasement of language – Pshaw!

Exactly why, Big Brother Tone, *"must must must"* we? And exactly who – in this and so many other of your babbling presumptions – was, or would in your – er, uncompellingly postulated future have been, this supposed *"We"*?

The most likely reality of what this 'choice' will mean is very different, according to Dexter Whitfield, Director of the Centre for Public Services:

> ". . . It requires schools, like hospitals and other public services, to compete against each other. Money will follow the chosen placement of pupils (or patients or other 'customers'), forcing a separation between client and contractor, and establishing a 'procurement culture' in which private and voluntary sector providers bid to take over service delivery . . . It erodes the potential for collective responsibility and solidarity between individuals in favour of a competitive individualism" (– from *'Articles of Faith'*, Red Pepper No. 139, March 2006).

Whitfield concluded with the warning that this marketisation process will continue unless we challenge ". . . *the very principle of applying market forces to services whose whole rationale is the use of public money to meet social need in a democratically accountable and responsive way".*

Long self-heralded Education Reformer Blair's insistence in July '04 that Top-Up Fees are a Top Hole Thing, despite his manifesto commitment of three years before *not* to entertain their imposition, once more gave the lie to New Labour's ever less convincing claims to be consolidating parliamentary democracy.

How can any credence be retained by the notion that the British public has a say in what any government does in our name, just because we're still free to cast a single vote roughly once every four years, when the premises on whose basis such votes might be cast are so summarily shredded by their architects, once these have captured the vote?

Page 21

". . . the people it rejected . . ."

One year on from the election, Dr Ross McKibbin of St John's College, Oxford, an expert on Labour Party history, observed that "Social Inclusion seems to be working a damn sight better up than down" (Sunday Telegraph Review p1, 26/4/98) – whilst the late lamented Tony Banks MP had noted at the outset, "They've had 18 years to fuck the country up. We've had only two days. And we're not doing badly . . ." (*'The Wit & Wisdom of Tony Banks'*, ed Iain Dale, Robson Books 1998).

Page 22

"In 1996, in Singapore . . ."

– Guardian 6/1/96, p7. Tony Blair's visit to Singapore was seen by many as the beginning of his election campaign. He paid tribute to the autocratic Singapore leader Lee Kan Yew, notorious for his merciless approach to law and order, saying that his views "very much reflect my own philosophy". In his speech Blair heaped lavish praise on the marketing success of the so-called 'Tiger Economies'.

Two years later these same economies plunged into collapse and chaos, threatening to pull Britain and the other Western nations down with them. When in the autumn of 1998 the Japanese company Fujitsu closed down its government-subsidised British plant in Sedgefield, Blair's own Teesside constituency, the Prime Minister was eager to stress that, rather than being anything his government could redeem, this was *". . . an unavoidable consequence of instability in the Far Eastern markets . . ."* (Daily Telegraph, p1, 16/8/98).

". . . The People's *Party . . ."*

Blair's speech to the Labour Party party in London's Royal Festival Hall at dawn on 2 May 1997 was reported in full in *'Were you still up for Portillo?'* by Brian Cathcart (Penguin '97). When the new Prime Minister went on to dub Labour *". . . the party of all the people – the many, not the few; the party that belongs to every part of Britain, no matter what people's background, or their creed, or their colour"*, he was cheered to the rafters by his assembled flock.

Page 23

"WEALTH CREATOR: 'HEY, LOOK, GUYS – HAVE SOME MORE' . . ."

Nicola Jennings's cartoon appeared two mornings after Stephen Byers, Blair's arch-'modernising' Trade and Industry Secretary, had declared in his Mansion House speech of 2/2/99, that *". . . Wealth creation is more important than wealth distribution"*. This sounded to many like an unequivocal attempt to dump off one of the central planks of the Labour movement's original platform.

In a Guardian Endpiece (p15, 6/12/99), Roy Hattersley MP suggested "two possible interpretations":

". . . One is that New Labour does not care for the poor. Mr Byers is far too immersed in the techniques of 'the project' to say that publicly. The alternative explanation is that he

really believes that when the economy expands the poor automatically share in the new prosperity. I have news for Mr Byers. That is what used to be called the 'trickle down effect' – a theory so obviously absurd that even the right wing of the American Republican Party no longer use it as an excuse for widening disparities of income.

"Free markets are notoriously unpredictable but one thing about them is absolutely certain. The people who go into them with the most are likely to come out with more. Without active redistribution, the gap between rich and poor will constantly widen. A radical government balances growth and redistribution against each other. Often they go hand in hand. Occasionally efficiency has to be sacrificed for equity."

". . . 'Old Labour' ideals/ erased . . ."

David Wighton provided an oblique take on this in the Financial Times on 23 October 1998, under the headline: *'Mandelson plans a microchip off the old block: The Trade and Industry Secretary is enthused by suggestions that the UK could build its very own Silicon Valley'*:

". . . Perhaps it was the Californian sun, but Peter Mandelson seemed almost intoxicated with the heady entrepreneurial atmosphere of Silicon Valley last week. *'We are intensely relaxed about people getting filthy rich'*, the Trade and Industry Secretary assured an approving group of senior executives at Hewlett-Packard during his fact-finding visit. *'As long as they pay their taxes'*, he added hurriedly."

Nearly eight New Labour years later, in *'Blair's Britain: only Profit matters'* (Guardian 3 May 2006, p29), Jonathan Freedland observed that ". . . deference is far from dead. It's just that now there is a new class to be deferred to – the aristocracy of wealth":

". . . A decade ago, thinkers around New Labour were dreaming of a new bottom line. Instead of companies pursuing only short-term gains for their shareholders, what if they started considering the wider interests of their 'stakeholders', including their workers, the larger community and even the environment? What if their success was not measured solely in pounds, shillings and pence, but in the social and environmental benefits they brought and costs they exacted? Wouldn't that be the true mark of a radical Labour government? That dream died . . . Only money talks, for in Blair's Britain, no less than Thatcher's, profit is to be worshipped: it is the only currency that counts."

Page 24

". . . the free milk/ of human kindness// . . . . Thatcher snatched . . ."

The future Prime Minister's best known act as Education Minister in Edward Heath's government was her removal of free milk from primary schools in June 1971. Until then it had been provided by local councils, funded from the rates. The nickname Maggie Milk Snatcher has stuck to her ever since.

As has – for Shakespeareans – the association with Lady Macbeth's disparagement of her husband (an early Wet?) for being "too full o'th' milk of human-kindness/ To catch the nearest way" (*'Macbeth'*, Act I, scene V, lines 15-16).

The European Union did try to bring back free milk, by means of a scheme whereby Local Authorities could claim 12p a pint subsidy from the EU Commission for milk provided to schoolchildren. Unhappily this was axed in December '98, in one of the Commission's economy drives, despite gross profligacies on the part of the New Milk Snatchers themselves. Huge ranges of butter mountains, for instance, were wilfully liquidated during the late 1990s whilst other parts of the planet stayed breadless. And at the end of New Labour's decade in office, still no free milk for schoolkids – or for anyone – at home. And still plenty of famine abroad – possibly still more, even.

Page 25

"measly pension, labyrinthine/ tax and insurance schemes . . ."

Despite the persistent dire warnings of Frank Field and of his successor in the Department of Social Security, Alistair Darling, that the Pensions system was in need of radical overhaul, no satisfactory action was taken on it over Blair plc's ten years in power.

The link between pensions and earnings, broken by the Tories in favour of a link with prices, had cost each pensioner about £25 a week. The move towards individual funds, embedded in New Labour's Stakeholder Pension Plan, had the effect of further entrenching inequality in old age. A reformed and revived SERPS would be much more efficient, and revive the redistributive process traditional to the British pensions system. As of 10 April 2000, pensioners were granted a derisory increase of 75p per week on the basic state pension – less than the average cost of a loaf of bread, and well below the average nationwide increase in earnings.

As Jeremy Hardy wrote in the Guardian of 13 May, 2000 –

". . . Labour might have entered government thinking: *'Now what did we come in here for?'* but pensioners are entirely clear about what Labour is supposed to do. Old people don't receive 75p with the words: *'Heavens, 15 shillings, all that lolly just for me? Why, I can put that towards a tin of faggots and still have no change from the government. Bless you, young sir'.* Old people are less apt to accept the media consensus that the government simply can't afford to do anything except throw money at public-private partnerships and computers that are supposed to facilitate welfare payments but don't work . . .

"Pensioners can do mental arithmetic. They know that if you add figures up they come to more. They know lump sums and free telly licences are tiny increases made to look generous. They know £20 would be £1,040 if multiplied by 52, but that at the end of the week it is £20. They know that tax relief doesn't help you if you don't pay tax . . ."

In the run-up to the June 2001 election, both Labour and the Tories seemed to go all compassionate towards pensioners – but the suddenly open-handed pledges looked, on closer scrutiny, more like ephemerally cosmetic surgery. That's to say, the rival parties were canvassing Senior Citizens from a last-minute panic regarding the vast number of potential votes at stake, rather than from a wholehearted concern for the aged. None of Chancellor Brown's complicated offerings and schemes, in particular, could conceal his resolutely mean-spirited refusal to contemplate restoring the link between pensions and earnings.

If this link had been maintained, then the single person's pension of £78 a week would have been £142 in the summer of 2006. The Report of the Turner Commission on pensions recommended restoration of the link. The Chancellor was still obdurate, but in a 'deal' with the Prime Minister (more reminiscent of coalition partners bargaining than members of the same party), it was agreed in May 2006 that the earnings link would be restored – but not until 2012!

While this means that the relative fall in the value of the pension will perhaps eventually be halted, it is still likely to leave 50% of pensioners reliant on means tested benefits as at present.

Given New Labour's back-tracking on previous commitments regarding single parent benefits, student top-up fees, et al, this rather unradical offspring of a temporary Blair-Brown marriage of convenience looks unlikely to survive as a policy six years on, even if a Labour government of any stripe in fact turns out to be in office then.

Ten days after the 2001 re-election, Rodney Bickerstaffe, President of the National Pensioners' Convention, pointed out (on page 19 of the Guardian of 22 June '01):

> ". . . The high turnout from pensioners was undoubtedly one of the reasons for the return of a Labour government. But older people now expect to see policies that will add real benefits to their lives. There needs to be more consultation and action. Many pensioners are confused by the complex rules surrounding the proposed pension credit. Of course they would welcome the chance to keep more of their savings – but they resent having to face a means test to qualify. The NPC is also disappointed that the government has no plans to introduce free personal care in residential and nursing homes. Every year, 70,000 people are left in the unenviable position of having to sell their homes, simply to pay for the care they need.
>
> "The only way to ensure that the needs of pensioners are met is by asking them for their views . . ."

On 25th May 2006 the Government put out a White Paper which readers could view via *www.dwp.gov.uk/pensionsreform/* – though to what extent this represents genuinely radical progress rather than another whitewash remains to be seen. Frank Field, Blair's first pensions minister, was not sanguine, commenting: "In 1997 British pensions were the envy of the world. Now they're the worst in Europe".

Page 25-26

". . . *What prospect beyond/ the random website chances/ of money-slots . . . . // – What use the hard-sold addictive routines/ of junk shopping . . .*" and ff

In an Observer article (4/10/1999) summarising his book on *'Karl Marx'* (Fourth Estate 1999), Francis Wheen wrote that –

> ". . . In Marx's vision of capitalist society, as in Swift's equine pseudo-paradise, the false Eden is created by reducing ordinary humans to the status of impotent, exiled Yahoos . . . All that is truly human becomes congealed or crystallised into an impersonal material force, while dead objects acquire menacing life and vigour. Money, once no more than an expression of value – a kind of *lingua franca* in which commodity could speak unto commodity – becomes value itself . . . To buy the alluring products of profiteers, we must become paid labourers; instead of living for our work, we work for our living. We are dragged into the social nexus of commodities and wages, prices and profits, a fantasy land where nothing is what it seems."

Page 27

". . . *Third Ways* . . ."

The vaporous concept of the Third Way was given its first airing by Tony Blair on 24/3/98: "And here let me say what I mean when I talk of a Third Way for New Labour", he said, and outlined a blandly managerial vision based on what he called "infinitely adaptable and imaginative values".

He spoke of the Third Way as "prudent discipline over financial and monetary policy . . . . focusing on education, skills, technology, high quality infrastructure and a welfare state which promotes work and makes it pay"; as "specific measures to tackle the scourge of social exclusion"; and as "a new emphasis on entrepreneurship and small business creation". This vision for Britain, the closest Blair has come to an ideological mission statement, was outlined in a speech given in French to the French National Assembly in Paris (available at *www.number-10.gov.uk/output/Page1160.asp*).

Unhappily, the tag has continued to elude precise definition, whilst continuing to string along with anything and everything Blair wanted pushed at any particular time. It threatened to stay "infinitely adaptable" (rather than "imaginative") for as long as he stayed in office.

The then French premier, Lionel Jospin, said that if the Third Way was between traditional social democracy and communism, he was *d'accord* – but not if it meant a compromise between neo-liberalism and social democracy. In his Fabian Society pamphlet published on 16 November '99, Jospin insisted that ". . . We can shape the world according to our values", and that free-market capitalism must be regulated.

Blair's Way tended to posit an extreme (if not yet quite owned up to) ultra-right neo-liberalism as one pole, and classical social democracy as the other. This Third Way has had a name for some time: Thatcherism.

Page 27-28

"New Deals . . . // . . . 'welfare/ to work/ for all' . . ."

'Welfare to Work' was unveiled in September 1997 as the government's considered philosophy regarding benefit and unemployment. From the premise that those in work should not need welfare, the theory progressed to the proposition that the removal of welfare would automatically bring about full employment. This leap of illogic managed, if nothing else beneficial, to fulfil Blair's instruction to his then Social Security ministers (Harriet Harman and Frank Field) to *"think the unthinkable"*.

Chew beyond the beguilingly alliterative soundbite and Gordon Brown's designating it a "National Crusade" and you got, as so often with New Labour catchphrases, an indigestible demagogic idiocy signifying nothing more radical than rearrangements of bureaucratic and financial goalposts: 'Welfare to Work' = 'No Welfare to Work'.

– Or as Steve Bell's cameo of the Chancellor's not-so-caring reform has it, atop page 27: *"NEW DEAL For The Unemployed . . . . . . FUCK ALL For The Unemployed"*.

And equally sadly, the substance of the government's vaunted New Deal in no way emulated Roosevelt's life-enhancing New Deal for Americans in the 1930s. But darker duplicities of that decade were evoked by the projected *"Environmental Task Force"* – almost exactly the language with which Adolf Hitler reduced unemployment statistics in Germany. The St Albion's parish was supposed to believe that this Deal and Force involve some kind of choice for, and covenant with, those who sign up for it – whilst those who can not, do not, or will not get paid work, are left to fend for themselves with the presumed just deserts of their incapacity and/or cussedness (i e, as said above, sweet f a).

What New Labour's so-called "Flagship" New Deal amounted to, in effect, was that those who had been claiming benefit for more than six months were automatically provided with either training or work. This work has tended to be in lowly positions with large companies which signed up to the New Deal. Such companies were persuaded to take on the long-term unemployed by the provision of government top-ups to cover the extra wages.

Thus every party plugged into the scheme was assumed to be happy. The companies benefit from an influx of cheap subsidised labour. The government receives the gratitude and goodwill of big business, whose well-being it reveres as being so vital to its own. And the hitherto unwaged folk hooked in to the scheme are awarded a fiscal framework to their existence, however unsuited these new labours may be to their respective needs and abilities (– cf the quotations from Karl Marx in the note to pages 25-26 on p263; from D H Lawrence on pp30 and 53; and from Dorothy L Sayers on pp270-271).

In practice, more of the unemployed have been offered training than jobs. The training burnished New Labour's image and enriched the trainers with fat contracts. But the most it actually provided for job seekers were pretty scant and superficial qualifications for pretty random and drab opportunities. The net result has been a consolidation of the mean-spirited *Ill*-fare State, with ever more adversarial policing of claimants and withdrawal of benefits, rather than a more caring, communal or fastidiously functioning society.

Anne McElvoy, in the Independent Wednesday Review (24 May 2000), pilloried

". . . the threadbare claim that the New Deal has bestowed 191,000 new jobs on young people. A full quarter of these return to state benefits within three months, an undisclosed number after six, and the standard of training supplied is as bad as it was under the Tories' make-work schemes. A tight labour market protects the Government from disagreeable scrutiny on these points. But sooner or later, the truth will out . . ."

– As indeed it did. On 14 May 2007 Frank Field's Report for the think-tank Reform declared the New Deal *"a woeful failure . . . and betrayal"*, having blown £3.5bn on overseeing an *increase* of 70,000 17-to-24-year-olds out of work to half a million, since the scheme was launched in 1998.

See also the notes following *'J'Accuse . . . Gangmaster Brawn'* on pp400-410.

Page 28

". . . *you might get as rich / as BAe Systems* . . ."

– see pages 367-368, and also pages 430-433

". . . *or Marlboro Maggie* . . ."

Margaret Thatcher, Blair's predecessor and admitted inspiration, contrived, in her retirement, to garner enormous amounts of money from the tobacco industry. In 1992 it was reported that she had accepted a £550,000 consultancy with Philip Morris, the multinational corporation which produces several best-selling brands of cigarette, including Marlboro, across the world (Sunday Times, p1, 19/7/92). Three years later the Morris Corporation paid for the ex-Prime Minister's 70th birthday party (London Evening Standard, p1, 14/9/95), and by 1996 her annual income from the company was estimated at £500,000 (Daily Express, p3, 19/6/96). Certified figures are unavailable, as Baroness Thatcher has adamantly refused to make any declarations in the Lords' Register of Interests – although (or because?) this was founded in the wake of the Conservative sleaze scandals of the mid-1990s.

". . . *or Bernie Ecclestone* . . ."

The announcement in November 1997 that the avowedly comprehensive ban on tobacco companies' sponsorship of sport, promised since before the election, would not apply to Formula One motor racing, was met with widespread despision.

The first reason given was that such a ban would be detrimental to British jobs, in that the

Formula One industry would simply relocate to more smoke-friendly countries.

A more convincing ground for the exemption emerged when journalists exposed the business involvement in Formula One of the then Public Health Minister Tessa Jowell's then husband, David Mills.

This was superseded in turn by the revelation of a one million pound donation to the Labour Party prior to the '97 election by Bernie Ecclestone, President of the Formula One Constructors' Association.

Both Ecclestone and the government insisted that the two transactions were entirely unrelated. Blair went so far as to appear on television and maintain that as he personally was "*. . . a pretty straight kind of guy*", no one need worry about anything (Guardian 10/11/98, p1).

But the dissembling that surrounded the affair was far from straight. When the Neill Committee on Standards in Public Life investigated it, Blair ostentatiously insisted that the money should be returned to Ecclestone in order to counter any, er – "*appearance* of wrong-doing"!

Ecclestone was loth to accept it back, claiming that ". . . I was surprised by the stupidity of the Labour Party" and that "It's not fair" (Sunday Times, p20, 5/4/98). The Party was immediately bailed out with a replacement million donated by another of Tony's cronies, Robert Earl of Planet Hollywood.

266

THE CHEQUERED FLAG

Philip Webster and Andrew Pierce reported in the Times which ran the Brookes cartoon above on 12/11/97 that:

"... A top to toe reform of the way Britain's political parties are funded was promised by the government last night as it struggled to wipe away the taint of sleaze surrounding its decision to exempt motor racing from any tobacco advertising ban."

Pretty slack progress, then, in that at the time of this book's going to press nearly a decade later, loans and donations for peerages, cash for favours, mutual benefit cronyism and overall sleaze-merchandising have become all the more solidly, widely and cynically entrenched as the names of the Blairite political games, despite that long ago promise.

A chequered flag indeed. *Plus ça change, plus c'est la même chose.*

It turns out that two-thirds of Formula One racing drivers at the 1998 French Grand Prix were simultaneously struck by Repetitive Strain Injury, notorious for causing permanent disability.

Jeremy Laurance, Health Editor of The Independent, reported on 10/8/99 (front page – *'Formula One is the fastest way to get RSI'*) that, according to Dr Emmanuel Masmejean and colleagues in the British Journal of Sports Medicine, "Its frequency is worrying . . . . The incidence of wrist and hand problems among sportsmen and women in the general population is estimated to be 25%, compared to the 63% found among the drivers . . ."

Despite all this, Formula One motor racing – and subsequently, televised snooker – went on advertising their sponsorship by the lung cancer industry to countless squillions of suggestible viewers. Did this not expose the senior public servant who went on sanctioning it, whilst claiming that the nation's health was a top priority, as – um – 'a pretty crooked kind of guy'?

In the summer of 1999 I was amazed to hear that definitively crooked guy, Lord Archhole, whingeing on BBC Radio 4 about how televised snooker could not survive without the sponsorship of tobacco advertising.

My own projects (such as New Departures publications, Poetry Olympics festivals, Jazz Poetry SuperJams) are still barely surviving on a shoestring after nearly five decades of gruelling spadework – but nonetheless struggle to go on making such inroads as we can manage, worldwide. If I crawl to cigarette firms and get their advertising to sponsor televised New Departures, Poetry Olympics and jazz poetry gigs, arts circuses and bandwagons, magazines and books, will the government turn the same blind eye on these sponsorships as it contributed to the promotions of Formula One and snooker?

Then again – no such deal could be a lucky strike for these enterprises, if the money had to be contingent on our contributors and performers being seen ardently chain-smoking on page, stage or screen, as the twice-running world snooker champion Alex 'Hurricane' Higgins, among many others, was induced to do. Amelia Gentleman reported in the Guardian of 27/7/1999 that Higgins

> ". . . was encouraged to smoke certain brands on television and players were given free cigarettes. [He] has undergone 44 doses of radiotherapy, and had surgery to remove a cancerous lymph node in his neck. Speaking in Dublin, he described himself as 'a living example of the dangers of smoking . . . They've had their advertising for a song for 25 years. Snooker players have died of cancer. Tobacco is addictive. None of these boys were forewarned' . . ."

So far from cementing what the New Labour government had promised as "the cornerstone" of its policy on nicotine *before* the 2001 election, the bill to ban tobacco advertising was conspicuous by its absence from the first Queen's Speech of the second term, on 20 June 2001. John Connolly of Action on Smoking and Health restated the obvious in the Guardian on 22/6/01, p19:

> ". . . It is just not possible to meet the Government's target of 1.5m fewer smokers by 2010 without banning the advertising that keeps them hooked."

Six months earlier, Alan Milburn, the then Health Secretary, had told MPs that ". . . Smoking is the biggest public health problem, and it is essential to get this law on the statute books . . ."

The ban had actually been promised in New Labour's 1997 manifesto. In January 2001 Milburn claimed that ". . . Where the previous government failed to act, this government will now do so. We will act to protect children; we will act to reduce smoking; we will act to save lives". However, as of another nine months later, no government action on nicotine had in fact been mooted.

So much for the Labour re-election manifesto's prime commitment to "radical reform". Could the 2001 Government's postponement of such avowedly crucial legislation be related to the fact that the cessation of tobacco advertising and sponsorship would vastly diminish the tax revenue on this one hundred million pounds-a-year business?

According to the Daily Telegraph's City Comment (*'Smoking does no harm at all to health of the nation's coffers'*) on 8/7/2001, p38, ". . . In Britain, smokers cough up about ten billion pounds a year in duty and VAT". It would seem that the Government was more hooked on the perpetually simmering teats of this munificent milch cow of – er, wealth creation, than on targeting for a dramatic reduction in the number of people smoking their life expectancy away.

The Health Act 2006, which got Royal Assent on 19 July 2006, has cleared the air around some of these state-sanctioned exploitations (see *www.opsi.gov.uk/acts/acts2006/20060028.htm*). Yet, as of early 2007, the tax revenue from nicotine sales, like that from the nationwide sales of other highly dangerous (though legal) drugs, notably alcohol, continues to be garnered by the Treasury of a government which is actively encouraging round-the-clock boozing, gambling and other pretty unhealthy addictions.

This government also continues to use such taxes to subsidise UK arms manufacture and exports. An administration more interested in facilitating optimum life cycles than in maximum profits would surely invest taxpayers' contributions in the curing and healing of human bodies from the consequences of destruction, rather than so ruthlessly using them to increase those unhealthy consequences.

"Birmingham's Roman Catholic Cathedral / . . . as rich as the Church of England . . ."

As of March 1998 the Cathedral was holding shares worth £25m in Lucas Varity and in Rolls Royce, two companies that profit from the sale of arms. When challenged on the issue, and on similar investments by other cathedrals and churches, the General Synod put forward a spokesman, Steve Jenkins, who enlightened journalist Ian Burrell: ". . . A mistake that people make is to assume that as a church you must be opposed to arms manufacture" (Independent, p1, 23/3/98). So much for *"Thou shalt not kill"*.

In February 1997 the Church of England's investments in GEC, the major arms manufacturers, were valued at £14m. This was justified by the Church in the following terms:

> " . . . Being an investment fund whose responsibilities must be met year-in year-out, the exclusion of entire sectors of the market is, given our size, not generally the first step taken in executing ethical policy if we are to achieve the consistency of return required."

A similarly prevaricating and time-dishonoured line of bullshit was reeled out to pretend that the exported armaments could be guaranteed to be used by their purchasers in self-defence only – though the Church did disingenuously admit such anomalies as that:

> ". . . monitoring is complicated by the diversity of modern large companies. For example, distinctions between products used for defence related and non-defence related purposes are often blurred. The distinction between offensive and defensive equipment is also often unclear . . ." (Church of England Commissioners' Press Release, 27/2/97).

So that's alright, then. The blurred distinctions and unclarity that govern the arms trade can go on being echoed, endorsed and exploited in the blurred and unclear language and practice of Britain's leading churchmen.

It would seem that the prime concern of some of Christ's Ministers in Albion today is to outdo our currently prevailing Apostles of Mammon in being as shrewd as serpents (– though not, alas, as innocent as doves – cf St Matthew 10, 16).

For balance, I should mention that by the autumn of 2006 the C of E's Ethical Advisory Group had cleaned up this and allied unsavoury aspects of the Church's act, avowing that ". . . We do not invest in any company that promotes pornography or supplies armaments. Investment is also avoided in any company, a major part of whose business activity or focus is gambling or the supply of tobacco products, alcoholic beverages or military equipment".

It's also clear from hearing and reading their words, and observing their actions, that the hearts and minds of Archbishops Rowan Williams, John Sentamu and their ilk are in a very good place.

Nevertheless, other oft-heard mouthpieces for various branches of contemporary Christianity, and for many other religions, still have a heck of a lot to answer for.

Quite a number of the official lines I have heard and read have gone backward rather than forward from the socio-moral evasions observed more than sixty years ago by Dorothy L Sayers in her incisive volume *'Creed or Chaos and Other Essays in Popular Theology'* (Hodder & Stoughton 1940, Methuen 1947):

> "The unsacramental attitude of modern society to man and matter is probably closely connected with its unsacramental attitude to work. The Church is a good deal to blame for having connived at this. From the eighteenth century onwards, she has tended to acquiesce in what I may call the 'industrious apprentice' view of the matter: 'Work hard and be thrifty, and God will bless you with a contented mind and a competence'. This is nothing but enlightened self-interest in its vulgarest form, and plays directly into the hands of the monopolist and the financier. Nothing has so deeply discredited the Christian Church as her squalid submission to the economic theory of society. The burning question of the Christian attitude to money is being so eagerly debated nowadays that it is scarcely necessary to do more than remind ourselves that the present unrest, both in Russia and in Central Europe, is an immediate judgment upon a financial system that has subordinated man to economics, and that no *mere* adjustment of economic machinery will have any lasting effect if it keeps man a prisoner inside the machine.

> "This is the burning question; but I believe there is a still more important and fundamental question waiting to be dealt with, and that is, what men in a Christian Society ought to think and feel about work. Curiously enough, apart from the passage in *Genesis* which suggests that work is a hardship and a judgement on sin, Christian doctrine is not very explicit about work. I believe, however, that there *is* a Christian doctrine of work, very closely related to the doctrines of the creative energy of God and the divine image in man.

> ". . . If man's fulfilment of his nature is to be found in the full expression of his divine creativeness, then we urgently need a Christian doctrine of work, which shall provide, not only for proper conditions of employment, but also that the work shall be such as a man may do with his whole heart, and that he shall do it for the very work's sake. But we cannot expect a sacramental attitude to work, while many people are forced, by our evil standard of values, to do work which is a spiritual degradation – a long series of financial trickeries, for example, or the manufacture of vulgar and useless trivialities."

Page 30

". . . life is lived in work/ unless you're a wage-slave./ While a wage-slave works, he leaves life aside/ and stands there a piece of dung . . ."

– See again Dorothy L Sayers in *'Creed or Chaos'*:

> ". . . The modern tendency seems to be to identify work with gainful employment; and this is, I maintain, the essential heresy at the back of the great economic fallacy which allows wheat and coffee to be burnt and fish to be used for manure while whole populations stand in need of food. The fallacy being that work is not the expression of man's creative energy in the service of Society, but only something he does in order to obtain money and leisure.

"A very able surgeon put it to me like this: 'What is happening', he said, 'is that nobody works for the sake of getting the thing done. The result of the work is a by-product; the *aim* of the work is to make money to do something else. Doctors practice medicine, not primarily to relieve suffering, but to make a living – the cure of the patient is something that happens on the way. Lawyers accept briefs, not because they have a passion for justice, but because the law is the profession which enables them to live'. . ."

If the aim of many British working lives has changed at all over the last six decades, it has tended to mean a change for the worse. And such changes, notably since Thatcher and Blair held sway, have tended to be implanted from the top (as witness the examples cited in the note to "– *countless lives reduced / to job market / investment statistics*" on page 284).

"Flower-piece II" by Richard Hamilton

This oil painting, one of a series Hamilton made between 1971 and 1974, is reproduced in colour in '*Richard Hamilton*', published by the Tate Gallery in 1992 in celebration of their Hamilton retrospective of that year. Pages 173-174 of the book's Catalogue section feature diverting notes about these Flower-pieces, such as the following:

". . . While he was working on the plates for an etched version of 'Flower-piece II' at the studio of Aldo Crommelynck in Paris, Sonia Orwell, a close mutual friend, saw Hamilton's motif for the first time. She took him by the arm, led him apart from the company and sternly said, 'You know Richard, life's not all shit and flowers'. Hamilton found the remark, and the tone of motherly concern, hilarious, but reflected that without the 'not' her opinion became profound: life was truly 'all shit and flowers' . . ."

Page 31

". . . *As packaged dung / whizzes along . . .*"

– cf the talking statues of political leaders made of compressed shit in the late lamented Alexander Zinoviev's '*The Yawning Heights*' (1979), and the talking arsehole in '*The Naked Lunch*' by William Burroughs (1959)

". . . *only* Hype / *springs diurnal . . .*"

– cf Alexander Pope, '*An Essay on Man*' (1733), Epistle 1, lines 95-96:

> "*Hope springs eternal in the human breast:*
> *Man never Is, but always to be blest.*"

". . . *save us* '. . . victorious, / happy and glorious' . . ."

Cf the British National Anthem: "*Send her victorious, / Happy and glorious, / Long to reign over us: / God save the Queen . . .*"

One of this book's motifs (adapting *The Waste Land*'s main theme) is salvation – but "God save the Queen"?

To where exactly is this God supposed to be "Sending her victorious" etc – and from whence?

The anthem's doggerel lyrics have puzzled me since early childhood. They presuppose that the Monarch is poised at the verge of some dire débacle from which (s)he needs saving. But the famous English reserve – or something – seems to go on conspiring against any exploration or explanation of what this fate might be.

– A nationwide acknowledgement of the extraordinary anachronism of a contemporary Queen's or King's pomp and inflated circumstance, perhaps?

"this promised/ once and future/ (still could be) pleasant/ green land"

– cf the last verse of William Blake's hymn in the Preface to *'Milton'* (1804), Plate 1:

> *"I will not cease from Mental Fight,*
> *Nor shall my Sword sleep in my hand*
> *Till we have built Jerusalem*
> *In England's green & pleasant Land."*

Page 33

"GORDON COMES OUT . . . 'WE ARE A PRIVATISER'. . ."

Chris Riddell's 1998 image of the winsomely breast-plated, pearl-necklaced and heavy-metal armoured "Iron Chancellor" aptly evokes the shade of Boadicea Thatcher selling off the family silver – with a nod to pyramid-corseted 'material gal' Madonna – appearing as it did just after Gordon Brown had announced in the Commons his sale of twelve billion pounds' worth of state assets to an incredulously silent Labour backbench. Chris's thinks-bubble speaks parallel volumes, echoing the original handbagger's occupational self-glory when – subsuming Victoria Reginahood – she announced: *"We are A Grandmother"*.

Thirteen years earlier (on 8/11/85) the emphatically non-socialist ex-PM Harold Macmillan had told the Tory Reform Group that selling state assets would no more provide lasting economic solutions than selling family silver does. Mrs T's unbending monetarist yoke went on to privatise various potentially profitable public services – the railways, British Telecom, the steel industry, et al.

Page 34

". . . 'tough choices' . . ."

'Hard choices' and 'tough choices' are among the buzz-phrases Tony Blair and his henchmen have resorted to most frequently. Early deployments of both featured in Blair's address at the ERM Environment Forum on 27 February 1996 (*'The New Environmental Agenda'*, February 2006) and also in his Introduction to the Labour Party's Election Manifesto of 1997.

Unfortunately, in most cases where these slogans were acted on, the choice tended to be soft on whatever Blair wanted at a particular time, and hard on the majority of the working population it affected.

". . . 'smarter' bombs"

– This unpleasant epithet provoked Spike Hawkins to draft a memo on behalf of a healthier meaning of 'smart' – and also, a healthier international community:

> *"Dear Mr Bush*
>
> *A smart bomb*
> *would stay*
> *at home!"*

". . . deathly job-stunted lives . . ."

Cf D H Lawrence's poem:

'WHY — ?'

> *"Why have money?*
> *why have a financial system to strangle us all in its octopus arms?*
> *why have industry?*
> *why have the industrial system?*
> *why have machines, that we only have to serve?*
> *why have a soviet, that only wants to screw us all in as parts of the machine?*
> *why have working classes at all, as if men were only embodied jobs?*
> *why not have men as men, and the work as merely part of the game of life?*
> *True, we've got all these things*
> *industrial and financial systems, machines and soviets, working classes.*
> *But why go on having them, if they belittle us?*
> *Why should we be belittled any longer?"*

While Russia may or may not have got rid of the Soviet system, President Tone would have UK citizens believe that we're all equally middle class now – or classless, even – thanks to New Labour.

If only!

Since May 1997, Blair, Brown, Straw, Irvine, Blunkett, Prescott, Mandelson, Falconer, Hoon, Reid and the rest of the so-called Project's manipulators have imposed scheme upon scheme to ". . . *screw us all in as parts of the machine*".

Why should we slave on as mere cogs in the machine, when it's the machine that's supposed to be serving us?

Given the new millennium's unprecedented abundance of food, drink and shelters, of transport and communications facilities – of just about every raw material and technological development worth sharing – what excuse can governments have for continuing to treat men or women as ". . . *only embodied jobs*"?

Let's make the most of the high tech that's clearly useful. But let's stop suffocating ourselves by labouring on in the mercenary stranglehold of soulless jobs, for nothing more than the man-made job machine's sake.

Why have advertising?

Why have thousands of firms competing against each other to produce the selfsame goods?

Why keep transporting those same goods from one part of the country, or one part of the globe, to other parts of the country, or other parts of the globe, from which more of the selfsame goods are also being transported, in turn – and quite frequently being transported to the selfsame place from which more of them are simultaneously being transported back?

A case in point was dryly and wryly noted by the late lamented E F Schumacher (in his posthumously published *'Good Work'*, Cape 1979):

> ". . . When you travel up the big motor road from London you find yourself surrounded by a huge fleet of lorries carrying biscuits from London to Glasgow. And when you look across to the other motorway, you find an equally huge fleet of lorries carrying biscuits from Glasgow to London. An impartial observer from another planet would come to the

conclusion that biscuits have to be transported at least six hundred miles before they reach their proper quality . . ."

Why push or hard sell any product at all?

– Including political parties?

Why have party funding at all?

If a political party's aim is to best sustain the country and the planet, it will prove this by what it plans and says and does, not by spin or advertising or selling.

How were the Labour Party's grounds for re-election in 2005 improved by a hair's breadth in consequence of a vast publicity campaign – or, indeed, of Mrs Blair's expenditure of £7,700 on her coiffure in the course of that brief but exorbitant campaign?

If a product or an initiative or a movement is any good, it won't need to be lavishly hair-styled or expensively talked up.

If it's no good, it needs to be withdrawn, until it justifies its restoration to public use by properly serving its avowed and demonstrably worthwhile purpose.

Why soldier on in meaningless, boring or soul-destroying jobs, for no better reason than the profit-fixated calls of the advertising industry, or the fancy-hairdressing industry, or the lung cancer industry, or the job industry, or the arms trade, or the exploitative money-machines, or the vested interests of career politicians, or any other waste of human energy, time or resources?

Why, respected and less respected world leaders, should any human being in the 21st Century be belittled any longer?

Once such mindless calls to treadmills of pointless wage-slavery are called *off* for good, we will be far better placed to get on with living and working in creative fulfilment, harmony and peace.

Page 38

"I'M ASKING YOU TO *SPONSOR THE UNSPONSORABLE!*"

Steve Bell's cartoon appeared in the Guardian after the second of Blair's promised "welfare road shows" to sell the government's message on 28 January 1998. The Bleeder had told 400 party members at the Vauxhall Recreation Centre in Luton that New Labour's radical *(sic)* welfare reform would "lift the most vulnerable people out of poverty and into work".

As of nine years later, this plan had failed to translate into contemporary fact – perhaps unsurprisingly, given the market driven (and driving) priorities of the fairground barker's wagon and pitch, as so trenchantly debunked by Bell.

See also the first few paragraphs of the note on p264 to "*New Deals . . . welfare to work for all*".

Page 39

". . . *its new Foreman, Comrade Blair . . .*"

– cf the revisionist variation on '*The Red Flag*' I remember hearing raucously chanted oft-times in my schooldays:

> "*. . . The working class can kiss my arse,*
> *I've got a foreman's job at last . . .*"

"On 10th December '97/ Britain's single parents/ chilled to hear . . ."

The cutting of Single Parent Benefit on 10 December 1997, engineered by Blair's own vaulting ambition, gave a dramatic indication of the manipulative presidential style that was to characterise his subsequent years at the helm.

The night of the crucial vote found his nibs unable to get to the House of Commons, owing to a prior engagement at Number Ten where he was hosting a reception for 'national treasures' beloved of The Sun and the Daily Mail, like soap star Liz Dawn, DJ Chris Evans and Beatle imitator Noel Gallagher. Paparazzi snapped our People's PM swigging champagne with millionaires at the very hour that a pittance was being clawed away from the poor by his sidekicks in Parliament.

Most of the MPs who did make it to the House toed the party line on the lone parents' bill, but a significant rump of Labour MPs refused to support it, whilst the official opposition – recognising the policy they had always supported but never dared propose so blatantly – gave the government their wholehearted support. The poles had been switched.

This betrayal – indeed, complete reversal – of all that Labour had traditionally stood for, is what started me writing this book. It would have been near-impossible for my son and I to survive without the Benefit for the first year or two after the loss of Frances Horovitz to cancer, when she was 45 and Adam only 12. So I well know just how much difference this did make to at least one lone parent, when the concession was well in place.

It was probably hardly ever enough for any single parents and children to survive on reasonably in or of itself. But its casual cancellation only six months after the (one thought) transformative Mayday '97 election result could hardly have been bettered if Blair's express purpose had been to cement the continuity of Thatcherite Pay-your-way-or-get-lost Monetarism.

Which, ten years later, it does seem to have been all along – and to so widely anti-social a degree, damn it.

Even the official spin-machine headed by Messrs Campbell and Mandelson was forced to concede that the policy had been *"badly presented"* – the worst sin, it seems, in the New Labour bible.

Blair's method of damage limitation repackaged a creepy sacrificial rite from the Old Testament, seeking to cover up his neglect of communal responsibility by laying the blame on a relatively innocent beast of burden. His personally selected scapegoat was the luckless Social Security Secretary, Harriet Harman, upon whose head all opprobrium was briskly heaped.

Since Harman was well known amongst lobby correspondents as one of the few cabinet members prepared to have her departmental policy determined by Gordon Brown's then minimal Treasury handouts without demanding more, one deduces that the real culprits for this act of penny-pinching spite and persecution were lurking elsewhere – and are presumably doing much the same at the time of my finishing this book nine-and-a-half years later.

Harman was finally cast out into the wilderness in the summer of '98, to be seen bearing away with her all (anti-)social iniquities of which the government might have been accused.

She was replaced by one of Brown's deputies, the eminently conforming and prudent Alistair Darling. A limited – and for many single parents, a callously dysfunctioning – replacement for the lost benefit had been given in the budget that spring, with a 20% increase in Child Benefit. Gordon Brown claimed that he was acting to "end the poverty trap" (Times, p2, 16/7/98) – ineffectually, many felt – and woefully late in the day.

With his introduction of the *'Working Families Tax Credit'*, Brown was at pains to emphasise work over parenthood. The scheme went some way towards helping single parents financially, but only for as long as they stayed in officially recognised employment – i e, only for as long as they stayed away from their children.

It looked and felt like yet another case – as with New Labour's treatment of pensioners, the disabled, students, and public spending in general – of this government's apparently incorrigible technique of:

(1) snatching away, or threatening to snatch away, a major (sometimes indispensable) source of survival;
(2) then withdrawing the threat, or seeming to give (some of) the support back – usually after a lot of hot air and bureaucracy;
(3) soliciting applause for compassionate reforms.

– This methodology strikes me as a near-plausible explanation of Blair's otherwise nebulous notion of 'The Third Way', so widely proselytised as the most special and unprecedented free gift in New Labour's policy hamper for a Greater Britain (*'gift'* in the German sense of that word perhaps, i e, 'poison').

Page 41

". . . *'Would you cut lone parents' benefit?'* . . . // . . . *'Of course not'* . . ."

Under the headline *'Leopards that will spring out on Labour'* (Independent, 22 January 1997), Polly Toynbee recounted how Peter Lilley, the Tory Social Security Secretary, pounced like a veritable leopard after Gordon Brown had promised that, if Labour were elected the following summer, they would spend no more on each department than the Tory government had budgeted for over the next two years.

Toynbee pointed out that the then ". . . Tory government itself would never have managed to stay within those limits". Her article began by summarising

> ". . . what Lilley has done: in the Budget the Chancellor announced that the Lone Parent Premium (£5.20 extra for single parents on income support) and One Parent Benefit (£6.30 for working single parents) will be axed. It was a neat ploy, signalling moral disapproval of single parents while saving £100m a year.

> "Harriet Harman, the shadow Social Security Secretary, protested that the cuts would hit the weakest, but otherwise no great cry went up. The silence was eerie. Once, hundreds of thousands would have been out on the streets in protest, but times have changed: people are resigned to government callousness, or simply don't care.

> "*Single parents account for most of the huge growth in poverty. They are the most vulnerable group, so cutting their benefits is dangerous cruelty. To cut the premium that helps those in work is plain madness . . . This is one of the most monstrous things this government has done.*

> ". . . This is the Tory Social Security Secretary's trap: to make these cuts he must consult his Advisory Committee, then put a Bill through Parliament. That cannot be done before June – by which time Labour could be in power. So will Harman, as her very first act, implement these cuts, or will she find £100m to plug the gap that Brown is committed to keeping at its present level?"

Toynbee proceeded to pop this leading – er – multi-million pound question: ". . . 'Will she or won't she introduce Tory legislation to cut single parents' benefits?' – 'No, of course not', she says".

Eleven months later, the Conservative MP Simon Burns referred Parliament to Toynbee's interview with Harman, recalling (Hansard, 10 December 1997) –

". . . the argument that was made throughout the country by the Right Hon lady before the election, that a cut in Lone Parent Benefit would continue or increase the poverty of children and lone parents. If that is true, why has the Right Hon lady reversed her argument?

"This sorry tale takes another twist that is embarrassing for the Government and a damning indictment of the Labour Party which, before the general election, promised anything to anyone to win power. The Secretary of State attacked the measure when it was introduced and promised to reverse it if Labour was elected. On 22 January 1997 . . . the Right Hon lady said categorically that she would not implement the cuts that were proposed by the Conservative Government. That interview contained a black and white commitment not to introduce those changes, but the Secretary of State has broken that commitment by asking her Hon friends to vote against the new clause and amendment No. 1.

"It would be wrong to single out the Secretary of State for Social Security and not mention her Right Hon friend the Prime Minister. I assure the House that his hands are not altogether clean on this issue either. As Leader of the Opposition, the Right Hon gentleman was just as guilty of raising the electorate's expectations. There is no point in the Prime Minister trying to justify his behaviour on the policy with speeches such as the one that he gave on Monday at Stockwell Park school, where he limply said: *'We are accused of breaking promises we never made, often by opponents who introduced the very measures they now criticise us for not reversing'*.

"But the Right Hon gentleman did make a promise to lone parents. He went on to say: *'Do not let anyone fall for the nonsense that Labour priorities are Tory ones or that we have done just the same as them'*. The Prime Minister has done the same as us over lone parents, and he cannot escape from the mess as easily as that, because he made the commitment to lone parents that he would not force through the changes."

Meanwhile the Labour MP for Glasgow Maryhill, Maria Fyfe, had written in the Morning Star about the cuts in lone parent benefit as follows:

". . . People voted Labour because they believed that there were alternatives. Lone parents took heart from our stance when these matters were debated during last November's budget.

"Labour members spoke passionately against these cuts, aided by a very useful briefing issued by our shadow Social Security team, viz —

'Since One Parent Benefit is not taxed, it helps to bridge the gap between welfare and work. Its abolition will make working lone mothers worse off and will discourage work amongst this group. Lone Parent Premium recognises that lone parents face additional costs in bringing up their children. They do not have a partner's time or income to help with children' . . ."

Promises, promises.

The situation was anatomised by Joan Smith in *'She's Minister for Women, so who needs chauvinists?'* in the Independent on Sunday (14/12/1997):

"On Thursday [11 December] I happened to be talking to a Labour backbencher who opposes his government's cuts in benefit to lone parents. As he shook his head in despair, and remarked on Harriet Harman's lamentable performance in the House of Commons, I realised something both of us had forgotten. Ms Harman, as well as being Social Security Secretary, is also Minister for Women. When I mentioned this fact, we broke into what I think is known as hollow laughter.

"Ms Harman's appointment, supposedly a ground-breaking move by Tony Blair's government, was revealed in the heady days immediately after the general election. But the announcement of the setting up of a Whitehall Women's Unit, and a Cabinet sub-committee chaired by Ms Harman to look at the way in which decisions affect women, was delayed until four weeks later – by which time it looked dangerously like an afterthought.

"At the time, Ms Harman wrote an article in the Guardian about her role as Minister for Women, arguing that women 'want a government they can trust, a government that delivers'. So I think it's reasonable to ask which Ms Harman stood up in the House on Wednesday night [10 December '97], sometimes close to tears because of barracking from her own backbenchers, and attempted to justify measures which will hit some of the worst-off women in society? [*True Joan, but quite a few men too, in fact; including me as was – see the fourth paragraph of page 275 above, MH*]

"The one who believes British women have had such a raw deal from previous governments that they need a special minister, namely herself, to defend their interests against hard-hearted politicians whose first interest is saving money? Or the one who, as Social Security minister, controls a high-spending department whose budget she is determined to slash, regardless of the consequences?

"Back in June, I pointed out in this newspaper that Ms Harman appeared to have been given a title but virtually no money, which was bad enough. I also asked how she intended to reconcile two ministerial roles which were so obviously in conflict with each other. This week we got the answer. Ms Harman's mission to save money overrides all other considerations – and she has consistently refused to address the question of what should happen to those women who cannot or do not want to get jobs until their children are older.

"You would think, to hear Ms Harman talk, that all single mothers live in metropolitan areas where jobs are plentiful and transport is easy. 'Lone mothers want to work, for a better standard of living for their children', she has insisted. But this is far from being the whole story, as a single mother living in a rural area told a Radio 4 programme this week. The only jobs available to her are in a distant town, making the cost of travelling and childcare prohibitive – and much of the work is seasonal.

"From April, a single mother who takes a seasonal job and is laid off at the end of it risks being treated by the DSS as a new claimant – and may find herself up to £10.25 a week worse off. If Harriet Harman, as Britain's first Minister for Women, is unable to grasp such details, an honourable course is open to her. She should resign at once."

She did not. She just went on meekly doing her bossmen's bidding, till they decided they'd milked her breast-plate and mouth-piece dry, and dumped her.

Nine years of New Labour misrule later, in *'Benefits threat to lone parents'* (Guardian 31/1/2007) Tania Branigan reported on how the government – whilst continuing to splash untold millions of tax revenues on arms and wars – was as concerned to bash lone parents as it had been at The Project's inception:

". . . Single parents who refuse to seek work could face cuts in benefits, the Work and Pensions Secretary warned yesterday, arguing that increasing employment was the only way to meet the government's goal. John Hutton [is] requiring lone parents '. . . to take employment when their youngest child reaches 12. At present they can claim benefits until the child is 16. We will need to go further in challenging existing assumptions about who should be in work – and at what point' . . ."

But Jane Ahrends said, on behalf of One Parent Families, that two-thirds of single parents with children aged between 11 and 16 were already working, and that –

> ". . . The majority amongst those who are not working usually have very good reasons for not doing so. A third of divorces happen when children are in that age category. It may well be that single parents decide that their priority must be to stabilise family life, and to be at home with their children. Most single parents want to work when the time is ripe for them and their children. But there are very high barriers for them, particularly in the absence of affordable local child care."

Chris Pond, director of the One Parent Families group, added that one quarter of otherwise unemployed single parents of 11-to-16 year-olds were caring for disabled children; and that many others of them were preoccupied with ". . . simply trying to provide stability in the aftermath of a family break-up". His conclusion was – what one might hope democratic governments would understand – that ". . . *Lone parents want help in getting over the hurdles they face when they are ready to [go out to] work, not further impoverishment when they are needed at home*".

More of the latter can only escalate still further the UK's current record incidence of child and one-parent family poverty – and hence intensify the overall extremes of imbalance between the situations of a number of obscenely over-affluent Brits, and those of far greater numbers of their more or less hopelessly insolvent fellow citizens.

One in every four British children was living in poverty as of February 2007, when the UK also came bottom of a UN league table of the twenty-one most developed countries which compared state by state treatments of the worst-off, and especially of children. The front and inside pages of both the Independent and the Guardian of 14/2/07 quoted the previous day's Unicef report on the wellbeing of children and adolescents: ". . . Children growing up in the UK suffer greater deprivation, worse relationships with their parents, and are exposed to more risks from alcohol, drugs and unsafe sex, than those in any other wealthy country in the world".

While Britain boasts one of the four strongest economies on the planet, surely the government needs to prioritise radical redistribution for emergency rescue operations on these fronts, rather than whipping single parents (many of whom are already worked off their feet at home) to get on their bikes and chance their arms on random jobs (many of which are quite probably going to be pretty unrewarding on any level).

According to the charity for the homeless, Shelter, 94,000 families were without a home at the beginning of 2007, and 134,000 children were in desperately temporary accommodation. Plus the London Child Poverty Commission's 2007 Report clocked 700,000 children below the poverty line in the city – two in five – with many families having to survive on less than £150 a week (see *www.the londonpaper.com* and the front page of its 28 February '07 issue). With a human basics record this abysmal, how could the nation's leaders have been spending one minute of their time and one penny of our money on "Winning the Olympics" – and then a whole lot more on crowing about it and continuing to multiply the overweening expenses attached?

". . . *this same so-called Leader/ . . . declined/ to limousine his arse/ to grace the debate – or rather, farce/ in Parliament . . .*"

– In the same Independent on Sunday article (14 December 1997) cited above, Joan Smith deconstructed the People's PM's modus operandi as follows:

> ". . . What a busy old Prime Minister we have these days – a Renaissance man who could find the time to share a joke with Chris Evans and Zoë Ball on the very evening that Labour

MPs were threatening to vote against their government. How happy Cherie looked, embracing Liz Dawn, who plays Vera Duckworth in *Coronation Street*. How willingly Tony signed an orange which Chris Evans said he would give away on his Virgin Radio breakfast show the following morning. How thrilled the Blairs must have been to meet Edna O'Brien, John Mortimer, John Thaw and Kevin Whately – and all at a cost to the taxpayer of only £3,000, roughly equal to a week's cut in benefit to 290 single mothers from next April.

"Malcolm Bruce, the Lib Dems' diligent Treasury spokesman, has forced the Government to admit it spent £7.4m on hospitality between 1 May and 30 September – more than a million pounds a month on receptions and drinks parties. The Ministry of Defence alone has managed to use up £2m in this way, while Wednesday's bash at Number 10 was the sixth such event hosted by the Blairs since the General Election.

"It is obvious to anyone outside the Blairs' charmed circle that this kind of socialising is in the worst possible taste, when the government is perceived by many ordinary people to be abandoning its commitments to single parents, students from poor families and the disabled.

"How many of us realised, when we voted Labour on 1 May, that we were landing ourselves with the years of Champagne Tony, a Prime Minister with so many stars in his eyes that he is no longer able to make simple connections?"

Page 43

"*. . . plastic-souled bossmen / appoint plasticine-doll groupies . . .*"

Cf Lynn Barber's interview with Harriet Harman in the Observer (31 May '98):

"It is accusations of her being 'docile' or 'acquiescent' that seem to annoy her most. Perhaps she realises too late that in being an obedient Blairite, she has entirely lost any popularity or personal credibility she might once have had. Time and again, she told me that she was never docile, never acquiescent.

"And yet, she also told me:

'. . . You know, in the old days in Opposition, the worst thing you could do was to say something that then made a story run. I'll never forget I was doing a series of local radio interviews, and we got to Radio Cumbria, and suddenly, at the end, the interviewer asked me something about Sellafield. Now, I kind of knew about it, but I didn't know what the line was. I wasn't doing Environment at the time, or Energy, and I actually thought that if I say something that creates a frenzy among the environmentalists, or the people working in Sellafield, this will be a real problem. So I kind of felt myself choosing to just sound completely ignorant. Because the people listening might think Bloody Hell! What an airhead! – but at least it wouldn't go anywhere, it wouldn't cause problems for my colleagues . . . But I think problem-avoidance has meant that sometimes I've created a situation where I look as if I've got a problem myself!'

"This must be the purest exposition of Mandelsonian politics: you have to know 'the line'. If you don't know the line, you are not allowed to speak. You are not allowed to have views, or even knowledge, of anything outside your brief. Better to fall on your sword and say that you have never heard of Sellafield than to express a non-line view about it. It is a remarkable tribute to her docility, though not perhaps to her common sense, that she went along with it so wholeheartedly. And now she complains that she is seen as an automaton."

In fairness to Ms Harman, readers should note that she performed a creditable series of *volte-face* after her eviction from government. In January 2001, for example, her Child Care Commission Report called for the state to provide new mothers with a wage for three years, and also with generous tax relief to help cover child care arrangements.

Page 44

TWO BELL CARTOONS

The upper cartoon fans out Blair's initial would-be winning Happy Family hand: Pooch Prescott the Household Pet, Mr Carrot the Corporate Accountant, Ms Stick the Social Worker, Mr Broon the Banker's Runner, Mr Dome the Dickhead, and Mr Teeth the Taskmaster – whip at the ready, eyes aglare and unsteady.

On 10 December 1997, forty-seven Labour MPs voted against the Government's proposed cuts to lone parent benefits, and many more abstained. None of Blair's Cabinet was in the House of Commons that night to support Harriet Harman in face of this backbench revolt.

The lower picture, based on the painting (and HMV trademark logo) by Francis Barrauld, appeared after hapless Harriet was summarily dispatched from her Cabinet post in Blair's first major reshuffle.

David Brindle commented in the Guardian on the day this cartoon graced the same paper (28/7/98), that: ". . . Welfare reform will remain at the heart of the Government's agenda, Downing Street insisted yesterday after removal of the Ministers who were supposed to modernise the 100 billion pound Social Security system. The departure from government of not only Harriet Harman, whose demise had been widely predicted, but also Frank Field, leaves a vacuum where Labour had promised a hive of activity and creative thinking . . ."

Steve Bell himself (in *'Bell's Eye: Twenty Years of Drawing Blood'*, Methuen 1999) was more explicit in confronting the oppressive hypocrisies and duplicities that motivated these slippery shifts of policy and personnel – under the headings *'Blair's Bollocks* . . . . . . *Social Exclusion'*:

> ". . . New Labour social policy seemed suspiciously like Old Conservative social policy, being short on material benefits and long on exhortation. Harriet Harman, the Minister for Social Security, pushed through the policies, including the withdrawal of certain benefits . . . and was later dismissed for being unpopular . . ."

Page 45

"Blair replaced her as Minister/ with A(nother) Darling . . ."

– namely Alistair Darling, who continued as an obedient Cabinet mainstay in various capacities throughout the subsequent nine years of reshuffles

". . . a course/ in compassion/ imagination/ spirituality/ fellow feeling . . ."

Other useful exercises, apart from *'The Message'* of Jeni Couzyn quoted on Pages 46-47, might be derived from *'Ancient Wisdom, Modern World'* by Tenzin Gyatso, the Dalai Lama (Little, Brown 1999).

According to Sarah Anderson's review of this in the Spectator of 5/6/1999 –

> ". . . He observes that those of us living in materially developed countries are less satisfied and less happy, and often suffer more, than those people in less developed countries; in the

societies we have created, loneliness and alienation are rampant, and we have made basic affection for other human beings harder and harder for ourselves. Science and technology give us instant results, and so we have dug ourselves into a situation where immediate and visible outcomes are what we expect; this is the very opposite of a life which contains spirituality and prayer, which both have largely invisible and long-term benefits.

". . . We can do without religion, but his ethics do not allow us to do without the basic spiritual qualities . . . If we could only follow the Dalai Lama's advice to the world for the new millennium, and cultivate a commitment to the principle of universal responsibility and unconditional love, not only would we as individuals become happier and more compassionate, but we would at the same time be making a significant contribution to the welfare of society."

Page 46

". . . and growth, *they are shouting*, growth . . ."

— see *'Small is Beautiful'* by E F Schumacher (1973):

". . . In a sense, everybody believes in growth, and rightly so, because growth is an essential feature of life. The whole point, however, is to give to the idea of growth a qualitative determination; for there are always many things that ought to be growing and many things that ought to be diminishing . . .

"In the excitement over the unfolding of his scientific and technical powers, modern man has built a system of production that ravishes nature and a type of society that mutilates man. If only there were more and more wealth, everything else, it is thought, would fall into place. Money is considered to be all-powerful; if it could not actually buy non-material values, such as justice, harmony, beauty or even health, it could circumvent the need for them or compensate for their loss. The development of production and the acquisition of wealth have thus become the highest goals of the modern world in relation to which all other goals, no matter how much lip-service may still be paid to them, have come to take second place. The highest goals require no justification; all secondary goals have finally to justify themselves in terms of the service their attainment renders to the attainment of the highest.

"This is the philosophy of materialism, and it is this philosophy which is now being challenged by events.

"We shrink back from the truth if we believe that the destructive forces of the modern world can be 'brought under control' simply by mobilising more resources – of wealth, education, research – to fight pollution, to preserve wildlife, to discover new sources of energy, and to arrive at more effective agreements on peaceful coexistence. Needless to say, wealth, education, research and many other things are needed for any civilisation, but what is most needed today is a revision of the ends which these means are meant to serve. And this implies, above all else, the development of a life-style which accords to material things their proper, legitimate place, which is secondary and not primary."

Page 52

"*Capital / Interchange Dungheap . . .*"

By an amazing coincidence, the Head Office of Waterstone's Booksellers is situated on Capital Interchange Way, Brentford.

When the authentic book-lover Tim Waterstone opened his first store in Old Brompton Road in 1982 with £6000 of redundancy pay-off from WH Smith, it was a welcome street-boost for literature. Over the next few years Waterstone went on lining the shelves of his rapidly multiplying branches with nothing but quality titles.

Unhappily the mega-marketing zeitgeist insinuated from government on down over those and subsequent years managed to cement the foundations of a New Philistia throughout the UK. And this has juggernauted from bad to worse in contaminating Britain, under Blair's New Labour, to even more corrosive profit-or-die debasements than those so wilfully spread by Margaret Thatcher.

Tim Waterstone sold his chain to Smith's, the philistines who sacked him, for £9m, but then in 1998 bought back into the company he had founded, fronting a consortium with HMV. Three years later, however, "worn down by disappointment with the way management were running Waterstone's", he stepped down again. He told the Times how disenchanted he remained with Britannia Marketspeak's ". . . lack of understanding of what the Waterstone's brand was about. Waterstone's has moved into the mid-market, chasing discounts and pushing Jordan biographies".

One of the few surviving pioneers of independent publishing in Britain, John Calder (who turned 80 in January 2007), knows to his cost, and to that of everyone interested in authentic literature, just how philistine this marketplace has become. In *'Pursuit: The Uncensored Memoirs of John Calder'* (Calder Publications '01), he remarked that –

> ". . . The publishing boom that people talk about now is just a few titles that are for one reason or another in vogue. But overall there has been a massive decline. Waterstone's are selling about 10% of their range of ten years ago. And any book that doesn't sell after a month gets returned immediately. The availability of books is hopelessly limited, and little is being translated from other languages. What we have now is exactly what I'd hoped all my life to prevent . . .

> "The growth of Waterstone's was a disaster once its management fell into the hands of administrators who knew nothing about books or about the needs of the general book trade. The need to be the biggest and to have the largest slice of the cake led them into policies that lose money all round, including a catastrophic discounting policy. Many booksellers can no longer afford to sell the slower-selling quality books aimed at the most educated of their customers.

> "This has been happening at a time of widespread dumbing-down, an unadmitted conspiracy between politicians, newspaper proprietors and commerce. People increasingly know less, read less, learn less of import from the media, and trust to a growing general prosperity (which cannot possibly last) to cushion their lives. And all this at a time when the need to be aware, to be able to think independently, to understand what the politicians are doing, rather than just hearing what they are saying, has never been more important . . ."

Page 54

'London Summer'

– written by Frances Horovitz in 1967, after picnicking, dancing, lovemaking and walking in Hyde Park, Kensington Gardens, and the surrounding byways of Paddington, Bayswater and Notting Hill

". . . *oomphatic/ overdubbed/ multitrack// orgasm . . . // . . . of 'How High The Moon'/ recorded for fun/ back in '51 . . .*"

– Les Paul and Mary Ford were early pioneers of multitrack recording. Bing Crosby had given Paul one of the first reel-to-reel tape recorders made by Ampex. On *www.salon.com* Frank Houston recalls that –

> ". . . While Paul was on the road with Ford, he realised that if he added a recording head, he could record multiple parts, anywhere. The pair began recording on tape. Their first multi-track hit, a cover of *'How High the Moon'*, was released in early 1951 (Capitol 1451), reached Number One, and went on to sell 1.5 million copies. Paul made a chorus of Ford's voice and filled every pause with his refined country-jazz licks. Ford's silky vocals put flesh on Paul's studio wizardry, which included twelve overdubs. No one had ever heard anything like this before; it was the sound of the future. 'Les Paul was the first person to turn me on to the guitar', Rolling Stones bassist Bill Wyman once said. '*How High the Moon* had terrific verve, proof at last that pop could provide stylish instrumental inventiveness' . . ."

Page 69

"– *countless lives reduced/ to job market/ investment statistics// – wilfully disinherited/ from the peaceable kingdoms . . .*"

– as witness for example Tony Blair's typical marketspeak pitch, in a Radio 4 Today programme interview on 4/11/2006, plugging yet another of his Big Investment initiatives, this time seeking to encourage youngsters to sign up for a career in science, which *might* (my italics) just hit bingo – meaning, quoth Our Father:

> ". . . *You're a worldwide tradeable commodity in the job market* . . ."

The trailer advertising the BBC1 TV series *'The Apprentice'* dutifully picked up this sort of baton several times a day over the two to three weeks running up to its broadcast in spring 2007. First Sir Alan Sugar was heard exulting that " – One of you is here to get a Six-Figure Salary Job", followed by the ardent voices of job-market candidates thrilled to have been shortlisted in the race to become his latest – er, *'tradeable commodity'*, with soundbites including " . . . I'm giving up everything to get this: this is what I deserve, though", and "We work until we bleed, and *we batter the hell out of everybody else*".

The question begged by all of these incentives remains, what prospects are left for "everybody else" – ?

". . . *the early beat Super-Tramp,/ W H Davies . . .*"

– see Davies's *'The Autobiography of a Super-Tramp'*, 1908

Page 73

"*Is there Life beyond the Gravy?*"

– cf Stevie Smith's story anthologised in *'At Close of Eve'*, 1947

". . . *fuüüms-bø-wo-rö-thé-tZeh/ – ooorrgh . . .*"

– adapted from the *'Ursonate'* ('Primal Sonata') composed by Kurt Schwitters between 1921 and 1932. This first-begun of Schwitters's abstract pieces, a classic of sound poetry, owed its initial conception to Raoul Hausmann's phonetic poem of 1918 which opens with the line *"fmsbwtäzäu"*. Schwitters adapted this to *"Fümms bö wö tää zää Uu"*.

Page 77

". . . a politics of courage, honesty and trust . . ."

– from the new Leader's Speech, Labour Party Conference, Blackpool, 4/10/94

"Where any view of Money exists/ Art cannot be carried on/ . . . but War only"

– the top line of William Blake's inscriptions to *'Laocoön'* (*c.* 1818-1820 – reproduced on p140)

"All men are ready to invest their money . . ." and ff

– from T S Eliot's *Choruses from 'The Rock'* (1934), Part I – spoken by The Rock

"Make perfect your will . . ."

– as B C Southam notes in his *'Student's Guide to the Selected Poems of T S Eliot'* (Faber 1968, '87 and '94), this echoes "many Biblical injunctions to serve God willingly, to become perfect in one's determination to serve God".

I would add, ". . . to serve '*God or whatever means the Good'* . . ." (Louis MacNeice's phrase in *'Meeting Point'*, 1939).

". . . take no thought of the harvest, / But only of proper sowing . . ."

– cf Matthew 6, 34: ". . . Take therefore no thought for the morrow . . ." The Biblical metaphor instructs humankind to live a spiritual life without regard to its rewards or punishments.

See also *'The Achievement of T S Eliot: an essay on the nature of poetry'* (Oxford University Press, New York 1935, enlarged edition 1958) by the Harvard University English Professor F O Matthiessen, with C L Barber. Matthiessen acknowledged "the great benefit of conversation" with Eliot during the seven months from October 1932 to April 1933, when the poet visited Harvard as Charles Eliot Norton Professor.

Matthiessen inferred, sometimes quoting Eliot verbatim, that *'The Waste Land'* drew from – among other sources – Jessie L Weston's *'From Ritual to Romance'* (Cambridge University Press 1920):

". . . He found the specific clue to the dramatic shaping of his material when he read in Miss Weston of the frequent representation of the mystery of death and rebirth by the story of a kingdom where, the forces of the ruler having been weakened or destroyed by sickness, old age, or the ravages of war, 'the land becomes Waste, and the task of the hero is that of restoration', *not by pursuing advantages for himself, but by giving himself to the quest of seeking the health and salvation of the land.*"

Cf Blake's inscription to *'Glad Day'* (*c.* 1794):

*"Albion rose from where he labourd at the Mill with Slaves
Giving himself For the Nations he danc'd the dance of Eternal Death."*

Page 79

". . . a transatlantic Dunciad . . ."

The four books of Alexander Pope's mock-heroic satire *'The Dunciad'* were composed and first published between 1726 and 1742. At the end of Book IV, the poem's *Genesis*-in-reverse climax

sees the transmission of truth – by the government, the arts, the sciences, religion and education –
choked under the ubiquitous strangleholds of Dullness, Indolence and Corruption:

> ". . . Nor human spark is left, nor glimpse divine!
> Lo! thy dread empire, Chaos is restored;
> Light dies before thy uncreating word . . .
> And universal darkness buries all."

– How unlike the public life of our own drear scene . . .

Page 80

Portraits, clockwise from upper left: Seamus Heaney, W B Yeats, Philip Larkin, John Keats

Page 81

". . . Behold: / 'The Poetry SuperLeague'. . ."

This caption was first foisted on the printed world around 1987, to puff Les Murray as ". . . one of
the finest poets writing in English, one of a superleague that includes Seamus Heaney, Derek
Walcott and Joseph Brodsky".

In the London Review of Books of 5 November 1992 (Vol 14, No 20), the late Donald Davie
deplored this as –

> ". . . astonishingly vulgar, and I suppress the author's name to spare his blushes. But if we
> reject the notion that poets can be ranked internationally like sprinters or discus-throwers,
> still we must take note that this is how Les Murray is rated by the makers of reputations.
> Accordingly his views are likely to be influential and sedulously promoted . . ."

Newsprint, broadcast media, and reputable literary publications such as British Book News and
Poetry Review did indeed plug the notion of "SuperLeague" (and the star billing of this particular
quadrumvirate) to the skies. In consequence the reign of "Super" and "Big League" promotions of
these, as of lesser talents, continues to thrive, with the "spin-off" effect that poetry itself (inspired
speech, pure art, mental war) is misapprehended, devalued and marginalised.

The continuing "growth industry" of poetry prizes and competitions, dangling their baits of ever
bigger money to be won, consolidates such philistinism. It marginalises the true gold standard for
poetry – the vocational aspiration to write well as its own incentive and reward.

The journalistic SuperLeague brand of hype has also slithed abroad a presumed association, damn
it, with quite different activities of my own.

In September 1980, in some despair at the Little-Englandist/Larkinite takeover of official
poetry in Britain (coinciding as it did with mounting xenophobia, yuppiedom, and an attempted
boycott of the Moscow Olympics by the milk-dry boss cow ThatchSnatch), I launched the Poetry
Olympics festivals.

The issue of New Departures (No. 12) which doubled as a programme for the launch event at
Westminster Abbey on Friday 26th September 1980, featured work by and dedicated to Brodsky,
Heaney and Walcott, among many others from many countries. In the editorial to this issue, 'Per
ardua ad Olympiad', I took pains to contradistinguish the impetus of the projected Poetry Olympics
movement from the bathos to which the largely unsporting Olympic Games had sunk – i e, of
servitude to commercial investments and nationalistic power struggles (– see pp317-320).

Poetry Olympics celebrates poetry as something everyone on earth can do together; equally, as something which clarifies the competition with *oneself* rehearsed by each poet in the making, and in the performance, of each poem. Yeats reflected in 1924 that ". . . We make poetry out of . . . the quarrel with ourselves".

And Blake wrote in 1826, annotating his copy of Wordsworth's *'Poems: Volume 1'* (1825):

> *"I cannot think that Real Poets have any competition. None are greatest in the Kingdom of Heaven; it is so in Poetry."*

My editorial to *New Departures* #12 concluded in a debate with Heaney on precisely this subject of not compromising, as he saw it, with "the world which disregards or is inimical to poetry – the world of big promotions, business, etc", or with the way "the whole Olympic thing has become debilitated by politics". I answered that our impulse planned to reclaim the Olympic rubric for "Real Poets" and living arts productions – which over these twenty-seven years we have done, albeit only in the smallish ways afforded to us. (See also the fifth paragraph on page 438.)

Another honourable, and largely satirical-parodic use of the sporting world trope, was ventured by my American namesake Mikhail Horowitz, in his booklet *'Big League Poets'* (City Lights Books, San Francisco 1978).

This baton was then taken up by the Petersfield bard Chris Sparkes, and published in his collection *'Kissing Through Glass'* (Mighty Conqueror Publications, 1986), and in *'Grandchildren of Albion: Voices and Visions of Younger Poets in Britain'* (New Departures, 1992). In this incarnation Chaucer, Milton, Wordsworth and Keats are brought back to active life in the baseball arena, with erudite panache, good humour and decorum.

Thus, in the righteous Superleague according to Sparkes, Geoffrey Chaucer was –

> ". . . a great slugger back in the days when the wild boar sniffed the arboreal breeze in unpolluted Engelond. Unlike many superstars, he suffered no shame nor ignominy in numbering himself with the hoipolloi, the nondescript, the ne'er-do-wells and the vulgar. Nor was he hoodwinked by the uppity kits of holy rollerball imposters. He preferred the simple benign Persoun whose runs reached to houses far asunder.
>
> "His finest match was the oft-recalled epic in which he completed twenty-three home runs on the way to Canterbury, culminating illustriously in one giant whomp over the Cathedral with his wine-dark bat. When he saw a loose and juicy volley whistling down the track, his eyes twinkled in his head like stars on a frosty night . . ."

Then again –

> ". . . The big thing about Long John Milton is of course how he managed to play without a decent pair of goggles. Concerning his technique in this, apart from playing with a runner, about as much as anyone ever got out of him was his enigmatic *'stand and wait'* – which is only what all sluggers do anyway . . . Well might the Puritan Green Shades' backfielder Andy Marvell marvel at how Long John – *'Through that wide field . . . he his way should find'*.
>
> "Currently seeded fourth in the world computer rankings, he is one of the top contenders for the Triumvirate of Megabards, and due to the enduring inspiration of his hits, his name has been given to the sag wagon physio's favourite pick-me-up: *"MilTonic"*. Also the white dubbing for Big League boots, now called *"Meltonian"*, may have derived from his pure upstanding stance.
>
> ". . . He always played strictly according to the book, never demeaning himself by pandering to the gallery. Accordingly, his style was stiff – but Long John trained hard, and rehearsed some serious updates from the ancient Hebrew courts (though, not

Radix Chaucer, inspecting a bat:
"Eek, all this new-fanglenesse!"

Long John Milton —
Steaming one in as of yore

Codger Wordsworth — another crossbat
heave through the daisies

Babyface Keats, having been struck
on the jaw

surprisingly, he lacked his predecessors' fluid rhythm). His side-show act included Minor League Roman Rules, and he was Roman Rules secretary for Oli Crombie's team (the Ironside Puriniks), a position won on the merits of just one dedicatory and obsequious lap around the ballpark.

"In his last wallop, Long John's art had ironed out the major flaws, and his Sampson re-run is one of Big League's masterpieces. He was back in Classic form, showing know-how, stamina and sheer poetry."

Furthermore –

"Codger Wordsworth . . . had a droopy, sombre, sulking stance, as though he'd always just been out first ball, yet he was the game's all-time arch bragger. He wrote to one fan who helped pay his subs that his hits would be 'efficacious in making men wiser, better and happier'. Imagine passing that round the bleacher-stand.

"Another annoying thing about him is the impression he gave of putting his own interests before the team's, often dictating matters to his wife or sister (who was just as good a player in her own right in the Women's League). And he made his partner Coleridge, himself a great player and umpire, feel – so he said – 'a little man' . . .

"He is the only English Big Leaguer to have written an autobiography, and that without a ghost writer. The truly great contribution from Codger lay in helping to ease Big League out of its 18th Century straitjacket. After his Continental tour his average was ebbing, what with slick Prose taking over the game's dominance. Yet decades later whole teams of bards really started picking up on some of his rural riffs.

". . . It wasn't Codger's wit that pulled in the crowds (he was never known to burst a single joke) – but for all that, Big League could do with a space-age Wordsworth to free itself from the chains of the new Academy, for many of whom it's not worth cutting down trees to make pitches.

". . . Portraits of his grumpy head are still familiar in Lakeland gift shops. As he did slog an incredible number of historic boundaries, League bores the world over never stop bickering about whether his bid for the Immortality Score has ever been equalled, so his place in Pitchers' Corner is well earned."

And, lest we forget –

". . . In his short but dynamic career, Babyface Keats was a familiar sight out training on the grounds of Hampstead Heath. He is well-known for his obsessive studies of the grandmasters of Big League underneath his school-desk, and for his subsequent imitations of the numbers Petrarch flowed in, and also of Eddie Spenser's and Bill Strat-Shaker's styles, as well as for his own controversial techniques.

"He thrilled to watch many an airy clout clamber through the clouds, and there's an interesting legend that, after being knocked out by a high celestial body-line ball one time, he got a notebook out and started scribing scribbles and odd jots about a nightingale.

". . . After a minor incident following a club meeting in 1820, he spat out some blood and declared, 'That drop of blood is my death-warrant'. Just a year later – after a mere quarter century's hungry generation – his elegant clouts must no longer soar.

"He got his last game in just before going to Italy for the final five months of his untimely cursed career. Babyface is buried in Rome next to a couple of team-mates – obituaried with a riddle in Roman rain."

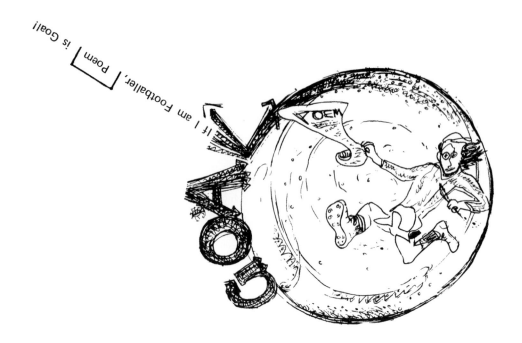

See also *'The Wolverhampton Wanderer'* (Latimer New Dimensions, 1971), my mock epic sequence which traces analogies between soccer players and road-running bards. One self-portrait I drew for that book, with the caption *". . . If I am Footballer, POEM is Goal!"*, seems to have presaged the Poetry Olympics torch I was to raise a decade later.

Blake and Yeats are surely right in holding that the ultimate competition in creative work is with and against oneself, and that "Real Poets" have no competition against each other. Their poetic reality and perch on Parnassus reside in the uniqueness of their respective achievements.

Keats is not better – or worse – than Bob Dylan.

Nevertheless, I do prefer the work of some poets and artists to that of others. And of course, often prefer some individual works or actions to others, on the parts of authors I generally like.

For example, many of the official laureate verses I've read by Poets Laureate strike me as pretty banal. Conspicuously so in the case of most of those by Ted Hughes, as distinct from most of his gauntly luminous and voluminous non-bespoke writings.

A lot of the occupational offerings of Hughes's successor as laureate, Andrew Motion, sounded to me like grovelling lip-service to New Labour's pseudo-liberal agenda – until, on 9th January 2003, the Guardian ran his *'Causa Belli'* across the top of its front page:

> *"They read good books, and quote, but never learn*
> *a language other than the scream of rocket-burn.*
> *Our straighter talk is drowned but ironclad:*
> *elections, money, empire, oil and Dad."*

The Guardian's John Ezard reported that Motion

> ". . . said yesterday that the leaders' rhetoric hid 'several of the motives which are actually driving the thing forward. In other words, it's as much to do with oil, imperialism and a sort of strange father fixation [on President Bush's part]. They are not being candid'.

"*'Causa Belli'* is a Latin phrase meaning 'causes, motives or pretexts of war'. The poem is based on an antithesis between *'They . . .'*, the leaders, and *'Our straighter talk . . .'*, that of doubters in conversations among the public.

"In the poem, the doubters' voices are *'drowned'* by the leaders. But their arguments are also described as *'ironclad'* because, Motion said, 'they will endure'.

"Motion's most famous precedent for doing this as poet laureate is Alfred Lord Tennyson. Tennyson included in his poem *'The Charge of the Light Brigade'* the controversial and popular lines '*. . . the soldier knew / someone had blundered'*."

With candour in mind, it was all the more refreshing that *'Causa Belli'* and Ezard's article about it, headed *'Poet Laureate joins doubters over Iraq'*, appeared in the same issue of the Guardian as the first interview with the ex-Education Minister, Estelle Morris, following her resignation on the ground that she was ". . . not up to the job". This feature was headed with her insistence – hitherto voiced by all too few (New Labour) MPs – that *"Politicians must admit to failure . . ."* Good for you Estelle.

On the premise that on the one hand, many politicians and lawyers are more bent on turning an expeditious trick to their own advantage than with expediting long-term social needs (let alone the enduring truths a poet's muse traditionally represents)

– and that on the other hand, many poets are as humanly vulnerable as anyone else

– I penned the following reflections on poetico-political commonality and divergence in that war-blighted spring of 2003:–

> *"Poets are the unacknowledged legislators of the world"*
> (P B Shelley, *'A Defence of Poetry'*)

Some poets are politicians,
     some are truth-hounds, some electricians.

Andrew Motion's butler voice, elocuted diction
     smoothing out every crinkle of latent friction
     came on stern and upstanding across the air,
     Saint Sincere
     ventriloquising Tony Blair
               – till his true Muse
     took the worst news
     to his heart
           – and his art
     cut a rug of its own
     out from under
     the New Labour circus's
     rig-mastered top spin
     to dig a firm heel
            in agin
     our People's PM's fatal flaw,
     that vainglorious lust
     for power through war.

Nigglemouthed Northern bloke of the folk
     Sean O'Brien throws testy punches
                        as fraught
    as yer pit bull terrier John Prescott,
    [ex-]Old Labour mascot, caught
    yapping and snapping illegible twixt
    his duplicitous surplus of homes, Jags and lunches
    – egged on by protesters, mixed
    party lines, tribal tags and wild hunches
    – see how he seethingly splutters and hisses
    and mutters and bristles and hits out
                      – and misses
    as steadfastly bedward he munches.

Don Paterson's Charles Kennedy with a skinful of nag.
Tom Paulin on telly's Ann Widdecombe in drag.

But not all living bards are chess-move politicians.
Wendy Cope's Glenda Jackson.   C A Duffy's Clare Short.
Geoffrey Hill's a broody Gwyneth Dunwoody.
Pinter bleeds for peace in a righteous moody.
Kathleen Raine's milk of paradise
    could still feed our needs.

Seamus Heaney's Richard Taylor – wise, concise
    neighbourhood physician.

Tony Harrison's Tony Benn,
    a mouthful-of-nails electrician
    as nifty dispensing home truths in bulk
    as debunking Dome myths of that ilk
    spun by Mandy Pandy
    and those wiggling worms of the silk,
    fatboots Charlie, merry Derry
    and Cherie-laced counsel
    for the President,
    Kubla Tone.

Johns Hegley and Agard, R McGough and Grace Nichols
    – like stand-up poets
    Michael Moore, Mark Thomas,
    Harry Enfield, Rory Bremner
    and Johns Bird and Fortune –
    pay unprogrammed attention
    to the real life that crackles
    hard songlines into action.

Let's give thanks for such troupers
    who give satisfaction

with the bonus of laughter
Stevie Smith and Betjeman quested after

— and with no Party Card or flag
save the insights and truths
of inspiration unfurled
to arm them for a deeper
legislation of the world.

". . . The best *Irish poet / since Yeats*"

— thus spake Robert Lowell, in perpetuity

". . . The best *letters ever / since Keats*"

— thus quoth Professor John Carey, in the Sunday Times

Page 82

". . . *like / . . . Alexander Pope on speed*"

— from an article in Punch (25/ 7/1980) by Alan Brien. This was Brien's impression of the poetry performance Heathcote Williams contributed to a modestly titled *'World's Best Jam'* session Live New Departures presented at Ronnie Scott's Club in London on Sunday 20 July, 1980.

Page 84

"*The World's Media / is One jealous Moloch. / / His Performance Degree decrees . . .*"

If '*media*' is properly understood as the plural of '*medium*', this should read ". . . *are* one jealous Moloch". But Moloch the '*tyrannical object of sacrifice*' (Concise Oxford Dictionary, 1990) seems to have consigned this fine point — along with many other fine linguistic, moral and aesthetic points — to His-story's sacrificial shredding-bins.

See also the excerpt from Allen Ginsberg's '*Howl*' against Moloch on page 10, and Ginsberg's interpretation of Moloch in the note to page 10 on p247.

". . . *Tropic of Hypertitis*"

— cf 1933-1945, when Henry Miller diagnosed the transatlantic malaise as '*Tropic of Cancer*', '*The Air-Conditioned Nightmare*', etc, etc

Page 87

"*Art is Long*"

— cf the aphorism coined by the Greek physician Hippocrates, ". . . *ars longa, vita brevis*" ("art is long, but life is short")

"*Henry Kissinjure*"

In 2001 the pioneering radical publishers Verso brought out '*The Trial of Henry Kissinger*', a 190-page investigation by Christopher Hitchens. In the book's preface, Hitchens states that he confined his brief ". . . to the identifiable crimes that can and should be placed on a proper bill of indictment":

"These include:

1.	The deliberate mass killing of civilian populations in Indochina.

2.	Deliberate collusion in mass murder, and later in assassination, in Bangladesh.

3.	The personal suborning and planning of murder, of a senior constitutional officer in a democratic nation – Chile – with which the US was not at war.

4.	Personal involvement in a plan to murder the head of state in the democratic nation of Cyprus.

5.	The incitement and enabling of genocide in East Timor.

6.	Personal involvement in a plan to kidnap and murder a journalist living in Washington DC."

Several paradoxes, of a kind one has learned to observe as increasingly commonplace over the last twenty-five years, alas, have danced attendance on the shameless promotions of Dr Kissinger's continuing public saleability.

– Paradoxical that this architect of so ghastly a scale of global bloodshed goes on, as he has done for yonks, banking mammoth fees from countless speaking engagements;

– paradoxical, to say the least, that such a person was offered, and had the chutzpah to accept, the Nobel Peace Prize in 1973.

The North Vietnamese diplomatic representative Le Duc Tho was offered it simultaneously, on the rationale that both men had successfully negotiated "an end to the war" in Vietnam. But Le Duc Tho declined, pointing out that his country was not yet at peace. The war continued in Vietnam until 1975.

The award of the Nobel to Killinger for services to peace prompted the wondrously iconoclastic singer-satirist Tom Lehrer to stop writing songs. Satire was no longer possible, said Lehrer, in a world which gave Dr K the peace prize.

Kissinger is on the books of New York's Harry Walker Lecture Agency, who plug him as follows:

"At present, Dr Kissinger is Chairman of Kissinger Associates Inc, an international consulting firm that has represented some of the world's most powerful multinational corporations . . .

"Dr Kissinger tours the world describing how America should relate to various regions and countries. Having spent much of the 1970s and 1980s in or near the corridors of power, practising realpolitik at the State Department and National Security Council, Dr Kissinger presents his own analysis of the special challenges the US faces in the new century."

According to Amy Wilentz's article in Time Magazine ('*Visions of Lecture Lucre*', 18 April 2005), Kissinger commands a fee of $18,000 per speech.

Francis Wheen noted in the Guardian of 10 December 1997 that –

" . . . Last month, almost unnoticed, Dr Kissinger popped in to Number 10 for a chat with the Prime Minister. The only mention of this historic encounter came in a brief item from the Press Association, which noted that 'he and Tony Blair are friends'. According to a Downing Street spokesman, the two men spent half an hour ' . . . looking across the spectrum of international relations'.

"It's quite a spectrum. Let us recall the fine words of this year's Labour manifesto: 'Labour wants Britain to be respected in the world for the integrity with which it conducts its foreign relations. We will make the protection of human rights a central part of our foreign policy'.

"Perhaps Blair and Kissinger discussed violations of human rights in East Timor, which has been occupied illegally by Indonesian troops since 1975. The invasion took place just one day after Kissinger and President Gerald Ford visited Indonesia – and, as his biographer Walter Isaacson has revealed, Kissinger 'knew from US intelligence of Indonesia's planned action, which violated the laws governing its purchases of American arms, but . . . was quietly content to permit the Timor rebellion to be suppressed, so the administration did nothing to stop the invasion'. More than 100,000 residents of East Timor (almost a seventh of the population) were killed. After returning to Washington, the Secretary of State 'raised a little bit of hell with his staff' – not because of the deaths, by which he appeared unmoved, but because the State Department had sent him a memo pointing out that Indonesia's use of American weapons was an outrage which would require an embargo against Jakarta. 'That will leak in three months', Dr K raged, 'and it will come out that Kissinger overruled his pristine bureaucrats and violated the law . . .'

"Since Tony Blair is a polite host, no doubt he avoided embarrassment by steering the conversation away from those areas where his guest had disgraced himself. But, rather like Basil Fawlty trying not to mention the war, he must have found it hard to think of anything else to talk about. Cambodia? A definite no-no, since Kissinger bombed its citizens to smithereens without troubling to inform the American Congress. Cyprus? Another taboo subject: as Christopher Hitchens proves conclusively in 'Hostage To History: Cyprus From The Ottomans To Kissinger' (Verso 1997), the old boy was directly responsible for the island's partition.

"On 13 August 1974, Kissinger declared that the Turkish community needed 'a greater degree of autonomy'. Like the Indonesian government a year later, the Turks recognised a green light when they saw one; the very next morning their army set about occupying the whole of northern Cyprus – creating the pariah state that is now best known as Asil Nadir's bolt-hole. Since Kissinger's betrayal of Cyprus was aided and abetted by a Labour government in London, Blair would probably wish to forget the whole business.

"Angola, Chile, Bangladesh? No, no, no: Kissinger brought death and destruction in all these places. I hope Blair kept well away from China, too, where Kissinger displayed his own commitment to the 'protection and promotion of human rights' by defending the Tiananmen Square massacre in 1989 ('no government in the world would have tolerated having the main square of its capital occupied for eight weeks by tens of thousands of demonstrators') while modestly forbearing to declare his own financial interest as a negotiator with the Chinese government on behalf of H J Heinz, Atlantic Richfield, ITT and other American corporations.

"As Walter Isaacson points out, '. . . Kissinger's relationship with the Deng regime was such that he could bring clients and guests to China and be met by the top leadership, a highly marketable asset'. Quite so: why let morality stand in the way of the all-conquering market?

"And now that Kissinger can be met by the 'top leadership' in London, he becomes more marketable than ever.

"Let us be charitable. Tony Blair may be an innocent who paid no attention to world affairs throughout the 1960s and 1970s – though you'd think someone in Downing Street would vaguely remember Kissinger's name and sound the alarm.

"Or Blair may believe that the deadly Doctor has mellowed with age and become a benign international statesman: New Labour, New Kissinger.

"It won't work. You can put a great white shark into a goldfish pond, but it remains a shark for all that. I'm reminded of the wise remark from an American politician when Kissinger's old chum Tricky Dicky was attempting, yet again, to relaunch himself as the New Nixon: 'There is no new Nixon. Only the old Nixon, a little older' . . ."

On 5 April 2006, BBC 4 screened 'The Trials of Henry Kissinger', a documentary based on Christopher Hitchens's abovementioned book, at the suitably ungodly hours of 1.05-2.25 am. The BBC issued the following press release in advance of this film's premiere:

". . . 'Henry Kissinger is a war criminal', says firebrand journalist Christopher Hitchens. 'He's a liar. And he's personally responsible for murder, for kidnapping, for torture'. What is Hitchens on about? He could be talking about the lawsuit currently under way in Washington DC, in which Kissinger is charged with having authorised the assassination of a Chilean general in 1970. Or he could be referring to the secret bombing of Cambodia in 1969. Or perhaps Kissinger's involvement in the sale of US weapons to Indonesian President Suharto for use in the massacre of one third of the population of East Timor in 1975.

"Featuring previously unseen footage, newly declassified US government documents, and revealing interviews with key insiders to the events in question, 'The Trials of Henry Kissinger' examines the charges facing him.

"The film tackles the question of whether principles of international law applied by Americans to their enemies are applicable to Americans, *or whether these laws are only written for the losers of conflicts*. It is at once an unauthorised biography and a look at the sparks that fly when an honoured American statesman is charged with war crimes."

Whilst on a flying visit to London on 24 April 2002, Kissinger faced calls for his arrest for having instigated, aided and abetted the war crimes committed by US forces in Vietnam.

On the same date, America's accusation that the IRA had sent members to Colombia to train Marxist rebels in terrorism were denied by Sinn Fein, who claimed the men were *"eco-tourists"*.

In spite of a number of such attempts at making Dr K answerable for some of his misdeeds, not one of them has actually taken effect to date.

The most concerted attempt at obtaining his prosecution, on the part of the family of Rene Schneider, hit the buffers early in 2006. The Associated Press reported its final demise on 17 April 2006, as follows:

"SUPREME COURT TURNS DOWN LAWSUIT OVER DEATH IN 1970 OF CHILE'S ARMY CHIEF

"Washington: Schneider v. Kissinger, 05-743.

"The US Supreme Court refused on Monday to revive a lawsuit that accused former Secretary of State Henry Kissinger of responsibility in the 1970 death of the head of the Chilean army.

"Family members of Gen. Rene Schneider filed the lawsuit in 2001. It claimed that US officials encouraged a plot to kidnap Schneider, during which he was killed.

"The suit claimed that the US government and Kissinger, then President Richard M. Nixon's national security adviser, were guilty of violating US, Chilean and international law.

"A lower court dismissed the case."

Another case, it would seem, of when the law is an ass, assholes prevail.

"Will the world ever be rid of Henry Kissinger?", asked Washington Post editor Bob Woodward in an interview on CBS-TV's *'60 Minutes'* on 1/10/06 – adding: ". . . If we can't put him in jail, can we at least force him into retirement?"

Woodward's *'State of Denial: Bush at War, Part III'* (Simon & Schuster, October 2006), reveals that Kissinger has been a major adviser to both President Bush and Vice President Cheney about Iraq from well before the US-led invasion. He had met with Bush between fifteen and twenty times, and with Cheney three or four or times that number, roughly once a month.

What is more, Dr K, infamous for his defining role in prolonging the Vietnam War, seemed still to be stirring its ashes – and even intent on rekindling them in Iraq. Apparently, Kissinger's main message to the White House has been from the outset, and – still more amazingly – went on being in early 2007, despite the unabating anarchy and carnage in Iraq, that ". . . *Victory is the only meaningful exit strategy"*.

Woodward found this ". . . fascinating. He's almost like one of the family . . . And Kissinger is fighting the Vietnam War again because, in his view, the problem in Vietnam was that we lost our will".

Dubbya too has continued to parrot the Victory mantra, over and over. Yet – whilst the scale, intensity and death-toll of bloodshed and destruction have increased over the weeks and months and years on all fronts in Iraq, much as they did in Vietnam – neither of these senior statesmen, nor anyone else, has come up with even a tentative definition of *what* Victory (victory by whom, over whom?), nor of *how* this presumed Victory would be "meaningful" (whether as "exit strategy", or anything else potentially helpful to any human).

– State of denial indeed.

At the outset of his presidency, Bill Clinton countered press allegations that he had smoked cannabis at Oxford University with one of the soft-soap get-out clauses he was to turn into a trademark survival kit: *". . . I didn't inhale"*.

In the late 1990s Clint fended off various accusations of having indulged in various cycles of extra-marital sex with similarly brash and spurious prevarications. The most notorious and widely circulated of these was his cigar-slimy smartass protestation that *". . . I did* not *have sex with that [Monica Lewinsky] woman"*, on the ground that what he did have was (allegedly) oral sex only.

John O'Sullivan told the Sunday Telegraph that the President apparently ". . . assured Ms Lewinsky that, according to the Bible, oral sex is not adultery and therefore OK".

This sickly-sweet-talking dick-headed ex-Prezza, not hitherto highly or widely regarded as a literary alumnus, was booked to speak at the Hay-on-Wye Literature Festival of 2001 for a fee of £100,000. Suzi Feay reported in the Independent (27 May '01) that when he belatedly showed up, the man famous for regarding the serial receipt of blow-jobs as "not having sex" –

". . . received a slow handclap last night for keeping 1,300 people waiting for more than three-quarters of an hour to hear his thoughts.

"But 90 minutes later, the former US President received a standing ovation for a performance which took in references to his 'good friends' Seamus Heaney, Nelson Mandela and King Hussein of Jordan . . . and a last-minute tribute to Dylan Thomas."

When I heard about this unseemly booking, I was astonished at the extent of adulation for such an unspeakable rogue on the part of UK literati I would have sussed as less gooey and more discriminating in their choices of fantasy lovers or folk heroes.

The likes of otherwise ostensibly reasonable and literate friends such as journo John Walsh or novelist Debby Moggach (who confided to me that the smarming Bull ". . . presses all the right buttons for me") seemed unable to conceive of superlatives sufficiently high-flown to account for this vastly world-debilitating conman's endlessly postulated "charisma" (something at no point at all discernible to me).

There seems to be no limit to the extremes of b/s to which the Bull Merchant par excellence is prepared to go in the cause of lining his pockets on the basis of such oustandingly slimeball credentials.

For a one-hour so-called "keynote speech" at London's Royal Albert Hall entitled 'President Clinton: Leadership for Future' (on 26/9/2006 – some six years after he had ceased to be President), the suet-spouter was billed as ". . . one of the most colourful (sic) politicians of the 20th Century", and the cheapest seats were priced at (Rear Circle) £60, and (Rear Arena) £120.

And on 24/2/2007, Radio 4's Today programme reported that Clinton's speaking engagements had yielded twenty million pounds in fees since he stopped being President, plus another thirty million on top of that in donations to his Clinton Foundation. Sic Transit Whoria.

". . . obscenely price-tagged 'culture heroes' . . ."

Another revealing aspect of *"the manufactured schmooze/ of 'prestige' . . . suck-ins/selling deadly humbug'n'cover-up brokers"* – and of this particularly revolting broker in special – appeared in the Western Mail three days after his grandstanding at the Hayfest (29 May 2001):

"NO CHEER FOR WHISKY PRODUCER AS CLINTON ASKS FOR FIFTY GRAND.

"A Welsh whisky maker turned down a visit from former US President Bill Clinton – when he was asked to fork out £50k for the privilege.

"Abergavenny farmer Ben Jones says he received a call from a member of Mr Clinton's entourage saying the ex-President would love to drop in and sample his traditional whisky.

"But delight turned to dismay when the farmer was told that '. . . *an endorsement would cost around £50,000*'.

"Mr Jones, who began reproducing his grandfather's whisky recipe five years ago, said 'I told him I couldn't afford it and would have to see what my wife had stuffed under the mattress'.

"The former art lecturer was told in the call from a man organising Mr Clinton's visit to the Hay-on-Wye Festival that the former President would be passing and had heard about Danzy Jones whisky.

"Mr Jones, 54, said '. . . I was told Bill likes whisky and would like to call in. I didn't believe it at first and did 1471 on the phone and called back'.

". . . It then emerged that he would be looking for a fee. I was told the ex-President '. . . *had to earn a living*', and that 'a figure of £50,000 had been mentioned to a distillery in Ireland'.

". . . It was there the discussions ended. 'I was taken aback' said Mr Jones, whose grandfather, Danzy, produced the whisky '. . . by adding herbs and rosehip syrup to his toddy' in 1890."

If the Hay Festival were interested in non-tabloid culture as distinct from would-be Celebrity Big Brother promotions, why not invite Ben Jones to give a talk on his granddad's Danzy Jones Whisky?

Even without the bonus of some locally distilled whisky tasting, this would surely be more worth a £100,000 fee for Ben and, equally, more worth the £100 per ticket Clinton-punters forked out for the brown-nosing orgy on 26 May '01.

See also *'No One Left to Lie to: The Values of the Worst Family'* by Christopher Hitchens (Verso 1999).

". . . or Cherie la Bouche . . ."

See Gordon Rayner's résumé on Cherie Blair's lecture'n'chat fees in the Daily Mail on 11 March 2006:

"BLAIRS' FOUR MILLION POUND MORTGAGES.

"Loans on four properties leave the Prime Minister and his wife paying an astonishing £16,000 every month.

"Despite this Mrs Blair's earnings would have been enough to keep the couple in the black last year. The Premier's wife made an estimated £140,000 from her career on the international lecture circuit, including £100,000 from a highly-controversial six-date charity tour of Australia and New Zealand.

"Her speaking fees are thought to have dwarfed the amount she earned from legal work, which she has cut back considerably in recent years. Figures released last year showed

Mrs Blair was paid £26,448 for legal aid work in 2003-4, compared with £178,068 in 1999-2000. A single evening's work on the lecture circuit, however, can earn her as much as £30,000.

"Mrs Blair will defy her critics and embark on another moneyspinning tour tomorrow. She will fly to the United Arab Emirates to give a speech on the leadership role of women, before going on to Florida for at least one engagement. She is due to speak at the Society of the Four Arts, an upper-crust club in Palm Beach, on Tuesday. Tickets for 'An Afternoon with Cherie Booth' cost £15.

"Earlier this week Mrs Blair faced demands to hand back her [£100k] fee for the Australian tour after it emerged that just eight per cent of the takings from her Melbourne appearance went to the children's cancer charity in question, a breach of local laws which say the figure must be at least 40 per cent.

"A Downing Street spokesman said last night: 'We have no comment to make' . . ."

In June 2005 la Bouche cashed in on her husband's meeting with George Dubbya in Washington DC, to the tune of £30k for a 90-minute talk.

Affairs of State

It cannot have escaped the Blairs' notice that, now himself is retired from the UK Prime Ministry, he too might be open to suggestions of a gig or thirty thousand on this easy-peasy gush circuit and – hey presto! – their dream of an afterlife as property development tycoons could be realised once and for all. Or more likely, just for them and theirs.

Eleven months later, Rayner reported ('BLAIRS BUY HOME NUMBER FIVE', Daily Mail 3/2/07, pages 1 & 4) that –

". . . The Blairs have exchanged contracts on an £800,000 mews house behind their £3.65 million London townhouse . . . Despite owing around £4 million on the four properties they already own, the Blairs have borrowed even more to buy their new property, taking their mortgage debts towards the £5 million mark. The news once again raises the question of just how the Blairs can afford their property investments, which will soon involve repayments of up to £20,000 per month. Homeowners will also be intrigued as to how the Blairs have been able to borrow the equivalent of twenty-five times the Prime Minister's salary."

In their personal property developments, as in various of Blair's government policies, the Cherie'n'Tone philosophy of 'Keep piling up the assets and pay later – or maybe, legal fiddles permitting, never' – has propounded for the best part of a decade: *"It's the rich what gets the money . . ." ad nauseam* (or even, if they go on getting their ways, *ad infinitum*).

Page 88

". . . off-rhyme rabble-rousing rasp-tentacled sounds . . ."

Having whilst unexpectedly hospitalised decided that he would reinvent himself as a newborn yet preternaturally accomplished People's Bard in 2000, the multi-millionaire magazine salesman Felix Dennis proceeded to proselytise his mission for what he understands to be traditional verse over hundreds of UK and US media.

The mission has been flagged on two main fronts: Dennis regards himself as the only living poet concerned to restore the prosody and forms of ancient Greek and Latin verse, and equally the only one likely to convey ". . . a dialogue on subjects that matter to nearly all of us".

Rhyme, he never tires of declaring, is the essential tool and prerequisite by whose means halfway decent verse can pass muster in our time.

I have many problems with this recurrently propounded (English Public) school of so-called thought about the craft – more often propounded by folk who are not demonstrably among its more skilful practitioners: Auberon Waugh and Boris Johnson come unbidden to mind.

Another recent old-bunkum champion was Stephen Fry, who inflicted 390 pages of largely ill-informed pseudo-Parnassian moonshine upon the coffee tables of his fan-base in *'The Ode Less Travelled'* (Hutchinson 2005).

Knowing perfectly well how to rhyme and measure stresses, as Shakespeare, Milton, Blake, Eliot, Auden, Lawrence, Ginsberg, Hughes and Plath did – just as Picasso, Bacon, de Kooning et al knew how to draw, and Bartok, John Cage and Charlie Parker et al knew how to write or play straightforward tunes – does not mean that any worthwhile poet, painter or musician needs to do those things, again and again, in every part of every work.

Felix Dennis's published verse output to date consists of pompous page after monotonous page of tiddly-om-pompotonous thumpety-thumping, and often quite grotesequely strained end-of-line couplings – such as *"ladies/babies", "amongst/once", "subsidy/Italy", "lemons/Netherlands", "shells to me/ mystery", "stoppages/sausages", "jury trials/British Isles"*.

Unhappily, most of the pieces in Dennis's first two mega-noisily published collections, though voluminous in quantity and size – provide a pretty irrefutable vindication (for those who might want or need it) of Milton's distaste for the (mis)use of rhyme for rhyme's sake, as ". . . the jingling sound of like endings" and ". . . the invention of a barbarous age, to set off wretched matter and lame metre".

". . . *the sanitised crap-can/ of Brit market forces/ had pitched around language// since it firmed up its money-mouthed/ . . . brain-twisting/ preda-/tory spam/ with her barrenness/ of Granite Ham . . .*"

— Gerald Scarfe opened his '*Scarfeland: A Lost World of Fabulous Beasts and Monsters*' (Hamish Hamilton 1989) with the following account of "The Sabre-Toothed Ptorydactyl":

"Long ago, I had heard of the mystical Labyrinth, home of the MinorTories and Labourytes, where the decisions that sway lives are written in stone by incompetents. I had read strange tales of the wicked Ptorydactyl, whose graven image in the shape of two lions flanked the Labyrinth.

"Legend had it that the Ptorydactyl had built her eyrie high in the mountains, so at six-thirty one morning I shouldered my pack and set off to find her. During that day it rained; great thunder clouds hung in the leaden sky.

"After an exhausting day's climb I neared the summit, made camp on a perilously narrow ledge and settled down for the night. I fell into an uncomfortable sleep. When I awoke at five-thirty the next morning it was bitterly cold: with fumbling fingers I opened my sketch pad and prepared to wait . . .

"As the morning light from the slate-grey sky spilled across the barren Downing mountains the Ptorydactyl busied herself about her eyrie. There was much to do. She tidied her hair and sharpened her razor bill. She must make herself look nice – sympathetic, no, caring was the word today. She wanted to create a caring image when she opened her first DIY hospital. A brilliant idea, a DIY hospital, no staff, just do it yourself medical equipment. You chose your op, picked up the necessary equipment, paid at the automatic cheque-out and simply did your own operation. It would give old and sick creatures with a defeatist point of view a new incentive, give them some get up and go.

"As I watched from a safe distance she launched herself from her icy ledge and her leathery wingtips scraped the hard crust of snow in the Westland valley. There were those who said that her gimlet eyes were blind to suffering but what, indeed, about the time she cried the crystal tear for her father, that split the earth asunder when it fell – maybe she could do that again. She would try. She had a Capodimonte model of the dear creatures who fought for her in the Falklands which sometimes brought a lump to her throat.

"I picked up my sketch pad and followed as the Ptorydactyl, carried on the fierce winds of monetarism, sped over the great North-South divide in the direction of the Labyrinth, where her baying Minortories obediently waited. She amused herself by diving briefly to scatter a clutch of Pinter hedgehogs. She had crushed the union dinosaurs and squashed the Galtieri slug (Gotcha!), what was a mere hedgehog? Definitely not 'one of us', dear. Her mocking laugh echoed across the dead valley, 'Frit Frit!' she shriekd. 'Frit Frit!' At the Labyrinth the dead Howe sheep and a hurd of Douglasses skulked nervously."

Page 89

"*The Sitwells* . . ."

— i e, Edith, Osbert and Sacheverell

". . . the history / of publicity . . ."

– from F R Leavis's *'New Bearings in English Poetry'*, 1932

"Dennis's bluster / rich wine-pumped / with fake lustre . . ."

Felix Dennis has freely admitted that he paid Hutchinson to publish his first collection *'A Glass Half Full'*. His preface to its successor, *'Lone Wolf'*, rants at me for being underwhelmed by the début volume – and asks what I thought the book-launch celebrants at his shrewdly titled *"Did I Mention the Free Wine?"* reading tours were up to: *". . . pretending* to listen to poetry?"

Since Dennis's own press releases boast that *". . .* over 20,000 glasses of French wines were served to audiences in thirty-two American and British cities" on his second such cork-popping tour, my instinctive answer has to be: *". . .* Most of them, yes indeed – stonedly pretending".

Certainly at the two initial London launches I attended (at the In & Out and Groucho Clubs), roistering gaggles of Free Wine Tourists were so smashed on the vintages in constant circulation that their ability to appreciate anything else – let alone anything fine-tuned – was visibly curtailed.

Admission to all these events was not only free, but explicitly solicited in heavily concerted national press advertising campaigns pitching the appeal of free wine very hard indeed, almost to the exclusion of poetry. Can one not fairly deduce that a good number of those who drank it in found the courtesy purchase of a book, which cost a tiny fraction of the value of the hooch consumed, a small price to pay for such a one-off orgy of fine wine bibbing?

All that Felix's pretensions to musehood have proved so far are that yes, anyone and everyone with enough money can buy a publisher; and yes, that one can also buy so-called fame and acclaim of a kind. And that extensive media coverage is always on offer to big spenders – and that one can even get hard-drinking revellers to buy one's books in the course of a 'thanks-for-the-free-wine' party spirit (though not necessarily to read them).

One thing that no amount of money can buy, though, however hard sales forces try – and however high pricey wines may dizzy 'em – is a perch on a tip-top branch of any *bona fide* Elysium. That height can only be earned, as Keats put it, by the production of poems that grow *". . . as naturally as the leaves to a tree"*.

As long as hype is pushed over truth, the likes of Felix Dennis will stay irredeemably money-mouthed, stuck in the affluent traffic of birdless wheeler-dealing.

Here's wishing him readier access to those harder-won reaches of the poetic pursuit, potentially attainable once all market values have been left in the office.

W H Auden made the point in his locus classicus, *'The Cave of Making (in memoriam Louis MacNeice)'*:

> *". . . After all, it's rather a privilege*
> *amid the affluent traffic*
> *to serve this unpopular art which cannot be turned into*
> *background noise for study*
> *or hung as a status trophy by rising executives,*
> *cannot be 'done' like Venice*
> *or abridged like Tolstoy, but stubbornly still insists upon*
> *being read or ignored . . ."*

"Felix D's . . . pretension / to poetico-moral largesse / falls flat on its face / — a fraudulent mess . . ." and ff

I composed detailed deconstructions of Dennis's ludicrously overblown claims to be the justly best-selling poet of the Noughties – one for BBC Radio 3's *The Verb*, and another in an open letter to him on pp69-70 of Prospect magazine, March 2005.

The opening of that article can, I am told, be accessed via Prospect magazine's website (*www.prospect-magazine.co.uk/article_details.php?id=6742*). Prospect headed the piece *'Swindling the Muse'*, on which wording I was not consulted. But the phrase fairly sums up one of the main thrusts of my case against Felix's poses for his own would-be reputational advancement, and his contemptuous beefs against the worthier poetic aspirations and achievements of others.

An in-depth absorption in the writings and *bons mots* of Auden might just prove transformative for this wayward windbag – just possibly paving the way for him to arrive at seriously new byways, highways and skyways of versification – ways beyond the hackneyed presumptions of his giant ego.

I'm thinking of the Auden who taunted the arrogant self-absorption of mountebanks who *". . . to wow the audience utter some resonant lie"*.

As James Fenton has noted (in *'A voice of his own'*, p4 of the Saturday Guardian Review, 3/2/07), ". . . This connected in [Auden's] mind with an abuse of political power, something he castigated . . . He associated it with fascism and the manipulation of the crowd".

"Speak not to me of Craft as Art untaught . . . // . . . A walk within an old cathedral . . . / is worth all the Picassos / ever bought"

Although lines two and five of this F Dennis versicle neither rhyme nor scan, the quaintly antique inversions, diction and pseudo-metrically constrained line breaks (unironically E J Thribbish in their clumsy self-consciousness), only serve to underline the false antitheses and coercive superficiality of the "dialogue on subjects that matter" which Felix has claimed to be provoking with his avowedly plain-speaking craft.

How on earth such coarsely splintered prose, and such attempted playing off of two given anti-philistine goods ("old cathedrals" and "all the Picassos") *against* each other, can contribute to dialogue on subjects that matter to most, is a question he might do well to examine.

My impression is that it was his preconceived concern to gild that cathedral walk with bells that rhyme – *"untaught / bought"*, *"brush / hush"* – which heavy-footed the exercise inexorably down the valley of the shadow of bluntly uninspired (English Public) schoolboy death-to-the-poem.

". . . 'MTV Party', 'Designer Labels' . . . // . . . 'I've had my eye on luxury goods' . . ."
– from Murray Lachlan Young's very slim first volume, *'Casual Sex'*, 1997

". . . media fixing lands / a palpable hit / for the creeping currency / of well-marketed shit . . ."

My aversion to Murray Lachlan Young, Felix Dennis and their coevils is concomitant with my objections to the philistine zeitgeist the likes of Tricky Dick Nixon, LBJ, Reagan, Bush Sr and Thatcher established, and Clinton, Blair, Putin and Bush Jr have wallowed in, exploited and extended, as suited their respective predatory purposes.

No doubt M L Young, Felix D, Stephen Fry et al are not completely without talent, and certainly the worlds of poetry can accommodate myriad constituents. But the forces of PR and commerce that brought Dennis and Lachlan Young to the public fore, have left that public with little or no enrichment to the enduring canons of poesy, only clanking examples of how rigidly marketspeak slots in to rule, within and also (on occasion) beyond its own aspirations.

These aspirations are likely to be in many ways about as far removed as you could get from any original caves of authentic poetry making. A crucial soundbite in point which exemplifies this degeneration, to my mind, was what Tony Harlow, marketing director of EMI, told a – er, seminal quorum of press and media personnel, when launching Murray's unprecedented record deal in June 1997 –

> ". . . Taking on a new young artist is always a risk. But we think he's a brilliant poet
> . . . We could have sold him as a performer, as a stand-up comic, or as a poet . . . but
> after talking a lot with him, *we decided that poetry was the best way to go.*"

M L Y's having graduated from the allegedly "First Media Performance degree course in the world" presumably counted for as much as the alleged brilliance of his verse in winning him the role of MTV-Poetry Wunderkind (– viz, an acquiescent dummy readymade to be reinvented, tailored and orchestrated as yer Naughtiest '90s Jack-the-Cad, and pumped straight through every popmost stage, screen and recording pipeline the hard-nosed marketing departments could rig or access).

The engineering of quantum leap sales and publicity by such manipulations seems to be just about the only 'art' genre both Old Tory and New Labour have been happy to take on board – and be taken on board by.

So when Nigel Reynolds, Arts Correspondent of the Daily Telegraph, effused in his front-page resumé of the 1997 Arts Year ('Arts & Books' special, 27/12/97), that *". . . Poetry had a terrific year"*, on the basis of M L Y's supposed achievement, I could not help wondering just how much poetry of 1997 the effuser had actually been aware of or read.

The only rationale Reynolds gave on behalf of the poetry of 1997's terrificness was that ". . . A Byronesque boy, Murray Lachlan Young, stunned the world by signing up with EMI for a Million Pounds to make discs of his poetry".

This was of course a barely disguised rehash of exactly what Tony Harlow and Young's publicity people had prepared for the arts news and media to rehash.

Perhaps prompted by a pseudo-literary 'tip-off' from Murray's manager, Grant Black, who was quoted characterising his 26-year-old protégé as *"very Byronesque"* in the Telegraph on 26 June '97, the marketeers had mega-plugged Young as *"The New Byron"*, permed his hair, and dressed him up to look like a Channel Five/Sky TV notion of a wicked latter-day Byron gone clubbing.

Unfortunately for poetry, if not for commerce, the young Young wrote more like a Loaded lounge lizard setting up a soft touch – as witness the quotation on page 91. If you do sample that, you'll probably be glad of the elixir of the first stanza of old Byron's *"She walks in beauty, like the night . . ."* quoted above it, to abet your speedy recovery.

For anyone who prefers poetry to the bullshit that "stuns the world", the New Byron's published output of 1997 could have served just one useful purpose I can think of – the function yer actual Byron assigned to the grave of the Peterloo exterminator, Lord Castlereagh:

> ". . . Stop, traveller – *and piss.*"

When Lachlan Young's publicity machine was stitching up the media, I received many more calls for interviews, quotes, articles, broadcasts and the like than have come my way over all the half century of my life's work with poetry and the arts.

How come? I'd let slip to a single newshound the fact that my heart leapt *not* up when I beheld the so-called Poetry Superstar's technicolor yawns of verbal diarrhoea spewed from inescapable supersynchronised superphoto-ops in super-newsprint, superglossy-mags and superprime-time slots on radio and telly. As if poetry were getting a look-in, rather than Big Business as usual. Or SuperBigger than ever, alas.

The objection to such Cash-in Young rackets is much the same as that to Lady Thatcher – except that she never posed as a poet. Marlboro Maggie got loadsamoney for her services to nationalist ship-sinking, high-falutin lecture-tours, lung cancer and every old Thatcher iron. Murray got it for puffing corny pop trivia, pseudo-hip naughtiness, cocaine in the burbs and any Young MTV jingle. Both were contractually committed to obsolescent lies – the lingua franca of selling at Nillennium.

1997 was a grim year for truth because, despite their electioneering pledge that things could only get better, New Labour's bosses, in league with the media, focused on the PR rhetoric of ruthless profiteering, top-geared to the market placement of everything and the enduring value of nothing. Tory spending plans were retained, as were the heavily subsidised arms and nuclear industries.

At the top of the refurbished pyramid, a thumping fiddler sat ensconced to multiply his offshore millions as Paymaster General, and a posturing Lord Chancellor lavished £650,000 of taxpayers' contributions on swanky renovations to the Lord Chancellor's Palace of Westminster rooms – rooms he'd be leaving for someone else to redecorate again after another couple of years.

In the unhallowed nether depths, however, the well-being of worker-ants and those, er . . . less well-connected citizens dependent on pensions, grants and other benefits, was abruptly and cruelly undermined.

It was also a tough year for literature because so many fine writers died, including the eight commemorated on pages 94-95. Not one of these was mentioned in the Torygraph's review of The 1997 Arts Year.

In the run-up to that year's National Poetry Day, the Independent of 6 October '97 ran a piece by the poet Michael Glover about the promotion of Murray Lachlan Young – "a performance poet who has penned very little save for his signature on a few lucrative contracts" – headlined *'What's he worth on paper?'*:

> "Any graduate of the world's first degree course in media performance (said to be available exclusively from University College, Salford), would know that timing is all. And therefore Bantam Books is quite right to publish *Casual Sex and Other Verse*, the much-hyped first book by the performance poet Murray Lachlan Young, at the beginning of a week when the media's attention will be focused on poetry, culminating in National Poetry Day on Thursday. It is a week in which feverish swarms of poets will be descending on Bristol, Manchester, London, Glasgow; in which schoolchildren will be hard at work producing poems at least as long as the Bayeux Tapestry; and in which serious poems will interrupt serious discussions on the airwaves.
>
> "But how serious will Murray Lachlan Young's efforts seem beside all the rest of this nationwide activity? The undeniably serious aspect of the affair so far is the figure that he is said to have commanded from EMI for a recording contract – £1.1m – and a second one

from MTV for £250,000. These sums of money (the recording contract alone being worth double the amount awarded to Seamus Heaney for the Nobel Prize for Literature) are extraordinary: no poet since Tennyson has commanded such sums.

". . . Now, at last, the hype is over. On the page, the work is trite and clumsy in the extreme; crude, self-preening doggerel in the Belloc-cum-Hood mode with a naughty, late-20th-century fizz about its subject-matter, which ranges from snorting cocaine to suicide, from outing heteros to casual sex.

"The test of any good poem is whether or not it deserves to be re-read; whether its language and its mood haunt us. This book-simulacrum can be read in 30 minutes flat, and it would require a mightily self-destructive act of physical and intellectual application to wish to pick it out of the waste basket.

"Some of the time the world is all zip, bop, wow! . . . At other times, in those moments between the moments, time seems to take a little longer. That's when the real poet, sometimes impecunious, occasionally curmudgeonly, shoulders through, fresh from the inner dark of himself (or herself) and others."

See also 'BIFF! BANG! POW! Michael Horovitz lays into Murray Lachlan Young and lays out the alternative' on page 32 of Poetry London Newsletter 31 (Autumn '98, ed Pascale Petit & Greta Stoddart).

Page 93

"Will Shakspeare . . ."

This is the spelling with which the Bard's burial on 25 April 1616 was recorded in the parish register of Holy Trinity Church, Stratford-upon-Avon. The entry is reproduced in facsimile on p421 of 'The Oxford Companion to Shakespeare' edited by Michael Dobson and Stanley Wells (OUP 2001).

Page 94

". . . The only riches, the great souls . . ."

– the last words of D H Lawrence's essay on Whitman (Chapter XII, 'Studies in Classic American Literature', 1923)

Page 95

". . . Selling gets to be more of a habit than using . . ."

– William Burroughs, 'The Naked Lunch', 1959

Page 96

". . . Wholly Communion/ Poetry Incarnation . . ."

See my editorial 'Afterwords' to the 'Children of Albion' anthology (Penguin 1969 – pages 336-342 and 355-363), for a detailed account of this best-ever-attended reading in Britain, which took place on Friday 11 June, 1965.

The event was recalled as "ground-breaking" – in that it marked the highest profile UK emergence of the supranational love generation – in 'Days in the Life: Voices from the English Underground 1961–1971' (Heinemann, 1988), the book of interviews Jonathon Green conducted with "101 quintessential 1960s groovers", and also in Green's more tendentious personal retrospect, 'All Dressed Up: The Sixties and the Counter-Culture' (Cape 1998, Pimlico 1999).

See also my Introduction to 'The POW! (Poetry Olympics Weekend) Anthology' (New Departures #21-23, 1996, pp 5-6); a good half of 'The POT! (Poetry Olympics Twenty05) Anthology (ND #36-37)', which celebrates the fortieth anniversary of the 1965 megagig and illustrates the diverse changes which evolved around international poetry and society throughout these years; and Peter Whitehead's *cinéma vérité* film of highlights from the evening, 'Wholly Communion' (available on DVD for £10 including p&p, from Hathor Publishing, 7 Broom Way, Kettering, Northants NN15 7RB – or via *www.peterwhitehead.net*).

Whitehead's book of the film, including texts of the poetry and prose by Gregory Corso, Harry Fainlight, Lawrence Ferlinghetti, Allen Ginsberg, MH, Ernst Jandl, Christopher Logue, Adrian Mitchell, Alex Trocchi and Andrei Voznesensky performed in 'Wholly Communion', went through several editions published first by Lorrimer Films and then by Hathor, some of which may still be available from antiquarian/Collectors' Item specialists or via cyber-sales.

". . . *Tonite let's all make love in London* . . ."

Peter Whitehead used this line for the title of another movie and a fantasy novel (– both relate to the 1965 Albert Hall poetmeet, and both are available from Hathor at the Kettering address and website given for 'Wholly Communion' above).

Page 97

". . . *Art cannot be carried on* . . ."

– cf page 77, the note to it on p285, and the facsimile reproduction on page 140

". . . *but War only*"

– cf Jean-Jacques Rousseau, 'Du Contrat Social' (1762): ". . . The state of war cannot arise from mere personal relations, but only from property relations."

Page 98

THE FALKLANDS

In 'Drawing Blood' (Little, Brown 2005), Gerald Scarfe annotated this drawing, 'Aggression Must Not Be Seen To Pay', as follows:

"General Galtieri of Argentina seizes the British Falkland Islands and Thatcher sets sail.

"The *General Belgrano* was sunk with the loss of more than three hundred lives. The ship was outside the 200-nautical-mile exclusion zone and heading away from the Islands when it was torpedoed . . ."

Page 99

"GOTCHA!"

– Gerald Scarfe's characterisation of 'The Greedy Baboon' in 'Heroes and Villains' (Hamish Hamilton 1989) itemises this creature's qualifications for the Bestiary of the Beastliest as follows:

'THE GREEDY BABOON *(Mechanical Digger)*
Habitat: Australia, USA and Great Britain.
Cry: Gotcha!
REMARKS: This Wapping great monster eats trees and regurgitates them as pulp to dull the

mind, stupefy and numb brains and addle thoughts.

Obsessed with mammary glands. Sky's the limit."

Scarfe's documentation of his first sighting of The Baboon is similarly revealing:

". . . The powerful grey silhouette of the Greedy Baboon appeared walking on all fours along a nearby ridge and lowered himself gingerly onto his favourite rock. He sat deep in thought for some while and then plucked a struggling employee from where he was clinging amongst his soiled and matted fur and, after a few moments' contemplation, popped him into his mouth, chewed and then spat him out. Then he rose and I saw the miracle that thirteen million others saw every morning. The Sun shone out of his bottom. It was astounding. His multicoloured buttocks shone with dazzling headlines: 'SOD OFF FOREIGNERS', 'A BONK A DAY KEEPS THE DOCTOR AWAY!', 'GOTCHA!', 'POOFTER ELTON ATE MY ARGIE' and 'THE BIGGEST TITS IN SPACE'. The baboon had no shame."

Page 100

". . . the Saatchi punk slag and bone yards . . ."

Cf the late lamented Jeff Nuttall, in an interview he recorded with John May at London's Chelsea Arts Club in December 1984:

"Saatchi & Saatchi is the sophisticated application of the work of Andy Warhol.

"It was Warhol who conducted a career in 'art' as an artist without any art. All you have to do is to observe the motions of the art market and you will be held to be an artist. He was the first guy to see that the last thing you need to belong to the art market was any art. Photographs of bean cans will do.

"I thought rather more of Warhol when I wrote *'Bomb Culture'* [1967] than I do now. I think Warhol is quite simply a highly conservative monopolistic businessman – and that's all he ever was.

"Indeed, with the much more sophisticated commercial techniques of Saatchi you may actually demonstrate that money doesn't need goods. This is the whole thing about capitalism – money without goods.

"So you have in London now, a huge, eloquently empty building with near as damn it fuck-all on the walls, and the only thing about these almost absent things on the walls of this almost empty building is that they're tremendously valuable. Therefore their importance is their expensiveness, and their expensiveness springs from their importance, and a good manipulator can set up that kind of absurd circular gathering momentum.

"If you make the initial payment of a vast sum of money for something which almost doesn't exist, whatever you slam that money down for immediately becomes 'important', and people will go on paying that amount of money or more for it.

"Furthermore, people will lose interest in anything of substance, because nobody's paying that kind of money for all these lumps of colour and all these things which actually give you meaty physical pleasure. What you pay money for is the fashionable void.

"Art has been seriously disrupted by that and it is, in fact, one way in which the bomb-owning, war-waging, competitive industrial society can defend itself against a viable art with any kind of teeth and any kind of cultural power. By immediately making fashionable and valuable that art which is completely not there, art which is completely void."

Other excerpts from this interview, *'Bomb Culture Revisited'*, are to be found in the anthology of *'Jeff Nuttall's Wake on Paper'* (New Departures [#]33, 2004). Further excerpts from the actual recording are included in the compilation of Nuttall's jazz cornet-playing, singing, and spoken wordsounds, *'Jeff Nuttall's Wake on CD'* (NDCD 34/New Departures [#]34, 2004).

"Maggie/ . . . quit her throne – and saw/ . . . what an unfunny/ new (not so wonderful)/ world this can be . . ."

Margaret Thatcher resigned after eleven years as Prime Minister on 10th November 1990, when it was brought home to her that the Conservative Party hierarchy no longer supported her as leader. On leaving Downing Street she reflected to the assembled media corps and cameras, with a histrionic tear in her voice, that *". . . It's a funny old world"* (Daily Telegraph, p1, 11/11/90, et al).

". . . loveless Goddess of Money and War/ with socialism pulped/ to glop through her maw . . ."

See *'The Secret Assassination of British Socialism'* by Jeff Nuttall:

". . . If Thatcher knew how to usurp the realm of floating imagery, Blair recognised that the route to success lay in the continuation of the monetarism Thatcher had established, and that his means to this success would have to be the fluidity of verbal definition that has sprung up through Structuralist jargon and computer-speak. If you can file and call it 'storing to memory', if you can transfer and call it 'downloading', if you can call the Dionysian 'abject', and revolution 'reconstruction', if you can call a slump a 'recession', then you can call consumer capitalism 'Labour'. Before this you must step into the Labour leadership at a time of crisis; then you must rely on the tacit hope of Labour voters that your piece-by-piece abandonment of Socialism is an electioneering strategy to be mercifully rectified after the election. Finally you must convince the disillusioned new Tories, Dome-bred and nourished on fashion, image and 'attitude', that Labour, a mere word, is banner enough under which to continue the Thatcherite principles of brute careerism and greed.

". . . 'Attitude' comes, beneath the Dome, to mean animation, rhetoric, hyperbole, hubris and gaga optimism, and is, of course, as empty as Blair's smile which is proving, as catastrophes accumulate on Indian frontiers, in French provincial town squares, in hospitals, schools and prisons, as irremovable as that of the late Reginald Bosanquet.

"But emptiness is the Post-Modern mode. The void, rectangular spaces of the Saatchi gallery, the slack, unlined, unpatterned and untextured fabric of the perpetually casual dress-style, the vapid nursery humour of successful sitcoms, the gap-headed infantilism of football fanatics and acid-house ravers, the rigid and dedicated refusal of all thought, passion, love, wit or honour are the first necessary elements in the style of our time, and Blair has found out how to embody it.

"Thus, like Thatcher, he will remain in power far longer than we can afford him, wreaking havoc merrily in all our quarters until we must face reality because fact will be all there is left to face, the fact of the blood on our own hands in Kosovo, the fact of Milosevic's victims dispersed beyond their own frontiers, the fact of the Chinese nuclear arsenal. Fabrications will run dry under the Rock and Roll Dome and there is a great big nothing at all in the Millennium Dome to revive them . . ."

– Extracted from *'Art and the Degradation of Awareness'*, Calder Publications 2001 – and also included in *'Jeff Nuttall's Wake on Paper'* (New Departures [#]33, 2004).

Page 101

". . . *media moguls . . . slimy chancers, / legal fiddlers, shameless sharks / / and more than a few / Big Business bosses . . .*"

Cf Nick Cohen's résumé of *'The tiny group that controls us all'* (New Statesman 8/5/2000):

> ". . . When half of the largest 100 economies in the world are corporations rather than countries, the business class is the real élite. It's a strong argument I like to think, but the dominant market ideology drowns it out. How can executives – and, by extension, the Blunketts, Straws and Blairs who ape them – be élitist?
>
> "The consumers are sovereign, aren't they? If businesses didn't give them what they wanted, they would be out of business. Businessmen who make it aren't sinister, but far better tribunes of the popular will than mere elected politicians. Opprobrium is reserved for the cynics who prefer freedom of information to PR; élitists who prefer juries to focus groups; forces of conservatism who prefer representative parliaments to shareholders' meetings; and reactionaries who prefer citizens to consumers.
>
> "Thus, Blair has not only brought unelected commercial lawyers into government but Lord Levy of the fundraising parties, Lord Simon of British Petroleum, Lord Macdonald of Scottish TV, the tautological Lord Sainsbury of Sainsbury's and other similar 'forces of modernity and justice'. Thirty-five per cent of the appointees that the first Labour government in a generation placed on advisory task forces are businessmen and women. Two per cent are trade unionists. David Blunkett wants business to run state schools. John Prescott wants business to run air traffic control. Gordon Brown's Private Finance Initiative gives extortionate amounts of taxpayers' money to private builders. Then the politicians who can't manage a thing themselves whine about cynicism and the decline of deference . . ."

Seven years after it was written, this indictment still holds water. The offer of honours and a seat in the legislature via a peerage to Party donors, and to some of the climbing clamour of property speculators, second-hand car dealers and concomitant riff-raff who have funded the City Academies, add emphasis to Cohen's complaint.

Page 102

"*For that / . . . thou shreddedst state welfare / from those most in need . . .*"

The obvious objection to New Labour's projected redesign of the Welfare State was, and still is, that it narrows down the options of those at the bottom of society in order to balance the books for those at the top – or even to help multiply their assets. Those incapable of presenting any opposition have been consistently bullied, whilst jobs, honours, handouts and favours have seemed ever available to those considered powerful enough to threaten the government's supremacy, and/or to reciprocate or consolidate its largesse.

"*. . . at the* end *of the day . . .*"

This is one of those rancid clichés politicians tend to access when playing for time and/or having nothing to say. Hence John Steinbeck defined a politician as: ". . . someone who approaches every problem with an open mouth".

". . . hallowed overworlds/ . . . of museums and high art . . ."

Before the Budget in April 1998 there was much speculation that extra Treasury funds would be made available to reduce the need for admission fees to those national museums and art galleries that had introduced them (in particular the popular and child-friendly museums in South Kensington). Comparisons were drawn between attendance figures in those that remained free, such as the National and Tate Galleries in London, and those which charged admission.

The far smaller Tate Gallery in St Ives, for instance, anomalously went on charging £3.90 a head. Much was made of the inevitable decline of "quickie" visits by punters uncertain of getting their money's worth. In the end a suitably New Labour compromise was struck, pledging enough money to keep those museums which had not yet begun charging, to go on not doing so in the future. Thus the government got its fix of PR gloss, and nothing changed on the ground.

These doublethink patterns have been repeated over and over *ad nauseam*. Culture and education are hard sold as commodities and investments, to be assessed and administered for their profit-making potential, yet at the same time savage cuts and measures are threatened that would curtail and exclude the participation of underclasses in them – only to *seem to be* modified or withdrawn later.

Such are the deceits under whose auspices our rulers would have us see them as magnanimous and caring.

". . . our great British heritage// of survival of the toffest . . ."

– by contrast to a more committed salt of the earth Labour Party's agenda, as observed in Norman Mailer's Mail on Sunday report on the 1983 election:

> ". . . Michael Foot had a cogent point of view at least. It said: we are not here in the world to find elegant solutions, pregnant with initiative, or to serve the ways and modes of profitable progress. No, we are here to provide for all those who are weaker and hungrier, more battered and more crippled than ourselves. That is our only certain good and great purpose on earth, and if you ask me about those insoluble economic problems that may arise if the top are deprived of their initiative, I will answer *to hell with them*. The top are greedy and mean and they will find a way to take care of themselves. They always do . . ."

Page 103

"SAY FEES"

Bell's thinks-bubble succinctly identifies the subtext to Blair's oft-megaphoned prioritising of "The Three Es" in his first election manifesto.

The introduction of the initial £1,000 a year tuition fees provoked backbench rebellion, but not enough to hold it back. Like the betrayals of lone parents, pensioners, the disabled et al, it was a signal foretaste of the concerted oppressions that were to keep getting worse over the subsequent decade.

"new schemes . . . / . . . to help the bee's knees/ of agile youngsters/ to roust on spin fare . . ."

– cf the notes about *"skint students"* on pages 256-260

". . . er, well . . . // um . . . // . . . er . . . // . . . um — you know . . ."

The bluster of Blair and of his sullied ranks of hangers-on got less and less coherent as their bad faiths and dishonours in office got more and more widely exposed. The once brave new leader's pseudo-estuary, pseudo-colloquial inflections, would-be matey come-ons, and insertions of *"you know"* after *"you know"* into his rhetorical sermons and appeals on radio and TV, at the Commons Dispatch Box and at press calls, reached epidemic extremes after it became clear that his "Shock'n'Awe" Coalition with Dubbya over Iraq, so far from saving or democratising that country, had reduced it to a near-irreparable state of remorselessly bloodthirsty civil war.

The sound of phrases deliberately mangled — as though the literate articulation of mellifluous vowels and distinct consonants was a closed book to this self-professed educationalist (*"Iran is no' Iraq"*, for instance, and *"I don' trea' i' [the carnage in Iraq] ligh'ly"*) — became the ever more lugubrious sound of a slowly but inexorably sinking salesman in querulous adamant denial.

At the outset of his first term in office, Blair's trustworthy demotic "pretty straight sort of guy" image was sanctimoniously enhanced by his Allah-Campbell prompted soundbite giving 'his' reaction to the untimely death of Diana, Princess of Wales: *". . . She was [catch-in-throat pause] . . . The People's Princess"*. Asked on television by Michael Cockerell as to just how this pretend-fairy tale designation (which instantaneously cast Blair as The People's PM) was coined, he asserted, in impeccable Mockney: *"I' woz wha' I fel' . . ."*

In his interview with John Humphrys on the Radio 4 Today programme of 2 February 2007, Blair — unwittingly I presume — echoed Willy Loman in Arthur Miller's *'Death of a Salesman'* when he mentioned how in public life it pays *". . . to be [well] liked"*.

The globally reverberating tragedy of Blair parallels the more poignantly spiritual one of Loman, in their common (and commonplace) unquestioning pursuit of the fraudulent values of western commerce. Though Blair is of course also a classic case of the overreaching personal hubris that generates its own eventual decline.

In no longer being nearly as well or widely liked as he once was, the soon-to-retire PM was audibly starting to experience something akin to the beginnings of Loman's disastrous demise — albeit more sanguinely than Miller's travelling salesman, probably in part due to the safety net of the Blairs' more shrewdly calculated insurance and survival schemes.

Evasive temporising, slippery thoughts and murky motives are often revealed by people playing for time in murky, evasive, slippery speech. After a decade-long surfeit of exposures to this would-be world- and word-reformer's conversational gamesmanship — with its deceptively amiable, unctuously automated console of glottal stops, pretend-blokeish bar-room argot, pretend-good-neighbourly over-the-fence chitchat, and would-be schoolboy jokiness and charm — few walks of UK life seem to have survived its hectoring linguistic infections uncrippled.

This Blairspeak s(l)ickness was grimly intrusive from the first in the maunderings of not only Himself, but also of Blair's most sedulous apes — Mickey Mandelson, Hazel Blears and Tessa Jowell in particular (the latter became increasingly incapable of emitting even quite short single phrases without at least one *"you know"* interposing). But by early 2007 the disease had got so virulent that even some of its more incisive diagnosticians were manifestly duped as to its fundamental source. Kate Chisholm, for example, wrote in a radio review for The Spectator of 16-23 December 2006:

". . . I wonder whether Tony ('Education, education, education') Blair or any of his cohorts in the Education Department were listening to the BBC World Service's *School Day 24* last week. Children from all round the world were brought together in live link-ups as part of the BBC's 'Generation Next' week of programmes designed to give young people, aged from 12 to 18, the chance to air their views, dominate the agenda, talk to each other across religious and ethnic frontiers. Mr Blair might have questioned the success of those 'literacy hours' after hearing the kids from a school in North London alongside those from New Delhi and Dar es Salaam. It was not that the English teenagers were lacking in confidence or self-expression. What disturbed me was their inability (when compared to their Indian or Tanzanian counterparts) to phrase an idea, complete a sentence, without a *'you know'*, *'kind of'*, *'ummmm'*. Happiness, from Tanzania, was far better equipped as an English-speaker to convey what she was thinking, eloquently and purposefully."

How dismaying that an observer so acute in her characterisation of the ailment had not sussed that the prime mover of its malaise is Blair himself. Surely more than any other speech models of the day, it was his pseudo-spontaneous vagaries and dumbed-down sales talk mannerisms, so inescapably influential via the battery of 24/7 multi-media, which these impressionable teenagers were echoing. And so far from being a possible corrective, as of early 2007 he was just as zealously and ubiquitously audible as before, still unparalleled as the continuing *fons et origo* of the educationally subnormal New Britspeak styles Ms Chisholm was bemoaning.

No Blair speech or interview of the many I've seen and heard ever missed out on the slightest opportunuity for chameleonic upsucking, nor yet (sometimes simultaneously!) for pseudo-deferential talking down. Specious verbal bolsters and ingratiating assumptions of consensus with and from his auditors – *"sort of"*, *". . . obviously"* – were resorted to at every turn on which there was no evidence for this and that Prime Ministerial brushing aside of leading questions.

Thus in the subsequent Today programme interview about Blair's foreign policies on 22 February '07, John Humphrys challenged Blair's repudiation of cover-up by the US of their long predetermined plan to bomb out Saddam Hussein, whatever the costs, by reminding him how various authoritative sources had volunteered the extent to which all Intelligence had been bent. When Blair spluttered emphatic denials, Humphrys reminded him that the PM's own Head of MI6, Richard Dearlove, had observed back in July 2002 (eight months before the US-led invasion kicked in): ". . . There has been a perceptible shift in attitude in Washington. Military action is now seen as inevitable. *The Intelligence and facts are being fixed around the policy*".

Blair testily replied –

". . . Look, I was there discussing this with the American administration at the time, and I can assure you that the idea that there had been a – er, sort of – irreversible decision taken there, is one of those, you know, conspiracy theories that come in and out of this argument all the time. The fact is that we went back to the United Nations and went through an entire United Nations process on this."

– The crucial fact Blair took care not to mention is that, during this "entire United Nations process", he comprehensively *failed* to persuade the Security Council to authorise military action against Saddam's Iraq.

Although America was on course to invade with Shock and Awe, as both Dubbya and Donald Rumsfeld let slip, in order to humour Blair's little problem with traditional British and European legalities banning pre-emptive attacks on sovereign states, they agreed to co-propose a "Second

Resolution". Quite a lot of the other (Dis)United Nations did not consider that Resolution 1441 (whose breach by Saddam had been brandished by the US and UK as a sufficiently bloodied red rag to warrant anyone's charging at Baghdad with maximum concerted and deadly bomb power), in fact justified invasion – especially as Hans Blix's weapons inspection team said they wanted more time to arrive at an informed conclusion regarding Saddam's alleged WMDs.

Much hot air ensued at the UN, with measured cadences of chopped logic from Dominique de Villepin, and Joshka Fischer jumping up and down excitedly shouting "I am not convinced! I am not convinced", etc, etc. But the Second Resolution was never put to a vote because it soon emerged that it would not get past the other permanent members of the Security Council. France and Russia made it clear they would veto it, and China would almost certainly have done so too. So after what was indeed a long and, as it turned out, entirely pointless process, the US, with Britain and Spain in tow, went ahead with Shock and Awe to demolish Iraq anyway *without* a UN resolution, casually demolishing aeons of United Nations authority in that process.

The pearls of intelligible (if deeply spurious) blagging by Blair on the airwaves cited three paragraphs ago, shone only by contrast to the effluent of semi-verbal burble that surrounded them, such as ". . . I, you know, sitting here now, you know . . . the public kind of – you know – understand . . ."

– The two million-plus "*NOT IN MY NAME*" public who demonstrated against the projected UK-US invasion of Iraq with their feet, hands and voices on 15th February 2003 certainly did understand – all too well, sod it.

What we understood *after* that day of authentic (inter)national community was that, however clearly we might spell out our most strongly held thoughts and feelings, this country's US+Wealth+War-besotted Leader was never likely to acknowledge their existence. Any such acknowledgement would risk diminishing his approval-ratings with his more globally powerful fellow President across the Atlantic (so presciently captioned "The Sea of Error" by Blake).

Blair's "*you know*"-count in the 2 February 2007 interview with Humphrys amounted to no less than 34, whilst Humphrys's part of the dialogue conceded not a one. So in a less than 15-minute series of expostulations, our education-prone leader interpolated a minimum of two "*you know*" jabs per minute. (– Could this be how his subconscious defines Consultation?)

To probe beyond the desire to perpetuate something of the wells of English undefiled, it may be worth considering what other subtexts might be lurking beneath the onrush of these Blairspeak corrosions. When it sidled out from New Labour lips, much of the recourse to "*you know*" was clearly seeking to blur its recipient(s) into a vulnerable complicity with the perpetrator. Others seemed to be ushering their victim onto a presumed sofa of inclusion in the VIP lounge that had been occupied in eternity by this speaker so civil as to include the "*you know*"-er in the shared higher knowledge. Others again cuddled up to extract subliminal agreement from listeners or interlocutors who might be distracted by anxiety about *not* quite knowing whatever it is the speaker tells them "*you know*". Etcetera, etcetera.

My instinct is that, so far from reflecting easy-going and open-minded awareness and consideration of the listener, these (non)conversational stopgaps were often carefully rehearsed devices born of The Project's habitual concern with pitching for the lowest common denominator, in order to stay on top of the game – all games, and get its way – all ways, however sinister or draconian.

But the best laid plans of ulterior motivators are liable to fall into their own traps. The litanies of "*you know*", "*I mean*", and associated Blairite (non)verbal fits and (re)starts frequently suggest that their mutterer was projecting a headful of ignorance and confusion; was serving its mucky balls to an audience in the hope that an ill-defined policy manipulation might reap a benefit from anything at all anyone else might conceivably know getting served back in turn to – er, top it up.

". . . the best ever/ (though lumpen/ Lottery-buttressed)/ state of the Arts . . ."

In June 1997, the newly elected government opted to continue with the Conservatives' main millennium project, the Dome at Greenwich, at a cost of £758m. One of the conditions, however, had always been that *no* public money was to be used to fund the scheme. It was calculated that income from commercial sources would amount to £359m, leaving a shortfall of £399m.

Enter the rebranded and reappropriated National Lottery, which the Conservative government had set up in 1994, with the proviso that its proceeds were *not* to be used for public projects. In autumn 1998, it was revealed that 33% of all lottery funds, under the rubric *'New Opportunities Fund'*, were earmarked for Government Projects – including the Millennium Dome at Greenwich.

Blair's commandeering of this money meant not only that the Dome would be much less burdensome financially, but that a highly lucrative top-up fund was made available to draw on whenever the need might arise.

The proportion of funds going to charity and the arts was found to have gone down, in consequence of this, from 20% each under the Conservatives in 1996-1997, to a mere 16.6% under New Labour in 1997-98 (Guardian front page, 7/10/98).

Central to the Dome Scheme was its transport strategy, which relied on constant use of the Jubilee Line extension to the London Underground network for 64% of its expected visitors. This development, running vastly over budget (at approximately £2.7 *billion* in mid-1998), was largely funded from public money (– cf Lord Rees-Mogg's detailed review of this in the notes to *Page 107* on pp320-322 hereafter).

The monumental banana-skin of the Dome's *annus horribilis* 2000 defied countless attempts on the part of satirists, cartoonists, critics and enemies of the enterprise to keep pace with its daily pratfalls and seemingly insatiable financial liabilities.

Nevertheless, the government, like some inexhaustibly wealthy Mafia capo endlessly squeezed by an inexhaustibly profligate mistress, coughed up to bail it out every time.

The 'New Opportunities Fund' should, strictly speaking, have been rebranded the 'New Opportun*ISM* Fund'.

As of spring 2007, a distressingly similar pattern has been evolving in relation to the similarly nationalist-triumphalist London Olympic Games scheduled for summer 2012. The original budget of £2.375bn, *"rigorously costed"* (quoth Tessa Jowell) in July 2005, had nearly quadrupled only twenty months later, to £9.3bn. As with the ever-doomed Dome, the National Lottery was to be unceremoniously pillaged yet again, Ms Jowell told Parliament on 15 March 2007, for another £675m this time round, on top of its initial £1.5bn commitment – with who knows how many further instalments for how many further alleged, dreamed-up or grandiloquently indulged costs to come? (See *'Good causes to be plundered to fund soaring cost of Games'*, pp1, 6-7, 12 and 14 of the Daily Mail, 16/3/07).

It beggars belief that the politicians allegedly forgot that there would be VAT on the costs. But I find even more sickening the scale on which they refused to learn from such a currently still glaring precedent as the Greenwich Dome disaster. Let them belatedly see some light, aim a lot lower financially, and a lot higher artistically and socio-equitably.

Masses of applications for the funding of struggling but demonstrably worthwhile arts projects, including many of my own, have been rejected for Arts Council and Heritage Lottery funding on the grounds that their budgetary plans are not contingency-conscious or Forwardly Planned enough. "Remember", we have kept being sternly told for decades, ". . . This is public/government/taxpayers' money: you applicants, like us commissars, need to be accountable for every penny, so, sorry, no dough. But do try again when you can make your figures add up immaculately" (– a typical time-dishonoured government-dictated Catch 22: if the potential incomes and expenditures balanced up, no grant aid would be needed).

Is it not high time for the dispensers of national moneybags to remember, in their turn, that many of these applications have been for grants of roughly £1k to £15k towards projects costing up to twice those amounts, as a guarantee against impossibly dramatic losses of quality, resources and expenses to the respective creator-organisers and artistic personnels?

– And also, to deal with the fact that it is, all too ironically, these sorts of grass roots projects which will be granted less financial or other support than ever because of Gargantuan spendthrifts like the governmental dreamers-up, and then incorrigible serial toppers-up, of both the Greenwich Dome and the Stratford Olympics.

As to the 2012 Olympic Games per se: why pay countless consultants, accountants, architects, builders, police et al for inflating a vast new stadium bubble in Stratford, when Wembley Stadium, at which I well remember the 1947 Games taking place perfectly smoothly, has just been revamped at colossal expense? Surely it would not cost millions more to restore a running track and the few other extras that facilitating athletics events will require?

If various parts of East London are to be revitalised, surely it makes more sense to keep that a separate, and again less costly, 'from-the-bottom-up' enterprise with authentic long-term benefits, unadulterated or besmirched by any aspect or contingency of the definitively obsolescent Games. (– More on this occupies pages 426-427.)

After the seventeen days (27 July to 12 August) in 2012, a stadium of mammoth grandiloquence will be as useless to the existing inbuilt community of the Lower Lea Valley as the Dome has been to that of Greenwich.

In 'Olympics jobs boom "will not help poor Londoners" . . .' (Guardian 23/3/07) Andrew Culf quoted a report by the London Assembly's Economic Development, Culture and Sport Committee which cast heavy doubts on the government's assumption that the escalating budget for the Games was justified because it would produce 50,000 new jobs around the Stratford Olympic Park. The Committee's Chair, Dee Dooley, pointed out that 60% of the local population were unemployed, and 25% had no qualifications: "In this area of London that has been characterised by deprivation for generations . . . the last thing we need is another Docklands", where so few of the new jobs or buildings have improved the situations of that locality's previous working population, let alone regenerated its underclasses.

Damian Hockney, leader of the One London party, also warned (– as opposed to Tessa Jowell's blithe parliamentary pledge on 15/3/07 that ". . . We have the Olympics pouring in millions of pounds into this area") – that he foresaw ". . . No new permanent jobs would be created for local people. The construction work will go to cheaper East European labourers, not local firms".

And amidst a chorus of complaints from the sporting enterprises hard-hit by all this misappropriated-for-the-Olympics gold, Derek Mapp, chair of Sport England, said that (– so far from Jowell's assumption that the Games will be ". . . the best catalyst for galvanising the participation of young people in sport") – the diversion of £54.9m of his outfit's income

> ". . . seriously endangers a sporting legacy from the 2012 Games. The true loss would be £223m, because almost £3 is levered in for every £1 invested. In the best case scenario 186,000 fewer people would be taking part in sport. Grass roots sport has benefits of reducing obesity and crime. This is an unfit nation, and we are the biggest tool for change, yet we are being cut . . ."

The huge lottery and other funds lavished upon these rabidly over-competitive, over-commercialised Olympics need to be curtailed and stopped from ripping off still further the multitudes of deeper-rooted, homegrown, unhyped – and hence all the more deserving and needy – ongoing sports and arts activities. Much as the Greenwich Dome fecklessly pissed away huge fortunes the long-standing Greenwich Theatre was closed for lack of a trickle from, so Stratford's own Theatre Royal, where Joan Littlewood had planted the first British community theatre workshop and playhouse more than half a century before, was among many local concerns in crying need of modest fundings withdrawn to bloat still more grossly the greedy shark Games.

High time to learn, politicos and profiteers, that Big Money does *not* breed high quality. Vast sums blown on such definitvely short-lived flashpoints insult and rob the taxpaying and lottery-punting population, and trample into toxicity the ancient, but widely traduced, Olympic drive for a global *Healing* of the Nations.

Unhappily, the terms with which Ms Jowell tried to distract the Commons, on 15/3/07, from the bottomless hole she and Blair have landed us in, drew on the selfsame New Labourspeak lexicon of hifalutin Big-Sell crassitudes which had tailored the Dome for perennial perdition: *"We should see this as an investment, not a cost . . . These will be Legacy Games! . . . Never will I apologise that we had the Vision* (sic) *and the confidence to go for it and Win* (sic) *the Games for London!"*

Pray pause, Madam Mediasport, and your successors – consider the unholy messes and frequent standstills London's transport systems, postal services, healthcare, security and overall ecology were labouring under as of five years ahead of the Games. – Pause and consider also the mixed blessings, curses and congestions an influx of masses more nationalist-triumphalist visitors are likely to bring with them and leave in their wake. This governmentally loud-hailed "Win for Britain" will need a lot more concern for the true supra-national glory of athletics, sportsmanship and other living arts, and a lot less clinging to PR lies and scams in pursuit of financial, chauvinist or political profits, if it is to end up benefiting humankind any more than the BlairoDome has done.

Investing a lot less on a much smaller-scale Games could perhaps just about salvage not only the temper and detail of the seventeen days in 2012 to foster a more harmonious transnational equilibrium, but also feed back something of that spirit – *bona fide* regeneration of organically communal culture – to enlighten all the days before and after the showbizzy flag-fanning frenzy as well.

But 'Let's go for broke on Super-Gambling' promoter Jowell was quoted on the front page of the Guardian on 23 April '07 as trying to reassure protesters, whose hard-earned existing sports and arts projects were being curtailed or demolished by the disconnection from Lotto funds she had hi-jacked for 2012, with two still more staggeringly duplicitous suggestions. To wit, that "– The

Lottery [will] have first call on *the profits from the sale of land after the Olympics*"; and that those she was currently depriving should "– Look at the safeguards we have put in place to meet your concerns [and] *see it as more of a loan to the Olympics . . .*"

Ho hum. Considering that it took New Labour six years to sell the Greenwich Dome – and that only by parading the militantly inartistic, unregenerative and later withheld bait, that it could become the UK's first Supercasino – it is hardly on the cards that the people of Stratford will want their home turf to remain simultaneously bottomed-out and reft asunder by the nation's most overblown Super-Sports Centre, nor that buyers for this summarily put-upon land will be queuing up to offer massive prices for it.

And considering the Blairs' and Blairites' record on property developments and loans – such as Tone'n'Cherie's multiple mortgages; the leaky onshore and offshore estate finaglings of Mandy and Geoffrey Robinson; loans and cash for peerages and other rewards; not forgetting Tessa Jowell's and ex-hubby David Mills's own transactions with never-never land – these notions of temporary loans in lieu of future bonanzas must surely qualify for some of the heaviest hammer-blows on the multinous nails upon New Labour's disgrace-festered coffin. – A number of these have been documented elsewhere in these notes (for instance, regarding the Blairs' incorrigibly cupidinous and dodgy-seeming accumulations of properties, and re similar slithy tovings on the parts of their acolytes, see pages 300-302, and 373-374).

As of April 2007, I am 72, and will quite likely not be around in five years or more, or otherwise not in much of a position to reap or do much with Ms Jowell's hypothetical payback. And it is no comfort to reflect that it is equally likely that she herself will no longer be authorised to broker anything much after – or even possibly for some time before – the Games in July-August 2012. It also seems quite possible that what she has already brokered in relation to them may be neither carried out, nor particularly respected by her successors. And in addition to all this, since her policies and prognostications have altered so frequently, swiftly and drastically over the previous year-and-a-half, what trust can one seriously put in these so-called *"safeguards . . . in place"* of which she prated in 2007 actually being honoured during or after 2012?

Page 105

"*. . . the polluted bottom/ of the toxic bog/ well sussed by Mogg . . .*"

– i e, Sir William Rees-Mogg. On page 16 of the Times of 2 October 2000, he exposed the Government's commitment to the Greenwich Dome as '*A shoddy gamble that never stood a chance*':

"*. . .* The scandal of Greenwich is not going to go away. According to Lord Falconer of Thoroton himself: 'Since May 1997, the Government has answered over 1,100 parliamentary questions; there have been numerous debates and five select committee enquiries'. There will be many more . . .

"The Government, including the Prime Minister, admits that there was over-optimism in the concept, disappointment in the outcome, inadequate administration, poor financial reporting and a huge overrun of losses which have had to be met out of lottery funds . . .

"The Government has, however, developed a new defence for its conduct. Eight days ago Tony Blair said that the Dome might be disappointing but that it had contributed to the regeneration of the Greenwich area. This defence has also been made again by Lord Falconer. He expressed the belief that, if one were to come back in a number of years, one would see a picture of regeneration. Not without another billion pounds or more, would be my estimate.

"I was surprised by what the Prime Minister said, so I went to see for myself how much regeneration had taken place on the Greenwich Peninsula. I had viewed the site by boat, a year or two before the Dome was completed, and had then seen that the whole peninsula was a derelict area, with a couple of empty gasometers and a small oil refinery sticking up out of an industrial wilderness.

". . . The Greenwich peninsula is in substantially the same state as it was when I last saw it. It is still a dismal and derelict industrial landscape. As I walked towards Greenwich College along the side of the Thames, I saw amazingly few signs of life. There were fierce signs warning children

not to enter the empty sites, but no children; there were warnings of guard dogs, but no guard dogs; there were coils of rusting barbed wire. I passed only three people, a driver walking towards his truck, and a blind man being pushed in a wheelchair by another elderly man. I saw a single duck swimming gloomily in the dirty river. In the mile between the Dome and the *Cutty Sark* that was all. Yet opposite were all the tall new buildings around Canary Wharf. The North bank has been redeveloped. The South bank has not.

"The whole site consists of some 250 acres, of which about 50 have been taken up by the Dome itself. During the time that the North bank was being developed, the Greenwich peninsula site was also available for redevelopment and was, in fact, considered by a large number of potential developers. In the past week I have been telephoned by two friends who happened to have been involved separately in looking at the site. One was most impressed when he flew over it in the late 1980s, the other discussed a possible scientific use for it in the early 1990s.

"Both proposals fell down because the site was too heavily polluted by the residues of more than 100 years of gas production, of chemicals, of oil refining, of steel production. On the second occasion, the developer had even spent some of his own money to put down some boreholes, which established the existence of poisonous metals, including lead and arsenic, going down to a level of 30 feet. There are also toxic and carcinogenic chemicals.

"This developer estimated that the greater part of the poisoned soil would have to be removed. In all it would amount to a billion cubic feet. There would be great difficulty, as well as cost, in finding a place in which to dump it. Removing the land which supports the rusting seawall, which already looks fragile in places, would probably mean that the wall would have to be replaced. One estimate was that the building of a new wall, on its own, would equal in cost the whole economic value of the site.

"Any plan for redevelopment has to face this difficulty; if the developers of a decade ago found it prohibitive, what has changed? The construction even of the Dome itself did not include excavation of the contaminated soil. The Dome site was scraped to a depth of 18 inches, a membrane was laid, and covered in hardcore and concrete. Greenwich Council would give the Dome only a limited, 12-month planning consent, for exhibition purposes. The rest of the site has not even been scraped and covered as far as one can see when one walks around it; scrape and cover is not safe enough for residential use.

"Pollution is now recognised as a much more serious environmental and health hazard than was appreciated even in the early 1990s. The contamination of the Greenwich site will already have spread through the water table to adjoining areas. There is a responsibility on the owner in law to compensate people injured by this contamination, or those whose properties are reduced in value. It is doubtful whether the whole site, or the Dome site on its own, could be sold to anyone without a guarantee against the damages which might arise from the underlying pollution.

". . . There was another project to provide a new Underground link between East London and Westminster. Somehow that project became entangled with the Greenwich site, without the pollution problem having been resolved. On top of that came the National Lottery, with its vast funds outside Treasury control, in essence irresponsible money. These funds were made available to the Millennium Commission, which decided to spend them on the Dome. This crazy bamboo scaffolding was ill-designed to bear any weight and it has fallen down.

"There are wider issues. The Millennium Commission has spent money on keeping the Dome open which should have been spent on proper purposes. Lottery funds are public money, and need to be controlled as such.

". . . It is no defence to argue that the Jubilee Line has at last been constructed, or that it is a very handsome architectural achievement. The location of the North Greenwich station was determined by the site. Unless the problems of the site can be solved, the line itself may be in the wrong place.

". . . Four questions had to be answered; they reflect on both the present Government and on its predecessor.

"How did they think that the pollution problem, which was known to everyone who had ever dealt with the site, would be solved?

"Why did they proceed with the extremely expensive plans for the Jubilee Line and the Dome without having established that the site could, in fact, be cleared?

"Why did the Government proceed without having secured a major developer, who had been sought unsuccessfully for a decade?

"Why did it go ahead without having a development plan in place?"

Six years later, on 20 September 2006, Lord Rees-Mogg wrote to me that: ". . . I never got answers to the four questions. They still seem to me to call for answers".

"20 YEARS ON . . . . . . 2 YEARS OLD"

This vintage double portrait by Bell first appeared on May Day 1999 on the cover of a Guardian Weekend special issue featuring a bran-tub of Steve's cartoons, headed *'Thatcher: the poison in my pen'.*

It was two years to the day of Blair's landslide victory, and also marked twenty years since Thatcher's advent as Prime Minister.

On page 190 of *'Bell's Eye'* (Methuen 1998) Steve Bell had written, under the heading *'True Bollocks'*, that —

". . . The true bollocks of Blairism lies in the fact that, while wishing to appear to be addressing the problems of poverty, inequality and lousy public service provision, it's doing the precise opposite and addressing the problems of capital. The main problem of capital is labour. This is why image is peculiarly important to New Labour . . .

"And so it goes on . . . Thatcher's triumph is complete, her legacy safe in the hands of, paradoxically, a Labour government."

The same Guardian Weekend magazine included the vision above, of Blair in one almighty supersponsored spin, with Deputy P M Prescott capsized in his wake, pug-legs akimbo, and a still worse splatted parent/minder with baby and babywalker still more immobilised — and presumably unnoticed — by the maniacal Whizzer.

Trading standards officers had warned parents on the day before to stop using ten models of babywalker, and urged manufacturers to recall models they said had failed the safety test. Hence the weird whirligig wheelie-frame in which Bosser Blur is depicted propelling himself — or perhaps more precisely, which is propelling him.

Both of these toons highlight the 'psychotic glint' in the birthday boy's eyes, recalling the verisimilitudinous control-freaky feature that also hallmarked Bell's many caricatures of Thatcher.

Page 108

'HOMEWORK'

Peter Brookes drew this for The Times of 22 April '98. New government guidelines had decreed that four-year-olds should spend 20 minutes a day on homework, and 16-year-olds two-and-a-half hours – whilst Frank Dobson, then Health Secretary, was jeered by nurses when he apologised for phasing their wage rise, and admitted that New Labour's public sector pay policy was no better than that of the Tories had been.

Dobbo also refused to rule out having to phase the following year's nurses' pay as well, if economic policy so dictated.

As of nine years later, the fate of the NHS looks largely (and governmentally) consigned to the random hazards of increasing, if creeping, privatisation.

One infers that yer average sixteen-year-old might have worked these problems out more effectively – perhaps even in about two-and-a-half hours.

See also the notes to "underpaid nurses" on pages 252-254.

Page 109

'Tony goes Tory' drawing by Peter Brookes

In July 2001 the former Labour Minister Peter Kilfoyle, MP for Liverpool Walton (who resigned from the Government in 2000 in protest at its betrayal of traditional Labour values and heartlands), published a cri-de-coeur in the party journal Renewal, warning that ". . . Failure to bare our political soul makes us little different from the Tories, or any other collection of superficial, self-seeking opportunists".

Kilfoyle accused Blair of deserting his 1995 conference commitments to social justice, equality and freedom of opportunity, and called for more truly radical policies of redistribution by – for instance – renationalising Railtrack, pitching the economy towards have-nots, and raising the minimum wage to a figure more in line with the minimum cost of living.

Kilfoyle's article amplified the growing disenchantment of party faithfuls with the New Labour Project's undemocratic cronyhood, unconcern for workers' rights, and increasingly Stalinist authoritarianism, by urging Labour to ". . . respond to its own inner voices, reflecting the party of conscience, belief and empathy which Labour is."

"Where Nye Bevan, John Smith / and countless true Labour workers / fought . . . / for nationwide health, you / – Tory Blair – arselicked and spun / more like Thatcher, / / avid / for privatised wealth . . ."

– see the last four paragraphs of my note to "The envy of the world" on page 328 below.

The New Labour manifestoes of 1997 and 2001 emphasised a determined commitment to free healthcare for all, and to the banning of private enterprise tobacco advertising. But the imposition of this ban, and the provision of basic healthcare for all citizens, were not implemented after either election.

Meanwhile the Cancer Research Campaign calculated that, until the government enforced a ban, smoking would continue to lead directly to the premature deaths of some thirteen people an hour around the UK.

The Blairite health ministers Yvette Cooper and Alan Milburn did keep on reiterating the well-known fact that smoking kills. But the Tobacco Advertising and Promotion Act was not implemented until July 2005, when international tobacco sponsorship (of Formula One, World Snooker, etc) was officially banned. This brought the UK legislation in line with the European Union directive agreed on 2 December 2002. But various exemptions, weaknesses and loopholes still remained (see *www.ash.org.uk*).

And as of March 2007, Blair plc's continuing programmes of unilateral privatisation, and of support for the US's pre-emptive warmongering, remained blandly unreformed from the overall Carry On Killing policies of the entire New Labour decade.

Page 112

". . . (unironically)/ Disneyfied folly . . ."

The Dome Secretary, Peter Mandelson, visited Disneyland in Florida in January 1998 to seek inspiration for what was then his pet project. In his speech plugging the Dome at the Royal Festival Hall (see *www.number-10.gov.uk/output/Page1158.asp*), Tony Blair spoke of the Millennium Experience as being "Exhilarating like Disneyworld, yet different."

He stopped short of indicating the nature of either the exhilaration or the difference.

See also the notes to *"The envy of the world . . ."* on pages 327-328, and those to *'J'accuse . . . Mandy Mouse the Dome-broker'* on pages 329-335.

". . . deep-rooted, widely cherished/ (and far less costly)/ arts in progress/ to survive . . ."

In February 1998, as the steel towers that would form the structure of the Millennium Dome rose overhead, nearby Greenwich Theatre announced its imminent closure in consequence of the axeing of its Arts Council grant with no reason given.

The Dome was costing a minimum of 758 *million* pounds to build, despite the fact that its role as a New Millennium exhibition space was scheduled to function for *no more than a year or two*. The Greenwich Theatre had been a much loved centre of the South East London drama community for *over three decades* of palpable hits, yet the Arts Council grant for its final year was 210 *thousand* pounds.

Short-term would-be profiteering Big-Time Dome £758m: Socially Dedicated for All-Time Greenwich Theatre £0.00. — How artistic was that?

The Greenwich Theatre managed to reopen in autumn 1999 after a vigorous campaign by locals, with grants from Greenwich Council and the Greenwich Development Agency. London Arts chipped in with grants in 2002 and 2003, but since then it has stayed open mainly by virtue of finance from the local council, local businesses, friends and angels.

There's regeneration for you, Domebrokers. Volunteered and created by — and replenishing — the local community, but in no way inflicted upon it with a Babel Tower of megahype, comprising a kind of bribery, as was the definitively rootless Dome itself.

See also the notes on *"new/ millennium// experience . . . . . company"* on pages 424-427.

Page 113

". . . connect/ Nothing with nothing . . ."

— Eliot, *'The Waste Land'*, III, lines 301-302

"In London town did Kubla Tone/ a stately treasure-dome decree . . ."

On 26 June 1997, David Blunkett, then Minister for Education and Employment, confided to his audio diary (published by Bloomsbury in October 2006 as *'The Blunkett Tapes'*), that –

> ". . . The millennium exhibition issue is worth recording, because in the middle of the first Cabinet discussion on it Tony had to go to the parliamentary church service, and we were left in the air. He had made it clear that he wanted the millennium exhibition to go ahead, but I would say that 80% of the cabinet were against it; 10% were against but trying to be positive about what might go into the exhibition if it had to go ahead (which was my position); and the remaining 10% – principally Harriet Harman and Margaret Beckett – were in favour.

> "After Tony had left the room John Prescott took the chair, and it was very awkward for him because Tony had really made it clear that he was going to go ahead whatever we said . . ."

". . . the greatest/ day out/ on Earth . . ."

– from Blair's PR speech for the Millennium Dome at London's Festival Hall (of which more below).

In Part 1 of Michael Cockerell's TV trilogy *'Blair: The Inside Story'*, broadcast on BBC2 on 20/2/2007, the ex-Number Ten Press Officer Lance Price recalled how –

> ". . . even then, in the early years of the Blair government, we were talking about legacy issues, legacy items. I can remember a discussion with David Milliband – now in the Cabinet, he was then Head of the Policy Unit at No. 10 – talking about *what symbols would be part of Tony Blair's legacy, and one of those was the Dome.*"

The film then panned to Blair's first PR Campaign for it, crooning his bizarre resolve to memorialise the brave new nothing-very-much at the then unmonumental Greenwich site:

> ". . . *However easy it would be to say no to this, it would be a real failure of imagination and vision.* We are going to take a grip on this, we are going to drive it through. *We're going to make sure there is a permanent legacy. We're going to make sure the costings are right.* We've got to do it – *it's the right thing to do . . .*"

– Whereupon viewers were proffered a soundbite from Peter Mandelson, appointed by Blair, said Cockerell, ". . . to take charge of the Dome which they hoped would be like the pyramids were for the Pharaohs": ". . . *If the Millennium Dome is a success, we will never be forgotten".*

H'm. The film cross-cut back to Blair blaring: ". . . It is not going to be torn down. *It will be a lasting asset for the country, and I am sure that this really will be the greatest show on Earth".*

These were the media fairground barkings and barterings of men consumed by delusions of grandeur frothed up by their own hopefully Sky-rocketing publicity machines. The words Success, Career, Legacy, Money were never far from their lips – for all that what the chaps were claiming to be renewing and extending was nothing less than Britain's Imaginative and Historic Destiny. – And, in Blair's case, on top of all that, the cementing in Greenwich of a Disney Fantasia of Heaven on Earth from whose – er, Visionary Airstrip the entire planet would be saved forever, thanks to New Labour's Modernised brand of (post-)Christian Capitalism.

The talk they were talking sought to dumbfound and reward our daily breadwinning (and Lotto-losing) with a Dome of Domes that would bring up to date and transcend the achievements of Will Shakespeare, Christopher Wren, J M W Turner, Isambard Kingdom Brunel, Winston Churchill and Jesus, all rolled into one.

The walk the wretchedly exorbitant and toxic tent actually turned out to walk, over the New Labour decade, has been unparalleled only for its unstoppable multiplicity and extravagance of local, national and international embarrassments.

Page 117

"The envy of the world . . ."

Blair renewed his full and effusive backing to the Dome project in a speech at the Royal Festival Hall on 24 February 1998. This prime South Bank Centre venue was carefully chosen, in order to bank on the continuing legacy of the 1951 Festival of Britain. Government publicists were keen to promote the Hall's alternative but seldom used title of *'The People's Palace'*.

But the Festival Hall is still functioning as a truly popular concert arena and arts centre more than half a century on. The life expectancy of Dome's day as the advent of a cultural (r)evolution *"to make a Difference"* expired like the air from an overblown balloon on the New Year's morning after it had so pompily opened the night before.

Jonathan Glancey reported in *'Back to the future with Dome of the Seventies'* (front page, Guardian 25/2/1998), how the Prime Minister saw the Dome –

". . . as a national rallying point, designed for a nation in which, by 2000, we will all subscribe to the New Labour creed: 'This is our Dome, Britain's Dome. And believe me, it will be the envy of the world'. Mr Blair's speech was an attempt to raise sponsorship . . . [but] why should the future have to look like sets from the Thunderbirds TV show or the Teletubbies? . . . The Prime Minister, though, is not to be deflected: 'I want every child in Britain to take from [the Dome] an experience so powerful and memories so strong that it gives them that abiding sense of purpose and unity that stays with them through the rest of their lives'. But not all children wish to conform, and it has often been Britain's non-conformists – Wollstonecraft, Blake, Brunel, Sinclair, Issigonis, Ruskin, Morris, The Beatles – who have pushed British creativity to new and far limits . . . The best of British thinking in 2000 and beyond is likely to be somewhere other than the Dome. It may even be in the far from hollow heads of young people who, brought up in the age of mass entertainment, branding and corporate ideologies, wish to think for themselves."

Blair's February '98 speech concluded with the ominous words, *"The bandwagon is beginning to roll"*. He was prescient. On the very next day a £12m sponsorship deal for the Dome from Rupert Murdoch's Sky TV was announced, and – surprise, surprise – Murdoch's hitherto derisive Sun newspaper came out in euphoric favour of the project: ". . . Now that we've seen inside it, we just can't wait for 1 January 2000 to arrive. The plans for the Millennium Experience are dazzling . . ." (*'The Sun Says'*, p7, 25/2/98).

– And this notwithstanding the fact that nothing resembling *"plans"* for the Dome's content had been laid at that point – only unnaturally gigantic and premature eggs of smelly PR gunk. The whole Millennium Experience story displays the fatal flaw of the New Labour "Project": its addiction to careerism, advertising and spin over commitment, hard-selling over quality control, meretricious aspirations to style over enduring substance, and finance beyond the greedy-gutsiest dreams of avarice over mind, heart and soul.

Thus even in December 1999, when the PM must have had crystal-clear knowledge of the Dome's, er . . . limited social usefulness – let alone inspiration – for the future, he nevertheless blithely reduced his basis for a second term of government to yet another sales pitch for this ultra-hubristic folly: ". . . *It is the first paragraph of my next election manifesto . . .*" (– see Daniel Foggo and Susan Bisset's review of the year in the Sunday Telegraph of 24/12/2000).

As for the Dome being . . . *"the envy of the world"* – Blair may or may not have been aware that this is the phrase with which Peter Laslett chose to sum up the effect of the BBC's Third Programme (as quoted in the Cambridge Review for 12 October 1957): ". . . a service which is literally the envy of the world".

The late Humphrey Carpenter reused it for the title of his survey of the network, *'The Envy of the World: Fifty Years of the BBC Third Programme and Radio 3, 1946-1996'* (Weidenfeld & Nicolson '96).

As the Third Programme (and – to an arguably lesser extent – Radio 3) was always dedicated to 'braining up', the world citizens Blair conjured up as being envious of the Dome before it had been built (let alone occupied, opened and revealed in all its artistic inglory) would have been Sun-bedazzled dope dreams away from those who had envied the Third Programme.

Certainly, neither Radio 3 nor the Third Programme were ever mentioned – let alone invoked – in the Prime Minister's many pronouncements on either the Dome or the so-called Third Way. And equally certainly, the BBC's Third Radio communications look to remain of more enduring benefit to posterity than either Blair's Dome or Blair's Way.

And so, in spades, do the giant steps taken over the last half century by Britain's National Health Service.

Blair could hardly have been unaware that *"The envy of the world"* is also how the NHS has been captioned ever since it was established in 1948.

It was an extraordinarily heartless manoeuvre for a new Prime Minister to have chosen this particular phrase in order to boost what turned out to be his first government's most perverse and sustained misuse of broadly public money, whilst at the same time auctioning to bits his country's most essential public service – and the very one to which the phrase had authentically attached for so long.

The Dome was never meant to be more than a short-lived opportunistic exploitation of the masses. On the other hand, the aspiration to provide free health care to the whole population, funded from general taxation, continues to justify world envy – especially, one hopes, on the part of truly democratic citizens of the USA (and this despite the Blair Corporation's seemingly incorrigible preoccupation with following the ultra-materialist American Way on all fronts, including the provision of health services at ruthlessly competitive prices).

". . . *a Healing/ of the grapplement of nations* . . ."
– see the note to *"For healing the nations"* on page 449

"... *a row of fir trees / twelve hundred kilometres long* ..."

– included in Mark Honigsbaum's '*Only Better Than Hanover*', which detailed the millennium celebrations round the world that "... make Greenwich look like a mean time" (Spectator, pp13-14, 4/7/98)

J'accuse ... Mandy Mouse the Dome-broker

I had that Mandy in the back of the pool once – no kidding!

It was a few months before his fall from high Notting Hill estate.

We were both leaping about, the only two males amid a bevy of women in the Saturday morning Wet Workout hour at the local pool. Suddenly our instructor called, "Grab a partner everyone", and Mandelson happened to be nearest to me – sleek and resplendent in green-and-yellow Paisley patterned jockey trunks.

The group was enjoined to adopt a wheelbarrow posture, with one partner stretched flat on the surface of the water whilst the other stood twirling the supine one by the armpits. Having just noted the vastly disproportionate outlay on the Millennium Dome underwritten and overseen by the human putty in my hands, and mindful of what so many struggling artist friends and organisations could do with a tiny fraction of those millions of pounds, I'm afraid the temptation to give his windpipe a sharp squeeze flickered into my head.

But the moment passed, and I meekly submitted my supine frame to be wheelbarrowed by him in turn. Had he sussed what was in my mind, God knows whether I'd be sat here now to tell the tale.

My objection was never to a shifty politician borrowing from a shifty multi-millionaire to upgrade his personal property developments. It's to the way shifty politicians sold dreams of similar riches via lottery winnings to millions of citizens understandably dissatisfied with their lot. And it's to the way the massive proceeds of this cheapo gambling pitch were slimeballed into massive investment in the massively philistine triteness of the Dome.

Both Lottery and Dome should, by any reasonable trade description act, be rebranded Opiates of the People.

In the Gospel of Dome according to Saint Pooter Mandelson on multi-plug TV in his missionary year of 1997, we were told: "... It's going to be *a tremendous advertisement*, which will show that *Britain is leading the rest of the world* into the next millennium ..."

Come off it, Mister flag-waving used-Tory vehicle salesman. If any nations can be said to be "leading the world", are not nuclear-free Brazil, Egypt, Ireland, Mexico, New Zealand, Sweden, and the other countries not yet afflicted with potential radiation (because they're not stockpiling or testing bombs), striking the only viable path for our species to follow – if *homo sapiens* is to survive?

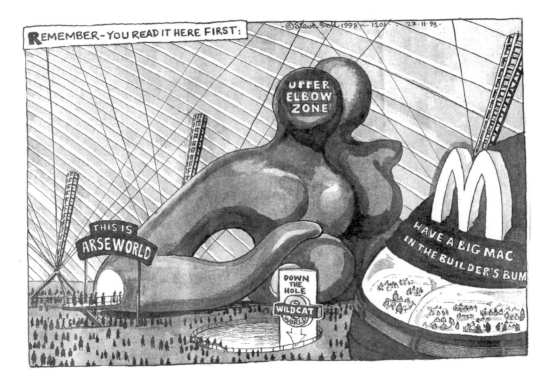

So please tell us, Oh Big Spenders-on-our-behalf, just *how* this advertisement showed Britain to be "leading the rest of the world"? Precisely what was it an advertisement *for?* To *where* did it lead non-Brits, Oh World Leaders, and to what purpose, pray?

"If the Millennium Dome is a success, we will never be forgotten", you spouted, and " – If it's a failure, we will never be forgiven". Hard to beat for sheer shameless glitz-questing adspeak, gushing on autopilot. In grabby New Labour's vainglorious hands, the Dome was bound to be an advertisement for little more than for advertising itself.

– Precisely how, Prime Panhandlers, did you and your ilk measure Success? Massive outlay, massive profits, rave reviews, big attendances, triumphalist chauvinism – ? Such unquestioning, narrow, smugly self-aggrandising aspirations sealed this project's constitutional failure as art, culture or social improvement from the moment yous took it over and on. As Bob Dylan sang in *'It's Alright Ma, I'm Only Bleeding'*: ". . . Advertising signs . . . con you/ Into thinking [you] . . . can do what's never been done/ [You] can win what's never been won . . . // Propaganda, all is phony".

Much as the proliferation of armaments, national prides and violence only adds a gruesome compound interest to the global suicide process, so the unregulated piling up of commodities, monopolies, and stock-in-trade rivalries will go on setting up ever more sitting targets for destruction, doomed from the outset by their innate mutual competitiveness.

If you doubt this book's inference that the unholy alliance between arms proliferation and money-worship accelerates the ever more widespread corrosion of our humanity, pray consider more closely the case of Mandy's Second Going.

In February 2001 various big shots in government and the media decided to get worked up about a disclosure that struck impartial observers as a pretty routine wisp of New Labour networking. In the spring of 1998 the Indian billionaire Srichand Hinduja's application for a British passport got preferential treatment shortly after Srichand and his brothers had offered four million pounds to embellish the Dome's so-called Spirit Zone, which had no sponsors at the time.

The more enduring ironies of what seems to have happened did *not* hit the headlines – for example:

– that the supposedly spiritual sector of Britain's millennial starship was anchored to the swag of hard-nosed arms traders who were facing bribery and corruption charges in their native land;

– that UK naturalisation of these profiteering clansmen was eased through swiftly and smoothly whilst multitudes of less wealthy (but also less obviously suspicious) characters who were seeking citizenship – or even just temporary refuge in Britain – were being kept out, turned away, kept waiting month after month in wretched conditions and circumstances, or – at best – obliged to undergo humiliating investigations;

– that of all the Dome's plethora of blank, bland and boring areas, the (renamed) Faith Zone was famously the blankest, blandest and most boring.

So another vast question hovers still – Spectral if not Godlike – over its remains: *where did all that money go?*

Is it lost and gone forever – as is the way of all hype, sooner or later, consumed by its own avaricious exhaust – ?

What is plain to see, Saint Prater, is that your own fiscal and political history brings home only the futility of amassing ginormous financial backing, with so little in mind to do with it beyond flaunting the banalities of spivs who've amassed ginormous financial backing.

It's liable to leave those who build on it in discredit of one sort or another – sometimes for life, with all manner of unforeseen knock-on effects on other people and other concerns drawn into such exclusively profit-fixated speculations.

In the course of "*Showcasing the Nation's achievements*", New Labour's multimillion-subsidised 'New Millennium Experience' contrived yet again to avoid like a plague the nightmare and doomsday realities of the affluent society's rejects

– that's to say, those Brits and non-Brits impervious to marketing, and thus excluded from "the Nation's achievements" and from the tiniest share or place in the razzmatazz – or in the costly Faith Zone, even.

I mean the homeless, the unemployed, the disabled, the bombed-out and dispossessed – become fugitives, refugees denied refuge, asylum-seekers refused asylum

– all the lonely people – unassuming, disadvantaged, powerless people

– humble people scouring the wastelands, to whom the Dome tossed no change, whom your Millennium Experience only taught yet again to "*. . . expect / Nothing . . .*"

– categorically ditched from the orgies of glad-handout spending, to try to reassemble –

"*. . . the broken fingernails*
of dirty hands . . ."

at which Eliot looked askance on Margate Sands in his '*Waste Land*' of 1922

– cut dead by Middle Class Britain at Millennium; left to tear what was left of their lives to nerveless shreds

– left to suffer, and pay the cost of, the broken promises of furtive minds, (un)ambitious men.

– Men inordinately ambitious for themselves, that is – but manifestly unconcerned about the sinking prospects of the neediest, whose well-being they were elected to represent along with everybody else's.

Blair, Twaddler, Lord Fatboots and their pals risked boring even paid-up believers shitless, with their unceasingly bathetic sales guff about The Millennium in general and The Greenwich Dome in particular being our (i e, the people of Britain's) Biggest Break Ever for some sort of ultimate state of grace.

The 1996 Chambers 21st Century Dictionary defines the millennium as '. . . *a future period of a thousand years during which some Christians believe Christ will rule the world*', and also as '. . . *a future golden age of worldwide peace and happiness*'.

Surely any project seriously seeking to fulfil either definition's lofty aspiration would need to aim a lot higher than either a further inflation of plutocratic bank balances, or so reekingly bogus an icon to Britain's pretensions to – er . . . Leading the World.

On the contrary, it would surely harness all available assets in order to forestall the adverse effects on the whole planet of arms dealing, wars, world poverty, hunger and diseases, pollution, nuclear waste and weapon proliferation, global warming, the profits-over-safety priorities of privatised transport systems, and hundreds of similarly datelined emergencies that cry out for action from anyone in power who can *"make a difference"*, Christian and non-Christian alike.

If Lord Jesus were planning His Second Coming, would He have located it in our would-be Lord Copper-bottomed Temple of Mammon on this eco-poisoned Greenwich timeshare?

– If only . . .

Christ's situation around London today remains for the most part (as it appears to do around most of the pseudo-civilised world) as Adrian Mitchell perceived it in 1959 in *'Quite Apart from the Holy Ghost'*:

> *"Jesus is stretched like the skin of a kite*
> *Over the cross, he seems in flight*
> *Sometimes. At times it seems more true*
> *That he is meat nailed up alive and pain all through.*
> *But it's hard to see Christ for priests. That happens when*
> *A poet engenders generations of advertising men."*

"Successful only because/ SO *much lovely lucre was well bonded . . ."* and ff

Apart from (and long before) the ever-swelling tides of commercial sponsorship, £260m was budgeted for the construction and infrastructure of the Dome, and £198m for the provision of its contents. A further £95m was allowed for its running costs during the year 2000. Opinion polls cited by the organisers claimed that twelve million visitors – nearly a fifth of the UK's population – would schlepp to Greenwich at their own expense and part with upwards of a further £15 to enter 'The People's Dome'.

This was the fast-talking hook – or rather, con-trick.

The Dome turned out to have cost taxpayers and lottery investors many millions more than any of these guestimates (£600m on the building alone) whilst getting massively less support from punters than its prestige-and-fortune-hunting promoters had, in their arrogance, banked on (less than half of the twelve million predicted).

In July 2000 the structure and the site were scheduled to be hastily sold off for a knock-down price, since by then the hollow banality of their claim to harbour the mega-flagship of UK achievement could no longer be gainsaid even by its most dogged governmental partisans. The mammoth débacle will presumably help bring home the hollowness at the fundaments of the 'Enterprise Culture' to many who might otherwise still be liable to fall for its anti-cultural commercialism.

The day after the imminent sale's announcement, the Guardian reported (p3, 28/7/00) that –

". . . The Millennium Dome was, in effect, given another £53m hand-out by the government last night when it was revealed that more than half the proceeds of its sale to a Japanese bank will go towards offsetting its debts."

In 'Second-hand Dome', the same day's Independent Review bade a cool

". . . Welcome to the Flog-it-off Cheap Zone. The £105m that the Japanese bank Nomura has spent buying the Millennium Dome at Greenwich sounds like a good deal of money. It is. But it looks a little less impressive next to the £800m or so of public lottery money that was poured into the project that was supposed, in the gushing words of Peter Mandelson, the absentee father of the Dome, to 'blow your socks off'. Instead, we now know that it has merely blown a dirty great hole in the coffers.

"Now Nomura plans to turn the site into a 'premier resort', with some of the zones retained and the worthiness expunged. No longer will visitors feel that they are on a journey round the mind of Mr Mandelson. It may thrive.

"But the abiding feeling remains that we have sold off not so much the family silver but the national Tupperware."

However, the Japanese merchant bank, which had indeed contemplated turning the Dome into a giant urban amusement park, suddenly got cold feet about taking over the so-called Leadership-of-the-World base in Greenwich.

It seems that their socks were indeed blown off, by the scale of the cash crisis, the low attendance figures and the impenetrably murky accounting, all of which had been concealed from them – as might have been expected of a shady Tupperware wheeler-dealer, but hardly of such a Joe Public-cum-government sponsored icon of the New Age.

Five years later, Richard Wray (in 'No place like Dome for major new venue', Guardian 26/5/05) reckoned that the Dome "has cost the taxpayer about £330 million to maintain since the Millenium Experience closed at the end of 2000".

In 2002 the site was finally sold to the American tycoon Philip Anschutz – on the condition that a share of any profits should go to English Partnerships, who manage the Dome.

In July 2004, a £550m deal was struck to ". . . turn the dome into a gambler's paradise with gaming tables, 900 slot machines and a 600-bed hotel", according to Nick Cohen (in 'Place your bets', Observer 25/7/04): ". . . The permanent memorial to the 1997 new Labour government's celebration of capitalism will be a casino."

The contrast between the Dome's business-fixated (dis)continuity and that of the architecture and artistic beacons that inspired and outlived the 1951 Festival of Britain, whose Muse-halls still grace the South Bank today, could hardly be more marked.

Nevertheless, this new Dome of Philistia, rebranded 'The O2' (= Zilch Mark Two?), did look as though it might at last flench some income from the thus far spectacularly loss-making venture.

One small but persistent fly, however, remained lodged in the projected emollient: UK gambling regulations forbade such (Super)casinos.

What an amazing coincidence then, that the Gambling Act narrowly squeezed through Parliament by Culture Minister Tessa Jowell in April 2005 did away with prohibitions against, yippee – how did you guess – (Super)casinos!

Very Cultural of the Ministress, that. You can seek elucidation of this typically Blairite finagle via *www.opsi.gov.uk/acts/en2005/2005en19.htm* (– though by no means all is revealed there . . . .).

Another year on, Rob Evans (Guardian p7, 25/7/06) reported that Greenwich had edged into the lead as the Casino Advisory Panel's favoured site for Britain's sole Supercasino, ahead of both Glasgow and Blackpool. Earlier that month the Deputy PM, John Prescott, had been entertained at his new buddy Anschutz's Texas cattle ranch.

On 5 July '06, Prescott fended off accusations of underhand dealings on Radio 4's Today programme, claiming that he had needed to schmooze Anschutz because "he is a guy . . . turning a poisonous bit of land into one of the best creators of regeneration that we've seen".

Prescott's tone conveyed an understandable degree of incredulity that he had at last found someone who actually wanted the Dome, "which everyone said was a liability".

His further assertion that Las Vegas glitz and bling would bring further regeneration to Greenwich was reminiscent of a buoyant Billy Bunter barely able to believe his luck regarding the gigantic postal order seriously at hand.

I have news for Messrs Prescott, Falconer, Blair, Mandelson, Tessa Jowell and the rest of the used-Dome sales team and promoters of gambling who have kept brandishing the R word to try to gild their shady deals with a socially benign-sounding gloss.

The eleventh edition of the Concise Oxford English Dictionary (2004) defines 'regenerate' as meaning: 'to regrow; to bring new and more vigorous life to an area or institution; to give a new and higher spiritual nature to . . .'   Also, when used as an adjective, it means 'reborn, especially in a spiritual or moral sense'.

It is in these senses that Shakespeare's Globe Theatre, Milton's 'Paradise Regained' and Blake's 'Jerusalem' were conceived as regenerative by their respective authors.

One of the saddest ironies that has beset the money-fixated New Labours Lost on the Dome, and also the Olympic Game-plans to date, lies in the little known fact that throughout the 1960s my dear departed and genuinely visionary, Shakespearean, Miltonic and Blakean friends, Joan Littlewood and Cedric Price, were busy laying inspired and intricate plans for a homegrown Fun Palace on the Isle of Dogs. They designed this to be a grass roots people-friendly arts, work, play and leisure centre – though not necessarily a money-spinner.

Cedric's credentials from heaven as an innovative architect whose Leonardo-like dreams were rooted in realism, and Joan's trail-blazing Theatre Workshop community ensemble productions at the Theatre Royal Stratford and elsewhere, had both achieved rather more than either the governments or the Arts Councils of the 1950s and '60s had done, in the matter of regenerating many parts of London.

They were unable to get the Fun Palace off the ground – or rather, onto that ground, or any ground – because of the moral apathy and political antagonism the project's blueprints elicited from the governments, Arts Councils and other sponsors of the time one might have hoped would be supportive.

The latter's main objection and fear seemed to be that the project's would-be creators had no particularly commercial aspirations for it. They wanted London to have a Palace for Fun instead of the for-money priorities of just about everything else being set up by officialdom.

Nadine Holdsworth devotes pages 32-36 of her *'Joan Littlewood'* (Routledge 2006) to the Fun Palace story, and quotes Joan's proposition in a 1964 New Scientist article that

". . . Those who at present work in factories, mines and offices will quite soon be able to live as only a few people now can: choosing their own congenial work, doing as much or as little of it as they like, and filling their leisure with whatever delights them."

Nadine Holdsworth recalls the duo's original conception:

". . . Littlewood's and Price's plans for a Fun Palace aimed to meet these new demands. Describing it as both a 'university of the streets' and a 'laboratory of pleasure', Littlewood envisaged the Fun Palace as a multi-use space housing a series of short-term, frequently-updated activities dedicated to pleasure, entertainment, communication and learning.

"During the 1950s and 1960s, social and cultural theorists such as Richard Hoggart and Raymond Williams were concerned that Welfare State educational and cultural policies, alongside American-dominated commercially-produced consumer culture and mass-media communications, were resulting in passive audiences. In contrast, Littlewood wanted to provide opportunities to learn and experience culture beyond the commercial market-place and hierarchical institutions such as the BBC and the education system.

"By providing numerous types of activity, Littlewood hoped to encourage people to make active decisions about what inspired them, gave pleasure and stimulated their imagination, regardless of whether that involved high art, popular culture, direct participation or casual observation. Alongside opportunities for activities, cultural encounters, eating, drinking and socialising, Littlewood wanted a space akin to the great parks that facilitated strolling and a chance to watch the world go by."

See also *'Joan's Book: Joan Littlewood's Peculiar History as She Tells It'* by J L (Methuen 1994).

As said, a particularly sad irony, given that the amount of money that Fun Palace might have cost was probably less than one iota of what has been squandered at Greenwich over most of the past decade.

And unlike the Dome, the Fun Palace – by dint of having contained its own *raison d'être* beyond a quick-sell – would quite likely still have been in full swing today, and maybe tomorrow too.

But so it didn't go, yet again, damn it.

"*. . . whilst other countries/ turned green . . ."*

– but not with envy (see page 118 and the notes on pages 327-329)

"*Blue Meanie bosses . . ."*

In '*Yellow Submarine*', George Dunning's full-length cartoon film of 1968, featuring the images, songs and voices of the Beatles, the Blue Meanies are the arch-villains who want to rid the world of music, virtue and happiness.

Page 122

"*. . . QUEUE HERE FOR ARMPIT WORLD . . ." (Lower Picture)*

Steve Bell drew this when the proposed contents of the Greenwich Dome were first unveiled in February 1998. Michael Heseltine had instigated the project, Peter Mandelson became Labour's Minister with special responsibility for it, and Blair announced the exhibits and attractions with ultra-puffy proprietorial zeal: "Dream, imagine and return refreshed", he cooed regarding the '*Dreamscape Zone*'; the '*Body Zone*' would invite punters to ". . . Voyage into the human machine and learn how to get the best from it"; and the PM vouchsafed an extra-big thrill in the '*Transaction Zone*': "See how money and finance are changing your life".

H'm. We did come to see that, with all manner of vengeances, Mister Dome Marketeer (and doom marketeer-to-be). At least we also had the consolation of seeing – and disbelieving – with Steve Bell's eyes.

Page 123

"*BEST OF BRITAIN . . ."*

This Peter Brookes cartoon, and perhaps also Steve Bell's that parallels it on the lower half of page 124, with the pointed focus of the Blair-Child's gaze upon his Big – er, Godfather's – genital area, may or may not have had something to do with the withdrawal of the curiously grovelling infant from the New Millennium Experience Company's subsequent publicity images – i e, as distinct from their initial blueprint as reproduced on the upper half of the facing page 122.

"*The Emperor's Millennium Clothes"*

Gerald Scarfe's take on the Dome was glossed in '*Drawing Blood: forty-five years of Scarfe Uncensored*' (Little, Brown 2005), as follows:

"Simon Jenkins, the journalist, rang me to see if I would be interested in making some sculptures for the Dome. I was completely against the Dome, and thought it had the smell of failure about it from the start . . . They wanted me to work in a pavilion called the Self-Portrait Zone. Jennie Page, who was Chief Executive of the New Millennium Experience Company, said she felt that the Zone, which was intended to give a picture of who we, the British, are, was becoming rather self-congratulatory, bearing messages about what wonderful sportsmen we are, how impressively multi-racial we are, and so on. It would be my job to show the other side of the coin. For Sport, I made a beer-bellied, boot-headed football hooligan. I showed us as couch potatoes, watching a vomiting television, clutching a remote control and beer can, while we became part of the fabric of our armchairs. British Comedy, which I consider to be very scatological and *Carry On*, was a laughing lavatory, with boob eyes, condom hat, lavatory brush in one hand, sausage in the other and, naturally, trousers down.

"Jennie Page rang me soon after the Dome opened. 'It's absolutely ghastly', she said, 'British Comedy burnt down in the night'. I later learned that when Special Branch were checking the Dome for bombs before the arrival of Tony Blair at the Millennium Eve party, one of them had peered into British Comedy's lavatory-pan face and dislodged the seat, creating an electrical fault. Later, this short caused the laughing lavatory to burst into flames. 'Yes, it's terrible', Jennie went on. 'It's been taken away to be repaired, so – have you got another sculpture to put in its place? It's too embarrassing to have a gaping space in the Self-Portrait Zone'. 'Well,' I said, after some thought, 'I have got a rhino . . .' 'Splendid!' she said. 'Can we have it?' 'But what', I asked, 'has a rhino got to do with the British character?' 'Never mind about that. We can't have an empty space'. And so there the full-size Chichester rhino stood for the following month. When I was in there one day, a respectable lady visitor asked me what it was doing there, and I told her the story. 'Oh', she said, '. . . I thought it meant that we, the British, are thick-skinned and horny'."

Page 124

"*. . . the indestructible good sense / of Luther King's dream . . .*"

On 28 August 1963, Martin Luther King immortalised one of the USA's finest hours by majestically chanting his vision to the multiracial congregation of 250,000 foregathered at the climax of their historic Civil Rights March on Washington: –

"I say to you today, my friends . . . even though we face difficulties today and tomorrow . . . I still have a dream. It is a dream that . . . one day this nation will rise up, and live out the true meaning of its creed: '*We hold these truths to be self-evident . . . that all men are created equal . . .*'

"I have a dream . . . that one day on the red hills of Georgia, sons of fomer slaves and sons of former slave-owners . . . will be able to sit down together at the table of brotherhood.

"I have a dream . . . that one day even the State of Mississippi . . . a state sweltering with the heat of injustice . . . sweltering with the heat of oppression . . . will be transformed into an oasis of freedom and justice.

"I have a dream . . . that my four little children will one day live in a nation where they will not be judged by the colour of their skin, but by the content of their character.

"When we let freedom ring, black men and white men . . . Jews and Gentiles . . . Protestants and Catholics . . . will be able to join hands and sing . . . in the words of the old Negro spiritual . . . '*Free at last! Free at last! Great God Almighty, we are free at last!*'. . ."

Page 125

Pictures of, clockwise from top: a sandstone Buddha, William Blake's death mask, Martin Luther King, and Jesus Christ

Page 126

"*. . . adapted / from Woody Guthrie . . .*"

'*This Land is Your Land*', Guthrie's anthem of solidarity for the oppressed and dispossessed of

America, was hi-jacked by the reactionary George Bush Sr and flown as his Presidential campaign song in 1989 – and then again by his even more bigoted son who had it played in the Ronald Reagan Building in Washington at the victory rally to celebrate his re-election in November 2004.

Whoever lit on the song as a supposedly patriotic vote-catcher must have overlooked or – more likely – censored its sardonic last verses:

> *"There was a big high wall there that tried to stop me*
> *A sign was painted, said private property*
> *But on the other side, it didn't say nothing*
> *– This side was made for you and me.*
>
> *"One bright sunny morning in the shadow of the steeple*
> *By the Relief Office I saw my people –*
> *As they stood there hungry, I stood there wondering*
> *If this land was made for you and me."*

Many of the millions who voted against George Bush Junior in the US Presidential elections of 2000 and 2004 – notably those whose votes were not even counted – must still be wondering the same thing.

Presumably no-one in the Bush family or administration wanted to acknowledge that the song was originally composed by Guthrie in 1940 as a Marxist riposte to Kate Smith's corny and mega-plugged renditions of Irving Berlin's *'God Bless America'*, entitled *'God Blessed America'*. The refrain, which he later revised to *". . . This land was made for you and me"*, originally read *"God blessed America for me . . ."*

Speaking on BBC Radio 4's *'More than Just a Song'* on 13th and 16th August '06, Billy Bragg reminded contemporary listeners of how these closing political verses were excised from just about every version popularised via US mass media, concerts, kindergartens, schoolbooks and syllabuses, broadcasts and recordings (by everyone from The Weavers and Pete Seeger through Bing Crosby and The Mormon Tabernacle Choir to Bruce Springsteen) over the entire last half century:

> ". . . That's how it ends, with a question mark. The beauty, the ribbon of highway, the gulf stream waters, all that beauty, has this question mark hanging over it, which has been painted out.
>
> "Most of the official songbooks from the 1940s and '50s didn't have this in. It took the folk revival – Dylan, Arlo Guthrie [Woody's son], young kids seeking out Woody – to restore it."

The Independent's US correspondent Andrew Buncombe recalled his feelings on hearing the truncated song struck up by the Republican Party band and triumphantly warbled, fit to levitate the Reagan Building, in honour of Dubbya's re-election:

> "I was dumbstruck because I knew a little about this song, knew a little about Woody Guthrie's role in the American canon, a socialist singer, a man who promoted egalitarianism and fairness, and lo and behold, in the very bowels of the Reagan Building, they started singing this as a Republican victory song.
>
> "I have to say, having seen George Bush's last four years and the tax cuts, and the way in which he was giving money to the better-off in society, it did stick in the craw that *they* should be using this song of socialism . . ."

On the same radio programme, Woody's daughter Nora made the following comments:

> "As [Woody] was travelling across the country, he was seeing so many homeless people and

poor people from the great Dustbowl migration and the Depression and it just seems that, when you really were out there, things were awful – things were just terrible for hundreds and hundreds of thousands of people.

"If you can imagine walking into New Orleans the day following the storms there, and someone marching with a band singing *'God Bless America'*, you'd wonder what that meant actually, and I think Woody's reaction was to try to look into that and say 'What's really going on here, and does God have anything to do with it?'

". . . Woody really despised taking simplistic positionings. He felt that the country and many, if not most of the people in America that *he* was seeing, particularly the poor and homeless people, were out there – helping each other, feeding each other, giving each other lifts, doing amazing, supportive things for each other, filled with hope in the most horrible, horrible times.

"So on one hand you have this wonderful anthemic thing to the citizens of the country – to the people, and on the other hand you have an anger at, I suppose, the Government really, in not being there for the people because, as we know, it's supposed to be – *'for the people, by the people'* . . ."

Nora Guthrie is convinced that the song remains as empowering as ever:

". . . We're all rolling over, rolling our eyes and being sick to our stomachs at times, about the way this song is used and interpreted, and stolen by various and sundry parties – whether it's George Bush or the Ku Klux Klan, they've all tried to use it!

"If there's been a time to sing *'This Land is Your Land'* the time is now, in terms of the way Woody meant it, and what his intentions were, and the power that it would give people here in America, under our circumstances, to change things."

Page 127

". . . *Imagine all the people/ Sharing all the world* . . ."

In a typically bullish, thick-headed, clichéd would-be pooh-pooh job on John Lennon headed *'Come, all ye faithless'* (Spectator Xmas issue, 17-24 December 2005), Mark Steyn branded Lennon's *'Imagine'* a "paean to nothingness".

Steyn was rehashing Joel Engel's conjecture in America's *Weekly Standard* that the ex-Beatle's disbelief in heaven, hell or religion will ". . . produce a lot more Hitlers and a lot fewer Mother Teresas". Engel's article quoted from *'Imagine'* with ill-substantiated contempt:

> "*Imagine there's no heaven*
> *It's easy if you try*
> *No hell below us*
> *Above us only sky*
> *Imagine all the people*
> *Living for today* . . ."

"Okay, let's imagine that", wrote Engel –

". . . let's imagine six billion people who believe that flesh and blood is all there is; that once you shuffle off this mortal coil, poof, you're history; that Hitler and Mother Teresa both met the same ultimate fate . . . The fear of an afterlife where one will be judged has likely kept hundreds of millions from committing acts of aggression, if not outright horror.

Nothing clears the conscience quite like a belief in eternal nothingness."

These assumptions strike me as profoundly irrational, unrealistic and unhistorical. Hitler's massacres, and the acts of outright horror that preceded them over the centuries, and that have continued to desolate our planet to this day – sanctioned and coordinated by diverse religious/fundamentalist leaders, Crusaders, colonists, maniacal nationalists, empire-builders, ethnic cleansers and (suicide-)bomb contractors – were and go on being inflicted with the alleged full support of their perpetrators' respective so-called gods and visions of afterlife.

Furthermore, this song is far from nihilistic. *"Imagine all the people/ Sharing all the world"* can hardly be interpreted as pushing the "conscienceless belief in eternal nothingness" both Engel and Steyn try to palm their readers off with as Lennon's message. Indeed, Engel-Steyn's summary of the song lyric's essence is about as wide of the mark as could be.

'Imagine' sings for keeping faith *pro bono publico* – for the breathing body politic here and now. It sings that with Gods out of the picture, human kind alone are responsible.

– It sings that if indefinable deities, and insurance policies based on posthumous judgements, punishments and rewards, are removed from our moral consciousness, it is we ourselves who have to be 100% answerable for our ideas, policies and behaviour.

As Lennon said of his, Yoko Ono's and the flower-children's, draft-dodgers' and anti-bomb generation's continuing peace-and-love mission: *"We're trying to make Christ's message contemporary . . . If somebody stands up and smiles, and then gets smacked in the face, that doesn't invalidate the smile"*.

– A lot closer to the pronouncements and positive practices of Jesus and Teresa than to those of Hitler or bin Laden, innit?

As is the rest of Lennon's anthem for a better, more generously humanist universe:

> *"Imagine there's no countries*
> *It isn't hard to do*
> *Nothing to kill or die for*
> *And no religion too*
> *Imagine all the people*
> *Living life in peace . . .*
>
> *Imagine no possessions*
> *I wonder if you can*
> *No need for greed or hunger*
> *A brotherhood of man*
> *Imagine all the people*
> *Sharing all the world . . .*
>
> *You may say I'm a dreamer*
> *But I'm not the only one*
> *I hope someday you'll join us*
> *And the world will live as one."*

So far from the faithless stick-or-carrot alternatives of a presumed hopelessly fallen world – of either sinfully losing out on heaven, or earning brownie points to come – *'Imagine'* calls for the practical redemption of this earth from our time-dishonoured self-entrapments.

– So far from negativity, the song's lyric psalms seriously attainable visions of love, decency and civilisation over against the currently prevailing ones of retribution, inequality and destruction.

Satar Jabar, hooded blind and displayed on a box with wires connected to his body in Abu Ghraib Prison, Baghdad on 5 November 2003

Towards the end of 2003 and early in 2004 various rumours of abuse and torture of prisoners held in the Abu Ghraib prison, also known as Baghdad Correctional Facility, gradually slipped out to and via diverse people and media.

The acts were committed by personnel of the 372nd Military Police company, CIA officers, and contractors involved in the occupation of Iraq.

Internal investigations by the US army began in January '04, and reports of the mistreatments along with horrendous images of American military in the acts of abusing and torturing prisoners, came to wide public attention soon after.

On 28 April 2004 a *'60 Minutes'* news report, followed by Seymour M Hersh's revelation of the abuses in the 10 May issue of *The New Yorker* (which was posted online on 30 April) brought home to the entire nation, and the world, the degrees of degrading cruelty, humiliation and sado-pornography that had been conducted under the American flag in Baghdad.

See the notes to *Page 133* on pages 351-366, and to *Page 214* on pages 441-442. Also Mark Danner's *'Torture and Truth: America, Abu Ghraib, and the War on Terror'* (Granta Books 2005); *'The Torture Papers'* edited by Karen J Greenberg and Joshua L Dratel (Cambridge University Press 2005); and *'The Abu Ghraib Investigations'* by Steven Strasser (Public Affairs Reports 2005).

Where the US's least attractive enterprises lead – such as its recurrent obsession with Robocopping the planet – certain Britons seem compelled to follow. Even, alas, unto the abuse and torture of Iraqi prisoners under their so-called guard. The first such sequel that came to light (as reported on pp1 & 4 of the Guardian, 19 January 2005) had been enacted in May 2003 after British soldiers at Camp Breadbasket, a food depot near Basra, had captured a group of looters.

In June '03 one of the squaddies was intercepted trying to process a roll of film which had recorded horrific photographic evidence of the sadistic humiliation of these prisoners, such as soldiers suspending one man from the prongs of a forklift truck; trampling on the head and naked body of another; and forcing others again to simulate anal and oral sex, in poses sadly similar to those enacted in the course of the abuses photographed at Abu Ghraib prison.

The British Army court martial took place just one week after a US military tribunal had sentenced Corporal Charles Graner to ten years' imprisonment for stacking naked Abu Ghraib prisoners up into a human pyramid and then ordering them to masturbate while other servicemen and women took photos of his degrading tableau (see pages 352-353, and 441-442).

Four junior Camp Breadbasket soldiers were convicted, but several potentially revealing issues remained unaddressed – notably: why was no-one charged with forcing the Iraqi prisoners to simulate stigmatised sex acts? And why was Major Taylor, the camp's CO, not held accountable for his instruction to the squaddies to *"work them* (i e, the looters) *hard"*, in breach of the Geneva Convention?

Audrey Gillan reported in *'Four guilty, but questions remain'* (Guardian 24/2/2005) that the court heard

". . . how Breadbasket's commanding officer, then Captain Dan Taylor, had devised a plan, codenamed Operation Ali Baba, in which soldiers were to rise at dawn and go *'Ali Baba hunting'*. They were told to bring camouflage poles with them – allegedly for their own protection, but the court was told that they were used to beat the thieves . . . In spite of this being illegal, Major Taylor was promoted three months after the photographs were reported to the police. He was exonerated by the military five days before the court martial began."

Phil Shiner of Public Interest Lawyers, who represented a number of the men who described having been abused at the camp, protested that the military's conduct of the case amounted to a show trial, whilst his clients' statements suggested that the abuse was a lot more widespread than the court martial admitted. In *'Calls to reopen Iraq abuse inquiry'* (Guardian 26/2/05), Audrey Gillan quoted Shiner's view that the trial had been ". . . run to a predetermined script based on damage limitation. *It shows how the military cannot be allowed to investigate and prosecute themselves"*.

Gillan reported that statements from Phil Shiner's clients refused by the court –

". . . give a different picture to what happened in May 2003 than was put before it. One man, Ra'id Attiyah Ali, said he was not a looter and in fact worked in the camp and had an identification card to prove it. He claims he was beaten and tied to a pole for an hour and a half:

'. . . I saw the soldiers kicking and beating Iraqis. I saw the guy who was held in a net. I saw five Iraqis in their underwear holding milk cartons on their head.

I saw a soldier urinating on them . . . about eight soldiers.'

"Another victim claimed to be the man photographed tied to the forklift truck. He said '. . . There was a female soldier wearing shorts and vest, she held an aerial in her hand. She detached a horse-driven cart and attached it to one of the detainees. She started hitting him with the aerial and asking him to pull the cart.'

And another of Shiner's excluded witnesses, Aqeel Jasim Mohammed, said:

". . . I was kicked on my testicles which left a permanent damage. I am no longer able to perform the sexual act. I had to divorce my wife recently as a consequence. My lip was cut and my nose broken. We were like toys in their hands . . ."

In September 2006 another Iraqi prisoner abuse scandal came to trial. One of those charged, Corporal Donald Payne, pleaded guilty to a war crime charge of inhumane treatment of persons at the Basra Detention Centre previously used by Saddam's brutal secret police. Payne was its jailer. The court heard that he had "conducted" a 36 hour-long "choir" of nine prisoners, a treatment the prosecution described as "Cpl Payne systematically assaulting each of the civilians" (reported by Steven Morris in *'Court martial hears of corporal's "choir" of screaming Iraqi prisoners'*, Guardian 21/9/06).

Julian Bevan QC was quoted on BBC News (*'UK soldier enjoyed Iraqis' pain'*, 20/9/06) as alleging that Payne ". . . seemed to carry out his 'conductor' role without fear of repercussion":

". . . The choir consisted of Cpl Payne assaulting each detainee in turn by, for instance, hitting in their stomachs, kicking them and punching them wherever on their bodies, causing them to shriek out or groan in pain, their various noises constituting the music."

As in the Camp Breadbasket case, these abuses were exposed after another soldier filmed their cruel evolution (not as evidence but as a hoped-for trophy souvenir). According to Steven Morris, the video shows Payne putting the sack-hooded prisoners in "stress positions" outlawed in the Army since revelations of their inhumanity in a Northern Ireland detention centre in 1972.

The trial was also supposed to decide whether the Corporal was guilty of the manslaughter of Baha Mousa, a 26 year-old hotel receptionist who had been starved for two days, and then died from 93 documented injuries such as a ligature round his neck, four broken ribs, and crushed wrists. Morris recounted how the hearing was told that Baha Mousa –

". . . was singled out for beatings and held in a toilet. Cpl Payne allegedly pinned him to the floor with his knee in his back, grabbed his head and banged it against the wall. Baha Mousa slumped and stopped breathing. Medical help was called for but he could not be saved. He was found to have suffered 93 injuries including fractured ribs and a broken nose. He had also suffered asphyxia."

Another similarity with the Camp Breadbasket case is the way in which junior soldiers were facing graver charges than their superiors. A Times report suggested that the brutal treatment meted out by Payne was sanctioned by senior Army officers (*'The Army approved abuse of prisoners'*, Michael Evans on pages 1-2, Times 17/11/06). According to this report –

". . . Major Antony Royce, called as a witness by the judge in the case, told the court that he was instructed by those higher up the chain of command in Basra to use 'conditioning techniques', including putting prisoners in stress positions and hooding them, to prepare detainees for tactical questioning.

"He said that the advice had come from a senior Army legal adviser. Such techniques are against both the Geneva Convention and the Army's own rules of engagement."

It should surprise no-one that ill-treatment and abuse have taken place if the conditions for such acts are set in motion via dehumanising practices turned a blind eye to, approved, encouraged, or even ordered, by the top brass.

The six-month court martial closed on 13 March 2007 at RAF Bulford, Wiltshire, with acquittal for every British soldier charged, and the Army cleared of responsibility for Baha Mousa's death. The ten members of the Queen's Lancashire Regiment unit who were called to give evidence over 30 hours of cross-questioning, responded to leading questions with all of 667 reiterations of "I can't remember" and "I don't know". One soldier even claimed to be unsure whether he had been to Iraq.

Amnesty International was reported by Mark Townsend (in *'How Army's £20m trial failed to find the Killers'*, Observer 18/3/07) to have been "among those concerned that, once again, the chain of command had not been found guilty in an abuse trial". – And also, to have derived from the trial ". . . a legitimate apprehension that a cover-up has ensued".

Examination of the court records suggests that this was a considerable understatement. For example, one of the grounds for blanket acquittal was "Court evidence . . . that dozens of men may have joined in or witnessed the abuse suffered by Baha and his fellow captives", apart from the seven QLR men in the dock.

Other examples: Corporal Payne's lawyer William Bache claimed that his client ". . . *was simply doing what he was told*". The group under Payne had been named the Grim Reapers because they had made "the first kill" in Iraq. A barrister asked one soldier, "So . . . a sort of badge of honour for killing people?" – "I do not know", replied the witness.

Another soldier was asked fourteen times: "You and [the other] Grim Reapers spent the greater part of 14th to 16th September guarding these Iraqis, and you and your colleagues beat them relentlessly, did you not?" – and replied fourteen times: "I do not wish to answer that question".

Later on, the same soldier did admit to ". . . slapping detainees on the back of their heads about five times each when they fell down . . . with enough force to make them stand up. Each time they did moan, saying, 'Oh mister, okay mister, no mister'. . . At this time, they were all finding it hard to continue". Apart from this, and another who let slip that it had been ". . . *a free for all*" of beating and kicking in the Iraqis, all of the soldiers insisted that they could not remember what had happened.

No-one was found guilty of the killing of Mousa, nor of the near-killing of Kifa Taha al-Mutairi, nor of the gross injuries of the eight other Iraqi detainees, because no conclusive proof of precisely who had inflicted which fatal injuries could be ascertained. This is all the harder to credit given the abovementioned film footage of the abuses, plus the fact that the court testimonies documented by the Guardian journalists and by Mark Townsend all featured ". . . accounts of Baha and his compatriots lying semi-conscious in their own excrement . . . and kicked and punched repeatedly".

Among many other graphic evidences of pitiless violence retailed to the court, the diaries of Private Stuart Mackenzie, who was attached to the QLR at the time, stated how when one of the Iraqis punched back, the would-be self-defender was ". . . filled in immediately by about ten of us. He was bleeding, from his head, face and ears. He was battered from head to toe so we let him go instead of arresting him".

Mackenzie was dismissed from the Territorial Army in August 2006 for "gross misconduct". Here are further excerpts from the diaries, logged between 24 July 2003 and 15 September '03:

". . . Man caught and roughed up. Head under water. He is going to be ill . . . Leg and a winged [flung] Ali Baba into Shat al Arab [Shatt al-Arab canal] for stealing wood. Piss funny . . . Caught some Ali Babas. Leg and a wing three Ali Babas into river. Tried to row their boat *[float]*. Well hard . . . Ali Babas x 5 on boat moored on dry dock. 10 shots fired. 1 x Ali Baba 9 x soldier. 1 Ali Baba hit twice in chest. Moaning + dying. Artificial bleed. Died before being casevaced *[medically evacuated]*.

". . . Hostage beaten up – broken wrist, concussion, sore bollocks . . . Found 3 Ali Babas at WTP7. Beat them up with sticks and filmed it – good day so far . . . House raid, for hours, nothing found. Caught 3 Ali Babas – beat fuck out of them in back of Saxon. 1 had a punctured lung + broken ribs + fingers. 1 had a dislocated shoulder + broken fingers . . . Out a few times then to main for conditioning prisoners. *[words scribbled out]* all night – no sleep for them – about 3 hours for me . . ."

Questioned by the court martial about these escapades, Mackenzie only repeated, "Like I said, I cannot remember". And the same answer came likewise, over and over, when he was asked what he had originally written which had been rendered illegible by the numerous crossings-out of words and phrases in the diaries.

For example, the Prosecution asked ". . . You wrote down things which might show that you had been beating people up . . . that you were guilty of a crime: what is crossed out here?" – *"I do not remember what is crossed out".* ". . . There must have been a reason for this?" – *"I do not remember. Perhaps it was a mistake".*

In the aftermath of the murders and beatings-up of Stephen Lawrence and a number of other (British) Black and Asian citizens, and other cases involving non-whites, it was belatedly acknowledged that there had long been, and still was in the early Noughties, "Institutional Racism" pervading the British Police. As well as the stomach-churning activities recalled above, the liberal use of "Ali Babas" in these accounts, so reminiscent of similar uses of "Niggers" and "Yids" and "Wogs" mainly, one hopes, in times long gone by, would nevertheless suggest that similar afflictions are still pretty chronic amongst bully-boy-to-psychotic British Army groups and individual soldiers.

Two further entries in the Mackenzie diaries, covering the last two days and nights being (allegedly) investigated by the court martial, were a bit more circumstantially revealing than the rest:

"Monday 15/9/03. Still conditioning the terrorists *[sic]*. They are in clip *[trouble]* big time. Finally got back to camp at 13.30pm. Back to BG *[brigade]* Main for 10pm. The fat bastard *[believed to be Baha Mousa]* who kept taking his hood off and escaping from his plasticuffs got put in another room. He resisted *[words scribbled out]*. He stopped breathing. Then we couldn't revive him. *[words scribbled out]* What a shame.

"Tuesday 16/9/03. Still guarding the prisoners. Back to Camp Stephen for b/fast at 7.45am. Back to guard prisoners – took them to Um Kasar *[Umm Qasar]* . . . The others were just really beaten up. It's going massive. It's a SIB *[Special Investigation Branch of the Royal Military Police]* investigation. Murder."

Phil Shiner of Public Interest again, for the victims, drew attention to the public record of how the soldiers ". . . subjected the Iraqis to ritualised abuse including one 'game' that involved a competition to see who could kickbox the hooded detainees the furthest".

Shiner's summary underlined the blatant injustice of the Judge Advocate, Mr Justice McKinnon's, conclusions that whilst ". . . the evidence was clear that Baha Mousa's 93 injuries were sustained as a result of numerous assaults over 36 hours . . . None of these soldiers has been charged with any offence *because there is no evidence against them as a result of a more or less obvious closing of ranks*".

Shiner was understandably disgusted:

"Everyone who pleaded not guilty has been found not guilty. No one in command has been called to account. The video played in the court martial makes it very clear that unless you were stone deaf, if you were on that base you knew what was going on. We are talking here about torture, not some nuanced degrading of treatment.

". . . The outcome is a travesty. It gives the victims nothing. It raises more questions than it answers including: 1. Why were the other soldiers responsible not charged? 2. How could it be thought lawful to engage in hooding, sleep deprivation and stressing 35 years after the Heath Government banned these techniques? 3. Was the first battalion Queen's Lancashire Regiment the only battalion engaging in such disgraceful behaviour, or is this systematic abuse more widespread?"

The third question was answered, to some extent, in Mark Townsend's 18 March '07 Observer article:

". . . Ministry of Defence figures reveal that there have been 221 investigations into abuse allegations involving British troops in Iraq since the invasion four years ago. Of these, 198 were closed without further action, with others disbanded after further enquiries. Just six instances of deliberate abuse have made it to court. Until the Baha case, only one has led to convictions."

A further disturbing subtext emerged at the Bulford court martial when Brigadier Euan Duncan, director of the Army's Intelligence Corps, told the hearing that ". . . British forces were put under pressure by the US to use more forceful interrogation techniques". This tallies with recent information regarding US Army behaviour in Iraq. On the morning of 6 May 2007, BBC Radio 4 News broadcast the findings of a US Army Doctors' survey of the current attitudes of combat troops in Iraq. Apparently one in three of the US soldiers polled considered the torture of detainees acceptable, and one in ten admitted to having mistreated Iraqi civilians, by hitting or kicking them and damaging their property, without reason or provocation.

See the detailed accounts of US Military and CIA policies and practices in regard to renditions, detentions, (mis)treatment of prisoners including torture of many kinds and degrees in the notes to *Page 133* on pages 351-366. And see also *'They were celebrating beating us: Iraqi says British troops were as bad as Saddam'*, Guardian 27/9/2006; *'Soldiers "given go-ahead to break Geneva Convention" . . .'*, Steven Morris, Guardian 17/11/06; *'Britain's military court martial system was called into question last night . . .'*, Steven Morris and Audrey Gillan, Guardian 14/2/07.

Several of Britain's best selling newspapers made a deeply unsavoury meal out of the expense this long drawn-out case had incurred, and also out of the indignity of bringing senior officers into potential disrepute by allowing charges to be issued against them at all. The Daily Telegraph headlined its front page on 15th February 2007 *'Colonel "Victim of Witch-hunt" . . .'*, whilst the same morning's Daily Mail offered its front page imbibers a likewise insensitively phrased taster: *'As War Hero is cleared in Twenty Million Pound prisoner abuse show trial, the damning verdict on Ministers who made him a scapegoat . . .'*

The alleged victim and scapegoat may, as the Mail's headline suggested, have been a war hero on other fronts, but these particular outrages, inflicted by raging bullies whose Commander Colonel Jorge Mendonca was in mid-September 2003, were not his finest hours, by any standards.

What he was charged with was *"failing to ensure his men did not mistreat Iraqi civilians detained in Basra"*. The court martial persuaded itself – with shameful pseudo-legalistic manipulations – to concede that Mendonca, along with all of his men, had no case to answer, because the evidence had been covered up by the closing of ranks noted in Justice McKinnon's summing-up, as cited above.

Of the ten Iraqis, one was killed, another nearly died, and the others were dealt indisputably grievous bodily harm. A show trial indeed – stage managing another episode of craven victors' justice in operation. – What it showed was the British Army looking after its own, even unto those who were quite happy to allow innocent civilians in their guardianship to suffer horrendous assaults – and even get beaten to death – with impunity.

What calibre of journalists could mindfully find the Commanding Officer, and not the Iraqi wounded and dead, as having been made a scapegoat and fallen victim to a witch-hunt?

As to the cost, what sort of mentality could begrudge this £20 million, in the cause of carrying out democratic justice on behalf of citizens of the country whose well-being UK soldiers were supposedly there to defend (– albeit with the disastrous results reported daily over the years since the first day of bombardments on 20 March 2003, at the cost of so many *billions* of taxpayers' precious pounds more, to such daily hopeless effect)?

Let us reverse the seemingly limitless rise and rise of legal fees promoted by the lawyer-led Blair administration, and let us cop out for good from Britain's craven poodling to the US's military leads worldwide. But let's not give up on Iraqis and other victims of Transatlantic Coalition violence getting the same publicly witnessed justice as anyone similarly mistreated in the US or UK would get.

With this in mind, it was all the more distressing to read and hear the not normally loony Tory Shadow Defence Secretary Liam Fox quoted as opining on 15/2/07 that ". . . *A whiff of political correctness* hangs heavy over the case against Colonel Mendonca", and that ". . . those responsible for bringing the case *need an urgent reappraisal of their procedures and their motives*".

H'm. I urge Dr Fox to take an in-depth look at the enormous masses of irrefutable evidence that have piled up around the case – which sad to say seems in this respect to be an exception that proves the rule – and either to recognise, or substantively to disprove, that the Colonel was in this instance an officer who was quite expressly, on 14-16 September 2003, ". . . *failing to ensure his men did not mistreat Iraqi civilians detained in Basra*".

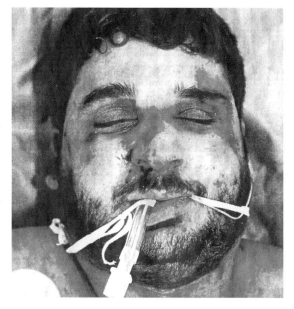

Let Dr Fox also take a look at the photograph of Baha Mousa with his family on page 349, taken before British soldiers got hold of him; and then take an equally close look at the one right here, taken on 16/09/03 in Basra mortuary, with the incubating tubes (applied in hopes of reviving and healing him) still in his mouth.

Let Dr Fox reappraise his own motives after thinking about the reaction of Baha's father Daoud Mousa, a colonel in the Basra police force, on first seeing his son's corpse:

> "I was horrified to see his body covered in blood and bruises . . . There was blood coming from his nose and mouth. The skin on one side of his face had been torn away to reveal the flesh beneath. There were severe patches of bruising over all of his body. The skin on his wrists had been torn off and the skin on his forehead torn away and there was no skin under his eyes either."

Let Dr Fox reflect on the RAF forensic pathologist's medical report on Baha Mousa's death:

> "The multiplicity of injuries and their widespread distribution is consistent with a systematic beating taking place over a period . . . the injuries are all consistent with the history that he could have been struggling on the floor. The mixture of grazes and bruises is indicative of a mixture of glancing blows against a firm object, and directly applied force with a blunt object."

The human rights charity Liberty have joined Phil Shiner in calling for an independent enquiry, in order, in the words of Liberty director Shami Chakrabarti, to hold ". . . Government and the highest level of the military to the highest accountability in a democracy".

In short, Dr Fox, such concerns are nothing to do with political correctness. It is the unaccountable courts martial system exposed by this manifestly bogus charade, which is in need of ". . . *urgent reappraisal of its procedures and their motives*".

What a pity that Dr Fox is not among those in agreement with Diane Abbott MP, who told a press conference for the Liberty initiative on 16 April '07 that ". . . MPs of all sides believe the best protection for our soldiers is the acknowledgement that we treat people according to the best human rights standards"; or with Ms Chakrabarti, that ". . . We will get past these difficulties by accountability, and by [making] the rule of law apply in Iraq and everywhere else".

On 30 April 2007 Donald Payne was sentenced to a year's imprisonment and dismissed from the Army for inhumane treatment of Iraqi civilians. His barrister Tim Owen QC postulated "a fundamental unfairness" in that Payne was being punished although "force – or the threat of force – [was] the only way to enforce the conditioning process" the soldiers had been ordered to execute (*'Britain's first War Criminal jailed'*, Steven Morris, Guardian 30/4/07). By most of the accounts presented, Payne's implementation of this process was fanatically excessive. He seems to have been deep into the habit of getting his rocks off by conducting "the choir . . . for the enjoyment and pleasure" of visitors to the detention centre. But the process itself, and also (what was again pointed up by Justice McKinnon) the ". . . serious failing in the chain of command all the way up to brigade and beyond" do seem fundamentally flawed, to say the least.

At risk of making quite a lot of new enemies, I put it to those who would prefer the mistreatment of these Iraqis and the death of Baha Mousa to have stayed hushed up, that they reflect on the ten years of near-limitless in-depth investigation, media prioritising, consequent mass public emotion and vast expenditure on every level that have been lavished, and continue to be lavished, on the tragic and premature – but presumably accidental – deaths in a Paris car-crash, on 31 August 1997, of Diana, Princess of Wales and Dodi al-Fayed. (I write this despite thereby winning also the enmity of Dodi's father. But then, as William Blake righteously riffed, *Mental* War is of the essence.)

Just about every premature death is a tragedy. But I put it to those who have belittled the ghastly fate of these ten Iraqis, that the slaughter of Baha Mousa, and the indignities heaped upon his comrades in Basra in September 2003, were *entirely wilful*, and deserve an at once more exacting and more compassionate kind and degree of (British) justice than they have been seen off by to date.

Like Diana, Baha was a parent. Ahmad al-Matairi told the September 2006 court martial that the last words he heard Baha Mousa shouting from the lavatory floor where he lay, slumped and asphyxiated by the concerted strains of Corporal Payne's Choir, were: "*My children will become orphans . . . my children, my children! . . . I am going to die . . .*"

May his soul rest in more peace than his body was granted by British soldiers. And may his widow and their two children fare better.

Page 130

"*Belsen Concentration Camp, 8 May 1945 . . .*"

My second-eldest brother, Leo Horovitz (1924-2003) was with the RAF in Germany at the end of World War II, and involuntarily witnessed the liberation of the Belsen death camp. Like so many who have experienced direct revelations of man's extreme inhumanities to man, he was traumatised by it for life. "Not a day passes" he would say, if anyone asked him about it, "when I do not remember the smell . . ."

Page 131

"*— Primo Levi*"

In 1942 Primo Levi was a 23 year-old industrial chemist working at a mine in the Italian Alps. Just when his 'fellow poet' Ezra Pound was thundering into the fullest flood of his anti-Semitic rants on Radio Rome (see the notes to *Page 161* and ff on pages 385-390), Levi was unable to go down to the town or even mingle with his fellow workers, because he was Jewish. In 1943, after going into hiding, he was captured as a partisan, and then as a Jew transported to Auschwitz.

On 10 January 1946 Levi wrote, in '*Shemà*':

> "*You who live secure*
> *In your warm houses,*
> *Who return at evening to find*
> *Hot food and friendly faces:*
>
>> *Consider whether this is a man,*
>> *Who labours in the mud*
>> *Who knows no peace*
>> *Who fights for a crust of bread*
>> *Who dies at a yes or a no.*
>> *Consider whether this is a woman,*
>> *Without hair or name*
>> *With no more strength to remember*
>> *Eyes empty and womb cold*
>> *As a frog in winter.*
>
> *Consider that this has been:*
> *I commend these words to you . . .*
> *. . . Repeat them to your children.*"

"*. . . Paul Celan's* 'Totenfuge' . . ."

— see the quotations from the late Michael Hamburger's translation of '*Totenfuge*' ranged to the right of pages 156-157, attributed in the note on page 383

"*. . . the* 'Shoah' *of Claude Lanzmann . . .*"

Lanzmann devoted twelve years of research and filming in Poland, Germany, Lithuania, Switzerland, France, Israel, America and elsewhere, to compiling his 565-minute history of the Shoah (modern Hebrew for '*catastrophe*').

The 'Shoah' film features testimonies and some re-enactments by ghetto and death camp victim-survivors, persecutors, 'administrators', workers and other observers.

It was released by Aleph/Historia in 1985 – as was the book of its script, by Librairie Arthème Fayard in Paris, and Pantheon Books in New York. In her preface, Simone de Beauvoir wrote –

". . . Neither fiction nor documentary, 'Shoah' succeeds in recreating the past with an amazing economy of means – places, voices, faces. The greatness of Claude Lanzmann's art is in making places speak, in reviving them through voices and, over and above words, conveying the unspeakable through people's expressions.

"Places. The Nazis' great concern was to obliterate all traces. But they could not wipe out all the memories, and Lanzmann has succeeded in ferreting out the horrible realities hidden beneath camouflage, like young forests and fresh grass. In ditches on that green field, trucks dumped bodies of Jews who had died of asphyxiation during the journey. Into that pretty little stream were thrown the ashes of incinerated corpses. Here are peaceful farms where Polish farmers could hear and even see what was happening in the camps . . ."

In the 'Time Out Film Guide' (Penguin 1991), Nigel Floyd wrote that

". . . . Lanzmann's meditation on the Holocaust is a distillation of 350 hours of interviews with living 'witnesses' to what happened at the extermination camps of Treblinka, Auschwitz, Sobibor, Chelmno and Belzec. Feeling that the familiar newsreel images have lost their power to shock, Lanzmann concentrates instead on the testimony of those survivors who are not 'reliving', but 'still living' what happened, and on 'the bureaucracy of death'. One of the two Jews to survive the murder of 400,000 men, women and children at the Chelmno death camp described his feelings on revisiting Poland for the first time. A train driver who ferried victims to the concentration camps is seen making that same journey to 'the end of the line' again and again; a retired Polish barber who cut the hair of those about to enter the gas chambers describes his former work; an SS officer talks about the 'processing' of those on their way to the concentration camps; a railway official discusses the difficulties associated with transporting so many Jews to their deaths. The same questions are repeated like an insistent refrain. The effect is relentless and cumulative."

Page 133

Humiliation of unidentified political prisoners at the hands of US Military in Guantánamo Bay, Cuba

The photograph was taken on 11 January 2002, one of the first days on which unidentified prisoners were blindfolded, handcuffed and foot-shackled into immobility by US military personnel in what had until then been known as Camp X-Ray, a prison area in the American naval base on Guantánamo Bay, Cuba.

The 750-plus all-male detainees from forty countries who have been held without trial or charge since January '02 in Camp Delta, as the hastily constructed concentration camp in Guantánamo was (re)named, were allegedly suspected of terrorist activities. On arrival at Camp Delta, the prisoners were told ". . . You are now *the property of the US Marine Corps*".

As the US refused to comply with international law, each of these men was denied his legal rights under the Geneva Convention. Whilst the US claimed that keeping them confined incommunicado in Guantánamo was an essential arm of the so-called War against Terror, it also irrationally insisted that the men were *not* prisoners of war. How Intelligent is that?

As long as the men never touched US soil, they were also automatically denied the rights guaranteed to criminals under the US Constitution, including the presumption of innocence until a trial by jury pronounces a guilty verdict.

Although Guantánamo Bay is a major American naval base, housing 3,000 military service members, civilians and their families, US courts do not consider it subject to US laws – or it seems, any laws – on the ground that the area has been leased to the US for $4,085 per year courtesy of a century-old treaty with Cuba.

The imperative for the Bush administration, as with the similar processes of prisoner abuse since 2001 in Afghanistan, Iraq, and various secret CIA 'renditions', was that those implementing the policies were kept well beyond the reach of any liability for war crimes.

Such are the democratic values and such is the religious civilisation which George Bush and Tony Blair have striven to set in stone – well worth the sacrifice, they decreed, of any number of lives, civilised and uncivilised, military and civilian alike.

In his Foreword to the paperback edition of *'Enemy Aliens: Double Standards and Constitutional Freedoms in the War on Terrorism'* (The New Press 2005), David Cole wrote that –

". . . After Abu Ghraib, the Guantánamo picture seems almost quaint – to borrow a term used by White House Counsel Alberto Gonzales in a memo to President Bush on 25 January 2002:

'In my judgement, this new [post-9/11] paradigm renders obsolete Geneva's strict limitations on questioning of enemy prisoners and renders quaint some of its provisions.'

"But there is a deep connection between that photo and the picture of the hooded and wired man standing on a box, perhaps the most well-known of the photographs of abuse and torture at Abu Ghraib prison *[reproduced on page 129]*. Once one denies the common dignity of one's fellow human beings, it is but a short path down the slippery slope to practices like torture.

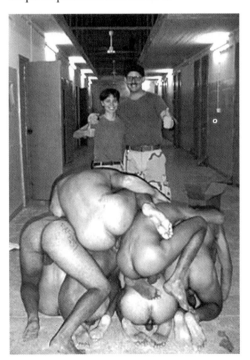

"At this point, it seems unlikely that anyone literally 'ordered' the worst of the sexual and other abuses visited upon Abu Ghraib prisoners. But if that is the case, Abu Ghraib shows that one need not *order* such treatment in order to *produce* it.

"The Bush administration has sought to dismiss the abuse as the work of a few renegade servicemen and women. The military has been slightly more forthright, attributing the abuse to a combination of factors, including the failure to train prison guards and to devote sufficient personnel to guarding the prisoners. But bad apples and omissions alone are unlikely to have produced such a widespread pattern of abuse – a pattern so accepted that one of the photos, of a group of naked prisoners piled on top of each other on a concrete floor in a sort of debased human pyramid, was used as a screen-saver on a computer in the US military intelligence office at Abu Ghraib prior to its disclosure to the outside world.

"Rather, what plainly seems to have brought on such abuse were directions from military leadership to 'set the conditions' for interrogation through such approved practices as sleep deprivation, nudity, exposure to extreme temperatures, and the use of dogs to induce fear. As one military investigation put it, 'what started as nakedness and humiliation, stress and physical training . . . carried over into sexual and physical assault'. The nakedness in particular, the investigation found, 'contribute[d] to an escalating "dehumanisation" of the detainees and set the stage for additional and more severe abuse'.

"When one begins to treat another human being as less than

PRICE $3.95   THE   2004
NEW YORKER

human, the norm of equal respect, so critical to restraining abuse, no longer serves its checking function. That should be the principal lesson of Abu Ghraib. Respect for the equal dignity of all persons must be a constraint on all anti-terror measures, precisely because there are such powerful temptations to disregard that mandate when confronted by fear.

"The details of the Bush administration's descent into torture are still being disclosed. New revelations are reported weekly. When historians look back, however, they will almost certainly identify the turning point as the evening of 28 April 2004, when CBS's '60 Minutes II' aired the first of the now-infamous photographs from Abu Ghraib prison graphically depicting the brutal torture, humiliation, and sexual abuse of Iraqi detainees by US military personnel.

"Those photographs, immediately disseminated round the world through the news media and the Internet, have become the iconic image of America's war on terrorism. It is an image – and a reality – that we cannot afford. It serves as ideal recruiting fodder for our enemies, and an obstacle to the cooperation we need if we are to protect ourselves from future acts of terror."

See the notes to *Page 129* on pp341-349, and also those about *'Terror in Abu Ghraib'* on pp441-442. Also: *'Voices from Guantánamo'* (pp1-2 & 30, Independent 6/3/2006); *'Should we fight terror with torture?'* by Harvard University Professor of Law Alan M Dershowitz (pp1-4, Independent Extra, 3/7/06); Dershowitz's *'Preemption: A Knife that Cuts Both Ways'* (Norton 2006); and *'Guantánamo is a US Torture Camp'* by Vikram Dodd (Khaleej Times Online, 18/1/2007).

And see also Moazzam Begg's *'Enemy Combatant: A British Muslim's Journey to Guantánamo and Back'* (The Free Press 2006). In February 2002 Moazzam was seized by the CIA in Islamabad and imprisoned by the US Military, first in their detention facility at Kandahar, then for a year in Bagram air base, and for another two years in Guantánamo Bay. He suffered much of this time in solitary confinement, and underwent more than 300 interrogations, as well as death threats, torture, and witnessing the murders of two other detainees. He was released early in 2005 without any explanation or apology.

The situation for the prisoners was of course – and remains in spring 2007 – *pace* David Cole above, far from *"quaint"*.

They have been held in small, mesh-sided cells for up to 24 hours a day. Lights are kept on day and night and there is no privacy. Inmates are allowed only 30 minutes of exercise on between three and seven days each week in the caged recreation yard (pictured on page 133) which measures a mere 9 metres by 7 metres. No visitors are allowed – and no photography excepting that officially ordained by the US authorities.

Each of the few prisoners who have been released to date, such as Moazzam Begg, has given profuse and vomit-inducing accounts of the merciless deprivations, bullyings, beatings, abuses and torture they and their fellow inmates were subjected to, frequently and without warning.

One might think that what little the outside world had discovered of what had gone on in both Abu Ghraib and Guantánamo should have been enough to enforce immediate and binding legislation against anything like it recurring. The more so in the name of trying to combat and overcome all conceptions and practices of terrorism around the globe.

Yet the continuing resort to torture by other US Military and so-called Intelligence, notably in many jails and transference locations manned by the CIA and the Pentagon, has been pretty irrefutably documented throughout the Noughties – but not, it seems, at all diminished by June 2007.

And this despite the screaming likelihood that any information or alleged "evidence" obtained during or after torture is, in the claws of that bestial means of elicitation, bound to be deeply suspect. There can be few human beings who would not blurt out whatever information they might gather is required by their torturers, rather than risk the immediate and savage disfigurement of their bodily or mental faculties, or indeed, of their lives.

On 13/10/2006, the BBC Radio 4 'Today' programme reported that

> ". . . US Marine Sergeant Heather Cerveney, who went to the [Guantánamo] base three weeks ago as a legal aide to a military lawyer, said in an affidavit that five navy guards described in detail how they beat up detainees. One sailor specifically said, 'I took the detainee by the head and smashed his head into the cell door'. . ."

Cerveney was appalled to observe and overhear this group of guards in the prison camp bar bragging and laughing about their recent brutal abuses of detainees, and vying with each other as to who had inflicted the worst damage.

On 13 September 2006 the UK's Lord Chancellor Charles Falconer called the Guantánamo concentration camp ". . . a shocking affront to the principles of democracy, a violation of the rule of law, and a recruiting agent for al-Qaeda" (quoted in a Guardian report by David Fickling). On the same day, the US's ex-four star general and secretary of state Colin Powell wrote to Republican Senator John McCain that ". . . The world is beginning to doubt the moral basis of our fight against terrorism".

See *'The inside story of Britain's shadowy role in the Guantánamo scandal'* by George B Mickum (pp1-3, Independent 16/3/06), and *'UK accused of Guantánamo collusion'* by David Batty (Guardian 18/9/06), who quoted Amnesty International UK's director Kate Allen:

". . . It's shameful that in four-and-a-half years the government has not insisted on independent medical examinations for long-term UK residents held in the black hole of Guantánamo . . . One of the detained, Omar Deghayes, is believed to have been blinded in one eye by guards at the camp."

See also *'Bush strikes a deal that lets him keep fighting dirty'* by David Rose (Observer 24/9/06), as well as Rose's detailed analysis in *'Guantánamo: America's War on Human Rights'* (Faber 2004).

Tony Blair, when asked in July 2003 what action could be taken on behalf of the UK residents held in Guantánamo, blandly replied: *"We have got very good information out of Guantánamo"*. However, on 22 November 2005 Blair told a House of Commons Commitee that *"Guantánamo Bay is an anomaly"*: not much of an admission, perhaps, until you remember it was made by Britain's major contender for the title of World Grandmaster of political anomaly finagling (– see pages 6-7, and the notes thereto on pages 242-247, for starters).

Leaving that to one side, it should be quite revealing to know in exactly what regards Mr Blair seriously thought that any information obtained from anyone subjected to any form of torture, was *"very good"*, on any level?

Terrorism is illegal warfare. Any opposition to terrorism which is not itself both legal and proportionate is bound to resemble – and in most cases, to swiftly become – yet another extension of the terrorism it sets up to overcome.

Acts of terror are often quite deliberate in targeting civilians and inflicting abuse, torture and premature death upon the terror victims. How on earth can such practices be overcome in the short term, or dispelled from the planet in futurity, by any form of counter-infliction of (illegal) terror, warfare, abuse, torture, or premature death upon any human being, however some such may be categorised as possible "enemy combatants"?

Moazzam Begg's *'Enemy Combatant'* recall of his terrible three years in US military captivity includes a photograph of the *"Entrance and check point leading to main cellblock in Camp Delta"*, Guantánamo. The billboard under the barbed wire fencing reads:

CAMP DELTA 1

MAXIMUM SECURITY

HONOR BOUND TO DEFEND FREEDOM

What honour or freedom has to do with it is a question anyone working at or accountable for the US's enterprise in Guantánamo needs to address. As John Milton wrote in *'Areopagitica'* (1644):

". . . Who ever knew Truth put to the worse, in a free and open encounter?"

In his Epilogue to *'Enemy Combatant'*, Moazzam reflects on some of the unanswered questions that loom in the wake of his experience of the presumed War on Terror:

". . . I have read Foreign Office letters to my father that maintain the Americans denied access to UK officials in Afghanistan, and yet I was interrogated by British Intelligence in these very places – places where people, in the same situation as me, were tortured to death.

"The sad fact is that they have acted duplicitously, immorally and unlawfully. It is not just their uncritical acceptance of and obedience to torturous conditions, régimes and physical restraint or worse. They were there by choice. These are the lessons of Nuremberg. You cannot simply be present in these circumstances and escape your own role. The definition of torture under the UN convention is the application of extreme mental or physical pressure by a state or an individual for the purpose of obtaining information. Any complicity in that, as well as direct application, is in breach of international law and is criminal by definition. The paradox is that whilst the government is unperturbed in using that information and depending upon it as reliable, it acknowledges too that information obtained through torture and duress is abhorrent to the British way of life.

"After 7 July 2005, Tony Blair said, 'We shall not allow the terrorists to change our way of life', but that is precisely what is happening. The knee-jerk approach to tackling terrorism pretends somehow that it is a new phenomenon in Britain because the war is an ideological one. The time allowed for detention without charge has already doubled to twenty-eight days, but Blair tried for ninety; plans for the closure of religious places (meaning mosques) deemed 'suspect' are in motion; new extradition agreements with countries that have torture as part of their unwritten convention, if not written constitution, have been signed; and, probably the most alarming of all: the accepted shoot-to-kill policy. I pray there are no more bombings, or our way of life will change again."

In 'CIA's Harsh Interrogation Techniques' on ABC News, 18/11/2005, Brian Ross and Richard Esposito itemised how the "Agency's tactics lead to questionable confessions":

". . . CIA sources described a list of six 'enhanced interrogation techniques' used, they said, on a dozen al-Qaeda targets incarcerated in isolation at secret locations on military bases in regions from Asia to Eastern Europe . . . including 'The Belly Slap'; 'Long Time Standing' (described as among 'the most effective' – prisoners are forced to stand, handcuffed and with their feet shackled to an eye bolt in the floor, for more than forty hours. Exhaustion and sleep deprivation are effective in yielding confessions); 'The Cold Cell' (the prisoner is left to stand naked in a cell kept near 50°, and is doused with cold water throughout the time in the cell); and 'Water Boarding' (the prisoner is bound to an inclined board, feet raised and head slightly below the feet. Cellophane is wrapped over the prisoner's face and water is poured over him. Unavoidably, the gag reflex kicks in and a terrifying fear of drowning leads to almost instant pleas to bring the treatment to a halt).

". . . 'The person believes they are being killed, and as such, it amounts to a mock execution, which is illegal', said John Sifton of Human Rights Watch. And the New York Times reported on 9/11/2005 that the techniques 'constitute cruel and degrading treatment under the [Geneva] Convention'. Former CIA officer Bob Baer added '. . . It is bad interrogation. You can get anyone to confess to anything if the torture's bad enough'."

– Not that such plain-spoken assessment and condemnation of these horrific practices seem to have had much effect on the likes of Dick Cheney, dubbed "Vice President for Torture" by the Washington Post. It was Cheney who led an aggressive campaign to grant legal amnesty to CIA personnel who had played any part in the interrogation of suspects at secret prisons, and who also lobbied hard to reduce US adherence to Geneva Convention bans on torture.

Suzanne Goldenberg reported ('Cheney condemned for backing water torture',Guardian 28/10/06) that Cheney told a conservative radio host who asked ". . . whether he was in favour of a 'dunk in the water' for detainees . . . that he was: 'It's a no-brainer for me' . . ." Meaning not, as most human beings with an ounce of compassion might suppose, a 'no-brainer' in that torture should be outlawed by every democratic, free and progressive state, but a 'no-brainer' in that US agents should be allowed to practice such sadistic cruelty, in ultra-secret locations, unmonitored and unobserved, and safely camouflaged under Cheney's hearty-sounding euphemism of *robust interrogation*. The Vice President's choices of phrase carried signal resonance (unintended, one would hope), considering the uses to which some of the informations elicited under torture have been put.

ABC News was told how the techniques had led to questionable testimonies aimed at achieving a cessation of the torture by satisfying the interrogators – and how directly some of the resulting misinformations had influenced the whole series of US-led bombings of and subsequent actions around Iraq:

"According to CIA sources, former al-Qaeda camp commander Ibn al Shakyh al-Libi, whom they had 'rendered' from Afghanistan to Cairo, made statements after two weeks of 'enhanced' interrogation that was designed to tell the interrogators what they wanted to hear. Sources say al-Libi had been subjected to each of the progressively harsher techniques in turn, and finally broke after being water boarded and then left to stand naked in his cold cell overnight, where he was doused with cold water at regular intervals.

"His statements became part of the basis for the Bush administration claims that Iraq trained al-Qaeda members to use biochemical weapons. *It was later established that al-Libi had no knowledge of such training or weapons and fabricated the statements because he was terrified of further harsh treatment.*"

– So utterly false testimony such as that yanked by a merciless application of the farthest extremes of torture imaginable fed the US's propagandising the notion that Iraqis trained al-Qaedans in the mechanics of biochemical warfare. And this in turn sexed up Dubbya's insistence that Iraq needed invading, with a view to purging al-Qaeda infiltration and the spreading of terrorism, violence, and ultra-pernicious weaponry around Iraq and the rest of the world. As of June 2007, Iraq and the rest of the world are seething with a daily and nightly increase of formal and informal al-Qaeda membership, with ever-spreading terror, violence and ultra-pernicious weaponry. Torture, though it only led to misinformations and worse torture all round, was the basic rule of the hideous game established at Guantánamo, and presumably ongoing via CIA and other renditions and agencies.

Britain is certainly among the countries which have turned wilfully blind eyes to its airports, including Prestwick and Luton, being used for refuelling by US planes on CIA prisoner-transference itineraries. Prestwick Airport was also used for US flights carrying weapons to be used in Israel's attack on Lebanon in summer 2006. And on 10 June 2007 pages 1 & 5 of the Mail on Sunday reported *Torture plane touches down at Suffolk airbase* (RAF Mildenhall).

Despite Margaret Beckett's admission, in a written response to a parliamentary question, that the UK Government was aware of a secret CIA prison network before Bush publicly admitted its existence in September 2006, Britain continued to drag its feet over the independent investigations into CIA renditions recommended to national parliaments by the European Union. Peter Walker reported (in *'EU states urged to investigate CIA rendition flights'*, Guardian 23/1/07) that the European Parliament's committee on CIA activities in Europe had condemned the "lack of cooperation" and "obstructive attitudes" of Austria, Italy, Poland, Portugal and the UK in response to its enquiries. The committee concluded that ". . . the serious lack of concrete answers to the questions raised by victims, NGOs, media and parliamentarians had only strengthened the validity of already well-documented allegations regarding secret prisons as well as would-be camouflaged flights".

The Guardian also revealed that ". . . In its [latest] 14/2/2007 Report, the European Parliament's committee on CIA activities in Europe said more than 1,200 CIA-operated flights had used European airspace between 2001 and 2005 . . ." – and that: ". . . Criticism of Britain for allegedly not cooperating with the Parliamentary investigation was removed from the Report at the insistence of Labour MEPs . . ." (*'EU countries ignored CIA terror suspect flights, Report says'*, 14/2/07). So much for freedom of information.

In the summer of 2006, the Council of Europe had published another detailed Report on collusions with CIA abductions and renditions on the part of European member states (*'Alleged secret detentions and unlawful inter-state transfers involving Council of Europe member states'*, Report of the Committee on Legal Affairs and Human Rights, 12 June 2006, Doc 10957). Based on first- and second-hand witness statements, the Report detailed the inhumane and degrading methods employed by American agents. According to its author Dick Marty, writing in the Explanatory Memorandum:

". . . No security measure justifies a massive and systematic violation of human rights and dignity. In the cases examined – whilst being conscious of dealing with possibly dangerous persons – the principle of proportionality was ignored, and with it the dignity of the person. In several instances, the actions undertaken in the course of a 'security check' were excessive in relation to security requirements, and may therefore constitute a violation of Article 3, ECHR [European Convention on Human Rights].

". . . Perhaps the most troubling aspect of this systematic practice, however, is that it appears to be *intended to humiliate*. Many accounts speak of these measures being taken despite 'strong resistance', both physical and verbal, on the part of the detainee. The nudity, forced shackling 'like an animal', and being forced to wear nappies, [are] offensive to the notions of dignity held by the detainees. It is simply not acceptable in Council of Europe member states for security services, whether European or foreign, to treat people in a manner that amounts to such 'extreme humiliation'.

". . . Personal accounts of this type of human rights abuse speak of utter demoralisation. The despair is greatest in cases where the abuse persists – where a person remains in secret detention, without knowing the basis on which he is being held, and where nobody apart from his captors knows about his exact whereabouts or wellbeing. The uncertainty that defines rendition and secret detention is torturous, both for those detained and those for whom they are 'disappeared'.

"Yet the ordeal continues long after a detainee is located, or even released and able to return home. Victims have described to us how they suffer from flashbacks and panic attacks, an inability to lead normal relationships, and a permanent fear of death. Families have been torn apart. On a personal level, deep psychological scars persist; and on a daily basis, stigma and suspicion seem to haunt anybody branded as 'suspect' in the 'war on terror'. Links with normal society appear practically impossible to restore.

"I salute the remarkable courage and resilience of those who have been held in secret detention and subsequently released, like Khaled el-Masri and Maher Arar. Both these men have spoken eloquently to us about what moves them to recount their experiences despite the obvious pain and trauma of doing so. From these words we must draw our own resolve to uncover the secret abuses of the 'spider's web' and ensure that they never again be allowed to occur."

The Report also included a number of "case studies" into the "unprecedented suffering" of those who underwent rendition, such as el-Masri, a German citizen of Lebanese descent who was, according to Marty, ". . . the victim of abduction and ill-treatment amounting to torture within the meaning given to it by the case-law of the United Nations Committee against Torture". He concluded that el-Masri's case "is the dramatic story of a person who is evidently innocent – or at least against whom not the slightest accusation could ever be made – who has been through a nightmare in the CIA's 'spider's web', merely because of a supposed friendship with a person suspected at some point in time of contacts with terrorist groups".

On 31 January 2007, the Associated Press reported that German prosecutors had issued arrest warrants for thirteen CIA agents who were suspected of kidnapping el-Masri three years before:

"Mr el-Masri says he was abducted in December 2003 at the Serbian-Macedonian border and flown by the CIA to a detention centre in Kabul, Afghanistan, where he was abused . . . He was released in Albania in May 2004 after the CIA discovered they had the wrong person."

Another individual singled out by Marty was Benyam Mohammed al-Habashi, an Ethiopian citizen and UK resident who was still incarcerated at Guantánamo Bay as of early June 2007. According to Mohamed's testimony, he underwent rendition from Pakistan to Morocco, where he was tortured in the most horrific manner. The Council of Europe Report quotes from his statement to his lawyer:

'. . . They came in and cuffed my hands behind my back. Then three men came in with black ski masks that only showed their eyes . . . One stood on each of my shoulders and the third punched me in the stomach. The first punch . . . turned everything inside me upside down. I felt I was going to vomit. I was meant to stand, but I was in so much pain I'd fall to my knees. They'd pull me back up and hit me again. They'd kick me in the thighs as I got up. They just beat me up that night . . . I collapsed and they left. I stayed on the ground for a long time before I lapsed into unconsciousness. My legs were dead. I could not move. I'd vomited and pissed on myself.'

". . . At its worst, the torture involved stripping Benyam naked and using a doctor's scalpel to make incisions all over his chest and other parts of his body:

'. . . One of them took my penis in his hand and began to make cuts. He did it once and they stood for a minute, watching my reaction. I was in agony, crying, trying desperately to suppress myself, but I was screaming. They must have done this twenty to thirty times, in maybe two hours. There was blood all over. They cut all over my private parts. One of them said it would be better just to cut it off, as I would only breed terrorists.'

". . . Eventually [– Council of Europe Report, point 207] Benyam began to cooperate in his interrogation sessions in an effort to prevent being tortured:

'. . . They said if you say this story as we read it, you will just go to court as a witness and all this torture will stop. I could not take any more . . . and I eventually repeated what they read out to me. They told me to say I was with bin Laden five or six times. Of course that was false. They continued with two or three interrogations a month. They weren't really interrogations – more like trainings, training me what to say' . . ."

The Report was adamant that the UK intelligence services colluded in this torture: ". . . During his illegal interrogations, [Benyam Mohammed al-Habashi] has been confronted with allegations that could only have arisen from intelligence provided by the United Kingdom".

The Report's damning conclusion was that the CIA's activities –

". . . carrying out several hundred flights and transporting illegally arrested persons without any scrutiny, can only point to the participation or collusion of several European services . . . even though . . . their methods were incompatible with national legal systems and European standards relating to respect for human rights.

". . . All of history shows that arbitrary decisions, contempt for human values, and torture have never been effective, have failed to resolve anything and, ultimately, have led only to a subsequent exacerbation of violence and brutality."

The cases of Benyam Mohammed, Bisher al-Rawi and Jamil el-Banna, all of whom were – or still are – imprisoned without charge at Guantánamo, were looked into by the All Party Parliamentary Group on Extraordinary Rendition. In an information session on 19 June 2006, Mohammed's lawyer, Clive Stafford-Smith, stated that his client

". . . was interrogated down in Morocco about various facts that could only have come from his former girlfriend here in London. And sure enough, his former girlfriend has been contacted by members of British security forces. He was confronted with stuff about his housing benefits here in Britain, and various other information that, again, wasn't coming from a Moroccan who made a few phone calls; that came from Britain."

This directly contradicts the Foreign Office's denial of responsibility, quoted in the Guardian of 6/8/2005 (Stephen Grey and Ian Cobain, *'Suspect's tale of travel and torture: Alleged bomb plotter claims two-and-a-half years of interrogation under US and UK supervision in "ghost prisons" abroad'*):

"Asked about the allegations, the Foreign Office said the UK 'unreservedly condemns the use of torture'. After consulting with the Home Office, MI5, and MI6, a spokesman said: 'The British Government, including the security and intelligence services, never uses torture for any purpose. Nor would HMG instigate or condone the use of torture by third parties' . . .''

The fact is that providing secret information to Morocco – criticised even by the US State Department for its human rights record – constitutes not only condoning, but *facilitating* torture.

As Dick Marty concluded: ". . . Since the purposes to which this information would be put were reasonably foreseeable, the provision of this information by the British Government amounts to complicity in Benyam's detention and ill treatment".

Mohammed's lawyer admits that his client spent time in a militant training camp in Afghanistan, and was picked up by the Pakistani authorities for trying to leave the country on a false passport. But if the West is to have any moral authority at all in the fight against terror, it can not conscionably use this sort of premise to justify such terrible abuse as Mohamed seems to have been subjected to – nor yet to support his indefinite detention without trial in the black hole of Guantánamo.

His fellow erstwhile British resident detainees, al-Rawi and el-Banna, appear to have been snatched on the basis of still flimsier intelligence cases against them. And although Bisher al-Rawi was eventually released from Guantánamo and returned to Britain on the 30th March 2007, his friend el-Banna remained incarcerated. Two months before al-Rawi's release, lawyer Brent Mickum had detailed the inhumane conditions of solitary confinement under which he was being kept (in *'Guantánamo's lost souls'*, Guardian 8th January 2007, *http://commentisfree.guardian.co.uk/brent_mickum/2007/01/post_885.html*):

"Bisher's world is a 6' x 8' cell in Camp V, where alleged 'non-compliant' prisoners are incarcerated. After five years and hundreds of interrogations, Bisher finally refused to be interrogated further. Despite the fact that Guantánamo officials have publicly proclaimed that prisoners are no longer required to participate in interrogations, Bisher is deemed non-compliant and tortured daily.

". . . While in isolation, Bisher has been constantly subjected to severe temperature extremes and other sensory torments, many of which are part of a sleep deprivation programme that never abates. Frequently, Bisher's cell is unbearably cold because the air conditioning is turned up to the maximum. Sometimes, his captors take his orange jumpsuit and sheet, leaving him only in his shorts. For a week at a time, Bisher constantly shivers and is unable to sleep because of the extreme cold. Once, when Bisher attempted to warm himself by covering himself with his prayer rug, one of the few 'comfort items' permitted to him, his guards removed it for 'misuse'. On other occasions, the heat is allowed to become so unbearable that breathing is difficult and laboured. For a week at a time, all Bisher can do is lie completely still, sweat pouring off his body during the day when the Cuban heat can reach 100° Fahrenheit, and the temperature inside Camp V is even higher.

". . . What the British government knows and the British public needs to know is that Bisher's treatment is designed to achieve a single objective: causing an individual to lose his psychological balance and, ultimately, his mind. Every aspect of Bisher's prison environment is controlled and manipulated to create constant mental instability."

Despite al-Rawi's release, Mickum's indictment remained deeply pertinent to the nine other British residents still held in Cuba, eight of them in solitary confinement, as well as countless other uncharged and untried prisoners. The lawyer also mentions "the calculated programme of cruelty" that ensures the censoring of any message of love from the family of al-Rawi's friend Jamil el-Banna:

"I have seen letters from Jamil's youngest children on my visits to Guantánamo, one-page letters that are heavily redacted by military censors. What is the offending language that the military has seen fit to redact? Language like 'Daddy, I love you' and 'Daddy, I miss you'. How do I know? Because on my instructions, Jamil's wife has saved copies of the letters her children sent . . . It is all part of a deliberate effort to weaken and destroy prisoners psychologically."

And yet, in the Guardian of 8/1/2007, Mickum pointed out that Britain –

". . . still refuses to demand the release of Jamil and [eight] other British residents. Neither [Mohammed nor el-Banna] will ever be charged; there is no evidence in the record I have received that can withstand even the slightest scrutiny. No court in the remotely civilised world would countenance convictions based on the evidence contained in [their] records. Moreover, Bisher's and Jamil's treatment has been so appalling, the Bush Administration would never allow it to be exposed to the world in a systematic fashion in open court. And, of course, some of that story directly implicates British officials."

Brent Mickum supports his claims with memoranda written by FBI agents at Guantánamo and released under the Freedom of Information Act. These "paint a grim and accurate picture" of the torture that the Bush Administration denies. He quotes from document #5053, dated August 2, 2004:

"As requested, here is a brief summary of what I observed at GTMO. On a couple of occasions, I entered interview rooms to find a detainee chained hand and foot in a fetal position on the floor, with no chair, food, or water. Most times they had urinated or defecated on themselves, and had been left there for 18 to 24 hours, or more. On one occasion, the air conditioning had been turned down so far and the temperature was so cold in the room, that the barefooted detainee was shaking with cold. When I asked the MPs what was going on, I was told that the interrogators from the day prior had ordered this treatment, and the detainee was not to be moved. On another occasion, the A/C had been turned off, making the temperature in the unventilated room well over 100°. The detainee was almost unconscious on the floor with a pile of hair next to him. He had apparently been literally pulling his own hair out throughout the night. On another occasion, not only was the temperature unbearably hot, but extremely loud rap music was being played in the room, and had been since the day before, with the detainee chained hand and foot in the fetal position on the floor."

On 16 November 2006, in a co-presentation I made with Moazzam Begg at London's Everyman Cinema Club, he surprised most people there by speaking of Guantánamo as in one sense –

" . . . the best of detention sites in the world, because it's the place you hear about, because it has access to the media. What you don't hear about are the ghost prisoners euphemistically known as 'extraordinary rendition'.

"We are talking about 14,000 people taken all around the world, some of those in Iraq but not exclusively so. It's akin to the people disappeared during the military junta in Argentina . . ." (– reported by Haroon Siddique in the Hampstead & Highgate Express, 23/11/06).

In '*Missing presumed tortured*' (New Statesman 20/11/06, pp12-15), Stephen Grey, the author of '*Ghost Plane: the inside story of the CIA's secret rendition programme*' (C Hurst & Co, 2006), retailed a litany of still more desolating revelations:

"On 6 September 2006, President Bush finally confirmed the existence of secret CIA jails. He added something chilling – a declaration that there were now '*no terrorists in the CIA programme*' . . . a statement which hinted . . . that the US has 'disappeared' prisoners to an uncertain fate.

"In the first years after the attacks of 9/11, thousands of Taliban or suspected terrorist suspects were captured. Just in Afghanistan, the US admitted processing more than 6,000 prisoners. Pakistan has said it handed over around 500 captives to the US; Iran said it sent 1,000 across the border to Afghanistan. Of all these, some were released and just over 700 ended up in Guantánamo. The simple act of subtraction shows that thousands are missing. More than five years after 9/11, where are they all?

"We know that many were rendered to foreign jails, both by the CIA and directly by the US military. But how many precisely? No audit of the fate of all these souls has ever been published.

". . . In early 2002, when the camp at Guantánamo Bay was opening up, I heard from a source close to the CIA that most of the media were missing the point. As cameras showed images of chained prisoners being wheeled across the base on trolleys, there was predictable outrage. But beyond Cuba was a concealed network of prisons around the globe that were becoming home to thousands more prisoners. The CIA had its own secret facilities, but many more were held in jails run by foreign allies.

". . . Why is it so sensitive to confirm what happened to these prisoners, to detail how many were transferred where and when? Why should a country receiving prisoners be so embarrassed? And why – when countries such as Egypt have come clean and said 'Yes, we received 70 to 80 prisoners rendered by the United States'– will the US itself not confirm what it did? Despite admitting, in general, that the CIA carries out renditions, *the US has yet to own up to a single specific case of transferring a prisoner to foreign custody*.

"The explanation for the secrecy is one that most of the CIA officers involved in rendition will quite freely admit – a transfer to places such as Egypt or Uzbekistan (a country known for boiling prisoners alive) will inevitably involve torture. And knowingly sending a prisoner to face torture is, under both US and international law, an illegal act. Revealing the fate of the missing prisoners may be just too politically embarrassing."

Stephen Grey summarises what he has been able to ascertain regarding the devastatingly cruel treatment of some of those "disappeared", including the case of Ibn-al Shaykh al-Libi already touched on in the report from ABC News by Messrs Ross and Esposito on pages 356-357 above:

". . . It was while he was under Egyptian interrogation that *al-Libi provided an important piece of 'testimony': that Saddam Hussein had an operational relationship with al-Qaeda*. It was an erroneous claim, since formally withdrawn by the CIA, *but was used as part of the justification for the war in Iraq*. Al-Libi's anonymous testimony was cited by Colin Powell before the United Nations. But no one mentioned where the intelligence came from.

"After his interrogation in Egypt, al-Libi was sent back to US custody in Afghanistan. But now he has disappeared. Perhaps he has been sent to Libya? He is certainly a more important prisoner than the vast majority at Guantánamo. Yet sending al-Libi to the Cuban camp, putting him on public trial and allowing him to tell his story, would be a political disaster. So he remains hidden.

"While the secrecy [around such disappearances] may protect the US from legal jeopardy . . . it also makes the threat of torture self-fulfilling. If you send a prisoner to Damascus, Tripoli or Tashkent, how can you hope to protect that prisoner – to ensure a fair trial or see that he stays alive – if you keep that rendition quiet? Secrecy protects the torturer; and it denies those innocent, those wrongly accused of crimes of terrorism and caught up in these renditions, any chance of justice.

"Last month Bush signed into law his new Military Commissions Act, which provides for the trial at Guantánamo of top al-Qaeda leaders. The act grants fewer rights to defendants than the Nazis got at Nuremberg. And yet, in this strange world, the rights now granted to men such as Khalid Sheikh Mohammed, the man who devised the 9/11 attack and who will now be brought to trial, still rank higher than the rights of the small fry, those much less significant players behind bars in foreign jails. In this new justice, the big terrorists are granted privileges, and the other missing prisoners, subtracted from the public record, are disappeared off the face of the earth. That's the mathematics of torture."

On 10 March 2007 the Pentagon proudly announced the first military trial of fourteen Guantánamo detainees, including Khalid Sheikh Mohammed, but, as Andrew Buncombe reported for the Independent on 14/2/07, these allegedly ". . . 'high-value' detainees were being examined by military lawyers . . . in private session, with the media and the men's lawyers excluded". Will anyone ever know to what extent any and all evidence, statements and 'confessions' used at these trials are the badly damaged fruits of torture?

The Pentagon later released an alleged transcript of Mohammed's tribunal, in which he laid claim to a raft of atrocities, including masterminding 9/11 and plotting thirty-one other bombings, successful or otherwise, beheading the journalist Daniel Pearl, and even planning to assassinate Jimmy Carter, Clinton and the Pope. But as long as the trials are held in closed session, without the normal rights of legal representation, it is difficult to see how such "confessions", at least partially derived from torture, can be afforded much – or any – credence.

Mohammed had been widely reported as conspicuous among detainees who had undergone waterboarding and other vile and illegal techniques of extortion at secret CIA jails. He was also neon-lit among those whose so-called *"robust interrogation"* had been championed by Vice *(sic)* President Cheney: ". . . Our ability to interrogate high-value detainees like Khalid Sheikh Mohammed [has] been a very important tool that we've had, to be able to secure the nation".

Amongst many international protesters against this, Tom Malinowski of Human Rights Watch was not just being cute when he turned Cheney's bold avowal on its befuddled (though – or perhaps because – patriotic), er, head: ". . . So, if Iran or Syria detained an American, the Vice President is saying that it would be perfectly fine for them to hold that American's head under water until he nearly drowns, if that's what they think they need to do to save Iranian or Syrian lives . . ."

Let us hope a comprehensively fresh uptake on all this was heralded on 29 March 2007 when the new and seemingly more answerable Defence Secretary Robert Gates said that Congress should find ways to close Guantánamo prison, and move the trials to the US, ". . . because no matter how transparent or open the trials, if they took place in Guantánamo, they would *lack credibility in the international community . . . because they have been tainted by the harsh treatment of detainees*".

However, the most recent documentations I have found suggest that this harsh treatment was only getting worse for the approximately 385 men still held in Guantánamo in early April 2007. An Amnesty International report, *'Cruel and Inhuman: Conditions of isolation for detainees at Guantánamo Bay'* (published 5 April 2007, AI Index: AMR 51/051/2007), estimated that about 80% of detainees were then held in solitary confinement.

This included those held in Camp 6, a new prison block which opened in December 2006, and which according to Amnesty ". . . has created even harsher and apparently more permanent conditions of extreme isolation and sensory deprivation".

Camp 6 has been described by the US authorities as "more comfortable" for its inmates. The fact is that prisoners are confined for at least 22 hours a day in individual steel cells with no outside windows and only a narrow strip of glass looking into an internal corridor. Detainees are utterly cut off from human contact, with even their guards only pushing meals through a slot in the door. There is no natural light or air, no communication without recourse to shouting under the door, which only leads to punishment. Even the mesh cages of Camp 1 allowed inmates air, light and the ability to communicate.

This "tightening of security" that has seen so many inmates languishing in solitary was reported to have been caused by the apparent suicide in June 2006 of three detainees – which some of the US military authorities saw fit to laugh off as "a publicity stunt".

Given the known effects of prolonged and extreme isolation on the human psyche, these measures are in effect nothing less than the tightening of a noose – of mental misery, insanity and suicidal tendencies – around the necks of those detained there. Suzanne Goldenberg reported (*'Guantánamo inmates in mass strike over new solitary cells'*, Guardian 10 April 2007) that the conditions of Camp 6 had caused thirteen inmates to go on hunger strike in protest. Since December 2006, these prisoners were being force-fed twice a day with plastic tubes inserted through their noses.

At Easter 2007, the ordeal of fifteen Royal Navy Marines and sailors ambushed, and then arrested, off the Iraqi coast by Iranian Revolutionary Guards on 23 March '07, had climaxed with their release and flight back to Britain on 5 April, after thirteen days of detention in Teheran.

On the following day, six of the navy personnel told how they had been blindfolded, handcuffed and kept in individual solitary confinements in cells measuring 8' x 6', interrogated night after night, and subjected to extreme "psychological pressures". They were paraded on Iranian Television, having been conditioned to 'confess' that they had culpably strayed into Iranian waters.

The question inevitably arose as to where else of late had similar mistreatments been described, photographed and filmed – shackling, hooding, isolation in minuscule cages, being pressurised to admit to guilts in response to coercive, threatful and potentially or actively violent captors?

– Where, but at the hands of the US Military in Guantánamo Bay, in Abu Ghraib prison, and via (CIA) renditions, and also – inflicted by Brits, as well – in Basra, and elsewhere in Iraq?

Admittedly, in none of these places or situations were prisoners displayed on television – though of course their nearest and dearest might have been happier if they had been – at least to be able to identify them and know that they were still alive. Admittedly also, none of the British sailors and Royal Marines seem to have suffered serious extremes of physical abuse or torture. – But several of them did grimly recall that they were made to fear that such extremes might just ensue at any point over the thirteen days and nights.

The UK media, especially the tabloid press, were vitriolic in their contempt for the Iranians' behaviour. Should we not rather be glad that all these Brits were set free without grievous bodily harm, and that none of them had to endure something worse than a few days' *intimations* of the diabolical horrors documented heretofore?

These presumably continued, all over the planet – and could still be continuing, even after the time of your reflecting on this, gentle reader. The Iranians – both in their volubly deplored (and disputed) aspiration to join the world nuclear weapons élite, and in this Royal Navy group internment (so mercifully ended without loss of life) – were in fact pursuing trails repeatedly blazed over the last sixty years and more by the USA, which has been so strident and threatful in opposing the Iranians' possibly comparable aspirations.

On 9 June 2007 pages 1 & 4 of the Daily Mail exposed the fact of *'TORTURE PRISONS: BRITAIN'S SHAME'*. See also *www.cageprisoners.com* – the human rights website which, as of 14 May 2007, displayed no less than twenty-four pages of entries under *"Renditions"*.

These range from *'Torture Flights: The Inside Story'* ("They could be walking the streets of Sweden, Italy, Albania, Indonesia or Pakistan. They are kidnapped in broad daylight, hooded, drugged, shackled and placed on a jet operated by the CIA. When they wake, they find themselves in countries such as Morocco, Egypt, Uzbekhistan or the others where torture is the currency of the interrogation room . . ." – Neil MacKay, The Sunday Herald, 16/10/2005) – to *'Outsourced Guantánamo: FBI and CIA Interrogating Detainees in Secret Ethiopian Jails'* ("The CIA and FBI agents have been interrogating hundreds of detainees at secret prisons in Ethiopia. Many of the prisoners were recently transferred there secretly and illegally from Kenya and Somalia. They are being held without charge or access to counsel . . ." – Anthony Mitchell, John Sifton and Jonathan Hafetz interviewed by Juan Gonzales and Amy Goodman in Democracy Now, 6/4/2007).

Not so much the War *on* Terror then, as the War *of* Terror.

Page 134

"the Christ / who whipped the money-changers / out of the Temple . . . . . . and pronounced them Thieves . . ."
– cf St Matthew 21, 12-13 (in the King James version):

> "And said unto them, *'It is written, My house shall be . . . the house of prayer; but ye have made it a den of thieves' . . ."*

Again, in John 2, 15-16:

> "And when he had made a scourge of small cords, he drove them all out of the temple . . . and poured out the changers' money, and overthrew the tables;
>
> > "And said unto them that sold . . . *'Take these things hence; make not my Father's house an house of merchandise' . . ."*

See also Mark 11, 15-18 and Luke 19, 45-46, for slightly variant accounts. Each of them, like Matthew, recalls Christ quoting the injunction from Isaiah 56, 7.

"*Once elected,/ the New Labour government/ immediately cut a further/ three million pounds/ from the public/ subsidies for arts . . .*"

Four years on, John Tusa asked (in The Times of 12 May 2001, p22):

". . . Can the Government's direct responsibility for the expensive banalities of the Dome or the fiasco of Cool Britannia be offset against the triumphs of Tate Modern, the British Museum or the Lowry Centre, all of which properly belong to the institutions and the people that delivered them?

"The Prime Minister says that the arts have now been incorporated into his political 'core script', but has anyone noticed the new conviction in his rhetoric about the arts?"

– The answer to both questions remained, as evidenced by every subsequent (p)re-election pretension and priority, an entirely predictable (and perhaps hence, in many quarters, barely audible) "*No*".

Another three-and-a-half years on, the Guardian of 14 December 2004's two lead stories concerned a "*Secret £1bn deal to insure Saudi arms contract*" (front page, by David Leigh and Rob Evans), and '*Arts funding freeze sparks fury*' (pp1 and 2, by Charlotte Higgins and Maeve Kennedy).

This issue of the Guardian also featured Higgins's account of how as from that winter, '*English arts bodies face[d] "devastating" £30m subsidy cut*' on p4, plus on the same page Kennedy's exposition of the '*Bleak future for heritage*' – and also, across the lower half of the same page, a symposium of disenchanted reactions and comments from Tusa, Michael Berkeley, Michael Boyd, Nicholas Hytner, Michael Grandage and Sam West.

Page 21's Leader comment, '*The Beggar's Opera*', consisted of an overall excoriation of the Treasury, and of the Department for Culture, Media & Sport, for the previous day's announcement which spelled the end of even the most modest increases in arts funding:

". . . Arts organisations were braced for a tough few years following the last spending review, but the decision to tilt the flow of funds so strongly from one sector (arts) to another (museums) goes against the grain. All arts and culture organisations ask for one thing: not bottomless pockets but reliable funding. Sudden sharp changes in who gets funds and who does not sets off a sea-sawing of resources.

"To make matters worse, culture secretary Tessa Jowell's comment that this settlement '. . . sits alongside expected income to the Heritage Lottery Fund' adds a worrying suggestion that *lottery funding has become a government proxy*.

"The real shame is that *the total arts budget is so small and its influence so vital. A Treasury which recognised real value for money would not dream of cutting it . . .*"

On the facing page (20) of this same 14/12/04 Guardian, stood Richard Norton-Taylor's exposé of how '*Britain is conniving in torture*'.

Six months before this litany of grim tidings was released, another Guardian investigation by David Leigh and Rob Evans had revealed ". . . corruption on a massive scale by Britain's biggest arms firm, BAe Systems" ('*Arms firm's £60m slush fund*', front and second page, 4 May 2004). The investigation reported payments totalling more than £60m to prominent Saudis, and –

". . . Most explosively, the documents detail £17m in benefits and cash paid by BAe, which is chaired by Sir Dick Evans, to the key Saudi politician in charge of British arms purchases, Prince Turki bin Nasser . . . BAe is trying to secure another £1.5bn of arms deals from the Saudi régime, following the sale of planes, missiles and warships worth £50bn to them over the past 15 years."

In December 2005, the Department for Culture *(sic)*, Media and Sport froze funding for three years, amounting to a ruthless cut of thirty million pounds. On 20 May 2006 Martin Kettle analysed, again in the Guardian, how *'The gulf between the arts and New Labour is growing wider'*.

How very sad that all this promotion of corrosive arms manufacture, trading and sleaze, and simultaneous derisory downscaling of support for the arts, has been supervised over ten years of government by a Prime Minister who has prated incessantly throughout each of these years of his *". . . passionate commitment to the values of civilisation"*.

". . . it automatically continued/ . . . to sponsor . . . lethal weapons/ . . . from the earnings/ of each British taxpayer/ – to the tune of/ . . . two hundred million/ pounds each year . . ."

The May 2004 report of the Report of the Campaign Against Arms Trade estimated the overall figure for the various forms of subsidy given by the government to the arms export industry to be around 890 million pounds per year.

In his 2001 Campaign Against Arms Trade Lecture, *'Subsidising A Deadly Trade'* (delivered at the London School of Economics on 9 April 2001, and published on the CAAT website *www.caat.org.uk* (search 'publications' and click on 'economics'), Sir Samuel Brittan pointed out that –

> ". . . The official estimate for British arms sales is that they amounted in 1999 to about four billion pounds per annum, or appreciably less than half a percent of the national income. A good academic estimate of the cost of government support has been £200m per annum. But *indirect support* for what is known as the 'Defence Industrial Base' *is many times larger.*
>
> Far and away the most important direct support comes from the Export Credit Guarantee Department (ECGD) which insures and finances export of capital goods. A former senior treasury official has publicly said that this department is too vulnerable to intensive lobbying by large corporations through their ministerial contacts . . ."

The ECGD effectively provides a subsidy when it agrees to guarantee a deal. This means that even when the buyer does not pay, the arms manufacturer gets paid – by the taxpayer. ECGD does recover some of its bad debts – but often only years later.

Sir Samuel had spelled out most of this, and more, in sharply revealing detail the year before, in *'Why arms sales are bad for Britain'* (New Statesman, 31/1/2000 pp 8-9, and on his website: *www.samuelbrittan.co.uk*) –

> "In a telling Times cartoon, a buoyant Tony Blair was shown exclaiming: *'PEOPLE WANT A HAWK'* (meaning a more determined military effort) in East Timor. On the side he was shown piloting one of the Hawk aircraft that the UK had been delivering to Indonesia for many years for the use of the country's military dictator, General Suharto.
>
> "The official defence was that these aircraft were supplied under a contract approved by

the previous Conservative government. This begins to wear thin when the same excuse is given for the resumption of deliveries of Hawk fighter spare parts for the government of Zimbabwe, after a brief suspension during the fighting in the Congo, in which Zimbabwe was heavily involved.

". . . So does an ethical foreign policy have to take second place to hard commercial realities? Do we have to accept the argument that, though many of these arms deals are undesirable, jobs depend on them and that if Britain did not promote them, other countries would take the orders instead?

". . . We should be on our guard when politicians defend dubious policies by declaring 'Jobs are at stake'.

"This is so whether it is an 'Old Labour' supporter wanting to promote manufacturing, a Tory spokesman talking about the employment provided by hunting, a 'New Labour' minister [Jack Straw, then Home Secretary] allowing Mike Tyson into the country because 'jobs are involved', or a business lobbyist pushing for arms sales to dubious régimes.

". . . It is often just those people who lecture us on the need for workers to change jobs, and who say that full employment cannot mean the same employment, who are most keen to promote the sale of arms.

"Such arguments are based on the myth that there is a lump of labour that is engaged in making specific products. Then, it is supposed, if orders or output are lost in one area they cannot be regained anywhere else. But people change jobs constantly. Well over three million people leave the unemployment register each year even in recession periods, over half of them for new jobs or training.

"Indeed, it is almost certainly easier for arms workers, many of whom have a wide range of valued skills, to find new jobs than it was for miners, whose training was far more specific.

". . . Arms sales do not represent, even in the narrowest economic terms, the best use of national resources. *They are so heavily supported by the taxpayer that there might actually be a gain in moving the workers, plant and technical skills to other activities that could pay for themselves.*

". . . Moreover, the ECGD provides 'packages for exporters of goods and services and political risk insurance' – in other words, taxpayer support for sales that would not pass muster on purely commercial terms.

". . . The damage inflicted by official arms promotion goes beyond the harmful potential of the arms themselves. Many other undesirable policies are rationalised in terms of the need to keep arms purchasers sweet. How else can one explain the extreme sensivitity in official quarters to any criticism of Saudi Arabia, and the pressure put on the BBC over *'The Death of a Princess'? . . .*"

Furthermore, as Elizabeth Young pointed out in the New Statesman two weeks later (*'Expect some new wars to prop up the arms industry'*) –

"The spreading consequences of the dispersion (the sale and resale) and the use of the arms require valuation. Remember the Stingers that the United States provided the anti-Russian Afghan 'freedom fighters', which continue appearing.

"Then what of the cost to the British taxpayer as a result of having to clear up the political, social, environmental and economic mess that follows the use of such weapons? What effect does the violence they fortify have on regional or general stability, and does that strengthen or weaken our diplomacy?

". . . Wall Street, rather than the Administration's understanding of the 'national interest', is now the arbiter of American weapons policy; and because the arms industry is one of those that (as they put it) 'educate' the Senate, American defence policy is being determined by Wall Street. Hence the desire for a national missile defence system, the costs of which to the taxpayer would be endless, but which would fund the industry for ever; and with the collapse of the Anti-Ballistic Missile Treaty, there is the possibility of other, ever more profitable arms races.

"We can certainly expect many more of the 'wars' that are so convenient in propping up demand for the industry's products. There seems to be no political justification, after nearly ten years, for the weekly (sometimes daily) Anglo-American strikes against targets in Iraq, other than using up expensive weapons that have to be replaced.

"Now that the precautionary principle has won the day in Seattle over the World Trade Organisation's free-trade mantra, let us also adopt it in relation to the arms industry and arms trade."

Seven years later still (autumn 2006), Tim Street of Campaign Against Arms Trade told me:

". . . CAAT estimates that UK arms exports receive a subsidy of around £890m per year. Given the 65,000 employees estimated to be working on military exports, the subsidy amounts to *over £13,000 for each job each year.*"

There are many other kinds of support for the arms industry, from attachés in UK embassies abroad overtly or covertly marketing UK arms, to tax concessions in areas short of work, etc, etc, ad nauseam.

One example of creepy support is the Defence Export Services Organisation (DESO). This began life as the Defence Sales Organisation in 1966, charged with ensuring that the government-owned arms companies did not lose sales to the USSR and France. Since the privatisation of the arms industry, this deadly marketing and PR department has continued to use public employees and taxpayers' money – 500 civil servants at a cost of £16.9m in 2004-'05 – to lobby on behalf of arms companies both at home and abroad.

These five hundred pen-and-sword pushers are headed by an executive on secondment from an arms company, as of early 2007 Alan Garwood of MBDA (part-owned by BAe Systems). One of his roles is to advise ministers on arms exports. With this kind of insider access to and from the heart of government, is it any surprise that outrageous ministerial decisions over arms and war have for decades now been offending the British public and provoking widespread misgivings, to say the least, regarding the consequent worldwide losses of limbs and lives, on top of such flagrant misuse of their hard-earned tax contributions?

The amorality of flogging arms to such euphemistically classified "emerging markets" as human wrongs-prone Iraq, Libya et al, was staggering enough. But DESO is also astronomically over-funded compared to its civilian counterparts. According to CAAT, ". . . relative to its share of total UK exports (which is less than 2%), DESO receives thirteen times the budget of the government organisation UK Trade and Investment, which promotes civil exports". (For more details about this, and further devastating expositions of blatantly unethical – yet state-authorised – arms, torture and war profiteering, together with details of how to join the campaign to shut down DESO, see CAAT's website: *www.caat.org.uk/campaigns/calltheshots*).

Why in heaven's name does Britain (to adapt one of Commander-in-Chief Blair's favourite, if exceedingly ill-worn, Prime Ministry Clarion Calls) have to go on trying to *"Lead the world"* on down such an irrevocably and infinitely murderous course?

One answer lies in the insidious programmes of socio-economic 'Modernisation' which have ruthlessly torn up community roots and egalitarian traditions. Witness the way Blair & Co have methodically dismantled the hitherto profoundly human and practical Royal Mail and Post Office networks, the National Health Service, dentistry, legal aid, national and local transport systems, free university education, support for the arts, etc, etc, whilst quietly widening the gaps between rich and poor, and simultaneously escalating the far less profitable and definitively inhuman arms and war industries.

These latter pseudo-Churchillian, jingoistic, hawkish and inhumane power projections have provided distracting cover for the unpleasant American Dream designs wished on the UK public, first by Thatcher and then by Blair and Brown, so that the merely mega-capitalist processes driving their so-called modernisations could be the more smoothly and thoroughly imposed.

The USA's concerns under Reagan, the Bushes and Clinton have conditioned their leading UK counterparts' voracious aspirations to comparable levels of national wealth and economic growth. And these preoccupations with economic supremacy have, paradoxically, kept both America and Britain heavily dependent on foreign investment. A major rationale for investment in the US is the fact that it constitutes a unified market with massive buying power.

A less obvious but increasingly telling reason for foreign investment is that prime players (such as China, Saudi Arabia, the Arab Sheikdoms, Malaysia and Taiwan) have an additional motive for putting money into the US economy: the urge to offset a potential threat.

If there were no such threat, however, this motive would vanish. American military might and the White House's seemingly incorrigible eagerness to go to war are essential preconditions of foreign investment, and hence of the US's economic success.

Apart from weaponry, American goods can not compete internationally, as is demonstrated by the US's continuously negative balance of trade. Without its commitment to arms and war proliferation, the American economy would decline dramatically.

High time then for the USA to open up and become a genuinely collaborative, non-coercive part and parcel of the United States of the Planet.

High time for all the governments and populations of the world, and not least the USA, to downscale all arms stockpilings, productions, activities and negotiations. Something on these lines could, given comprehensive global commitment, enable axes of nothing but good to develop.

As soon as this our (could-be) whole planet recognises the necessity of giving up on short-term nationalistic and military gains, in favour of concerted opposition to our mutual long-term enemies – global terror and global warming – internecine chess moves and tit-for-tat trampolines of violence would be cast aside.

Unless this alternative process can be set into fail-safe motion very soon, there is little likelihood that the worldwide human race will be capable of engineering a trustworthy basis for multilateral health, equitable sharing of the earth's rich resources, or peaceful survival in the foreseeable future.

"Round here it's upside-down . . . . / Cities scrap their peace accords and fight / And the murderous war-god ravens everywhere . . ."

– Virgil, *'Georgics I'* (30 BC), lines 505 to 511, translated by Harry Eyres.

Cf Eyres's praise of Virgil (on page 24 of the Daily Telegraph, 25 May 1999) as *'. . . a writer whose verse can be read as an elegy . . . for the Balkans war'*:

> ". . . there is no doubt that the whole spirit of the *'Georgics'* is deeply pacific . . . in deprecating war, and more widely in its passionate invocation of the laws that govern the planting of crops, the tending of animals, and the relationship between man and nature.
>
> "I feel Virgil, a shy and surely gentle man who spoke of the 'madness of the forum', was at the very least a temperamental pacifist . . .
>
> "Tears seem to flow on every page of the *'Aeneid'*. Driven by storms on to the shore of Carthage, Aeneas finds himself at the site of a new temple, on whose walls artists are depicting scenes of the Trojan war. The fact of art's bearing witness to barbarism leads him to utter (weeping the while, of course) the most famous line in the epic, perhaps even in Latin: *'Sunt lacrimae rerum, et mentem mortalia tangunt'*. It means something like this: 'Everything that happens does not go unwept: the fates of mortals touch the heart' . . ."

Page 143

". . . *The Poets light but Lamps*" and ff

– written by Emily Dickinson *c.* 1864

". . . all the Megabuck-spinning/ . . . at astral soft-soap admin level// . . . mass brainwash that launders / . . . and cleans up mass profits/ from murder and pollution"

Evidence John Kerry's reply on the 16/2/07 Radio 4 Today programme, when asked for *". . . a few thoughts about the censorship from the White House of scientists trying to talk about climate change . . . You told a Senate Committee recently that what's been happening in the White House was virtually criminal"*:

> *". . . We have a flat-earth caucus here in the United States Senate, [but] no scientific analysis that is peer-reviewed to legitimise that position. The White House has outright censored scientific reports. They kept our scientists from talking publicly. They have eliminated words like 'global warming', 'global climate change' from reports. It's been George Orwell's worst fears . . . a kind of Orwellian response to reality. When you do that, when you deny the truth to people, and you're sworn to uphold the constitution of the United States and represent our rights, and when you change reports to alter something that's true, that's unacceptable behaviour by any standard."*

". . . brainwash that bleaches/ ('. . . purer than pure'?) . . . // . . . the big lies of/ ('whiter than white'!)"

Tony Blair's first government came to power vowing to sweep sleaze out of British politics, but on 30 January 1998 Sarah Neville of Reuters cited an interview with that day's Yorkshire Post in which Blair tried to whitewash the "stifling of debate and . . . . gagging orders under which candidates seeking election in corruption-hit Doncaster and Hull are expected to refrain from public criticism of the party". The PM claimed that –

> *". . . The point is that we have had disciplinary problems in those two places. This is part of making sure we're whiter than white on this and we end up with a situation where people aren't bringing the party into disrepute in any shape or form at all . . ."*

This was an early indication of what became Blair's habitual weakness for blurring distinctions between blatantly evident nepotism, cronyism or corruption, and his administration's increasingly obsessive concern to suppress the possible exposure of any trace of wrong-doing in New Labour's supposedly squeaky-serried ranks.

Our Padre was mouthing a similarly (b)lathering resolution after the scandal regarding cash-for-access to Ministers via lobbyists broke five months later. The front page of the Times for 8 July 1998 quoted Blair's claim, in the teeth of revelations of access-fixing published in the previous Sunday's Observer (5/7/98), that –

> *". . . We have to be very careful that we are purer than pure, that people understand that we will not have any truck with anything that is improper."*

To adapt the Bard: methought the lad he did protest too much.

And the more so in view of the manifest impurities and improprieties that thickened the plots in and around New Labour over the subsequent months and years.

A few examples were cited by Peter Oborne on page 12 of the Spectator on 4 March 2006:

> *". . . In 1998, Downing Street announced that Sir Richard Wilson, then the Cabinet Secretary, had carried out an investigation into Peter Mandelson's infamous home loan. It suited Tony Blair politically to make this claim. But Wilson, who was on holiday with his family in Center Parcs, had done nothing of the sort.*

"Three years later, and Blair was at it again. Downing Street put it about that Sir Richard had sounded the death knell for Peter Mandelson, causing his second resignation as a result of the Hinduja passports affair. In fact Sir Richard had been on Mandelson's side. In this case moral cowardice, rather than political convenience, seems to have been the motivation. Tony Blair had made the decision to cut down Mandelson, and wanted to blame someone else.

". . . This time Gus O'Donnell is not just investigating David Mills and Tessa Jowell. He has been carrying out a premature post-mortem on the Blair government. What started out with the hope, the freshness, the pledge to be purer than pure has ended up in offshore tax havens, obscure hedge funds and allegations of corruption.

". . . The Prime Minister has always claimed to care for ordinary people . . . but he only really feels at home with the deracinated super-rich, and the Mills affair is a reminder of that.

"Three mortgages may come to define the Blair government. First we had Peter Mandelson's failure to declare his loan from Geoffrey Robinson in his dealings with the Britannia Building Society. Now we have the mysterious circumstances surrounding Tessa Jowell's North London home. Most curious of all is the mortgage, thought to amount to £2.5 million, on Tony and Cherie Blair's home in Connaught Square. How the Blairs raised that money, and pay the interest, has yet to be explained."

See also Peter Oborne's detailed account and deconstruction of 'The Rise of Political Lying' (Free Press 2005).

". . . suspect food . . ."

– cf T S Eliot, 'The Love Song of J. Alfred Prufrock' (1917):

". . . Do I dare to eat a peach?"

". . . to be cleared/ of fears and suspicions/ by publicly funded/ 'researches' controlled by// 'Corporate Welfare' commissions . . ."

Thus, for example, a report commissioned by the makers of Philip Morris and Marlboro (who control 80% of the tobacco market in the Czech Republic) to examine the overall cost of smoking in that country, pronounced that government profits from nicotine amounted to £104 million a year (Melanie McDonagh in the Sunday Times, 22 July 2001, page 17).

The report was exposed to Daily Telegraph readers (on 18 July '01, page 9) by Washington correspondent Ben Fenton, under the heading: 'Smoking deaths "can help your economy". . .' It based its deductions on the then considered predictable statistic that habitual smokers will die, on average, some five years sooner than their non-smoking contemporaries.

The ginormous savings, quoth the Philip Morris report, ". . . derived from not having dead smokers using up public services such as health care, hospital beds, old people's homes and pensions . . ."

Well thanks a bunch, Big Phil – and good night. As Pete Brown wrote, in 'Advertisement', 1960:

"Unhappy?
When you're dead
You'll grin all day."

And as the proverbial Robert Browning might have written, in 'Philip M Passes', 2001:

> Lungs in their oven —
> All's right with the worms.

Page 145

"Is THIS the most dangerous puppet in Britain?"

Tony Blair had sedulously sucked up to Rupert Murdoch's tabloid flagship, The Sun, since the outset of his mission. But the mutual suck-in wavered in June 1998 after Blair expressed sympathy for a European single currency. The paper ran a front page photo of the PM alongside the banner headline: *"Is THIS the most dangerous man in Britain?"*

Soon after the King of Spin had been so grievously outspun, the spun one was busy issuing a series of less enthusiastic soundbites than before on the subject of the single currency . . .

"It felt a lot closer . . . / to the 'fascist régime' / the Sex Pistols fired at . . ."

This suggestion, like the oft-mooted association of Alastair Campbell's propaganda methods with those of Joseph Goebbels, may seem an exaggeration. Some of the more extreme analogies of New Labour with the Nazi régime drawn by Stephen Bayley in *'Labour Camp: The Failure of Style over Substance'* (Batsford 1998), may also seem unwarranted.

But it has become more and more apparent that a kind of thought police enforcing 'on-message' views onto MPs, has certainly sought — and managed — to control public (dis)information and Parliamentary decisions (including lamentably inhumane resolutions regarding warfare and arms, health and the environment, education and the arts) since Blair's administration took office.

The controls might look casual or cautious, compared to those exacted by the blatantly vicious dicatorships of Hitler and Stalin, Saddam and Mugabe. However, in its insistence on unwavering conformity from every functionary who wanted to stay in favour, Blair plc was not all that far removed from those totalitarian impositions of (self-)censorship and 'party lines'. Witness, for example, the note on page 280 quoting Lynn Barber on Harriet Harman's admission of having ". . . *to know 'the line'. If you don't know the line, you are not allowed to speak . . .*"

Most free thinkers would surely endorse most of the points made in the course of Stephen Bayley's reflections on his six months as creative consultant to the Dome at Greenwich (despite the self-approbation and score-settling in which some of this book indulges). For instance, in June 1997, his first encounter with Peter Mandelson took place

> ". . . when Mandelson, pager attached and retinue in place, came to address the staff of the Millennium. He said something like 'I believe in art, design and excellence . . . *However,* I am a politician'. I chirrupped up something like 'So this means there are occasions when you don't believe in art, design and excellence'. People say it took minutes for the chill to leave the room."

'Labour Camp' was rebuked for the alleged anti-Semitism of Bayley's dubbing of the then Millennium-Meister *"Professor Mandelstein"*. It seems from the contexts of this nicknaming that the connotation was rather with *Franken*stein, as the projected Millennium Experience — for Bayley anyway — got increasingly monopolised by Mandy's increasingly monstrous caprices.

A surely unintended but faintly Jewish echo the 'Mandelstein' coinage suggests to me is of the marvellous musical boy Mendelssohn — a name redolent of the purity of artistic, intellectual and moral virtue to which precious little, if anything, in the Dome's conception or (dread buzzword) delivery has aspired.

Bayley's critiques of the new government's "siege camp mentality", and his citations from Helmut Lehmann-Haupt's *'Art Under A Dictatorship'* (OUP, 1954) – as that ". . . *authoritarian régimes of whatever colour tend to invest in bad art of a similar style*" – remain persuasive.

One exposure of the vulnerable nerves touched by Bayley's incisions came in the form of a spluttering and yes, audibly authoritarian dismissal of *'Labour Camp'* by Gerald Kaufman in *'The apotheosis of fatuity'* (Torygraph Arts & Books, 10/10/98), which shrugged off the book's merciless mockery of the Millennium Dome as an assault on ". . . *that facile target*" which added nothing to widely received opinions.

As Kaufman was the long-standing Chair of the Commons' so-called Select Committee on Culture and Media, it was he who actually had the – er, facility, to dismiss the said target itself. Instead, the Culture Ministry proved vastly material in empowering its realisation, and in keeping it open for all of twelve months, although the door takings over each of those months proved increasingly inadequate to recouping even the tiniest fraction of its costs. – Or did Kaufman mean that Bayley should have known all along that facileness is the name of New Labour's game *vis-à-vis* culture?

'Labour Camp' has it that

". . . as a solution which existed before the problem was properly stated, the Millennium Dome perfectly represents a culture where almost everything is sacrificed on the altar of presentation. The Millennium Experience is pure *kitsch*, one expression of a philistine government interested in a glib quest for easy solutions dressed in powerful symbolism. Another expression of the same intellectual and artistic deficiencies is a pusillanimous dependence on opinion research and on focus groups. These are not so much the articles of faith of our civilisation, as its articles of superstition. You cannot impose an architectural solution (on a Millennium or anything else) until you fully understand the problem."

As I see it, a major problem at Nillennium is that our rulers articulate so little appreciation or encouragement of the authentic creative achievement and potential that abounds around the UK today, albeit unsung by politicians.

Mandelson complained at the outset of his plugging the Dome that some Britons who were carping about it ". . . *lack a sense of greatness*: I think it's pathetic . . ." – and suggested that the Dome would put the Great back into Britain. The claim was transparently empty, considering it was made at a point when nothing had been mooted to be put into the Dome to achieve this dubious purpose. – Or did Mandy Mouse mean that it was the Dome's Emptiness which would of itself help those who *believed* in it to achieve that *"sense of greatness"*? The Emperor's Clothes, 2000 – re-running the Everly Brothers' *'Bye Bye Love'*, with its plangent, resonant – and, well, sort of great – cry of recognition: *"Hello Emptiness"* – ?

Come 2007, the song about the Greenwich Dome remains: *"What's Pathetic Now?"*

The contents that did transpire amounted, for most observers and visitors, to greatness of one kind only: a monstrously monumental waste of time, money, energies and resources. If only an understanding of genuine artistry – as conveyed by the joyous lilt of Felix Mendelssohn's music for *'A Midsummer Night's Dream'* for example, or by the potently potable punch of contemporary world music and performance poetry – had got a look-in, there might have been *some* less moronic future in that would-be Cool Britannia's nightmare.

As Bayley remarked,

". . . Whenever entire countries have attempted to invent or reinvent national identity, the results have tended to be sinister . . . That pseudo-events are so influential in public life is an inevitable consequence of a civilisation and a government obsessed with the media. Pseudo-events are complementary to the arcane but well-publicised practice of spin-doctoring. Each treats news as something to be invented and managed, not reported and analysed. Nowadays, when a politician speaks off the cuff, it causes alarm and surprise. There has been no opportunity for spin! It may be a real event, not an imagined one!"

Greatness at whipping up a biggest ever (albeit short-lived) spinning top with mammoth (albeit quickly splurged) monopoly dough is one thing – pathetic or brill, depending on your standpoint.

A genuine renaissance, such as the restoration-in-progress of living poetry to the global community, is quite another – the more truly great because the work force gets on with the job of its own volition, not because anyone is sponsoring, publicising, promoting, selling or – in a word – artificialising it.

"It made you a moron / – a potential H-Bomb . . . // . . . There is no future / in England's dream"

– from the alternative *'God Save The Queen'* by John Lydon and Glen Matlock (Virgin 1977), as is:

"We are the flowers inside the dustbin . . ."

Page 146

"Such a wow with your women . . ."

Hypocrisies developed from the outset, both inside and outside government, in attitudes to the record number of women MPs in the first New Labour administration. Whilst many Labour and feminist folk wanted to flash this as a victory for equal rights and the Women's Movement, media attention tended to focus on the women's appearance; on their dress sense (largely prescribed by party headquarters for electability and popularity); and on how niftily they juggled family commitments in tandem with their political careers.

Most middle-market media, presumably in cahoots with Blairite Spin Surgeons, sought to rebrand women's liberation 'Girl Power', in deference to the phenomenally successful marketing of five well-packaged Thatcher wannabes in tight costumes.

On the other hand (as reported in *'Artful MP attacks New Labour Stepford Wives'*, The Times 7/2/98, p18), the (then) Labour veteran Brian Sedgemore rounded on

". . . those female New Labour MPs who've had the chip inserted into their brain to keep them on-message, and who collectively put down women and children in the vote on lone parent benefits. Few have shown any interest in culture. I hesitate to say it, but a new Parliament replete with cultural inadequacies is no better than the old Parliament replete with artistic testosterone morons."

Tess Kingham, elected Labour MP for Gloucester in 1997, was one woman who certainly tried to engage with the ultra-manipulative Whip system and the oafish public-school-debating-club infra diggery-pokery of the Parliamentary Chamber. But she stood down from probable re-election in 2001, infuriated by such reactionary time-wasting rituals. In *'Cheesed off by willy-jousters in a pointless Parliament'* (Guardian 20 June 2001, p16), she spelled out some of her reasons:

"I am convinced that it is not a lack of women at the top that has turned off women voters – it is our outdated, polarised party political system, and a discredited House of Commons. Women are disillusioned: they see MPs indulging in yah-boo nonsense, point-scoring and silly games that have no relevance to their daily lives.

"After being elected in 1997 I relished the prospect of being at the centre of political debate with the opportunity for detailed scrutiny of legislation. What I got instead was days and nights watching opposition MPs endlessly thrusting their groins around the Chamber in mock combat with Labour ministers – achieving absolutely nothing. Among the glorious repertoire were tactics such as talking nonsense for hours, throwing out months of work on MPs' important private bills by simply shouting out 'Object', and spending inordinate time debating how long we should be debating. What a waste of effort and what an insult to our voters and taxpayers. One woman aptly named this 'historic' tradition of opposition 'willy-jousting'.

"I hoped the Labour women of the 1997 intake could change the system. I remember standing on the steps of Church House after the election victory for that ill-fated 'Blair Babes' photo and thinking: 'We'll show them!' This was never a realistic aspiration: there are still very few women MPs, less than 18% of parliamentary seats. According to the Inter-Parliamentary Union, Britain has 33 countries ahead of her in female representation. One would expect to see the Scandinavian countries in front, yet we also fall behind Monaco (22%), Laos (21%), Argentina (26%) and Croatia (20%).

". . . Most of the women who want reform, like myself, are quite capable of holding down demanding jobs and bringing up families. It is not that we cannot cope. It is simply that we believe parliament is *out of touch with the people, increasingly irrelevant to women's lives. The general election turnout seems to have made our point.*

"Tony Blair is content to see parliament wither because it increases the power of the executive and delivers an apathetic electorate, less able to challenge his authority."

What a wasted opportunity on the part of Blair's inflexible régime, preferring its women to remain bosses' babes, under men's thumbs, reinforcing the Leader's macho warfaring drift.

The Equal Opportunities Commission's 2007 analysis of women in politics reported no change after yet another six years of likewise daily male parliamentary predominance, with still only eighteen per cent females in Parliament, and the UK still at No. 33 in the world for women's representation in government.

". . . *three loud boos for the hype and schmooze . . .*"

— see pages 39-47, and Joan Smith's observations on pages 279-280, inter alia

Page 148

". . . *from Bambi deer* / / *to Bombardier Extraordinaire . . .*"

— see the note to *Page 186* on pages 418-419

Page 150

"*Bomb-blagging SuperStag . . .*"

— cf two definitions in the *'Concise Oxford English Dictionary'* (eleventh edition, ed Catherine Soanes and Angus Stevenson, 2004) —

"*blag*: an act of using clever talk or lying to obtain something.

". . . *stag*: a fully adult male deer; an adult male turkey; *chiefly N. Amer*: a man who attends a social gathering unaccompanied by a female partner; *Brit. Stock Exchange*: a person who applies for shares in a new issue with a view to selling at once for a profit . . ."

'BUDDIES'

Nicholas Garland's cartoon strip reveals how Britain's much-vaunted Special Relationship with the US was drawn on in a number of mutual cuddle-ups by the Bill'n'Tony tap-dance team.

Drawn on — and tainted by? — For example: committed socialists and anti-nuclear campaigners were not the only groups to be outraged when the Prime Minister decided to stay stumm over his deal with Clint the Bull to send weapons-grade nuclear fuel from the ex-Soviet Republic of Georgia to the Dounreay reprocessing plant in Scotland.

Page 152

"*Third Way's pop-tosh muzak . . . // . . . led nowhere clear/ save — awash with dosh/ — to get itself/ re-elected my dear . . .*"

Saint Anthony's most Divine Mission thus far, His official release (on the afternoon of VE Day, Tuesday 8 May 2001) of the first Election Date of the new millennium, was beamed live from a Southwark girls' school with the unctuously Double-Sainted name of St Saviour's and St Olave's.

This Annunciation bade fair to out-parody not only the wickedly exaggerated caricatures of His Reverend Do-Right style regularly aired on TV by the likes of Rory Bremner and Harry Enfield, but even the ludicrously sanctimonious Vicar in Private Eye's fortnightly *'Saint Albion Parish News'* columns (see page 381 below).

Playing for all He was worth the laddish Centre Forward-Captain and genial People's Guvnor, with a floodlit cross and a stained glass window behind him, Saint Tone shamelessly co-opted support from both Jesus Christ and multiculturalism – flanked on both sides by a supposedly adoring choir of mixed-race pupils, which cued him in with a mellifluous Hymn To The Future. Some of the girls, to their credit, were unable to avoid looking suitably embarrassed at having been corralled into this photo-call for the youngest-yet clutch of Blair's babes.

The most cringe-making moment, of many the shirt-sleeved Messiah lingered over in His sickly 20-minute spiel, was its grovelling peroration for "*. . . a fresh mandate for radical change*".

What on earth did He think the voters of exactly four years earlier had overwhelmingly elected Him in to do (for a term of five years, not four)? If Blair *had* fulfilled that mandate, He would not have been reduced to appealing for it again.

The Saviour's Sermon claimed that ". . . I stand before you today with *a sense of humility . . . .* because we know we still have so much to do".

The humble, honest and honourable course would have been to serve the full five years for which He was elected, and to achieve that much more of what He said He knew still needed doing *before* going to the country again.

In that case the electorate (– most of which had voted Labour in 1997 on the understanding that "*so much . . . . radical change*" would already have been implemented by summer 2001) would hardly have needed prompting, hectoring or spin to be persuaded to cheer Blair on to continue its implementing.

With his St Saviour's pose, the PM cut a figure closer to that of an insecure spoiled brat forever seeking reassurance, than that of a socially committed pastor whose popularly approved reforming actions had earned Him His right to mass allegiance.

Our would-be New Saviour further muddied His pitch for a Second Coming by prating that ". . . We are not yet *the leading nation in Europe* that our weight, prosperity and history demand".

Why do they demand it? *Who* – apart from King Tony – says that they demand it? Surely the "radical change" will be to play our equal part in the co-operative community of Europe, *as opposed to* competing for its leadership.

This aspiration to be "*the leading nation*" smacks of the banal values lampooned in Sellar and Yeatman's '*1066 and All That*' (Methuen & Co, 1930), with its justly lambasted battle of the would-be Big Shots to be "*Top Nation*".

It is this very aspiration which was, alas, pursued by both Hitler and Stalin – and has continued to preoccupy a lamentable gaggle of their latter-day heirs.

How can anyone in his or her right mind believe that harking back to the ghastly languages, ambitions, demagogy, materialistic arrogance and power assumptions of the British Empire, the Third Reich or the Soviet Union, is anything but the *reverse* of "*radical change*" for a better future?

Simon Hoggart (on the front and second pages of the Guardian, 9 May 2001) pointed out that –

> ". . . the Prime Minister had told us all that he was going into the campaign 'humble and hungry'. Fat chance. He'd already had lunch and as for the humble, well, he looked pretty pleased with himself.

"He walked in, just missing an estate agent's board on a shuttered shop: 'Principles: For Rent' . . .

"The sound of hushed singing wafted up from the choir. Only New Labour would start an election in the middle of a Madonna video . . .

"By the time he plunged into his address to the voters he'd lost his audience, who were whispering to each other, staring glumly at the floor, or fast asleep. It didn't matter. They were only the stage props. The whole event stank of spin doctors' sweat."

Or, as the Incumbent Vicar himself reported it in Private Eye's 'St Albion Parish News' on 18 May 2001 (Eye #1028, p18):

". . . It was in a spirit of real humility that last week I decided to take over our St Albion's Girls School for the day to brief the children and selected members of the local media on what a great job we at St Albion's have been doing!

"The reason why Mr Campbell and I had chosen our local school as the best place to put over our message was not an accident.

"After all, these children 'are the most important people in the parish' (apart from our local journalists, of course!).

"As I told them (with the flashbulbs of the St Albion Observer going off in my face!), 'You are the future – and so am I!'

"And that was a message they really appreciated! As one young girl said to me, 'We're so glad you came today, Vicar, because if you hadn't we'd have had to be doing double maths'.

"I was very moved by this, and by the girls' reaction to my whole speech. The way they sat there with their eyes closed, while I told them about public-private partnerships and our long term investment programme, showed how hard they were all concentrating!

"And at the end they were all completely silent (until Mr Campbell reminded them that they should show their appreciation by clapping!).

"We all then stood up and sang a new chorus which Mr Campbell had chosen for the occasion from the BBC's new song book 'Hymns Modern and Modern', and I accompanied it on my Stratocaster just to make the kids feel it was relevant to them in a very real way!

"I also took my jacket off, which might have been a bit much for the headmistress, but just because I'm a vicar, it doesn't mean to say I'm not cool, and the kids went wild!

"Anyway, here are the words of that hymn and I hope we will be hearing a lot more of it in the weeks to come:

'We are the voters of the future,
We are the children of today,
We are the leaders of tomorrow,
We're travelling the third way.'

(Repeat)

Yours (with a big X!)

Tony – "

Page 155

"*. . . indelible ache/ of* 'Black and Blue' *. . .*"

– this song is quoted from on page 183

"*Southern trees bear a strange fruit, / Blood on the leaves and blood at the root . . .*"

– opening lines of the searing ballad about lynching by Abel Meeropol, a white Jewish schoolteacher and communist sympathiser from the Bronx, who published it under the pen-name of Lewis Allan.

From 1939, when she first performed and recorded the poem, it swiftly became – and remains to this day – the unforgettable signature song of Billie Holiday.

In '*The Heart of a Woman*', Maya Angelou described Holiday singing '*Strange Fruit*' to her young son Guy, during a visit to Los Angeles in 1958 (one year before the singer's premature death):

". . . Billie talked and sang in a hoarse, dry tone the well-known protest song. Her rasping voice and phrasing enchanted me. I saw the black bodies hanging from the Southern trees. I saw the lynch victims' blood glide from the leaves down the trunks and on to the roots.

Guy interrupted: 'How can there be blood at the root?' I made a hard face and warned him, 'Shut up, Guy, just listen'. Billie had continued under the interruption, her voice vibrating over harsh edges.

She painted a picture of a lovely land, pastoral and bucolic, then added eyes bulged and mouths twisted, onto the Southern landscape.

Guy broke into her song. 'What's a pastoral scene, Miss Holiday?' Billie looked up slowly and studied Guy for a second. Her face became cruel, and when she spoke her voice was scornful. 'It means when the crackers are killing the niggers. It means that when they take a little nigger like you and snatch off his nuts and shove them down his goddam throat. That's what it means'.

The thrust of the rage repelled Guy and stunned me.

Billie continued, 'That's what they do. That's a goddam pastoral scene' . . ."

David Margolick's *'Strange Fruit: Billie Holiday, Café Society and an Early Cry for Civil Rights'* (Running Press, USA 2000, and Payback Press/Canongate, Scotland 2001) includes the New York nightclub MC's account of Holiday's mother objecting when Billie began singing *'Strange Fruit'*: ". . . *Why was she doing it?*" "Because it could make things better", Billie replied. "But you'll be dead", her mother insisted. "Yeah, but I'll feel it", Holiday said. *"I'll know it in my grave . . ."*

Page 156-157

> *"A man lives in the house*
> *he plays with the serpents . . . .*
>
> *. . . . your golden hair Margarete*
> *your ashen hair Shulamith*
> *he plays with the serpents . . ."*

All the italicised lines ranged to the right of these pages are from Michael Hamburger's translation of *'Totenfuge'* (*'Death Fugue'*) by Paul Celan (in *'Poems of Paul Celan'*, Anvil Press Poetry 1988).

Page 156

"– *murderous jihads* . . ."

– i e, the self-styled 'holy wars' of certain Islamic fundamentalists and fanatics against unbelievers, as distinct from (and often extremely opposed to) *'greater* jihad' meaning the inner spiritual struggle against sin or evil

". . . routinely inflicted/ more often than not/ with some version/ of God on call"

– cf Bob Dylan's *'With God On Our Side'*:

> *". . . The cavalry charged*
> *The Indians died*
> *Oh the country was young*
> *With God on its side.*
>
> *". . . now we got weapons*
> *Of the chemical dust*
> *If fire them we're forced to*
> *Then fire them we must*
> *One push of the button*
> *And a shot the world wide*
> *And you never ask questions*
> *When God's on your side."*

See also *'With God On Their Side: How Christian Fundamentalists Trampled Science, Policy and Democracy in George W Bush's White House'* by Esther Kaplan (The New Press 2004).

– Cf *'They Sit In Darkness'* by Adam Horovitz:

> *"They sit in darkness*
> *waiting their turn.*
> *As they say goodbye*
> *the whip drives them forward.*
>
> *Squat cubicle*
> *riddled with holes:*
> *'What is this Isaac?'*
> *'I'm not sure'.*
>
> 'Horovitz, Feist, those families forward'
>
> *as the gas seeps through*
> *and they panic, screaming*
> *to the overtures of Wagner:*
>
> *And*
> *they die,*
> *hundred*
> *by hundred . . .*
>
> *And the world sits in darkness*
>
> *and it is too late."*

("Feist" was my mother's – Adam's grandmother's – maiden name.)

"*. . . . The age demanded . . . .*"

– opening couplet of Section II of '*E P Ode pour l'Election de son Sepulcre*', from '*Hugh Selwyn Mauberley*' (1919-1920). This is the sequence in which Pound "*strove to resuscitate the dead art / Of poetry; to maintain 'the sublime' . . .* "

The last quatrain of this section recapitulates the theme:

> "*The 'age demanded' chiefly a mould in plaster,*
> *Made with no loss of time,*
> *A prose kinema, not, not assuredly, alabaster*
> *Or the 'sculpture' of rhyme.*"

Unhappily, both Pound and Eliot – in their endorsement, promulgation and embellishments of the anti-Semitism, Fascism, racism and misogyny prevalent across much of Europe between the two World Wars – did provide images of that era's "*accelerated grimace*" (see the quotation from Lyndall Gordon's '*T S Eliot: An Imperfect Life*' on page 387).

"*. . . the crazed purist / – vile ranter – Ezra Pound . . .*"

With "*purist*" I'm thinking of the perfect pitch of Pound's lyric syllables, the purity of his commitment to poetry, and of his critical *usefulness*: the passionate championship of particular artists and writers and civilisations, and the wide-ranging erudition worn so lightly in primers like '*ABC of Reading*' (1934), '*Guide to Kulchur*' (1938 and 1952), and in his concise, muscular essays.

In '*Everyone who was Anybody*' by Janet Hobhouse (1975), Gertrude Stein is quoted rather sarcastically branding Pound ". . . A village explainer, excellent if you were a village, but if you were not, not . . ."

However, intellectual communication in the West has often resembled the ways cultures develop in villages, as witness the continuing open universities of New York's Greenwich Village and the Latin Quarter of Paris. Furthermore, the potential foreseen by 'alternative society' pathfinders like Marshall McLuhan, for remaking the whole earth into a global village, is a plugged-in fact of life today (– for all that the insights and effects of its current governing explainers and ordainers may seem to leave almost infinite room for improvement).

The connections and insights to be garnered from Pound's best writings remain indispensable. Ernest Hemingway's assessment is at least as salutary as Stein's:

> ". . . Ezra was right half the time, and *when he was wrong, he was so wrong you were never in any doubt about it . . .*" (New Republic, 11 November 1936).

But when he was bad, Pound was not just very bad.

In his stomach-turning broadcasts of Fascist propaganda in support of Mussolini's social programme (including support of censorship) over Rome Radio during World War II, and in the virulent 'kike'-baiting rants even brought to the fore of his increasingly deformed (but less truly "free") verse, he was as foul-mouthed as the most vicious of Hitler's gangsters.

To be driven mad by a perception of humankind being drained of all integrity by power networks of usury, as Pound seems to have been, makes a sort of sense. There was a semblance of method, as well as apparently limitless malignancy, in his madness. But the objective historical fact remains that, although Jews have often dealt in moneylending with interest, usury was not a Jewish invention or monopoly, but a means of survival traditionally foisted on them by others.

In 'The Voice of Pound' (PN Review No. 138, for March-April 2001), Elaine Feinstein shows how Pound "actively contributed to the climate of opinion in which the Holocaust was allowed to happen":

> ". . . Though the Cantos begin in a dream of Odysseus, their obsession is history. The first world war had been caused, as Pound saw it, by the conflict of rival capitalist structures, and like many another man who had lost valued friends in the trenches, he had no wish to see another war. By the time he had begun to put his faith in the Social Credit theory of Major Douglas, however, his main wish was to take power away from the bankers, and by 1930 those he singles out are usually Jews.

> ". . . During the war, Pound broadcast at least 120 original editorial manifestos from Radio Rome from 1941 to 1943. It is worth pointing out that no one asked Pound to make any such broadcasts.

> "What he said, he said from conviction and not under constraint; and his convictions are Hitlerian rather than Italian Fascist. On 15 March 1942, in a broadcast aimed primarily at Britain, he said: 'You let in the Jew and the Jew rotted your empire . . . And the big Jew has rotted every nation he has wormed into . . .'

> "Pound saves his most vehement denunciations for 'a dirty bit of meat by the name of Gollancz' and Rothschild, Warburg, Schiff and Sief . . ."

"What relevance then", asks Feinstein, "can Pound have for the young poet writing now? Even the lovely canto which opens, 'With Usura hath no man a house of good stone' has to be questioned, since few of us would own any house without the power to borrow money against the purchase. Yet he was right about the threat to art posed by the commercial world. The quality of art diminishes when it becomes something that exists only to buy and sell. In a free market, it is easy enough to see that" –

> '. . . no picture is made to endure nor to live with
> but it is made to sell and sell quickly.'

In October 1967, at his home in Sant' Ambrogio, near Rapallo, the 81-year-old exile broke a reputed virtual silence of many years in an interview with Allen Ginsberg. In the course of this Pound volunteered, better late than never, that –

> ". . . At seventy I realised that instead of being a lunatic, I was a moron . . . The intention was bad, that's the trouble. Anything I've done has been an accident. Any good has been spoiled by my intentions. The preoccupation with irrelevant and stupid things . . . But the worst mistake I made was the stupid suburban prejudice of anti-Semitism. All along, that spoiled everything . . .

> "I should have been able to do better . . ."

(– Quoted in 'Ginsberg: A Biography' by Barry Miles, Viking, 1989.)

Eliot's anti-Semitism was less crazed, voluminous and blood-curdling than Pound's, but what little of it has survived on paper is just as banal and disgusting.

For Eliot, so compelling and so intensively (self-)proclaimed an ambassador for civilisation, to indulge in poisonous racialist stereotyping – and *to keep it in print over two decades after the Nazi death camps* – has called into question, for many, the whole mission of this influential authority on (twentieth century) culture.

Thus, in '*T S Eliot: An Imperfect Life*' (Vintage Books, 1998), Lyndall Gordon noted that

". . . Eliot once owned to a 'suspicious' and 'cowardly' disposition driven by a hidden force. In suspicious and worried times, it relieved him to hit out at common targets. It is often suggested that his anti-Semitism is too much a commonplace of the time to merit particular notice, but, as Anthony Julius points out (in '*T S Eliot, Anti-Semitism and Literary Form*', Cambridge U P, 1995), it was not inevitable in his milieu: Joyce, E M Forster, Middleton Murry and Aldous Huxley all countered it in different ways. It is also suggested that Eliot is at his most brilliant when he incited prejudice. On the contrary, I find Eliot banal in his caricature of the profiteering Jew as 'Money in furs' (conveniently forgetting that his own Blood forebears had dealt in beaver hats); banal in his snigger at upstart names of his own invention – 'Lady Kleinwurm', 'Lady Katzegg'; and banal yet again when he plants the Jew beneath the rats of a decayed Venice. Eliot saw himself above his age, looking beyond it as a prophet. In the hatred he incites for a Chicago 'Semite' from Vienna, forcing on us the 'protozoic slime' of Bleistein's 'lustreless protrusive eye', Eliot himself falls into the savagery of the age he affects to abhor . . .

"Exposés of Eliot are sharpened by his supremacy as moral arbiter, but we can't forget his vision of perfection. Hatred is common; perfection rare. In him, the two were interfused . . .

"What those who attack Eliot for anti-Semitism tend to overlook is what often goes with it: misogyny . . ."

Thus also, around 1950, Emanuel Litvinoff wrote, from a personally intimidated standpoint:

'*To T S Eliot*' –

"*Eminence becomes you. Now when the rock is struck*
your young sardonic voice which broke on beauty
floats amid incense and speaks oracles
as though a god
utters from Russell Square and condescends,
high in the solemn cathedral of the air,
his holy octaves to a million radios.

I am not one accepted in your parish.
Bleistein is my relative and I share
the protozoic slime of Shylock, a page
in Stürmer, and, underneath the cities,
a billet somewhat lower than the rats.
Blood in the sewers. Pieces of our flesh
float with the ordure on the Vistula.
You had a sermon but it was not this.

It would seem, then, yours is a voice
remote, singing another river
and the gilded wreck of princes only
for Time's ruin. It is hard to kneel
when knees are stiff.

But London Semite Russian Pale, you will say
Heaven is not in our voices.
The accent, I confess, is merely human,

speaking of passion with a small letter
and, crying widow, mourning not the Church
but a woman staring the sexless sea
for no ship's return,
and no fruit singing in the orchards.

Yet walking with Cohen when the sun exploded
and darkness choked our nostrils,
and the smoke drifting over Treblinka
reeked of the smouldering ashes of children,
I thought what an angry poem
you would have made of it, given the pity.

But your eye is a telescope
scanning the circuit of stars
for Good-Good and Evil Absolute,
and, at luncheon, turns fastidiously from fleshy
noses to contemplation of the knife
twisting among the entrails of spaghetti.

So shall I say it is not eminence chills
but the snigger from behind the covers of history,
the sly words and the cold heart
and footprints made with blood upon a continent?
Let your words
tread lightly on this earth of Europe
lest my people's bones protest."

And thus, more recently, in '*Marc Chagall,* Over the Town', Tom Paulin regrets

". . . how quite a few
critics of T S Eliot
choose
either to forgive or forget
those bits of verse
and one piece
of coldly sinister prose
that're about
his fear and hatred of all Jews"

– a just rebuke, as John Kinsella commented in The Observer (Books, 2 January 2000), to the way establishmentarian "complacencies . . . arise and then endure".

However, whilst the very sparseness of Eliot's spurts of Jew-hating venom makes them hard to forget, if one were convinced that they emanated from *fear*, ought one not *try* to forgive them? Rather than perpetuate the hopeless treadmill of racial and religious hatred? – The late lamented Michael Hamburger said in reference to his 1962 poem '*In a Cold Season*' ('*Ownerless Earth*', Carcanet 1973) about the State of Israel's death sentence on the notorious Nazi war criminal Adolf Eichmann: ". . . Mercy is harder than justice. Justice only buries the stench. Mercy clears the air".

". . .To have gathered from the air a live tradition . . ." and ff

– from the closing lines of Canto LXXXI by Ezra Pound, '*The Pisan Cantos*' (1945-1948)

". . . *Allen Ginsberg/ (– who'd learned from Pound . . . / to pull down* his *vanity) . . .*"

– see Pound's Canto LXXXI again:

> ". . . *Pull down thy vanity*
> *Thou art a beaten dog beneath the hail,*
> *A swollen magpie in a fitful sun,*
> *Half black half white*
> *Nor knowst'ou wing from tail*
> *Pull down thy vanity*
> > *How mean thy hates*
> *Fostered in falsity,*
> > *Pull down thy vanity,*
> *Rathe to destroy, niggard in charity,*
> *Pull down thy vanity,*
> > *I say pull down . . .*"

Pages 163-165

". . . *While preachers preach of evil fates/ Teachers teach that knowledge waits . . . . . // . . . . . . It's easy to see without looking too far/ Not much/ Is really sacred . . .*"

– from Bob Dylan's '*It's Alright Ma (I'm only Bleeding)*'

Page 166

". . . *Killers get high on/ the God of Science/ & cheer the big Arms Race on/ Kicking the globe in the head and/ puncturing its skin// Earth looks like it won't recover . . .*"

– a sadly persuasive premonition, for all that there is no arms race as such any more. The USA is racing with itself and no other nation can keep up: not surprising when you consider that America accounts for one-third of global military expenditure, plus 50% of global arms sales.

See also notes to "*No arms race/ is ever/ won/ for good*" on page 433, and pages 368-372.

Page 167

"*Shantih shantih shantih . . .*"

– the last line (433) of Eliot's '*The Waste Land*'.

His note on it begins: "*Shantih. Repeated as here, a formal ending to an Upanishad.*"

Page 168

"*Loud sing Goddam!*"

Cf '*Ancient Music*' by Ezra Pound (1917):

> "*Winter is icummen in,*
> *Lhude sing Goddamm,*
> *Raineth drop and staineth slop,*
> *And how the wind doth ramm!*
> *Sing: Goddamm.*"

This was Pound's adaptation of the opening of the anonymous thirteenth century *'Cuckoo Song'*:

"Sumer is icumen in —
Lhudë sing, cuccu!
Groweth sed and bloweth med
And springeth the wudë nu.
Sing, cuccu!"

See also the calypsonian John Agard's *'Weatherman'*, which begins:

"I am de weatherman
and dere's no dreaderman
in English company . . ."

". . . the Moneyburg Address . . ."

— adapted from Abraham Lincoln's Gettysburg Address of 19th November 1863, in which he proposed ". . . That this nation, under God, shall have a new birth of freedom; and that government of the people, by the people, and for the people, shall not perish from the earth . . ."

This is the Abraham Lincoln who, as a novitiate congressman, made a likewise eloquent, passionate and incisive speech in protest against America's unprovoked attack on Mexico in 1848.

It was aimed at the then President James Polk — but it might just as well have been written in March 2003, to expose the would-be smoke-screening opportunism of the widely dreaded George W (for War'n'Weapons proliferation-merchant) Bush:

". . . Trusting to escape scrutiny, by fixing the public gaze upon the exceeding brightness of military glory — that attractive rainbow, that rises in showers of blood — that serpent's eye, that charms to destroy — he plunged into war."

Page 169

'US ARMS INDUSTRY DIAGRAM . . . . . . SON OF STAR WARS'

Peter Brookes's strip neatly homes in on the hypocrises and cupidinous agendas that lurk behind the aggressively hard-sold US missile defence systems.

Presidents Bash and Blur made many indigestible meals of their alleged concerns for "the future of civilisation". Britain's People's PM's sycophantic deference to double-dealer Dubbya's most deadly Done Deals was aptly pilloried by one of our genuine People's Members of the European Parliament — the Green Party's Caroline Lucas (in the Guardian on 23/12/2002, p17):

". . . So Whitehall believes it would be 'silly' to think that this government might reject US pressure to site 'Son of Star Wars' missiles in Britain.

"Presumably it would also be silly to suggest that US attempts to win British support by offering 'commercial opportunities for British companies' means that the only ones to gain would be Bush and Blair's corporate allies in the arms trade.

"The Pentagon has spent 91 billion dollars on missile defence projects since Reagan's 1983 Star Wars speech. The prime beneficiaries of this wealth are a handful of major weapons contractors.

"Now British companies are being offered a slice of the cake. And — unless we succeed in stopping this madness — those same corporations will make even more grotesque profits from the ensuing new arms race.

"Instead of providing corporate welfare to defence contractors, the billions would be much better spent on building true security through addressing the root causes of conflict – the poverty and inequality that still stalk so much of the world . . .”

In 2000 and 2001, Britain spent a mere 0.32% of its Gross National Income on foreign aid. If Tony Blair wasn't just spinning another line when he said how much he hated war and wanted peace, why did he not put our money where his mouth was?

He could have made a start by banning all arms sales (which so often go to countries which can ill afford them, and/or could not possibly need them for any plausible 'defence' purposes) – and by vastly increasing the aid budget.

Pages 170-171

The provenance of this photograph is detailed in the second note to Page 234 on pages 450-451

Page 173

“. . . Marks of weakness, marks of woe . . .”

– from 'London', as per the reproduction from Blake's original hand-made 'Songs of Experience', 1794, on facing page 172

“. . . this time-dishonoured/ nation of shopkeepers . . .”

Cf Napoleon: “England is a nation of shopkeepers” – quoted in Barry E O'Meara's 'Napoleon in Exile', Vol 2, 1822

Cf also Adam Smith, in 'Wealth of Nations' (1776), Book 4, Chapter 7:

“. . . To found a great empire for the sole purpose of raising up a people of customers, may at first sight appear a project fit only for a nation of shopkeepers. It is, however, a project altogether unfit for a nation of shopkeepers; but extremely fit for a nation whose government is influenced by shopkeepers . . .”

Page 174

“ – to what new chartered ends . . .”

Cf the opening of Blake's 'London' (reproduced in facsimile from Blake's 'Songs of Experience' on previous page 172) –

“I wander through each charter'd street,
Near where the charter'd Thames does flow . . .”

In 'The Rights of Man' (Part 2, 1792), Tom Paine had scorned “charters and corporations” because they shat on the rights of the majority.

In 'Rereading: The invisible worm . . .' (Guardian Review, 3/3/2007), Tom Paulin interpreted Blake's 'London' as –

“. . . a cry of indignation against war and commercial abuse, against what we might call the military-industrial complex . . . Blake is attacking not just the church, but also the systems of abuse and hypocrisy that keep a corrupt society functioning . . . The 'chartered streets' refers to the system of commercial management that existed in the city. The same system extends into nature, too: the 'chartered Thames'. Blake is saying that even the ancient and unencumbered river is managed for profit.

". . . We know that Blake applauded the revolution of 1789 and wore the *bonnet rouge*, or red cap, in support of the revolutionaries. But when news arrived of the executions and the Terror, he threw the cap away in disgust. We can see these two political themes present throughout *'Songs of Experience'*. Blake is attacking the present system, but at the same time he's concerned about what will happen next."

In the Introduction to his edition of the *'Selected Poems of William Blake'* (The Poetry Bookshelf series, Heinemann 1957), F W Bateson also pointed out that

". . . In the poem's first draft the opprobrious epithet had not been *'charter'd'* but *'dirty'* (*'dirty street', 'dirty Thames'*), but by the time *'London'* was engraved for *'Songs of Experience'* the physical pollution had come to seem less oppressive to Blake than the spiritual tyranny exercised by the City of London, its boroughs and its incorporated companies. Magna Carta had once been a guarantee of English freedom, but by the eighteenth century the charters, from which not even the Thames was exempt, were empowering a minority of Londoners to impose their 'mind-forged manacles' on the rest of their fellow-citizens . . ."

No change there, then, under our own recent People's Primate's administration. As witness, for example, New Labour's efforts to consign London's unified tube train network to the outer darkness (in terms of the priorities of profits over safety) — to which Blair's habitual sell-outs to the highest private bidders had already dished the national rail system, perhaps irretrievably.

Parallel degenerations have gone on being inflicted, with increasing damage to the British public during New Labour's ten years in office, upon the UK's hitherto universally admired health, education, telephone and postal services.

It was momentarily amusing to read Chris Rogers's snort on page 27 of the Guardian, on 20 January 2005, that ". . . I will scream if I hear one more politician say *'deliver'* when they mean 'provide'. The only things that you can deliver are a baby, a speech or the post. Perhaps the 'Prime Minister's Delivery Unit' could give the Royal Mail a hand?"

— Ironic in that the improvident Tony Blair himself probably did as much as anybody to abuse the D-word in this vein — and doubly so in that he and his government had made it their business to dismantle our erstwhile efficient postal, BT and community services, whilst resolving to consign the limply looming local and general erections to the by then hopelessly unreliable Viagra of postal ballots. As long ago as the year 2000, Blair had got Parliament to approve the so-called Urban Reinvention Programme, designed to further fragment the hitherto efficiently, directly and occupationally interconnected mail delivery and Post Office networks.

Letters in the Guardians of 21 and 28 December 2004 (including one from me headed *'The Post Office's disastrous delivery'*, 21/12/04), noted that some sub-postmasters have seemed quite happy for their offices to close. A great number of these were certainly chuffed to pocket so-called redundancy payments — i e, bribes — in the region of £75k. Yet a number even of these, and of many others under threat of imposed closure, were then and more recently most *unhappy* that their corner shops, often built up over one or more generations, would thereby be disabled from staying in business on all of their customary fronts. Spokespersons for these were cited on 19 January 2005 in Oliver Burkeman's *'The Last Post'*, Guardian 2.

Just a month earlier, the same newspaper had featured on its front page and also on page 11 (Guardian 18/12/04) a feature about what it described as that winter's *"most desirable greetings card"*, which is still available (in full colour, with satirical logos by Satpaul Bhamra, and a self-sealing two-colour envelope – see *www.poetryolympics.com*). I produced this for our Lost Office Campaign against the 'profits-before-people' Post Office closures and Royal Mail cutbacks, which were – then as now – wreaking havoc with communications all over Britain.

Under the headline *'Pleas ignored as Post Offices go'*, Alison Benjamin wrote:

". . . One of Britain's most famous artists and a well-known jazz poet have teamed up to try to save a West London Post Office. David Hockney and Michael Horovitz have produced a greetings card to raise awareness about the plight of the Post Office in Westbourne Grove.

"Hockney, who used the Post Office when he lived nearby, has donated an ink and watercolour painting called *'People in the Street'*, which could be the corner where this Post Office is located.

"Horovitz has lived in the area for more than 40 years and was a regular user of this Post Office before its closure last month – despite a two-month campaign by local residents to keep it open.

"In the poetry greeting, entitled *'Lost Office'*, and topped by a broken heart, he accuses the Post Office of *'ponceing on the cancer of commercialism'* over the loss of *'this flower'd Grove's crown jewel'*.

". . . *'Here's barking at you, for dumping thus our prime community resource/With such base grovelling to Mammon's ruthless course'*, he writes.

"He fears the building will be sold off as luxury flats, boutiques, eateries etc *'. . . for the routine dross-market fate/ Of yet another multisquillion scoop for real estate/ Sharks'*.

"The Post Office denied there were any plans to sell the building. 'There's no question we have a policy of selling off properties in high rental areas to make a quick buck', said a spokesman: 'West London is very well served with post offices. There are eight within a mile radius of that branch' . . ."

– But this P O spokesman quoted by Benjamin as boasting eight still functioning offices within a mile of the Westbourne Grove/Portobello Road junction had not kept up with the government-owned Royal Mail's and Post Office Ltd's destructive

policies. For one thing, 222 Westbourne Grove had always been a Crown Office, not a branch. And of the six distantly neighbouring sub-Post Offices as were, three had been bribed to close down the postal part of their services. This in fact left only another three sub-Post Offices still open within one mile of where Notting Hill Post Office was, each providing only rudimentary services, plus only one fully functioning Crown Office, and this in the posh zone of Kensington Church Street.

For citizens without wheels in the Northern reaches of the – er, Royal Borough, or with wheelchairs only, a roughly two-mile trek to get letters, packages and parcels weighed and stamped; to get driving licences, passports, Recorded, Insured and Special Deliveries, and suchlike, sorted; to pay utility bills, do banking and other sundry business the Post Office has kept (expensively) advertising and urging them to do there – has meant the loss of the best part of a day, with inevitably stressful wear-and-tear all round.

Meanwhile those citizens with wheels in quest of the much fewer, farther between and obscurely restructured Post Offices (often in minuscule corners of Tesco, W H Smith and their motley ilk – and even in pubs . . .), endlessly multiply traffic congestion and parking problems. Furthermore, the massive queues consequent on these closures at each remaining office, most of which had been spilling out onto their adjoining pavements for most of each day for years before the closures, mean that the *minimum* wait for a transaction or enquiry at any of them tends to be thirty minutes or often still longer per visit.

These degenerations of Post Office counter services have exhausted the patience even of the likes of such normally good-humoured folk as stand-up comic Jo Brand, whose quick wit has lightened the tedium of so many a drear, dull and corny stage, radio and television show (as

for example when on Anne Robinson's 'Fantasy TV Dinners', Robinson queried, "Have you heard the statistic, Jo, that the average British male thinks about sex *once every seven minutes?*" – to get the instant riposte, "Yes I have. *Leaving only six minutes for football*"). However, the Independent of 27 March 2007 reported that, off-stage, caught up like most of us in the workaday grind –

> ". . . The blue rinse biddy guarding the stamps in Dulwich Village Post Office saw Brand last week. Clutching a jiffy parcel, she reluctantly joined the snaking queues's tail. A jovial old raspberry-cheeked man turned round and, spotting her, sweetly called, 'Got any gags, love? Feel like entertaining us troops in our hour of boredom?' Brand rolled her eyes, scowled, and told him to 'Fuck right off'. . ."

Can Christian sentiments like these be the fitting consequence of the superlative public service Royal Mail's 'new broom' chief executive, Adam Crozier, claimed he had turned round to become *"the best it has been for ten years"*?

Having used (and paid about a quarter of my income for) the postal services virtually every weekday for the last half-century, I can assure Mr Crozier and his colleagues that, in my experience, it has never been anywhere near as ineffectual and customer-unfriendly at any point over these fifty years, compared to the comprehensive deterioration since he took over and restructured – or rather, laid waste to – most of the things that had been most valuable and creditable about it, justifying the hitherto universally received opinion that it was "the envy of the world". Not any more, alas – thanks to the grotesquely uncaring cavalier self-serving smug-palmed greed of the likes of Crozier, Royal Mail chairman Allan Leighton, and their clutch of fellow unaccountable managerial moneygrubs.

My poem on the Lost Office Campaign greetings card describes the closure of Notting Hill Post Office as *"yet another scoop for real-estate/ Sharks"* because this classically beautiful stone building, which has served and held together the North Kensington community as a top-notch Crown Post Office since it was built for that purpose in 1908, was deliberately withdrawn from executing the *bona fide* Post Office activities at which it had so long excelled, for ever after. Should the DTI not now, with accurate trade descriptions in mind, rename such ex-postal headquarters *"Government Property Developments plc"*?

8,800 Kensington ratepayers signed a petition to contest and avert all of these closures, and Post Office Ltd responded by hiring Sir Michael Beloff QC for a fee of £35,000 a day, to see the campaign off, rendering it liable for costs starting at £5,500 – whose ruthlessly threatened escalation none of us, including the Royal Borough of Kensington & Chelsea Council, were in a position to contemplate underwriting.

So much for the government's avowed commitments to "radical reform of the public services" and "civilised values". One big-shot and affluent lawyer counted for more than the communications needs of 8,800-plus daily Post Office losers. How radical and civilised is that?

From 1908 until the end of World War II, the magnificent Westbourne Grove office had served its fast-growing community of homes, shops and social services so well that its name was soon adopted to cover the whole area, which had previously been known as Bayswater, Paddington and Portobello, not Notting Hill. The bus stop that immediately fronts what was the office has gone on being known by locals and driver-conductors, throughout the years since its closure, as *"Notting Hill Post Office"*.

The two photographs of the front of Westbourne Grove P O below (in Autumn 2006) and on page 398 (in Spring '07) hardly do justice to the building's defiant grandeur. Note the care with which Post Offices Ltd tried to paint out the words "POST OFFICE" engraved a century ago.

Could that have been because they were ashamed of having killed it, or because they sensed that this rubric staying there for the world to recall its history would prove unpopular as a selling point? Either consideration would make a suitably shameful kind of sense.

The cruelly premature termination of our Office's supremely fulfilled activities was speedily and illegally slipped through under cover of the Urban Reinvention Programme (which did *not* apply to Crown Post Offices), with an impossibly overnight-deadlined and utterly sham "Consultation Process" pretending to back it up. One of several revealing facts that were exposed during our failed High Court appeal was that this office had made a loss of just £68k in the previous year – i e, considerably *less* than the "Compensation Scheme" sum Post Offices Ltd were paying every sub-Post Office manager they could persuade in return for closing their businesses.

The building has stayed devoid of human occupation as of June 2007, two-and-a-half years since it was so summarily stripped of its functions. Presumably the companies had to go on paying astronomical Business Rate Council Tax for all these months. Yet another expanse of newly waste land still vacant, though still fully installed and raring to publicly serve.

An obvious, and far more reasonable recourse wide open to Post Office Ltd, does remain. It would be both practical and honourable: simply *to reopen*, and restore the still perfectly fit-for-purpose building to the discharge of its original and massively popular daily transactions.

Apart from the pressing local demands this would instantly meet – and be likely to rake in all-time high profits from, as this particular flowered corner has recently become one of the hubs of 'The New Knightsbridge' – it could also well prove to be the best piece of PR for the companies since Humphrey Jennings's film 'Night Mail' more than seventy years ago.

On page 46 of 'The POP! (Poetry Olympics Party) Anthology' (New Departures [#]25-26, 2000), I ran a paean of praise for the then Royal Mail and Post Offices of Britain entitled 'The Poetry of Stamps'. It began as follows:

> "Mention the words 'Night Mail' and older poets and poetry lovers alike will light up with a warm glow at the fortuitous twinning of W H Auden and the postal service. In 1935 Auden worked for the General Post Office Film Unit for six months, and the Post Office introduced him to Benjamin Britten. Two film collaborations resulted, one of which was Auden's composition of the verse commentary for this mesmerising film, which immortalised the nightly postal special from Euston to Glasgow."

The Guardian valiantly continued to feature editorial copy observing and questioning some of the worst such political and business corruptions which have continued to hit on nearly all British postal activities. Two letters it published on 7/1/2005, headed 'Profits and Losses', homed in on particularly practical points – although as far as any lessons learned by the bosses and the only shareholder, our wonderfully radical reforming government, seem to have been concerned, the writers (like hundreds or, quite probably, several thousands of others) might as well not have bothered.

The lead letter came from Barry Norman in Bradford:

> ". . . Why is this Labour government unable to see further than a simple balance sheet and unable to see the social costs and benefits of such things as Post Offices? They are much more than a place for cash transactions. This government talks about its citizens' responsibilities to society and each other. Post Offices are places where this is demonstrated at its best. It is where, if Fred has not been in for his pension this week, Tom gets to find out and goes to see if he is all right. They are a valuable hub of the community.

Author supporting his local Post Office, as requested

"The reason they are closing at such a rate is because of the switch to direct payments – something that has always been available for those who wanted it – which is a choice, something I thought this government was in favour of. The switch to direct payments is another example of this government bringing in legislation that affects the vulnerable and least powerful. There are many people who have felt threatened by letters from direct payments saying they will be visiting them because they have not arranged the switch from passbooks.

"The impression is that there is no alternative to opening a bank account. And when this is all complete people can look forward to being charged to withdraw their own money from certain bank machines. The government says the new system is to prevent fraud. If it wants to stop fraud it should look at the tax system with the same zeal as it looks at the benefit system."

Equally cogent was that day's second letter, from the novelist and playwright John Arden:

". . . The closure of Post Offices because they do not make money reminds me of the fairy tale of the boy who could not dig his master's garden because of the chilblains on some of his fingers. His master immediately 'rationalised' the situation: he chopped off the affected fingers, only to discover the boy was never able to handle a spade ever again. The Royal Mail is a public service, not a series of small businesses each trying to turn a profit. The service should be provided at an equal level in all of its offices for all of the public. It should have no more to do with profit than parliament or the law courts."

All too bizarrely, the few Post Offices left have taken to packing items you purchase in envelopes or wrapping that bear the legend: *"Support your Local Post Office"*. To which the rejoinder has to be: *"We would if we had one"* (– see photograph).

Toward the end of 2004, Post Office Ltd closed all five of the North Kensington offices it had pretended to consult local residents, business, Councillors and MPs about. Martin O'Neill's DTI Select Committee's *'Crown Post Offices Report'* roundly condemned ". . . the Post Office's unwillingness to be transparent and inclusive in the consultation procedures, and its unpreparedness to amend its plans in the face of reasoned argument".

In February 2005, a Post Office surveyor I buttonholed on sighting him taking photos of the main Westbourne Grove office, completely disused since the 10/11/04 closure, told me the company was hoping to lease out the building at high cost for non-postal business. This reverses the above-quoted notion Post Office Ltd's press officer confided to the Guardian, asserting that there was no question of their developing properties for commercial gain (surprise surprise).

It rather overlaps with the Royal Mail's bosses' ways of awarding themselves multi-million pound bonuses for seeming to show a financial upsurge for the company by sacking over one-third of the specialised and experienced work force, and sidelining the wages and pension needs of the remainder. Another case of public needs wilfully bypassed by a small gang of cronies who have simultaneously copied another of this privatising government's favourite gimmicks – i e, endlessly boasting of their commitment to public services. Commitment to serving themselves, more like.

On 18 May 2005 the Guardian's industrial editor Mark Milner reported that Adam Crozier had in fact awarded himself £184m ". . . on top of his annual pay, and a bonus of just over £700,000", and that ". . . Four other executive directors will share a further £3.7m under the Incentive Scheme, while Allan Leighton received £330,000 in bonus payments". In 2006 Crozier took home another £1,038,000. Yet in 2005 the Royal Mail's pension fund was £2.5 *billion in deficit*, and Milner also revealed that Post Office Ltd's loss over the previous year was £110m ". . . as it continued to suffer from the loss of income derived from paying out State Benefits".

And it got even worse. Leighton, who with Crozier was responsible for pulling the plug on these direct over-the-counter payments, along with the unplugging of so much else that was working so well, had the heartless hypocrisy, on pocketing his £330,000 bonus, to comment: ". . . We have a mountain to climb and *we've only reached base camp. The greatest challenge now is to bring about a complete culture change in the Royal Mail*". Ah, that supposedly redemptive c-word again, so beloved of the New Labour priesthood, who kept preaching how they were so – er, passionately determined to reform and regulate these wretchedly traduced public services.

– Well Allan, Adam, Government Owners & Co: you could begin by sharing some of those ginormous self-devoted payments with the girls and guys charged with doing your donkey work, and also by sharing some more of your ill-gotten gains with the Royal Mail and Post Office punters you've been charging such ever-increasing amounts for the very mixed blessings of the consequent grimly uneven, downscaled and far-flung services we have been left to make do with in return.

Dave Ward of the Communications Workers' Union spoke for the country when he railed against the ". . . disproportionate level of executives' bonuses compared to the workforce's: '*It is the workforce which has to carry out change . . .*" Nick Goulding, on behalf of the Forum of Private Business, found it ". . . utterly wrong-headed that the bonus structure appears to be linked to financial targets rather than performance targets. *It is performance that matters and it is performance which is not good enough*". And Postwatch too, on behalf of the millions and millions of Post Office losers, repeated what one might have hoped that company directors (– even directors as disgust-ingly greedy as those currently squatted so fatly on the postal business) would regard as the basic premise of their operations , i e, that ". . . *Customers care about the service they are receiving, not how much the company is making*".

On 28 February 2007, the Guardian and Financial Times reported that Adam Crozier was "calling for an end to all regulatory controls on bulk business mail, including lucrative junk mail:

'. . . the changes are needed to ensure the company's financial viability' . . ." The addition of advertising materials had been limited to a maximum of six items per door by door delivery. It looks as if we can expect a future where the few items of non-scamming post that may get through our letterboxes will prove barely findable amidst infinite paperfalls of unwanted advertising, whose revenue Crozier, Leighton and their fellow mafiosi of industry, along with our pretend-socially committed governments, seem to crave above all else, as their own unassailable private pension schemes. Let storm-felled trees exact fierce vengeance upon their conservatories, garden pools and gazebos – and bin-men leave their unrecycled garbage forever uncollected.

On 17 May 2007 the Government announced that another 2,500 Post Offices will be biting the dust by the end of 2008. The Trade & Industry Minister Alistair Darling told that morning's Today Programme this was because ". . . Less and less people are using the Post Offices. We need to do something about that . . . and reduce the network". – Eh? If a government closes 4,000 Post Offices, as New Labour had recently done, any fule kno less and less people will be able to use them. And anyone who thinks more people will use them because and after yet an*other* 2,500 Offices close, needs to stay out of office, period.

Post Offices to be shit in Southport are: Woodvale, Heathfield Road (Ainsdale), Marsh-side Road, Hillside and Lord Street South.

Southport Visitor

In the guilt-plated teeth of all this mindless neglect, let us nevertheless do what we can to revive decent and accountable postal systems local, national and international. You could help raise awareness and funds for this cause of restoring some genuine conviction and humanity into the services, if you wish, by ordering and distributing our all-purpose multi-coloured greetings card with David Hockney's painting, Satpaul Bhamra's logos, my poem and also the specially designed 'Lost Office Campaign' envelope. Please send crossed Postal Orders or cheques of £2 for one card and envelope, or £15 for ten, including p&p, to 'New Departures', PO Box 9819, London W11 2GQ, UK, and they will be addressed and despatched by First Class Post – and let us hope, delivered to you forthwith, Royal Mail willing.

"Mister Jobsworth's Friend . . ."

The Blair-Brown obsession with Full Employment has manacled New Labour to the cause of regimented (in)activity without value, meaning or use, beyond the fact of an income in return for the enforcement of frequently pointless chores or regulations. Hence the frequently automatic rejoinder, "It's more than my *job's worth* (not) to . . . . . ."

Wherefore *J'accuse* . . . *Gangmaster Brawn*

– for diluting and muddying the inborn desire of most humans to do a good job, and for equating it with his managerial desire to reduce each of us to a smoothly functioning cog in New Labour's Money + Jobs = Progress machine.

'*Brown declares War on workshy*', thundered the front page of The Times on 17 September 1999. The penalty for anyone unemployed who turned down any three jobs had been the loss of 40% of personal benefits. But – as if this wasn't oppressive enough – under Gordon Brown's latest New Deal there was to be a "*crackdown*" (sic), particularly aimed at "the young".

If the language of government makes its younger subjects seem criminal, some of them are going to start *feeling* criminal. Sooner or later they may think, 'Well, I may as well do what's expected of me', and get into a life of crime which might otherwise never have occurred to them. And the more stubborn and unreasoning an ass the law is experienced or perceived to be, the more understandable – and even reasonable – the inclination of people to break it without compunction.

Chancellor Brawn told The Times that under his imminent crackdown –

". . . they will lose two weeks' benefit after refusing one opportunity, four weeks' benefit after two, and six months' benefit after refusing a third. Previously the penalty for a third refusal was a six-week stoppage . . ."

This allows no leeway for anyone, of any age, who finds all three proposed jobs uncongenial, nor for the many already fully employed (often in work which provides longer-term benefits for our world, if not immediate ones) although this (self-)employment brings little or no income to the providers.

For example, the outstandingly talented Welsh poet and artist Nik Morgan, ten pages of whose experimental texts and visual art-works I published in *Grandchildren of Albion: Voices & Visions of Younger Poets in Britain* (New Departures 1992) has been forced to survive for the years 2003-2007 on no more than the minimal handouts his family and friends were able to spare. Here are some excerpts from a letter he sent me in March 2006:

". . . In the November 2002 budget Gordon Brown introduced the New Deal for the unemployed which involved compulsion and the threat of stopping benefit for failing to accept its 'help'. In March 2003 I was told that unless I followed the mandatory course of action suggested by the government, my Job Seekers' Allowance would be stopped. I refused to do this on the basis that their suggestions to get an unrelated job, go into business as an artist-poet, or go on a six-month computer course were inappropriate, and that the threat to stop my benefit was immoral and perhaps even illegal in terms of the Human Rights Act (European Convention on Human Rights).

"I submitted repeated appeals against each decision as the Department of Work and Pensions gradually stopped my benefit, but just before Christmas 2003 I was asked to redefine my job description. This was a definite shifting of the goalposts and when I defined my occupation as 'artist-poet' I was told I would not be able to claim Job Seeker's Allowance any more with this job description. I subsequently contacted you and later Baroness Helena Kennedy concerning this decision because the upshot is that if you have no money, you are coerced into doing what the State demands by the threat to your means of survival. Apart from anything else, this is not good for the Arts.

"During this time I had written to ex-Arts Minister Chris Smith MP who lobbied for a New Deal for artists-poets just like the already existing scheme for musicians who can claim under the present law. Unfortunately this fell on deaf ears as I later received a letter from Baroness Hollis of Heigham, Under-Secretary of State for Work and Pensions, informing me that I could no longer claim Job Seekers' Allowance because the job description I had given was not Class 1 employment of 40 hours per week minimum.

"I had also visited a Solicitor who was initially keen to follow up the case, but cooled somewhat when the prospect of Legal Aid for such a case receded. Only dead certs get financial aid these days, so I couldn't pursue the case without *pro bono* advice (someone willing to work for free). As this was not forthcoming, I couldn't pursue the legal case any further.

"I attended an Appeal Tribunal to fight the mandatory nature of the New Deal on the grounds that it violates several articles of the European Convention on Human Rights and is Orwellian in its ramifications for the poor, for artists and poets, and for citizenship in general. The Chairman said that although I had spoken with 'eloquence and altruism' he nevertheless had to follow the law and rule in favour of the DWP.

"Helena Kennedy felt that there was a majority view in the country, or at least in Parliament, that artists and poets should work for a living. That is, they don't see Art and Poetry as real work. It seems that money is the only thing valued under this system.

"When a person's means of support is cut off, it's an attempt to influence values and behaviour under the threat of insolvency and potential depersonalisation, alienation, and possible starvation. Gordon Brown claims that New Labour has improved the opportunities of everyone in this country without exception. I, however, am currently a quite specific exception."

– I myself am another. For most of my working life since leaving university in 1959-'60 I have been disqualified from state benefits, excepting the Single Parent allowance for a couple of years after Frances Horovitz died prematurely in 1983. Because the arts activities in which I have pursued my vocation were only rarely accepted as *bona fide* employment by the National Insurance system, and because when I have been paid it has usually been very little, my documented N I deductions and stamp payments were few and irregular. After I turned 65 in the year 2000, such income as I could scrape dwindled further, whilst the State Pension allotted me was minuscule owing, I was told, to the sporadic nature of my National Insurance contributions.

I noted wryly that on 25 October 2006 a posse of disgruntled pensioners descended on Downing Street with a petition for an increase of £30 per week in the basic State Pension. I would be overjoyed if my own pension could rise *to* a weekly £30. As of 2/5/07 it had risen to only £23.17p. Not that I'm not grateful. Every little helps, as the wren said peeing into the sea.

But if you should read this, Gordon Brown, please note that the subsistence opportunities of Nik Morgan and Michael Horovitz have remained emphatically *unimproved* under New Labour (– your heavily hyped tax credits are no help for our survival, since our incomes are far too low to be taxable; plus the fiendishly complex and uptight restrictions that your pension credit scheme's bureaucracies are tricked out with also include me out).

As for you Tony Blair, why on earth did your heavily hyped farewell speech about the arts at Tate Modern on 6 March 2007 want to lead off with the observation that British ". . . *children probably won't ever be artists*". – Quite a curse of a self-fulfilling prophecy, if your ten years' policy, of not recognising that art can be real work, is to continue under the aegis of those who succeed you as (Prime) Ministers. (See the notes on pages 254-256, and also those on pages 436-440.)

Nik has seen his specialist work opportunities definitively downgraded over four years to date – and he is by no means alone in this among writers and artists I know to be of well proven quality by the consensus of their mentors and peers. Very few of these have reached the publicly or governmentally approved status of so-called 'Big Names', nor any degree of state-approved 'Marketability' in the daftly competitive and largely philistine so-called free market stakes. Some of the finest artists and poets can be non-starters at business or self-promotion, whilst many who excel at moneymaking are not necessarily or particularly fine writers or artists.

Nik Morgan has produced a number of art works and poems which reflect on this unhappy marginalisation of his particular talents and creative potential – for instance:

"The Useless Poets' Social Security Society

Out of work bard in search of a yacht,
yawn at his sonnets and leave him to rot,
another statistic to block the machines
with battery hens in a junkyard of dreams.
It's money we want, and you off the books,
so you'll have to contend with our dirty looks,
loaded suggestions and double-talk schemes,
disgruntled queues of faded jeans,
just fill in the forms and you're on the right track,
there's shoes to shine and shelves to stack.
How can we help you to fit in with ease
polishing apples or minding your P's,
and knowing your place which is serving our teas?
So I'll tell you again in case you don't know it,
the last thing we need in this world is a poet."

Here are two more of Nik's poems, along with two of his drawings.

'Cannon Fodder' –

"Fate in the heart
of the common soldier,
such value to the country
that honoured rag of proper property
and in himself
counted of little importance
still young and cheerful head
bent on the enemy's guns."

'Burial'

*"A soldier's heroism
comes home
from the war."*

In 1963-64 in Khrushchev's Soviet Russia, the late lamented poet and translator Joseph Brodsky was repeatedly arrested, put on trial, and confined to mental institutions. He was imprisoned near Arkhangelsk in the icy Russian North from March 1964 until November '65, when he was released in grudging response to requests and demands from Russian and foreign writers including Anna Akhmatova and Jean-Paul Sartre.

Over the subsequent six-and-a-half years Brodsky was constrained to do no work except that considered "useful" by the authorities. Just four of his poems slipped past the censors to be published during that period. In 1972 his exile was enforced, and he managed to settle in the USA, largely through the good graces of W H Auden. Fifteen years later he was awarded the Nobel Prize for Literature.

Brodsky's persecution was conducted in terms grimly prescient of our inflexibly Brawny Gridiron's new cold war on the unemployed: that is, Brodsky was indicted as a *"workshy element"* and *"dangerous parasite"* for working at nothing but his poems and translations.

His February 1964 trial included the following exchange between the court and the accused:

"*Judge:* Who recognised you as a poet? Who enrolled you in the ranks of poets? *Brodsky:* No one. And who enrolled me in the ranks of humanity? *Judge:* And did you study this? *Brodsky:* This? *Judge:* To become a poet. You have not tried to enter the university where they give instruction . . . where they study . . . *Brodsky:* I did not think . . . I did not think that this was a matter of instruction."

Among the charges for which Brodsky was sentenced was the pre-Blair Blairism that:

"... Brodsky systematically does not fulfil *the duties of a [Soviet] citizen with regard to the production of material wealth ...*"

Around the same time that Brodsky and many of his contemporaries in the USSR were being sent to hard labour and/or prison, some of them never to return to writing (or even to re-emerge at all), the Geordie poet Tom Pickard was hauled before dole committees and councils in Newcastle on similar charges.

Pickard, then in his late teens, had wished only to continue developing the lines of work for which he had a proven talent – writing, and bringing writers, readers and auditors together via page and stage. All the officials concerned derided the idea of any of this qualifying as a Job.

Pickard was threatened with six months' imprisonment if he refused either to take what they regarded as "a proper job", or to attend a Rehab Centre for six months in order "to get back into the habit of working".

This is documented in graphic detail in Pickard's *'Guttersnipe'* (City Lights Books, San Francisco 1971). He managed to escape detention on the ground that he was "mentally ill". It's possible that the institutional aggravation did upset the balance of his mind. It's certain that the pile-up of frightening threats, withdrawal of benefits, and questioning of his life's work did nothing for his or his family's sense of "social security".

Basil Bunting and Tom Pickard at a Warwick University poetry festival in 1980

The Anglo-Stalinist Brawnspeak of this breed of state-licensed philistine bullying is exquisitely mocked in 'What the Chairman told Tom', a dramatic monologue the much missed Northumbrian bard Basil Bunting wrote in 1965:

> ". . . Poetry? It's a hobby.
> I run model trains.
> Mr Shaw there breeds pigeons.
>
> It's not work. You don't sweat.
> Nobody pays for it.
> You could advertise soap.
>
> Art, that's opera; or repertory –
> The Desert Song.
> Nancy was in the chorus.
>
> But to ask for twelve pounds a week –
> married, aren't you? –
> you've got a nerve.
>
> How could I look a bus conductor
> in the face
> if I paid you twelve pounds?
>
> Who says it's poetry, anyhow?
> My ten year old
> can do it and rhyme.
>
> I get three thousand and expenses,
> a car, vouchers,
> but I'm an accountant.
>
> They do what I tell them,
> my company.
> What do you do?
>
> Nasty little words, nasty long words,
> it's unhealthy.
> I want to wash when I meet a poet.
>
> They're Reds, addicts,
> all delinquents.
> What you write is rot.
>
> Mr Hines says so, and he's a schoolteacher,
> he ought to know.
> Go and find work . . ."

Poets and artists contribute enormous riches to the world, though often in quiet ways not measurable on the time-and-motion graphs of departments of trade, industry, wages and employment.

Poets and artists are not special kinds of people. Since each human being has an inner as well as an outer life, each human being is, potentially at least, a special kind of artist or creator.

With so much high technology reducing the need for manual labour, and with such vast resources, worldwide, available for redistribution, is it not high time world leaders broke up the mass-employment-for-money way of life, in favour of cementing a genuine international community?

If nations were truly united, a readjustment could be made almost overnight from the conscription of the poor into meaningless or destructive jobs, to the universal enjoyment of life and work for their own sakes.

If we must retain financial systems, let those with more assets than they can use pass the surplus on to their less fortunate fellow creatures. The Royal Family, for instance, might consider proving its socio-moral worth by converting half of Buckingham Palace into a refuge for some of this country's many destitute and homeless vagrants.

If the mind and the soul are to function, the option to do little or nothing can sometimes be of the essence.

If Gangmaster Brown freed himself from his computers, calculators, pagers and so forth, and awarded himself a spell on the dole, in which to do nothing but stand and stare at nature and beauty with W H Davies (as witness page 69), to loaf as Walt Whitman frequently and joyfully did, and to languish in the "diligent indolence" of imaginative daydreaming as Keats did on good days – then might we hear more melodious ditties from his lips.

Yea – if Brawnbrain could absent himself from nationalist Gridiron-mongery awhile, to ". . . *float on high o'er vales and hills*", guileless as Wordsworth's cloud – then might a vision of daffodils, real or imagined, envelop him in the natural remedy of their

> ". . . *never-ending line*
> *Along the margin of a bay:*
> *Ten thousand saw I at a glance,*
> *Tossing their heads in sprightly dance*"

– jocund beyond accounting, sprightly as the waves that *"beside them danced"* –

> ". . . *but they*
> *Out-did the sparkling waves in glee* . . ."

And if non-governmental Gordon proceeded on some couch to ". . . *lie / In vacant or in pensive mood*", having – like Wordsworth two centuries before

> ". . . *gazed – and gazed – but little thought*
> *What wealth the show to me had brought*"

– then might Brawn too recover the paradisal vision of

> ". . . *that inward eye*
> *Which is the bliss of solitude* . . ."

– and then might all at once the floral columns

> ". . . *Beside the lake, beneath the trees,*
> *Fluttering and dancing in the breeze* . . ."

conjure his mind up, up and away – to the infinite realms of gold

　　　　　　　　　　　　　　　　　　　　　　– gold, that is, way beyond party

fund banknotes and string vested interest rates

　　　　　　　　　　　　　　　　　　　　　– that the joy of God's plenty cast its light

through the narrow chinks of his counting cavern.

Then let even the darkest Brown machinations catch some wisps of that light where it beams, that a new generosity enter his soul and send mean spirits packing

    — to reflect, connect — and *absorb* the light
                                — and leisurely bathe in the daffodil-gold — splash awash and aflutter in the green and yellow, gold and rose red
                                        — in rainbow intelligence, as of a true golden treasury, social epiphany — to suffuse, bemuse and o'ercome thon lucre-soiled dour shadow self

    — and equip him to free less affluent, privileged or money-crazed folk from his cruel unquestioning crackdowns upon them: why should we all share the Goad-on Treasury's brief to lock us forever in the colourless oblivion of dead-end jobs for-jobs'-sake grief?

Oyez, verily yea — let those under way with work that suits their gifts
be delivered from recruitment by war chest shifts
                                    — from getting forcibly herded like beasts of burden into brawn-brainwashed armies, troops of wage-slaves — automatons — tramping out their days in dull and depressive routines — of rehearsing for wars, cracked down
                                        to drear statistics of martial orders, day after day
           in pursuit of no more than a foot soldier's pay — bribed to stay ever-ready to hit, to brawn-bash their opposite numbers — to grind others down, do *anything* — to get in the lead and stay well ahead — if only by doing the others down
                         to lower payslips, lower employments, dehumanised waste

    — what's the point Mister Brown, why have competition, why should *any*one lose out?

But *if* the human right to work *in one's own way* were restored, with wage slavery abjured, abolished — abhorred
                — *then* let Brown hearts too with pleasure fill,
                   and sundance with the daffodils!

Meanwhile, however, most of our well-heeled ego-blinkered leaders only got meaner all the while. It's as if the new élite, lacking the conviction or strength to lay the ghost of Ma Thatcher, had resolved to play safe and blandly restore her rotten core asocial mores.

    Wherefore: let's kick back hard against these stern "strategies" and arrogant *'Thou shalt Not'* prohibitions. Let's pitch our minds and works against philistine despots who insist that Britain expects every one of its subjects to drop every (un)employment with which we may need or prefer to fill *our* time, in order to swell the juicily jingling surfeit of *their* so-called "war-chests".

    This coinage, linking financial investment with war, revealed a hopelessly brutalised prospect: our National Governors boastfully swelling their chests with war against their own worst-off and weakest.

    And this miserly hoarding was index-linked, as it were, to the brazen sacrifice of sorely needed public spending on the overpriced and overstocked altars of New Labour's first term — whose main mission turned out nothing more than money management and staying in power.

    — This was confirmed rather than redeemed when, at certain panicked or politically prudential moments, an exceptional titbit was granted to high-profile pressure groups – as when Age Concern and other pensioners' representatives saw red at the niggardly increase of 75p a week proffered by New Labour to oldies for millennium year.

As soon as the concerted volume of Senior Citizen outrage signalled the concerted volume of votes to be lost, strategic white flags, in the form of *volte-face* concessions and promises of stupendous splurges next term, were swiftly hoist in a tizzy to realign the potentially floating codgers.

"War-chest" is unpleasantly evocative of the perennial right-wing stance on war typified by press headlines like: ". . . Copper prices picked up yesterday *as fears of a quick peace in Vietnam receded* . . ." (my italics – Daily Telegraph, 10 January 1967).

If the language of government characterises its subjects as war-bound, some of them are going to start feeling enmity, and are quite likely to become long-standing adversaries. In which case, Brawn and his ilk might come to an understanding of Blake's good sense when he wrote ". . . *Opposition is true Friendship*".

The Puritan work ethic has a lot to answer for. Inner-directed work for (inter)personal fulfilment – yes indeed. Forced labour for the mere fact of wages, or the mere fact of serving the State (". . . *with regard to the production of material wealth* . . .") – no thanks.

Unbridled Capitalism has a lot to answer for. The means by which profiteering bosses and 'growth'-obsessed administrations raise productivity are as debilitating today as when Karl Marx dissected their effects in *'Das Kapital'* (1867):

> ". . . They distort the worker into a fragment of a man . . . They transform his lifetime into working-time, and drag his wife and child beneath the wheels of the juggernaut of capital . . . Accumulation of wealth at one pole is, therefore, at the same time accumulation of misery, the torment of labour, slavery, ignorance, brutalisation and moral degradation at the opposite pole . . ."

Goad-on's edicts may add coin to the Treasury. They certainly impoverish the future of civilisation. War Chests ponce on wage slaves. They take us straight back to the soulless state observed by D H Lawrence seventy years ago, in poems such as *'Poor Young Things'* –

> *"The young today are born prisoners,*
> *poor things, and they know it.*
> *Born in a universal workhouse,*
> *and they feel it.*
> *Inheriting a sort of confinement,*
> *work, and prisoners' routine*
> *and prisoners' flat, ineffectual pastime."*

Turn again, Gangmaster Brawn, and *think* again – think more like a human being for once, for all, and less like an electronic calculator, so it please your grace and favour.

Alright, as well as loafing and languishing, Whitman worked as hard in his way as did Florence Nightingale in hers, to nurse, comfort and rehabilitate his grievously war-wounded countrymen; Lawrence was a schoolteacher for a time, and Bunting a spy and a journalist, among other (poorly paid) occupations. But the most valuable jobs done by each of these survive in their self-employed writings, which will always spread spiritual comfort, awareness, joy, enlightenment and inspiration.

Whose work is more use to the world (or even just to their countries) in the long run: that of Wordsworth, Keats, Whitman, Davies, Lawrence, Bunting, Brodsky, Pickard, Morgan, myself, and our successors today and in the future?

— Or that of the arms trade wage slaves and life-destroying Cruise-aiders you and the mercenary crew of your alter ego, Bomber Blair, would have every one of us become, Prison Governor Brown?

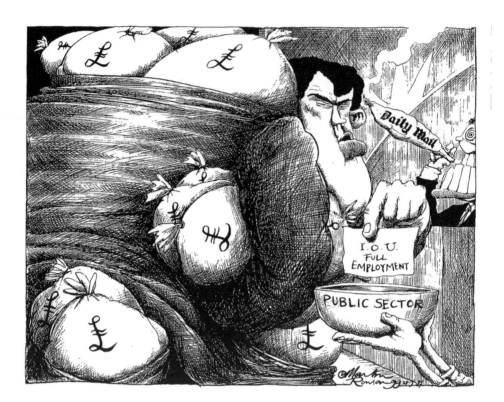

Page 175

". . . *Poetry Fetter'd Fetters the Human Race* . . ." and ff

— from the culmination of Blake's address *'To the Public'* on Plate 3 of *'Jerusalem: The Emanation of the Giant Albion'*, written and etched 1804-1820

Page 176

"NOT ONE OF US"

Richard Cole's cartoon depicts Messrs Blair, Chirac and Clinton aghast at the signs in early May '98 of India's aspirations to joining the nuclear weapons club. When both India and Pakistan test-exploded a number of nuclear devices in 1998, the USA led a chorus of condemnation from the established club member states

— and this despite the fact that North America is the only country to have actually dropped nuclear bombs throughout the last sixty years, with disastrous long-term consequences for countless Japanese, and for their cities of Hiroshima and Nagasaki.

The US had also conducted no less than 1,050 nuclear tests. Quite a few more, then, than India's and Pakistan's reported two to six each, as of March 2007 (*www.fas.org*).

Despite all this – indeed, without the hint of a reference to any of it, US economic assistance to India was stopped, and sanctions imposed.

However, the sanctions adopted by America against Pakistan were faded out when the Pakistani military dictator's support was solicited after the 9/11 attacks on New York's Twin Towers et al.

In March 2006 a deal brokered with India also sealed transatlantic approval of India's fellow membership of this wretchedly bomb-bedevilled club.

Page 177

". . . Britain's political leaders ape/ U S notions/ of war being fun/– and show wannabe Super-Star Warriors/ in Russia and China,/ North Korea and Iran,/ Israel, India, Syria, Pakistan/ – possibly even, alas, Japan/ . . . what to do to be reckoned . . . / World Cup calibre/ New-Age Guns . . ."

Polly Toynbee pointed out years ago (Guardian 23 August 2000, p22) that –

> ". . . Congress's refusal to sign the comprehensive test ban treaty last October virtually urges others to acquire their own weapons. The Bush camp talks of tearing up the 1972 anti-ballistic missile treaty. The insane national missile defence system . . . will end the old Mutually Assured Destruction policy by which the world survived the cold war. Costing $60bn, it works even less well than the 'smart bombs' of recent wars, but still arouses fear and anger in China and Russia. Zbigniew Brzezinski calls it the mentality of the 'internationally gated community' . . ."

The coincidental acronym of this Mutually Assured Destruction policy was always a reminder that it would only take a Dr Strangelove moment on the part of a single moronic or maniacal world leader with nuclear bomb power to assure the planet of, precisely, mutually assured destruction. As a Private Eye cover depicting Bush and Blair discussing Saddam Hussein's then-alleged WMD reserves had it – "Blair: *He's out of control and he's got nuclear weapons.* Bush: *What's wrong with that?*"

The WMD ambitions of a number of variously insecure and/or (would-be) hawkish states around the globe have clearly been raised by the US-led invasion of Iraq.

In 'A System Shaken' (Financial Times 10/10/2006), Quentin Peel and Daniel Dombey remarked that ". . . Today's combustible Middle East has become a part of the world where many countries appear to be seeking the option of developing nuclear weapons capabilities".

Peel and Dombey cited the view of former US Secretary of State Madeleine Albright, that —

". . . The message out of Iraq . . . that if you don't have nuclear weapons you get invaded, if you do have nuclear weapons, you don't get invaded . . . was hammered home by President George W Bush's decision to link Iraq, Iran and North Korea together in the 'Axis of Evil' . . ."

So much the worse then, for all world citizens, that the UN Non-Proliferation Treaty Review Conference in May 2005 paid such scant regard to the concerted pleas of the Mayors of Hiroshima and Nagasaki, and showed no movement whatever toward the goal of eliminating all nuclear weapons as mandated by Article VI of the Non-Proliferation Treaty (NPT), and also of the 1996 International Court of Justice Advisory Opinion on the Legality of the Threat or Use of Nuclear Weapons.

The widely reported development of battlefield nuclear weapons by the US, combined with its continued complaisance in the face of potential nuclear weapon deployment by American allies like India and Israel, contrasts starkly with the ratcheting up of tension with Iran over a danger of nuclear weapon development by that country. But as of May 2007, Iran's manufacturing or using Weapons of Mass Destruction is no more proven as real, let alone immediate, than were those of Saddam Hussein which were falsely claimed by the Gorge'n'Tiny show as necessitating the spring 2003 invasion of Iraq.

The bad faith of nuclear weapons states in not mounting any disarmament programme at all sends a clear signal to such states as Iran, which could realistically aspire to 'threshold status' and therefore indeed get on with developing the technical capacity to produce nuclear weapons.

In terms of the doctrine of 'deterrence', Iran might be thought to have a valid case for developing a substantial arsenal of bombs — that is, to deter potential trouble via the hostile US bases surrounding its borders in Turkey, Iraq and Afghanistan.

On 30 August 2006, so far from resiling from Bush's provocative placement of Iran atop his "axis of evil" hit list, the US proceeded to conduct its twenty-third subcritical nuclear test at the underground nuclear test site in Nevada, and yet again ignored the letter of plangent protest this elicited from the Mayor of Hiroshima.

At the same time, both Tony Blair and Gordon Brown explicitly volunteered their unequivocal support for the UK to acquire a new generation of nuclear weapons. The Trident missile system and the Vanguard submarines which carry them will need replacing by 2024, and a vote in Parliament on this undertaking was whipped through the House of Commons, with concerted support from the Conservatives, in March 2007.

Given the absence of any nuclear threat, this step is tantamount to embarking on a new arms race. It also locks the UK into another thirty years or more of so-called defence based on nuclear weapons.

Estimates of the cost of this Trident renewal vary from £20bn to £40bn, depending on what type of new missiles or submarines are chosen. The CND Alternative White Paper, 'Safer Britain, Safer World' (published November 2006 – see www.cnduk.org) put the huge potential waste of money into devastating but realistic social perspective, estimating that ". . . £25 billion is equivalent to 60,000 newly qualified nurses and 60,000 new secondary school teachers for the next ten years."

Planning approval was granted in January 2006 to upgrade the research laser at AWE (another unintendedly telling acronym – ?), the Atomic Weapons Establishment at Aldermaston in Berkshire. It seems that the upgrade of Trident, like Britain's so-called war on Iraq etc, etc, had been set under way quite a long time before its possibility was put to Parliament.

This continuing proliferation will reinforce immeasurably the no-win situation this earth's inhabitants have been locked into by the military-industrial nillennium, whose occupational bullying-power has shadowed humankind ever since it was first taken to its logical *(sic)* extremes by the USA's unprecedentedly massive, lethal and gratuitous terror bombings of Hiroshima and Nagasaki on the 5th and 8th August 1945.

The renewal of Trident breaches the UK's signed-up commitments to Article VI of the Nuclear Non-Proliferation Treaty (NPT), that: ". . . Each of the parties to the Treaty undertakes to pursue negotiations in good faith on effective measures relating to cessation of the nuclear arms race at an early date, and to nuclear disarmament, and on a treaty on general and complete disarmament under strict and effective control". Britain's upgrade will inevitably provoke and/or encourage similar developments on the part of various other nations.

If the Labour Government were indeed *"leading the world"* on as many fronts as it has so absurdly aspired to do, the question of where it might have led other states and (potentially) ferocious fighting forces from Albania to Zimbabwe, Israel to Iran, al-Qaeda to Hezbollah, is a pretty incomparably leading one. The attempted rationales that just about Anything Goes after 9/11 and 7/7 contain an under-explored underside: would-be democratic opponents of formal terrorism need to reckon more thoroughly with the implications of enemies some of whom are just as fulfilled by dying themselves, as they are by killing *their* enemies in the process. Furthermore, the explosive power of each Trident warhead is at least eight times that of the bomb dropped on Hiroshima. The price of some global "Intervention" of the kind so beloved of bold Bombardier Blair might just prove a "Deterrent" too near, even for the chronically war-hoarse likes of him.

The UK's unilateral extension of its nuclear capacities flies in the face of international law relating to war. Evidence, Professor Christine Chinkin and Rabinder Singh QC (of Cherie Booth's Matrix Chambers) recently pointed out that the deployment of Trident – and of any upgraded replacement thereof –

> ". . . would breach customary international law, in particular because it would infringe the 'intransgressible' requirement that a distinction must be drawn between combatants and non-combatants . . . If the envisaged use of force is itself unlawful, the stated readiness to use it would be a threat prohibited under Article 2, paragraph 4 of the United Nations Charter."

In 2005 Kofi Annan, then General Secretary of the UN, introduced the review conference for the NPT Treaty in New York by observing that:

> ". . . Some 35,000 nuclear weapons remain, with thousands still deployed on hair trigger alert. The objective of nuclear non-proliferation is not helped by the fact that the nuclear weapons states continue to insist that those weapons in their hands enhance security, while in the hands of others they are a threat to world peace. If we were making steady progress towards disarmament this situation would be less alarming. Unfortunately the reverse is true."

Page 178

"that 'Class of Men . . . / . . . whose whole delight / is in Destroying' . . ."
– from Blake's Preface to *'Milton'* (1804-1808)

Page 179

". . . the leading men / (playground bullies) / who fly too high / above themselves / and play God / / – men who've made machines / that hit and miss / their strongest hand / / and arms outstretched / beyond clear use / their holy trump / / – leading men who keep on / misleading / so-called servicemen / . . . . to be reduced, in war / to packs of hounds / to bay for blood . . ."

Cf Deuteronomy 4, 34:

> ". . . God assayed to . . . take him a nation . . . by war, and by a mighty hand, and by a stretched out arm, and by great terrors . . . that the LORD your God did for you . . ."

See also Deuteronomy 5, 15, and 7, 19.

". . . nobly decorous . . ."

See *'Dulce et Decorum Est'*, Wilfred Owen's first-hand bulletin from the trenches of World War I.

This classic rebuke to the glorification of patriotic man-against-man violence could also serve as a caption to any number of photographs and film clips from the front lines of many of the myriad disasters wished upon humanity by (non)humanity over the 80 years since it was written:

". . . If in some smothering dreams you too could pace
Behind the wagon that we flung him in,
And watch the white eyes writhing in his face,
His hanging face, like a devil's sick of sin;
If you could hear, at every jolt, the blood
Come gargling from the froth-corrupted lungs,
Obscene as cancer, bitter as the cud
Of vile, incurable sores on innocent tongues, –
My friend, you would not tell with such high zest
To children ardent for some desperate glory,
The old Lie: Dulce et decorum est
  pro patria mori."

Owen wrote to his mother on 16 October 1917: ". . . The famous Latin tag (from Horace, *Odes* 3.2.13) means, of course, *'It is sweet and meet to die for one's country'.* 'Sweet'! And 'decorous'!"

On 7 June 2007 the tally of UK service personnel who have paid this terminal price for Blair's Iraq adventure had reached 150. It is difficult to register this without also noting that so many more, who never enlisted in anyone's army, have paid with their lives for the Blair administration's active collaboration on the US's hawkish policies in Iraq and Afghanistan, not forgetting the strong-armed support both administrations extended to Israel to brook not a moment's ceasefire in its pitilessly savage thirty-three days and nights of bombarding Lebanon back into the Stone Age in late July and August of 2006.

Back in the dawn of New Labour's first term of office in 1997, the new Foreign Secretary Robin Cook proclaimed that Labour aimed to be *"a force for good in the world"* and to restore *"an ethical dimension to foreign policy".* These moral high-ground aspirations were soon tarnished by the series of shady deals, bribes, sales of arms to oppressive régimes, etc, etc, itemised throughout this book.

Suicide bombers have been unfailingly and definitively demonised as terrorists by Shock and Awe proponents, and of course indiscriminate terror is their general discernible effect, for all that it may not always be their aim. But it rarely seems to have occurred to the trigger-happy hardcore pushers of the so-called War on Terror that the pressure on flag-flying youngsters to risk their lives *pro patria* makes in itself, in its potential last resort, an allowance for suicide bombing or its equivalent – as took place for example in consequence of the ill-fated Charge of the Light Brigade.

Charles Kennedy's resolute opposition to the bad faith and suspect basis for the UK's following Bush's lead in invading and bombing Iraq in the spring of 2003 won him and his party many brownie points in my book of life. So I was all the sorrier to observe that not long after, he saw fit to sack Jenny Tonge from the then Liberal Democrat shadow cabinet, solely on account of her saying that she could understand how a Palestinian parent, whose children were under threat or had been damaged or killed, with little in prospect to live for, might be tempted to contemplate suicide bombing. This was surely not to condone that course of action, but rather to try moving towards a more principled, thoughtful and effective reassessment of dealing with that ever-increasing tendency.

Dubbya, Blur, and other (to my mind, hopelessly doomed-to-ineffectuality) protagonists of and apologists for counter-terrorist terror, would have everyone believe that all previous written and unwritten international rules of military, policing and intelligence engagement were irrevocably thrown to the winds by the destructions inflicted on the US East Coast on 9 September 2001.

But there is only one respect in which this time-dishonoured western militaristic hook, that

'. . . *There is no greater honour*' than to die for one's country, is distinguishable from the so-called faith with which trainee suicide bombers go on being indoctrinated in our time. Many of the last decade's conscripted and supposedly Robocopping coalition servicemen and women have been as safeguarded as possible from premature death, disaster or harm by staying high above danger zones, or armed to the teeth and maximum security-insulated within and around them – unlike many of those they are fully equipped to bomb, shoot or maim pretty indiscriminately when feeling threatened.

Flying, bombing and shooting under the War on Terror banner means 'our boys and girls' are indoctrinated and sanctioned to carry out murders, woundings and demolitions without being liable to charges of Terrorism themselves. How civilised, ethical, democratic, or even-handed a force for good, is such deregulated so-called warfare?

Bush, Blair and their spokespersons never stop putting out the line that what happened in the US on 9/11, and in London on 7/7, means that pre-emptive strikes against potential terror are not just acceptable, but a generally prioritised option, rather than the very last and indispensable emergency life-saving resort it should be.

How do they think this makes the Muslims, Arabs, and others threatened or hit by such strikes feel? I would have thought that the odds – especially given the recent histories and recurrent cycles of violence breeding violence in the Balkans, Asia, Africa, Northern Ireland and the Middle East – are that this policy is most likely to engender many *more* acts of terror and counter-terror, not less.

Readers who may think I am overstating the role of the arms trade may or may not like to know that between 1999 and 2004, UK arms sales almost quadrupled. The UK remained second only to the United States – though hotly pursued by France – as the greatest global arms exporter.

The public commitment to poverty relief and development in Africa by Blair and Brown contrasted starkly with British arms sales to that continent, which reached record levels at around the one billion pound mark in 2005, as was revealed by the pressure group Saferworld.

Areas of tension or so-called 'low intensity' conflict for which arms were licensed for export by the Blair government included Eritrea, Ethiopia, Algeria, Sudan, Zambia, Uganda, Namibia and Somalia.

How strange, again, that the head of this government throughout this period kept bemoaning the ongoing situation of Africa as ". . . *a scar on the conscience of the world*".

This accumulation of hypocrisies and of hard-sold licences to destroy and kill made Blair's complicity in the USA's brutal and illegal wars of invasion and occupation a virtually foregone conclusion. Their attempted justification on the grounds of promoting "democracy", "civilised values" and all the other intricately spun wordwebs of disinformation helped to thicken the smokescreens that kept some of the worst abuses of war-cover and victors' justice from wider public eyes, until after the irreparable damage had been done.

In view of all this foreign policy degeneration, it was not so surprising that the gradual escalation of a – er, 'culture' of gambling in general around the UK, plus the 2006-projected introduction of casinos here in particular, met so little resistance. Presumably this would be, in part at least, because so many citizens were so head-banged, demoralised and traumatised into feelings of powerless passivity, by the extent to which the Clinton-Blair-Bush coalitions gambled away so many innocent lives the world over.

Terror in Hiroshima, 1945

– see the notes to *"lost faces/ and bodies/ of Japanese generations"* on pages 433-434

Terror in Nagasaki, 1945

The photograph of Nagasaki Bridge is one of many that were taken by Yosuke Yahata the day after the demolition of her homeland by the second US atomic bomb drop, just three days after Hiroshima had been laid waste by its predecessor.

Over a third of the city was destroyed. Of the 52,000 homes in Nagasaki, 14,000 were destroyed and 5,400 seriously damaged. Only 12 per cent of the homes escaped unscathed.

It will never be gauged for certain how many people died in consequence of the atomic attack. By January 1946 the number who had done so approached 70,000, with around twice that number dead after another five years. At least 60,000 more were badly injured.

Page 182

"Down by the riverside/ gonna lay my weapons down . . . // . . . ain't gonna study/ war no more . . ."

The traditional lyric of this spiritual folksong more often gives *"my burden"*, *"my long white robe"* and *"my sword and shield"* as the items the singer is going to lay down, down by the riverside. However, on a recording I once had featuring vintage New Orleans trumpeter Bunk Johnson, it was mainly *"weapons"* he was looking forward to parting from – with the added poignant ambiguity of his pronouncing them *"weepins"*.

Like the "sword and shield" version, this sometimes put me in mind of the song's possible echo of Isaiah (as quoted in the first of my epigraphs to this book on page 9).

Incidentally, if either whoever walked off with my copy of this 10-inch Bunk LP (which also included further gruff, spirited vocals on top of his characteristic fierce, white-hot yet subtle trumpeting, on other trad songs like 'Ace in the Hole') is reading this – or if anyone else knows how or where I can obtain another copy of that 1950s album – please contact me via the addresses given on prelims page 4.

"Pale hands I loved/ Beside the Shalimar,/ Where are you now?// Where are you now?"

– from 'Kashmiri Song', set by Amy Woodforde-Finden (1860-1919) to one of the Four Indian Love Lyrics by Laurence Hope (1865-1904), from the latter's collection 'The Garden of Kama'.

After the publication of Hope's volumes of poetry, it was revealed that 'Laurence Hope' was in fact the pseudonym of Adela Florence Cory. Apparently the two women never met. Adela was married to Malcolm Hassels Nicolson, an Indian Army Colonel.

Where they all are now is anybody's guess. Heaven only knows, perhaps.

For Stephen Butt (*http://www.woodforde.co.uk/page54.htm*), *"Pale hands I loved . . ."* recalls the early Edwardian "love affair between England and Eastern poetry and music".

For me it brings to mind the delicate sensitivity, tenderness and immortality of the much missed poet, actor and teacher Frances Horovitz (1938-1983), whose life and work were infused by – among other things – a wide spectrum of Eastern poetry and music, and by all natural beauty:

"Pale hands, pink-tipped, like lotus-buds that float
On those cool waters where we used to dwell . . ."

Page 183

". . . *moon fades/ to a thumbprint// beyond the curtain/ at daybreak* . . ."

– cf the closing lines of Frances Horovitz's mid-1960s poem '*moon*':

". . . *sometimes I wish you*
no more than a thumbprint
on the edge of the sky"

Page 185

"*falling/ falling/ water becomes water/ over stone*"

– reproduced from Frances Horovitz's handwritten notebook of the mid-1970s; she used this observation as the title for her third volume of poetry, '*Water Over Stone*' (Enitharmon Press, 1980)

Page 186

". . . Man/ *at large* . . ."

Nicholas Garland drew the compelling double portrait above for publication on the day after Blair had told the Labour Party Conferrence (1/10/2002) that his government had not been bold enough in pushing through change. He acknowledged that protests had been voiced regarding military action against Iraq, but was unwavering in his support for President Bush. He maintained, in his most "passionate" *fortissimo*, that Britain must be ready to go to war against Saddam in the interests of peace.

Before Tony Boy got elected, he was often compared with Bambi in the (relatively) innocent early Walt Disney movie. After six months in office, and increasingly during and after his self-promotion as the Hawk of Nato over Serbia, Blair increasingly resembled the agency Bambi's mother most feared when, on hearing shots ring out, she told her fawn: "... *Man* is in the forest".

– And how much more so after a further eight years of ever more ardent and murderous war-mongering, with peace less and less in prospect – least of all in Iraq.

See also Peter Brookes's cartoon on page 148.

Page 187-188

"... uncontrollable/ hard floods of fire/ / falling/ / falling/ /   – bursting chemical tanks/ that erupt poisoned rain ..."

Cf George Monbiot's analysis of the long-term environmental implications of Nato's (vastly unvernal) Spring 1999 offensive over the Balkans in 'Nato's chemical warfare remains an obscene modern plague' (Guardian 22 April '99, p20):

> "This, in environmental terms, is perhaps the dirtiest war the West has ever fought ...
> Britain's Ministry of Defence told me yesterday that the bombers are 'keeping the risks of pollution to a minimum', but it was unable to explain how, while blowing chemical plants to pieces, they have achieved this commendable feat. Nato informed me that '... the smoke from these fires is barely comparable to the smoke caused by the Yugoslav attacks on several hundred villages'. It's clear that neither agency has the faintest idea of what it's talking about.
>
> "The chemical tanks ruptured by Nato bombers on the outskirts of Belgrade last week contained a number of lethal pollutants. Some held a complex mixture of hydrocarbons called 'naphtha', others housed phosgene and chlorine (both of which were used as chemical weapons in the First World War), and hydrochloric acid. As the factories burnt, a poisoned rain, containing hundreds of toxic combustion products, splattered Belgrade, its suburbs and the surrounding countryside. Broken tanks and burst pipes poured naphtha, chlorine, ethylene dichloride and transformer oil, all deadly poisons, into the Danube. Oil slicks up to twelve miles long wound their way towards Romania.
>
> "These toxins are unlikely to kill people immediately. But they will have soaked the soil across hundreds of square miles and percolated into the aquifers. The people of the former Yugoslavia, as a result, will be repeatedly exposed to them. Many of the compounds released cause cancers, miscarriages and birth defects. Others are associated with fatal nerve and liver diseases. The effects of the bombing of Serbia's economy equate, in other words, to low-intensity chemical warfare.
>
> "Nato's scorched earth policy, which seeks to destroy Milosevic's armed capacity by destroying everything else, places the Alliance firmly on the wrong side of the Geneva Convention. For a war which targets chemical factories and oil installations, which deploys radioactive weapons in towns and cities, is a war against everyone: civilians as well as combatants, the unborn as well as the living. As such, it can never be a just one."

"*– for eleven weeks of 'degrading/ Serbia's infrastructure'/ to rubble and dead flesh// – as directed by NATO's/ top couch potatoes . . .*"

Chris Riddell's cartoon, Michael Heath's on the facing page 189, and Andrzej Krauze's below allude to Operation Allied Force, aka the Kosovo-NATO War. This was Nato's military operation against the Federal Republic of Yugoslavia which was unleashed from 24 March to 11 June 1999.

Nato's proclaimed goal was to protect the Kosovo Albanian people from what it regarded as aggression by the military of the Federal Republic of Yugoslavia, Serbian paramilitary police forces and irregular militias allied to the Serbian government. The Yugoslav Government claimed that it was protecting the minority Serbian population of Kosovo against attacks by what the US itself had classified as a Terrorist Organisation: the Kosovo Liberation Army.

Operation Allied Force relied almost exclusively on the use of a large-scale air campaign to destroy Yugoslav targets from high altitudes. Ground units were not used, although their use was threatened near the end of the conflict. This approach was adopted to minimise the risk to the Nato forces and attracted considerable public criticism due to its relative ineffectiveness against mobile ground targets such as tanks and troop formations. Long-range Cruise missiles were used to hit a number of heavily defended targets such as strategic installations in Belgrade and Pristina. Civilian installations including power plants, water processing plants and the state-owned broadcaster were also intentionally targeted.

At the start of May '99, a Nato aircraft attacked an Albanian refugee convoy, believing it was a Serbian military convoy, killing more than 50 people. Nato admitted its mistake five days later, but the Serbs accused Nato of deliberately attacking the refugees. On the 7th May, Nato bombs hit the Chinese Embassy in Belgrade, killing three Chinese journalists and outraging Chinese public opinion. Nato claimed they were firing at Yugoslav positions. The United States and Nato later apologised for the bombing, saying that it occurred because of an outdated map provided by the CIA.

Then there was an attack on Serbia's principal TV stations and the bombing of chemical factories which resulted in major pollution incidents and loss of jobs.

The campaign failed in its proclaimed objective, in that thousands were killed during the conflict and hundreds of thousands more fled from the province to other parts of the country and to the surrounding countries.

A Nato-led peacekeeping force, KFOR, continued to maintain a precarious peace in Kosovo under the UN wing. Although another large-scale conflict between Serbia and Albanian Kosovans looks unlikely in the near future, the region continues to suffer the effects of poverty, widespread organised crime and ethnic tensions. Unfortunately ethnic hate was not defeated and it remains strong in Kosovo in early 2007.

"bombing out basic lifelines/ for fellow humans/ who've done nothing to warrant/ being sacrificed as scapegoats . . . // . . . as charred figleaves/ to camouflage/ one military hitman's/ sexual miscellania"

Under the headline *'80th Anniversary of the end of World War I'*, Julian Borger reported (Guardian, 11 November 1998) how –

> ". . . Washington ordered the rapid reinforcement of US forces in the Gulf yesterday and ruled out negotiations with Saddam Hussein over the Iraqi leader's decision to halt cooperation with United Nations weapons inspections. The decision to speed the flow of troops and armour to the Middle East was made at a meeting between President Clinton and his senior security officials yesterday. Mr Clinton telephoned Britain's Prime Minister Tony Blair *after* the meeting to discuss the situation."

Steve Bell wrote in *'Bell's Eye: Twenty years of Drawing Blood'* (Methuen 1999) of his disaffection for the resulting particularly ill-timed bomb-blast from what he dubbed the USA's "Lame Dick President" of the day:

> "1998 was an eventful year for President William Jefferson Clinton, characterised by the almost mystical connection between revelations concerning the activities of his unruly member and renewed bombing attacks . . .
>
> "One of the least tasteful of these attacks was the one that was launched on Baghdad on Remembrance Day, 11 November 1998. The drawing *[reproduced at the top of page 186]* was prompted by television coverage of poppies cascading down in silence from the Menin Gate at Ypres on that day."

As epigraph to his memento, Steve Bell revisited and updated a famous line from Laurence Binyon's much loved elegy *'For the Fallen (September 1914)'*:

> *"They shall grow not old, as we that are left grow old:*
> *Age shall not weary them, nor the years condemn.*
> *At the going down of the sun and in the morning*
> *We will remember them . . ."*

". . . *When will they ever learn?*"

– from Pete Seeger's song, '*Where Have All the Flowers Gone?*' (Essex Music Group/Bucks Music, London)

Page 193

". . . *the barbarous terrors/ of Hitler's 1940/ airblitz on London// and later/ his doodlebugs . . .*" and ff

I included an account of my family's experience of these in '*A Son of Abraham: Reflections on poetry, the Holocaust, my father – and what now?*' (Jewish Chronicle Literary Supplement, 12 January 1990, pages iv-v).

Page 194

"*What is that sound . . . / . . . maternal lamentation*"

– Eliot's '*The Waste Land*', V, lines 366-367

"*WOMEN WITH BEDDING IN BLITZED SUBURB OF BEIRUT*"

This photograph shows Lebanese women salvaging belongings from their demolished homes in Beirut's Southern suburbs on Sunday 16 July 2006.

Under the heading '*Israel steps up air raids after missiles hit Haifa*', Nicholas Blanford reported in the Times (17/7/06) that at midnight on Saturday 15 July Israeli warplanes had unleashed their fiercest bombardment of Beirut to date, devastating apartment buildings and blacking out much of the city.

On the same spread of the Times (pp6-7), Stephen Farrell and Yonit Farago reported Hezbollah's revenge with their deadliest strike in Israel up to then, shortly after 9am on Sunday 16 July, when eight Israeli Railways workers were killed by a Hezbollah missile that smashed through the roof of their railway repair yard in Haifa. Hezbollah's leader Sheikh Hassan Nasrallah said the guerilla group's launching of twenty long-range missiles on Haifa was ". . . retaliation for Israel's killing of civilians".

Israeli bombers in turn came back in the evening after the Haifa attack –

". . . to bombard Hezbollah's headquarters in Beirut and drop leaflets over Southern Lebanon warning residents to leave.

"Last night Israel launched eight raids in less than 15 minutes, firing ten missiles on a runway and setting a fuel storage tank ablaze. It was the fourth time the airport had been attacked since Wednesday 12 July.

"Other targets included Hezbollah strongholds in Dahiyah and the Eastern city of Baalbek, and Jiyah power plant in Beirut.

"Police in Lebanon said yesterday that 41 people had been killed in the preceding 24 hours, nearly all civilians. This brings the total dead in Lebanon to 148, against 24 in Israel.

"An air strike on a Southern village killed eight civilians including seven with dual Canadian-Lebanese citizenship.

"Last night's attacks came after the penetration of rockets deeper into Israel than ever before. They hit Afua, 33 miles [50km] South of the border, and a town near Nazareth.

"In the Southern city of Tyre 16 people were killed and more than 100 wounded. Witnesses said most of the casualties were caused by an attack on a building used by rescue workers. Tyre appeared almost deserted as residents took refuge in basements, much as their Israeli counterparts were doing a few dozen miles South."

The long-term effects of randomly far-flung quantities of unexploded ordnance (notably landmines and untold masses of cluster-bombs), and of the bombed coastal fuel storage tanks, are incalculable.

The swirling drifts of contamination seem unlikely to clear in the short-term, and their reverberating health hazards may or may not prove incurable. They were observed and felt almost immediately after as far away as the shores of Turkey and Greece.

What a pity that nobody in power seems to want to learn from the insane disproportion and horrendous repercussions of the gratuitous terror-bombings of Hiroshima and Nagasaki in 1945, or from more recent avoidable ecological disasters like the one which shrouded Chernobyl in 1986.

During the last three days of the war with Lebanon, the Israeli military dropped millions of deadly cluster submunitions over the South of the country, although they knew full well that a ceasefire was about to come into effect. Up to 30% of these tiny but particularly child-unfriendly death toys, uncharmingly known as 'bomblets', failed to detonate on impact, and thus became lethal mines primed to go off when disturbed. They remain lodged in the houses, woodpiles and – especially pernicious – in the fields, olive groves and fruit trees of Lebanese villages reliant on agriculture, and will continue to kill and maim the civilian population unpredictably and indefinitely.

The UN calculated that 100,000 of Israel's American-made cluster bombs remained unexploded in nearly 250 locations in Southern Lebanon, 90% of them dropped in those last few days of the war (– as witness Ewen MacAskill's report on page 15 of the Guardian, 30/1/07).

In 'Deadly Harvest' (pages 1-2, Independent, 18th September 2006), Patrick Cockburn cited independent monitors who had recorded 83 deaths from cluster munitions in the twenty-five days since the end of the conflict on 14th August 2006. The same report quoted an Israeli rocket-unit commander who told the Haaretz newspaper that "we covered entire villages with cluster bombs . . . what we did there was crazy and monstrous".

Whilst the UN and other organisations were still trying to clear the cluster bombs, the work was much too slow for the Lebanese farmers, who were watching their livelihood rotting on the branch. Chris Clark, the UN's Mine Clearance Programme manager, said they planned to complete the clearance by December 2007, but that cluster bombs would continue to turn up in the area "for decades to come" (BBC Radio 4 Today programme, 19 October '06).

Alongside the US Air Force, the RAF's personnel have also frequently been constrained to drop cluster bombs – which are in effect exceedingly un-storklike bundles of compressed mini-landmines – for example in the Gulf War of 1991, over the Balkans in 1999, and in Iraq since 2003.

The then Defence Secretary Geoff Hoon confided to Parliament on 3 April 2003 that cluster bombs were used only when it was "absolutely justified" because it would ". . . make the battlefield safer for our armed forces".

On the following morning's Today programme, he claimed that ". . . The very strong (sic) military advice is that they are essential". Presumably he mouthed this smarm because the Ministry of Defence had just, for the first time, admitted it had dropped 50 airborne cluster munitions in the South of Iraq, leaving behind up to 800 unexploded bomblets.

John Humphrys put it to Hoon that Iraqi mothers of children killed by cluster bombs would not thank British forces for this part of the Coalition's intervention. Despite many years of exposure to bullshit from arms- and war-pushing politicians, I could hardly believe my ears – but on listening back confirmed – that Hoon's reply was: ". . . One day they might".

Like similar apologists for longtime-dishonoured military non-solutions (for example the Nixon-Kissinger irrationale of bombing South East Asian villages to – er, they said – *save* South East Asian villages), Hoon was of course limply clutching the supposed salvation of Iraq as a fig-leaf to cover this manifestly futile deployment of barbaric weaponry. Endless cycles of premature deaths, destructions, displacements, grief and suffering are on Hoon's hands, and the hands of all those who profit from or condone cluster bombs as legal, reasonable, appropriate, or "essential" armaments.

In February 2007, Britain at last joined forty-five other countries in Oslo to co-sign the declaration calling for a Treaty banning cluster bombs. Unfortunately the USA, Russia, China and Israel refused to sign. For the umpteenth time, I was made ashamed to be Jewish by, on top of the overall inhumanity of Israel's July-August 2006 razing of Southern Lebanon, hearing Israel's main Foreign Ministry spokesman Mark Regev smugly reiterating, day after day, his autopilot mantra on being questioned about the relentless and indiscriminate (cluster)bombardments of the Lebanese: *". . . Nothing we are doing is illegal".*

On 2 March 2007, the UK Defence Secretary Des Browne announced that in future Britain would only resort to cluster bombs with special self-destruct features, saying *". . . We should strive to reduce civilian casualtiies to the minimum".* But the Lib Dem Defence spokesman, Nick Harvey, called on the MoD to scrap all cluster bombs, arguing that Browne had proferred a "dubious and misleading" distinction between "dumb" and "smart" cluster munitions:

> ". . . All cluster munitions are indiscriminate, and there are serious concerns that even so-called 'smart' munitions have a significant failure rate, making them a dangerous remnant of conflict and posing a serious threat. If the government is to fulfil its commitments, set out at the Oslo Conference, to prohibit 'cluster munitions that cause unacceptable harm by 2008', then it must ban *all* cluster munitions, without distinction."

See also the Cluster Munitions Coalition's website: *www.stopclustermunitions.org*, and Spike Hawkins's Letter to Dubbya regarding so-called 'Smart Bombs', in the note to *"smarter bombs"* on page 272.

Page 195

". . . new/ millennium// experience . . . company . . ."

The above words are incorporated from The (then) New Millennium Experience Company's super-sponsored (by funds from the National Lottery, British Telecom, Manpower, Marks & Spencer, McDonald's, Sky, Tesco, the Hinduja Bros, and other friends of – er, cultural regeneration, they'd have you believe) rubric in glossy brochures and widespread lavish TV and newsprint publicity throughout 1999, all stridently targeted: *"Towards 2000".*

Unhappily, like so many heavily nation state-promoted initiatives (notably massive military attacks, worldwide, in the names of defence, peace, civilised values etc, etc), this campaign took little or no stock of the universes after and beyond its sell-by moment.

The inescapably ubiquitous PR the NMEC circulated confidently boasted "The Millennium Experience will be . . . *the most spectacular millennial event anywhere in the world.* It will run through throughout (sic) the year 2000 . . . and *is expected to attract over 123 million visitors from the UK and around the globe".*

Furthermore, the blurbs anticipated that ". . . the National Programme will give everyone in Britain the opportunity to participate in . . . *projects that will make a lasting difference to our society";* that ". . . *the spectacular opening ceremony in the Dome on 31 December 1999 will herald the celebration of British ideas and technology";* and also – constantly repeated – that ". . . *the overall theme, embracing the optimism of Britain as we enter the new millennium, is 'TIME TO MAKE A DIFFERENCE' . . ."*

Eight years on, grandiose epithets like *"spectacular"* were still being flaunted, and others like *"regeneration"* abused, at every opportunity, by government and commercial spin-merchants. But the only *"lasting difference to our society"* or *"most spectacular millennial event anywhere in the world"* being hard-sold a propos of the Dome, as of New Year's 2007, was the prospect of the Greenwich peninsula becoming dominated by a ginormous Government Culture Department-sanctioned Supercasino, designed mainly to swell the already astronomical fortune of American billionaire Philip Anschutz.

Any Supercasino is inevitably going to further dissipate the smaller fortunes (and already all too dissipated mores) of diverse fortune-questing Brits and tourists. It will methodically multiply widespread addiction to gambling, and in so doing intensify various other similarly destructive addictions.

A *"lasting difference"*? The *"optimism of Britain"*? The so-called New Millennium Experience certainly wasted a vast amount of time and money – on not making any useful Difference at all

– on what amounted, as Jimmy Porter put it in John Osborne's *'Look Back in Anger'* half a century ago, to ". . . the Brave New nothing-very-much-thank-you . . ."

Like "whiter than white" and "purer than pure", the entire wilfully obsolescent, hypocritically unthought-through, fraudulently advertised cycles of fast buck-raking make one long for a few breaths (or ideally, infinite injections) of that authentic civilisation Mahatma Gandhi thought would be "a very good idea" seventy years ago.

Surely it is near-suicidal, as well as seriously inegalitarian, to consign the fates of fellow citizens to this kind of randomly drifting 'Place Your Bets' vision of Culture?

C'mon, for Chrissake – in such time and potential "Difference" as may be left to any of us – just quit stalling, once for all – and get seriously Serious, guys.

Las Vegas-style gambling clubs do *not* generate anything you could call *Regenerative*. They do not generate goodness, decency, rebirth, health, vigour, responsibility, beauty, wonderment or spirituality.

What they generate are other addictions, notably to booze, drugs, crime and prostitution, ugly buildings and practices, exploitation of women and cheap labour, the cynical ripping off of punters, related swindling and crime, gang wars and protection rackets, money-laundering, other vice, venality, and jackpot-fixated opportunism on all levels.

The overriding item casinos large and small are bound to want to generate is cash, cash, and ever more cash.

And this multiplication of gambling centres has been pushed by the mega-capitalistic New Labour government in a period when record numbers of UK citizens were stewing, and in some cases drowning, in potentially bottomless quagmires of personal debt. The least fortunate among us are the ones who will be the most beguiled by the Mephistophelean pitch of quick financial killings on offer via these super-gambling projects – and are the ones most liable to be ground down or killed by them sooner rather than later.

In the London Evening Standard of 30 August 2006 (under the heading, *'Delusions that still haunt the Dome: as a public inquiry begins today into the Dome's conversion to a Supercasino, one planning expert says this last gamble to rescue a doomed venture is no guarantee of regenerating the Greenwich peninsula'*), Paul Barker wrote:

". . . Even as his power draws to a close, the Millennium Dome comes back again to haunt Tony Blair. Today the supposedly independent Casino Advisory Panel opens its "examination in public" into whether an American owned Supercasino should be stuffed into the Dome. But it will not end the squalor, backdoor finagling and hype upon hype that the Dome now stands for.

"Time was when Blair saw the Dome as prime candidate for a boastful lead paragraph in his 2001 general election manifesto. Now new owner Philip Anschutz's company twists the words of clergymen in a desperate effort to try to drum up support for this unwanted project. What will it now look like if Blair leaves office with this albatross still around his neck?

"His deputy, John Prescott, has supposedly held earlier meetings with Mr Anschutz, without ever letting the dread word 'casino' pass his lips.

"But the biggest lie in the latest, sorry stage of the Dome's evolution is that the great hype of 'regeneration' – with thousands of companies and housebuyers supposedly beating a path to the dismal Greenwich Peninsula – could carry on under the Dome's new identity, regardless of actuality.

"Serious regeneration never really happened, even in the Dome's earlier history.

"This month, a mortgage broker assured me that those who bought into the peninsula in the pioneer days of Dome-touting have caught a cold. The prices, he said, sank back. Harsh reality set in. There's a problem of negative equity.

". . . Regeneration is one of the great clichés of our time. A theory grew up, especially among architects, that all you needed was to drop an iconic building into a rundown area and Regeneration would follow.

"Not so. Cities like London are highly complex organisms. They aren't Plasticine, to be moulded as the mood takes you. Streets and districts come hardwired with historical memories. The jury is still out on what the 2012 Olympics will achieve socially in East London, after the games close.

". . . In Greenwich, too, we can already see that the mills of regeneration grind exceeding slow. After all, the original Dome complex was supposed to regenerate the area, and has had little effect.

"True and *lasting regeneration . . . has to involve local ideas, local initiatives, local entrepreneurs, even local builders to have a chance of success.* That is what the Greenwich peninsula now needs.

". . . Blair preferred to see the contracts signed for a gaudy pleasure palace – rather than the infinitely more damaging TV images of surely most sensible treatment for the Dome: pulling the whole white elephant down. That would be a symbolic collapse too far for this iconic Blairite edifice."

In a follow-up piece for the same paper, published on the day that Manchester was announced as surprise winner of the Supercasino Lottery, Barker assessed the news that the deprived London Borough of Newham was to be awarded the consolation prize of a (unSuper) casino of its own ('*A Supercasino that London never wanted*', Evening Standard, 30/1/07, p13): ". . . By definition, the casinos are going to be located in places that people have decided, in their droves, they don't want to go. Otherwise, there'd be no need for regeneration. If you're a tourist wanting a night out in London, would you really go to furthest Newham . . . ? Newham will have to be cheaper. So jobs will be, mostly, marginal, transient, and underpaid".

The truth of the matter is, as Barker reaffirmed, ". . . for regeneration to work, the ideas must come from below, not from above. They must be flexible. And they must be nurtured locally" – i e, they must be grassroots schemes that return their profits to the local community, not centrally imposed leviathans whose tax earnings go straight to the Treasury.

What an irony that a prime – perhaps the only – example of 21st Century regeneration in Greenwich to date turns out to be the revival of the long-standing Greenwich Theatre. This local arts and community centre had been forced to close down in 1998 for want of its annual Arts Council grant of £210k, slashed that year to top up the voracious kitty of £758m clawed into oblivion by the Millennium Dome. Seven years on, the latter remains the National Embarrassment and sick joke, whilst Greenwich Theatre has re-established its central role in the area. At a tiny smidgeon of the cost, naturally. It would seem that feckless gambling was New Labour's main (mis)understanding of Culture from the outset . . .

Given the Blair Government's nonetheless continuing absurdly hyped delusions about Regeneration by Gambling, as a flagstone of its plans for radical reform, there was a further irony in the choice of Manchester for Britain's first Supercasino. Manchester is famous – and infamous – for more gang wars and guns, violent crime and vice, and widespread abject poverty, than any other city in the UK with the possible exceptions of London and Glasgow. And the Supercasino was to be built in the most poverty-blighted eastern corner of that city.

Luckily for non-criminal Mancunians, the House of Lords kicked out the entire benighted scheme on 28 March 2007, largely because a quorum of level-headed folk, including the Archbishops of Canterbury and York, pressed the point that one of the last things likely to spread authentic culture or regeneration was anything to do with gambling or casinos. Thank the Lord – or goodness, or providence, or something – for the Lords. Long may the obvious unwisdom of promoting a – er, culture of gambling and casinos keep those dangerous hotbeds of addictions away. But what a sign of the philistine times that the nation's Ministers and official Departments of Culture and Media needed Lords and Archbishops to remind them of such a glaringly self-evident point.

– To proffer a drop of credibility, if not consolation, to (Super)casino proponents, perhaps we should entertain the possibility that this policy initiative's communication was jinxed by a single misplaced consonant, and what they were talking about all along was *DEgeneration* by Gambling – ?

Page 197

"U-Turn On All This/ – or Die"

Nick Ut's photograph from 8 June 1972 shows Vietnamese children running down a road near Trang Bang after a napalm chemical attack on villages suspected of harbouring National Liberation Front fighters. The photo became a defining symbol of the international movement against US involvement in Vietnam.

The child in the centre of the picture, running naked after having been severely burned on her back, was Phan Thi Kim Phuc, then aged nine. South Vietnamese planes had dropped a napalm bomb on Trang Bang, which was occupied by Viet Cong forces. Kim Phuc joined a group of civilians and ARVN soldiers fleeing from the Cao Dai temple in the village along the road to safe ARVN positions. A South Vietnamese pilot mistook the group as a threat and diverted to attack it.

After taking the photo, Nick Ut took Kim Phuc straight to a hospital in Saigon, where it was thought her burns were so severe that she would not survive. But after 14 months in the hospital, and seventeen different surgeries, she returned home.

In 1996 Kim Phuc gave a speech at the US Vietnam Veterans' Memorial on Veterans' Day. She said that we cannot change the past, but can work for a peaceful future. In November 1997 she was named a UNESCO Goodwill Ambassador. In October 2004 she was awarded an honorary Doctorate of Laws from York University in Toronto for her work to aid child victims of war around the world.

Audio tapes of then-President Richard Nixon, in dialogue with his chief of staff H R Haldeman, reveal that Nixon questioned the veracity of the photograph, muttering that it may have been "fixed". After listening back to this tape, Nick Ut commented:

> "President Nixon doubted the authenticity of my photograph when he saw it in the papers on June 12, 1972 . . . That terrified little girl is still alive today and has become an eloquent testimony to the authenticity of the photo. The picture for me and unquestionably for many others could not have been more real. The photo was as authentic as the Vietnam War itself. The horror of the Vietnam War recorded by me did not have to be fixed."

Page 198

". . . What we actually have/ in pseudo-millennial Britain . . ."

– cf Nick Cohen in *'Cruel Britannia'* (Verso Books 1999): ". . . what we have in Britain is a consensus built around the prejudices of right-wing conservatism"

"thick with . . . opportunism, gambling, infinite greed"

In July 2006 Richard Caborn, Minister in the Department of Culture, Media & Sport expressed his concern (in a memo to Mark Davies, MD of Betfair, quoted in the Observer of 7/1/2007) that ". . . *Britain should become a World Leader in the field of online gambling"*. You might think that anyone staking this claim as something to write home, never mind boast about, was satirically fantasising as to the only more grotesquely pointless area in which the country could possibly take a pride in staying ahead of others than those Mandelson, Jowell & Blairites Inc had already flaunted as the UK's World Leadership Credentials (– i e, the Nillennium Dome, the most unaccountably expensive and nationalistic seventeen days of competitive athletics ever, and the out-hawking of the USA, Nazi Germany and the Soviet Union in Blair's endlessly re-avowed determination to stay on top of "The First Division of Nations Prepared to Intervene" with military actions whenever it struck him as "The Right Thing To Do").

– But no: Caborn was in thumpingly bureaucratic earnest. Perhaps not so surprising after all, given his Culture Ministressa Jowell's kinky preoccupation with turning the whole of Britain into a network of ceaselessly whirring government-promoted casinos.

But you might still wonder in just what creditable senses either casinos or online gambling qualify as either Sport or Media, let alone Culture? Presumably the prospect of potentially Big Money to spin off to the Treasury yet again curbed any tremor of conscience, sensitivity or concern regarding potential ill-effects on the population at large of being so wilfully drawn into gambling and its long-documented and inevitable concomitants – debt, money-laundering, drug-taking, pushing and addiction, alcoholism, prostitution, et al *ad nauseam*.

"A World Leader" – ? When Mayor Livingstone had paid the ex-CIA operative Bob Kiley millions for, by his own admission, "doing not much" as the so-called Consultant on London's ever-worsening transport problems – and when Blair had spent squillions more than that following *his* Leaders Clinton and Bush into so many murderous wars and other disastrous misadventures abroad, on what ground could the UK still pretend or aspire to be leading anyone anywhere?

Let our elected leaders rather do what they are elected for: sort out this little country's own child poverty crisis; unhealthy health and toothless dentistry services; educational inequities; ever-increasing urban violence (with knives, guns and gangs standing in for the missiles, bombs and armies being mirrored) – plus the onrush of anti-ecological exploitations on all fronts for quick profits and long-term misery.

– And then, after a concerted period of redistributions and palpably effective U-Turns, having spent not a minute or a penny on questing for status or publicity, Britain could possibly find itself, as an unsolicited and deserved but immaterial bonus, regarded as a halfway decent example, in some respects, by others.

". . . this government darkness visible/ clotted as Monsanto – thick/ as thieves in the night . . ."

For many years Monsanto, notoriously disgraced for its knowing and reckless (of anything but quick-sell profits) promotion of more or less untested Genetically Modified materials, was one of the largest manufacturers of PCBs. These are artificial organic chemicals that from the 1920s onwards were used in a wide range of industrial products, from capacitors to fertilisers and paint. In 2007 these are openly recognised as persistent organic pollutants due to their long-term stability in the environment. This means that they accumulate in top predators such as polar bears, whales and humans, where their toxicity can result in liver damage, reproductive problems, damage to the immune system, and possibly cancer. PCBs were eventually banned in 1986, but recently-released documents show that Monsanto knew about the deadly effects of the chemicals as early as 1953.

According to John Vidal (*'Monsanto dumped toxic waste in UK'*, Guardian 12 February 2007, pp1-2), ". . . Company chemists tested the PCB chemicals on rats and found that they killed more than 50% with medium-level doses" – and that each of the surviving rats was damaged. Vidal also reported that the company knew how the chemicals were accumulating in the environment, and contaminating fish, birds, wildlife, animals and human milk from 1965 – yet carried on manufacturing them in their Welsh factories, to the tune of 61,500 tonnes in Newport and Ruabon.

Equally worrying for UK residents and workers is the evidence, in the same issue of the Guardian, that Monsanto paid contractors "to dump thousands of tonnes of highly toxic waste in British landfill sites". A private Environment Agency report obtained by the Guardian showed that 67 extremely toxic chemicals, including Agent Orange derivatives, dioxins and PCBs that could only have been made by Monsanto, are leaking from Brofiscin Quarry near Cardiff. This landfill site, an unlined pit that was never licensed to take chemical wastes, came to national attention in 2003 when fumes escaped from the dump and covered the neighbouring village of Groesfaen. And this despite the fact that the site had been investigated between 1967 and 1973, after farmers reported poisoned cattle and deformed calves.

A pollution consultant, Douglas Gowan, filed a report for the National Farmers' Union which was never acted on, and last year reported how for four years from 1969 he witnessed ". . . not just landfill tipping in regular hours, but also dumping at night. I saw vehicles dumping slurry, liquids and tars, as well as . . . open drums. There is evidence of not only negligence and utter incompetence, but cover-up, and the problem has grown unchecked . . ." (*'The wasteland: how years of secret chemical dumping left a toxic legacy'*, John Vidal, Guardian 12/2/07, p9). In 1971 the United States banned domestic production of PCBs, but Monsanto continued producing them in Wales for six more years, with the blessings of British governments which had known of the environmental dangers throughout the preceding decade.

Internal Monsanto documents have revealed that the Newport factory was leaky to the extent that at one point it was "losing" 1.7kg (3.7lb) a day of some of the most dangerous PCBs. Vidal's Guardian reports quote –

". . . Herbert Vodden, a Monsanto physicist who tested how long the PCBs took to break down, [who] said the company initially lobbied the government to carry on making PCBs in the 1960s. 'They were very supportive', he said. And when Monsanto [finally] decided to pull out of PCB manufacture, '. . . the Department of Industry argued *against* us withdrawing them. *They came and told us that we should continue*' . . ."

Barton Williams, who owns the quarry, told Vidal that he has ". . . no idea exactly what lies below his land, or how dangerous it is: 'It's leaking, isn't it? It's the wrong colour'. . ." The waste dump reeks a nauseous mix of sick and sulphur when it rains, and a small brook gushes a vivid orange froth from it. Williams complained that ". . . The Environment Agency hasn't been open about it at all, and the Council didn't even tell me it was toxic waste when I bought the land. They only told the public three years ago".

The Environment Agency now accepts that both waste and groundwater around the Brofiscin site have been polluted since the 1970s, and that this situation will continue as the dumped metal containers continue to corrode and release their toxic contents. The lasting harm done by the continued production and unscrupulous transportations and disposals of such evidently long-lasting and harmful chemicals – let alone the continuing compound interest of unabated contamination – will not be reckoned for many years to come.

"thick with . . . sycophancy, cronyism, owed favours, bribery . . ."

Examples of these have become the norm since 1997, their absence the exception.

Measureless to man, woman and child have been the yawns stifled at the unstoppable onrush of favours for Tony's cronies, donations and loans for peerages, along with other honours, plum jobs and all manner of bonuses orchestrated by ultra-nepotistical New Labour in general, and Downing Street in particular.

The further corruptions around UK arms trading that have come to light, on top of revelations of how brutally exploitative the racketeering turns out to have been for yonks, make the Blair régime's incorrigible warmongering slightly more explicable, damn it.

The bribes that had previously been uncovered (see the notes to *Page 142* on pp367-368) were only the tip of the iceberg. A huge investigation by the Serious Fraud Office got under way in 2006 and dredged up evidence of British Aerospace bribes all over the planet.

For instance, *inter alia*: over £1m was paid to General Pinochet in Chile; a commission of more than £7m was paid to ensure the sale of two rusty second-hand Royal Navy frigates to Romania; the infamous and no-longer secret slush fund of more than £60m was used by BAe to lay on limos, prostitutes and luxury holidays in the cause of sweetening and paying off prominent Saudi Arabian officials and royals for lucrative arms contracts.

In November 2006 the SFO was poised, under the 2001 Anti-Terrorism, Crime and Security Act, to gain access to some of the Saudi royal family's Swiss bank accounts that would allegedly have shed light on cases of bribery by BAe in pursuit of its £43bn Al-Yamamah (which apparently means Dove . . .) contract with the Saudis. Yet on 14/12/06, following intensive lobbying by BAe, the Attorney-General Peter Goldsmith, and the PM behind him, ordered the investigation to be closed. The timing of Blair Cabinet-member Goldsmith's announcement of this cop-out to a near-deserted House of Lords on the same day as the 3-years' awaited Stevens Report on the deaths of Princess Diana and Dodi al-Fayed was to appear *and* the first police interview with the PM about loans for peerages *and* major Post Office closure news, suggested a 'Bury Bad News' element at work.

Blair claimed national security was at stake, and Goldsmith claimed the intelligence agencies' support. Unfortunately for Goldsmith in his by then customary role of playing Shakespeare's Buckingham the front man to Blair's Richard III, John Scarlett, the head of MI6, refused to endorse this, whilst Whitehall sources said ". . . there was *nothing* to suggest that the Saudis had warned 'if you continue with this enquiry, we will cut off intelligence'. . ." (*'MI6 and Blair at odds over Saudi deals'*, David Leigh, Richard Norton-Taylor and Rob Evans, Guardian, 16/1/2007). Meanwhile Robert Wardle, director of the SFO, disputed Goldsmith's assessment that it was likely that no charges would have been brought (see *'Fraud office disputes UK line on BAe'*, Jimmy Burns, Christopher Adams and Hugh Williamson, Financial Times, 16/1/06; *'Blair forced Goldsmith to drop BAe charges'*, Leigh & Evans, Guardian 1/2/07; *'Swiss launch BAe inquiry over money-laundering'*, Leigh & Evans, 14/5/07); and *'MoD accused: BBC says officials processed payments'*, Guardian 12/6/07).

The Attorney-General has, surprise surprise, repeatedly insisted that commercial considerations, such as the £10-£20 billion Eurofighter Typhoons deal that BAe and the Saudis were about to close just as the SFO turned on the heat, played no part in his sudden change of mind. If this were true, then why – like Winnie the Pooh denying he'd been at the honey though his snout was covered in the stuff – did he bother to mention it so emphatically? Ditto Blair's repeated denials that the closure order had nothing to do with the many UK arms manufacturing jobs that would otherwise be lost. According to The Guardian (p1, 7/6/07) Goldsmith had warned "government complicity [was] in danger of being revealed unless the corruption enquiries were stopped".

After his *"passionate"* 2003 resolution that Britain must bomb into Iraq because she would otherwise risk being missiled into by Saddam at 45 minutes' notice, and because 'twas *"the right thing to do"*, Blair was hardly one to command authority regarding national security. Surely national security depends very largely on maintaining the rule of laws up to which the nation has signed – ? As to the bleatings about job losses, for goodness' sake: *let such abhorrent jobs be lost instanter and forever.* When the Nazi gas chambers and death camps were finally eradicated, no politician or labour leader worthy of respect wasted tears or breath bemoaning the different work opportunities ex-concentration camp employees found themselves resorting to in consequence. (See the notes on pages 367-372, including Samuel Brittan's warning that "We should be on our guard when politicians defend dubious policies by declaring *'Jobs are at stake'*, etc, etc.)

Government officials were going to have to justify themselves before the anti-corruption body, the Organisation for Economic Co-operation and Development (OECD), whose Anti-Bribery Convention the UK signed in 2002. Since Article 5 of this *precludes* "considerations of . . . the potential effect on relations with another state", both Blair's and Goldsmith's would-be justifications for calling off the Strategic Fraud Office investigation were invalid and – er – fraudulent.

Following the whitewashes of the not-so-independent enquiries into the legitimacy of Britain's invasion of Iraq by Lord Button (aka the Hutton Report and the Butler Report), and given the fact that Peter Goldsmith had initially advised that this bombardment of a sovereign state would in fact infringe international law, the abrupt termination order against the SFO-BAe researches was all the more revealing of Blair's incorrigible hypocrisy, and his likewise incorrigible grovelling to moneyed Big Shots. – And all the more ironic, in view of the empty narcissism with which his government had gone on puffing its feathers for – er, integrity, for having steered onto the statute book in 2001 the very anti-corruption Act which the B-movieLiar sidestepped so hammily in 2006.

Ian McCartney, Blair's Minister for Trade & Investment, went so far as to declare (Guardian 26/4/07, p35) that ". . . We are proud of the steps we have taken in the last two years to implement the [OECD] Convention". This rang hollow in view of the Guardian's report (*'UK tries to sabotage BAe bribes enquiry'*, front page 24/4/07) that at its March meeting, the OECD's "36-strong panel announced detailed plans to mount a fresh official inspection of Britain because of the manner in which the BAe enquiry had been halted. It also rebuked the UK for failing to keep its promises to modernise its inadequate corruption laws, under which no one has yet been prosecuted". (See *'US protest on axeing of BAe probe'* by Jimmy Burns and James Boxell, Financial Times pp1 & 3, 22/4/07; *'BAe accused of secretly paying £1bn to Saudi prince – sanctioned by MOD'* by Leigh & Evans, Guardian pp1-3, 7/6/07), and *'BAe faces criminal enquiry in US'* (Guardian pp1-2, 14/6/07).

As of June 2007, the SFO was pressing on with investigations into various other BAe bribery and corruption allegations. For example, Swedish prosecutors had recently identified an Austrian Count based in Scotland as one of three agents suspected of being involved in alleged commission payments of more than £4m related to a £400m Anglo-Swedish deal to lease fighter planes to the Czech Republic in 2004. The SFO was probing BAe's use of a secret offshore subsidiary, Red Diamond, which was ". . . set up to pay worldwide commissions through Swiss banks" (*'Count named in BAe corruption inquiry'*, David Leigh and Rob Evans, Guardian 21/2/07).

Tony Blair never showed the slightest compunction about acting as a salesman for BAe. As well as lobbying in Prague in 2002, he went to Riyadh on a similar mission in 2005, etc, etc, etc.

He had also campaigned hard at home, forcing through, among other scams, Cabinet approval in 2001 to license the sale of an overpriced and definitvely unnecessary £28m military radar system to Tanzania, one of the world's poorest nations, in the face of opposition from Clare Short and Gordon Brown. In January 2007, Short used her parliamentary privilege to discover that the SFO had seen documents showing the Tanzania deal ". . . stank: No.10 insisted on letting this go ahead, when it was always obvious that this useless project was corrupt", she said (*'BAe's secret $12m payout in African deal'*, Leigh and Evans, Guardian front page, 15/1/07). This article reported that BAe's secretly owned offshore company Red Diamond covertly deposited $12m – 30% of the contract price – into Tanzanian middleman Sailesh Vithlani's Swiss bank account. (See also page 6, and the second note to it on pages 242-243).

Another shady arms deal undergoing the SFO's scrutiny that left Blair's face looking distinctly bad-eggy was the 1999 sale of Hawk jets to South Africa. The investigation encompassed alleged payments to a senior South African defence ministry official, as well as to John Breadencamp, BAe's agent in southern Africa. The conclusion of the £1.5 billion deal saw South Africa plump for a package of twenty-four BAe Hawk jets and twenty-eight Saab Gripen fighter planes, instead of a rival Italian offer at less than half the price. According to the Johannesburg Mail & Guardian, secret payments of nearly £80m were made to South African agents by BAe's Red Diamond and HQ Marketing units (*'BAe bosses named as corruption suspects'*, Guardian front page, 17/1/07).

As David Leigh wrote in the Guardian on 24/2/2007, ". . . Never has a major British company been confronted with such a parade of global corruption allegations as BAe. Why did they set up the Red Diamond subsidiary that never appeared in its published accounts, and was registered in the murky anonymity of the British Virgin Islands? Why did Red Diamond pay hundreds of millions of pounds into other people's Swiss bank account?" (See also *'The BAe Files'* on *www.guardian.co.uk/baefiles*)

I would add, is it not also long overdue for UK governments – avowedly opposed to arms proliferation – to answer to an independent enquiry as to why British taxpayers have for so long been charged, and go on being charged, for propping up such vile commerce which, apart from making no profits for them or for the nation, inevitably adds to the gross toll of human suffering and premature deaths all over the planet?

Page 199

". . . *Uncle Sam's leaden/ dreamless design/ of Mob-rule materialist/ world domination*"

– as indicated by Michael Meacher in his article '*This war on terrorism is bogus*' (Guardian 6/9/03, p21):

> "We now know that a blueprint for the creation of a global Pax America . . . entitled '*Rebuilding America's Defences*', was written in September 2000 by the neoconservative think tank, Project for the New American Century (PNAC). The plan shows Bush's cabinet intended to take military control of the Gulf region whether or not Saddam Hussein was in power. It says 'while the unresolved conflict with Iraq provides the immediate justification, *the need for a substantial American force presence in the Gulf transcends the issue of the régime of Saddam Hussein*' . . .

> "It says 'even should Saddam pass from the scene', US bases in Saudi Arabia and Kuwait will remain permanently . . . as 'Iran may well prove as large a threat to US interests as Iraq has'. It spotlights China for 'régime change', saying 'it is time to increase the presence of American forces in South East Asia'. The document also calls for the creation of 'US space forces' to dominate space, and the total control of cyberspace to prevent 'enemies' using the internet against the US. It also hints that the US may consider developing biological weapons '. . . that can target specific genotypes [and] may transform biological warfare from the realm of terror to a politically useful tool' . . ."

Page 200

In this photograph from the US Army Corps of Engineers archive, the Hiroshima bomb victim's skin was burned in a pattern corresponding to the dark portions of her kimono.

Page 201

". . . *No arms race/ is ever won/ for good/ after all* . . ."

– particularly when you are having it with your supposed allies, as is the case now, with the UK and other European nations so concerned to keep up with US military developments: a race they are doomed always to lose because of America's massively 'superior' military budget.

See also note to "*Earth looks like it won't recover*" on page 389.

". . . *// e v e r l a s t i n g l y // l o s t   f a c e s // and bodies/ of Japanese/ generations* . . ."

As long ago as 1967, James Cameron tried to awaken his readers (of '*Point of Departure: an Autobiography*', Arthur Barker) to the fact that the bomb dropped on Hiroshima on 6 August 1945 to sample its effects and keep the Russians out of Japan –

> ". . . was not, by the monstrous standards of the present, much of a bomb. It was an interesting consideration, when the anointed ostriches of Defence were speaking of the 'tactical weapon' as though it had the discrimination of a stiletto, that this 'tactical weapon' was precisely the atomic bomb of 1945 that we had equated with the wrath of God, that abruptly ended the life of 80,000 people one August morning.

". . . Some of us had been to Hiroshima, deliberately choosing an examination of the most spectacular, destructive, and almost certainly the wickedest man-made catastrophe ever known. The ferocious paradoxes of the place were symptoms . . . of the traumatic reaction of a community well aware that it had been made the guinea-pig of the most cold-blooded and terrible physical experiment in history (since the Japanese were as aware as anyone else that they were atom-bombed *after* their attempts to sue for peace) . . . a people whose minds, among the survivors, had been scarred into a compulsion to disguise, distort, forget."

Gore Vidal is another who has exposed (in, among other publications, the Times Literary Supplement of 10/11/2000, pages 16-17) –

"the great myth . . . that Harry Truman dropped his two atom bombs on Hiroshima and Nagasaki because he feared that a million American lives would be lost in an invasion (that was the lie he told at the time). Admiral Nimitz, on the spot in the Pacific, and General Eisenhower, brooding elsewhere, disagreed: the Japanese had already lost the war, they said. No nuclear bombs, no invasion were needed, since the Japanese had been trying to surrender since the May 1945 devastation of Tokyo by US B-29 bombers."

Truman's handwritten diary for 18 July 1945 mentioned the "telegram from Jap *(sic)* emperor asking for peace", and on 3 August '45 Walter Brown logged a meeting with the US Secretary of State James F Byrnes, Admiral W D Leahy and Truman at which all three agreed, "Japs looking for peace". Just three days later Truman ordered the demolition of Hiroshima, and on 9 August he unloaded the second atom bomb onto the blameless inhabitants of Nagasaki.

Why were the bombs dispatched? No doubt partly to discover just how lethal their effects could be. Vidal is among many who believe it was primarily ". . . To frighten Stalin, a suitable enemy for the US as it was about to metamorphose from an untidy republic into a national security state at 'perpetual war', in Charles A Beard's phrase, 'for perpetual peace' . . ."

The UK's foreign policies seem to have kowtowed to those of the US for most of the last half century. What Vidal wrote about Truman's attempted intimidation of Stalin, at the reverberating expense of civilian lives in Hiroshima and Nagasaki, feels grimly prescient of our own death-hawking gang's resolve to out-bully Milosevic, Osama bin Laden, the Taliban, Saddam Hussein *et al*, at such high-flown cost to so many scatter-bombed and Depleted Uranium-shelled citizens of the former Yugoslavia, Afghanistan, Iraq *et al*:

". . . Please no letters about the horrors of the Gulag, Stalin's mistreatment of the buffer states, and so on. Our subject is the serious distortions of the truth on *our* side and why, unless they are straightened out, we are forever doomed to thrash about in a permanent uncomprehending fog. Good morning, Vietnam!"

Page 202

"the dead tree gives no shelter, the cricket no relief . . . . // . . . . I will show you fear in a handful of dust"
– from Eliot's *'The Waste Land'*, I, lines 23-30. Cf "Life's but a walking shadow" – Shakespeare's *'Macbeth'*, V, v, 24.

Page 204

"– famed oily blood brothers . . ."

The continued link between oil-getting and blood-letting is painfully obvious. According to Michael Meacher (Guardian 6/9/03):

"... Until July 2001 the US saw the Taliban régime as a source of stability in Central Asia that would enable the construction of hydrocarbon pipelines from the oil and gas fields in Turkmenistan, Uzbekistan, Kazakhstan, through Afghanistan and Pakistan, to the Indian ocean. But, confronted with the Taliban's refusal to accept US conditions, the US representatives told them 'either you accept our offer of a carpet of gold, or we will bury you under a carpet of bombs . . .' (Inter Press Service, 15 November 2001).

"The UK government has confirmed that 70% of our electricity will come from gas by 2020, and 90% of that will be imported. In that context it should be noted that Iraq has 110 trillion cubic feet of gas reserves in addition to its oil."

– All the more reason, therefore, to hasten a seriously Green Revolution, harbinger of global redistribution and long overdue *post*-military navigations for timeship earth.

.

"An eye for an eye"

This paraphrase of Exodus 21.24 and Deuteronomy 19.21, oft-times invoked by George W Bush, has never resolved any human dispute satisfactorily, let alone enduringly. When acted on – as it has continued to be around so many troubled parts of the planet in recent decades – the barbaric injunction's main consequence seems to be more and more blind, maimed and killed people almost everywhere in the world, one way and another.

George Bush has repeated the vindictive mantra over and over since 9/11 in alleged relation to the calamities of that date. This exposes a lack of joined-up thinking on his part, and on that of his aides and speech-writers, in that whenever the support of embryonic stem cell research is mooted, the President has declared he would never *". . . destroy life to save a life . . ."*

I accept that two wrongs are unlikely to make a right. The question is, why don't Bush and his coevil-axe grinders and brain-dead eye-blinders accept it? Destroying lives, or eyes, to avenge previous destroyed lives or eyes, is a guaranteed 100% all-round no-win policy.

Page 205

"God bless/ AMERICA"

See notes to *"adapted/ from Woody Guthrie"* on pages 337-339

Page 208

". . . all those sexless/ military-industrial/ divisions"

Cf Dwight Eisenhower's speech of farewell as President to the American nation, on 17 January 1961:

"We now stand ten years past the midpoint of a century that has witnessed four major wars among great nations. Three of these involved our own country. Despite these holocausts America is today the strongest, the most influential and most productive nation in the world. Understandably proud of this pre-eminence, we yet realise that *America's leadership and prestige depend* not merely upon our unmatched material progress, riches and military strength, but *on how we use our power in the interests of world peace and human betterment . . .*

"Until the latest of our world conflicts, the United States had no armaments industry. American makers of plowshares could, with time and as required, make swords as well. But now we can no longer risk emergency improvisation of national defence; we have been compelled to create a permanent armaments industry of vast proportions. Added to this, three and a half million men and women are directly engaged in the defence establishment. We annually spend on military security more than the net income of all United States corporations.

"This conjunction of an immense military establishment and a large arms industry is new in the American experience . . . *In the councils of government, we must guard against the acquisition of unwarranted influence, whether sought or unsought, by the military-industrial complex. The potential for the disastrous rise of misplaced power exists and will persist.* We must never let the weight of this combination endanger our liberties or democratic processes. We should take nothing for granted. *Only an alert and knowledgeable citizenry can compel the proper meshing of the huge industrial and military machinery of defence with our peaceful methods and goals, so that security and liberty may prosper together.*"

Ike's warnings and the Kennedy-Kruschev Test Ban Treaty were not heeded by the administrations which followed the assassinations of J F and Robert Kennedy. The US military industry spread its eagle wings worldwide, and instead of staying harnessed by *"peaceful methods and goals"* and supportive of *"the interests of human betterment"*, America's increasingly aggressive marketing of multi-pronged weaponry wilfully recharged and extended global conflict, torture and war-machines.

In *'Blowback: The Costs and Consequences of American Empire'* (Henry Holt & Co, New York 2000), Chalmers Johnson observed, with extraordinarily alert prescience, that –

"One of the things this huge military establishment does is sell arms to other countries, making the Pentagon a critical *economic* agency of a United States government. Militarily oriented products account for about a quarter of the total US Gross Domestic Product. The government employs some 6,500 people just to co-ordinate and administer its arms sales programme in conjunction with officials at American embassies around the world, who spend most of their 'diplomatic' careers working as arms salesmen. The Arms Export Control Act requires that the executive branch notify Congress of foreign military and construction sales directly negotiated by the Pentagon. Commercial sales valued at $14 million or more negotiated by the arms industry must also be reported. Using official Pentagon statistics, between 1990 and 1996 the combination of the three categories amounted to $97,836,821,000. From this nearly $100 billion figure must be subtracted the $3 billion a year the government offers its foreign customers to help subsidise arms purchases from the United States.

". . . *'Blowback'* is shorthand for saying that *a nation reaps what it sows, even if it does not fully know or understand what it has sown. Given its wealth and power, the United States will be a prime recipient in the foreseeable future of all the more expectable forms of blowback, particularly terrorist attacks against Americans in and out of the armed forces anywhere on earth,* including within the United States."

Page 208-209

"– *dump sham economics* / / – *close off once for all* / *that frantic fast lane selling drive* . . . // . . . *Politicians* – *get real:* / – *forget 'leading the world'* . . ."

On 6 March 2007, Tony Blair read out a long (and even more self-approbating than usual) speech at London's Tate Modern gallery. The advance publicity presaged a speech about the arts in Britain, but it turned out to say next to nothing about the arts, and precious little about anything else excepting money. And most of that consisted of lies about money. Here are some fairly typical excerpts:

> "Before coming to government, I said that we would make the arts and culture part of our 'core script' . . . It was no longer to be on the periphery, an add-on . . . but rather it was to be central, an essential part of the narrative about the character of a new, different, changed Britain."

Blair then claimed that this centrality had been achieved by New Labour, and that we will "look back at the last ten years as *a 'golden age' for the arts*". — Er, well — ok, in that the commercial-viability-is-all ethic *(sic)* has imposed a clampdown on artistic nonconformity and risk-taking over these years. Under New Labour prescriptions and proscriptions, visible or potentially creative activities have found (– or, all too often, lost) their ways supervened by purely gold – meaning financial – standards only.

If they can be defined and incorporated as profitable industries they have been encouraged and harnessed. If not, they are categorically out of the frame – as witness Helena Kennedy's answer to painter-poet Nik Morgan (see page 402), when his benefit was withdrawn because he was determined to continue doing the job he loves, does well, and is best qualified for – *viz: Parliament does not see Art or Poetry as real work.* Morgan deduced that ". . . Money is the only thing valued under this system".

The Blair definitions and deformations of culture have indeed been central to the "different, changed Britain" his governance has left us with. Rampant Philistinism coupled with pseudo-Richard the Lionheart leads in foreign policy do not a Blake's Jerusalem build.

What has been "new and different" militarily qualified 1997-2007, with Blair's five wars alone far outgunning Thatcher's short (if mega-brutal) single one over her long years in charge, to be remembered and deplored as a 'deadly decade'. Whilst the artistic void over the Blair era, in terms of, er – "core" or "central" government nurturing, suggests a 'dross decade' as the more accurate designation.

The most obvious examples of core scripts and central government peripheralising *bona fide* artistic lights, on New Labour's incorrigibly materialistic level alone, have been the boosting of the Greenwich Dome and, latterly, of the seventeen-day Olympic Games of 2012, with each of their stupendous and utterly uprecedented fundings putting paid to thousands and thousands of genuinely artistic projects, despite their far less exorbitant needs.

Another of Blair's would-be bullet points on 6 March was that: ". . . A Nation that cares about art will be . . . in the early 21st Century, a more Successful one". My close scrutiny of this PM since before he grasped the helm has revealed not the slightest evidence that Blair cares about any serious art activity at all. ". . . Culture spans so many disciplines" he blathered, and ". . . I am very much aware of the contribution from every quarter". One wonders which quarters apart from market-ing, spin, *realpolitik*, hawking the planet and self-promotion he would be much aware of. As Catherine Bennett wrote in Guardian 2 on 8/3/07: ". . . Although we are all familiar with Blair's admiration for rock music, soaps, football and Shilpa Shetty, it is hard to recall his registering any interest, ever, in other art forms".

– There was no need for him to define how he measured success because where it was not explic-it, it was patently implicit in every breath of the speech: Success always = Big Money in New

Labourspeak. And thus, spake King Blag, ". . . *A new breed of entrepreneurial leaders . . . has shown that art is compatible with sound financial discipline.* Indeed, the public subsidy *produces a return*". – Come again? The biggest pseudo-arts project of His decade, the 2000 Millennium Dome, subsidised far above the hilt from tax, Lotto and some pretty dodgy corporate backers including arms merchants, produced an all-time record deficit, for which the public purses were still being raided in 2007.

Blair's Tate Modern speech also boasted that ". . . The Arts Council operates as an arm's length body, so that *the state is placed in the position of doing what it has historically done well – funding – and not what it has historically done very badly – control of the arts*". – As so often with Maestro Blur, this was a crunchy-sounding waffle of several toxic lies at once. Like most of its predecessors in living memory, but more so, Blair's state managed very well (as he – the prime policy architect, with Gordon Brown – was aware at all points) to control the arts quite definitively, by controlling and constantly curtailing subsidies to non-profit-making arts.

For instance: the proudly flagged 'New Opportunities Fund' and the National Lottery – both designed and committed to subsidise among other things, the arts overall, and the Arts Council in particular, with an express embargo on the funding of any governmental initiatives or emergencies – were in fact regularly mugged over this *"golden decade"* for the Greenwich Dome, and of late have gone on being mugged for the 2012 Olympic Games.

In 1998 the Dome's alleged pre-production costs gobbled up £*758 million* or more whilst, along with many hundreds of authentic arts enterprises nationwide, the long-standing and much-used and loved Greenwich Theatre had to close when its grant expectation of a mere £*210 thousand* was turned down as unaffordable.

Again: in 2006 the London branch of Arts Council England found itself too financially beleaguered to release a £5k grant against a fraction of the minimum likely losses on a Poetry Olympics festival, or a further £5k towards a bumper international New Departures anthology's printing costs – repeating four previous similar rejections of similarly small-scale potential grant aid between 1998 and 2004.

And the same sort of fate befell many similarly worthy arts projects and workers, mainly because – since the adoption and inflations of the Greenwich Dome, and then, as Blairites kept calling it, the "Winning the Olympics for London" *fait accompli* – virtually all bets for other London-based subsidy-seekers were sent packing, in favour of the near-infinite grandiose requirements supposed necessary to guarantee "Success" for the year 2000 in and out of Greenwich, and for the athletics events of 27 July-12 August 2012 in and out of the five boroughs in the Lower Lea Valley.

Blair's speech also smarmed that over 'his' ten years, ". . . *We have deepened our culture*". For my (minimal but hard-earned) money, he and his regiments of corporate gangsters and artistically clueless policy wonks have made it – made the very word culture, and public understandings of its desirable meanings – near-irrecoverably more shallow. Thus John Tusa observed (in *'Meddling Philistines'*, Times 2, 17 April 2007, pp14-15) that ". . . The word 'culture' in local authority speak has been debased to include swimming, walking and enjoying parks, almost to the deliberate exclusion of the visual and performing arts".

Many of Blair's Tate Modern claims would presumably have been denied by several of the Arts Ministers Blair had discarded for being too committed to raising the scope and support for artists at home, and to downscaling that for arms trading and wars abroad, such as Mark Fisher and Chris Smith. I can't see either of those agreeing, for instance, that ". . . *All of us in Government take great pride in what has been achieved this past decade . . .*"

Yes, some great(ish) arts productions have been achieved. But these have happened despite, not because of New Labour. What Blair's Camelotto-fixated cronyhood is responsible – and should apologise in eternity – for, are such degrading manifestations of non- or *Ugh*-culture as the *I'm a Celebrity / Big Brother / Fame Academy* brands of television wank shows, and the promotion of neo-American brute force as the first resort in addressing national and international crises.

On 15 March 2007 Tessa Jowell simpered to the Commons that the budget for the 2012 Olympic Games was to be trebled to £9.3bn – which she decreed meant that the Arts Council's contribution to the Games had to rise from £49.6m to £112.5m. – So much for the "arm's length" principle, and for Blair's lie regarding New Labour's magnanimous abandonment of what he said at Tate Modern "*. . . the state has historically done very badly – control of the arts*".

Arts Council England's chief executive Peter Hewitt commented that "*. . . The impact is likely to be felt across the whole of England, and disproportionately by smaller arts organisations, local projects and individual artists*". And the Heritage Lottery Fund was, in turn, having to lose £90m to the seventeen-day wonder in 2012. Dame Liz Forgan, chair of this hitherto authentically regenerative Fund, pointed out that "*. . . This will impact on our ability to invest in the nation's heritage at exactly the time it is being showcased to the world in 2012*". Another case of wilfully unjoined-up thinking. – Or rather, of perishing any thought beyond the most immediate and superficial self-interest.

Which control-fixated Legacy Hunter, then, in this situation, was not so much "*. . . The new breed of entrepreneurial leader [who] has shown that art . . . is compatible with sound financial discipline*", as someone whose game was to get away, along with his cronies, with playing the arts, media and sports cards as wildly and crookedly as suited the most flattering wish-fulfilment of his, er, Leading Place in History?

Such brands of finagling might be allowed less mileage to post-Blair Blurrites if the Departments of Culture, Media & Sport were separated into three autonomous and less blurrable policy units. At the very least, this might mean that no future Minister for Sport would get away, without being suitably derided and demoted, as 2007's Sports Captain Richard Caborn did, with not only fixing the government's approval and official registration of online gambling as a Sport, but with puffing this anti-cultiural fix round the media as a pastime in which "*. . . Britain should become a world leader*"! (Yes, it would be quite funny, if only he had not pushed it with such unironic pomposity – and if only it were not simultaneously *so* costly and *so* impoverishing.)

Blair's 6 March '07 address resembled most of his other PR-pitched speeches in not letting the media off without at least one of his own "Britain is Leading the World" sound-grabs. For Tate Modern it was: "*. . . The UK Leads the world in the take-up of digital TV*". – Wowee! Or rather: so what? If the UK's 1997-2007 leisure, pleasure and –er, culture seekers are indeed known the world over to be the most passive, square-eyed and intellectually obese cyber-potatoes on the planet, all the more discredit to you, would-be Leader-World Saviour supreme.

Astonishingly – even for Teflon Tony – he tried to ingratiate himself further with the Tate Modern audience, and with the arts supposedly in mind, by notching up as a big plus his information that "*. . . London is one of three global capitals for the advertising industry*". Here's a tip for you, Tone: before pontificating about the arts again, take for your head notes two insights laid down by William Blake two centuries ago: "*. . . Suffer not the expensive advertising boasts made by fashionable fools for contemptible works . . .*" – and: "*. . . Where any view of Money exists, Art can not be carried on, but War only*".

439

Given some liberal doses of humility and some in-depth applications of *aperçus* such as "A little learning is a dangerous thing", career politicians could benefit themselves and their constituents by actually taking *the arts themselves* seriously. Had Blair attempted this before mouthing off such a grotesquely insensitive and patronising-to-the-workforce AGM-type press release, he might have thought again about one passage in it in particular. A close examination and deconstruction of this passage might have engendered a profound reversal of many of the "core scripts" and "civilised values" and "radical reforms" he had stood for since becoming Prime Minister, notably the sacrosanct prioritising of free market capitalism, and of its knee-jerk military-bully boy reflexes when challenged.

At the outset of the speech, he declared:

> ". . . A country like Britain today survives by the talent and ability of its people. *Human capital is key. The more it is developed, the better we are. Modern goods and services require high value-added input* . . . So when more children get access to the joy of art, it is not the art alone that they learn . . . *They may never be, probably won't ever be, an artist."*

– There it is. You said it chum. And you said it only half a minute after pretending you believed that art was ". . . *no longer to be on the periphery, an add-on* . . ." Under the Blair régime, as attested in the Commander-in-Chief's last word on the next UK generation in relation to arts production: "They . . . probably *won't* ever be an artist".

What an admission, in an extended address purporting to congratulate the concerted developments, under the speaker's unwavering baton, of what he was claiming to have orchestrated for the arts during his decade in office. If our children probably won't be artists, because governors like Blair want them only to be wage slaves, *"Human capital"* to be *"developed"* into *"high value-added input"* – how will it be possible for any art to be made at all?

A prerequisite for art to carry on, Big Dummy Tone, is for artists of any proven potential to be *helped and encouraged to be artists*.

Towards the close of his speech, Blair claimed to "know that . . . many of you are nervous that the golden era may be about to end", and to insinuate that he could allay such anxiety, in that ". . . The Olympic Victory *(sic)* was a vindication of the cultural face we now present to the world. One of the main reasons we Won is that we projected an idea of what Britain is now, and what we will become in the future".

If that was in fact one of the reasons, it would seem to have meant that Britain was then (and will become, or go on being) represented by the most – er, Successful conmen and hustlers in the world. And if that is the case, then the sooner Britain comes off its high-whinnying horse, and consigns this ugly anti-cultural face called Blairism to the dustbin, and engages with all the rest of the world as *comrades to cooperate, work and play with*, not competitors to defeat, or lesser followers to lead, the better all round – with a potential new lease of lives for artists and the arts in this country; and one might hope, for plenty of new departures and arrivals in, from, to and around many other countries too.

See also the notes on page 317 and ff, and on page 367 and ff.

Page 210-211

". . . *nothing new/ American Centurions// ...... doom-booming cacophony/ of empire-preserving scams"*

See Michael Meacher's citation of *'Rebuilding America's Defences'*, in the note to *Page 199* on page 433. This, as early on as September 2000, documented the Bush cabinet's hegemonic 'Project for the New American Century' – namely, for the US to take total military control of the Gulf region – and indeed of the entire planet, cyberspace, and it would seem, of anything else in the universe that might conceivably be up for grabs.

Page 211

"... they that live by the Bomb/ perish by the Bomb ..."

– Cf St Matthew, 26, 52: "Then said Jesus . . . Put up again thy sword into his place: for all they that take the sword shall perish with the sword".

Page 214

Terror in Abu Ghraib

This, and the other photos (reproduced on pp 129, 178, 214, and 352) of the humiliations inflicted by US Military on Iraqi prisoners, should help convey to anyone who still does not understand, why – apart from the sanctions, invasions, bombings and occupations – so many people hate America, and particularly hate its various widespread interventions outside the USA.

Abu Ghraib, 20 miles west of Baghdad, was Saddam Hussein's most notoriously violent, oppressive, torture-prone and murderous prison. After the régime's collapse in April 2003, this huge complex became a US military prison. But most of the thousands of prisoners, including women and teenagers, were civilians – some of them suspected common criminals, some detainees suspected of "crimes against the Coalition", and some suspected so-called "high-value" insurgents.

In July 2003, a major investigation into the US Army's prison system in Iraq was commissioned, and a 53-page report by Major General Antonio Taguba was completed in February '04. This had not been meant for public release, but the New Yorker magazine obtained a copy. In its 10/5/04 issue, Seymour M Hersh's *'Torture at Abu Ghraib'* cited a selection of its many ghastly revelations. Taguba found that between October and December 2003 there had been many "sadistic, blatant and wanton criminal abuses of detainees" at Abu Ghraib by soldiers of the 372nd Military Police Company and by members of the US intelligence community – such as:

> "... Breaking chemical lights and pouring the phosphoric liquid on detainees; pouring cold water on naked detainees; beating detainees with a broom handle and a chair; threatening male detainees with rape; allowing a military police guard to stitch the wound of a detainee who was injured after being slammed against the wall in his cell; sodomising a detainee with a chemical light and perhaps a broom stick, and using military working dogs to frighten and intimidate detainees with threats of attack *[see photograph on page 178]* and . . . biting a detainee."

Hersh summarised the "stunning evidence" Taguba's report provided of these abuses, including "detailed . . . graphic photographic evidence". This showed, among other horrors –

> "... Private Lynndie England, a cigarette dangling from her mouth, giving a jaunty thumbs-up sign and pointing at the genitals of a young Iraqi, who is naked except for a sandbag over his head, as he masturbates. In another, England stands arm-in-arm with Specialist Charles Graner, both grinning and giving the thumbs-up behind a cluster of perhaps seven naked Iraqis, knees bent, piled clumsily on top of each other in a pyramid *[reproduced on page 352]* . . . Another photograph shows a kneeling, naked, unhooded male prisoner . . . posed to make it appear that he is performing oral sex on another male prisoner, who is naked and hooded.

"Such dehumanisation is unacceptable in any culture, but it is especially so in the Arab world. Homosexual acts are against Islamic law and it is humiliating for men to be naked in front of other men. Bernard Haykel, a professor of Middle Eastern studies at NYU, explained: '. . . Being put on top of each other and forced to masturbate, being naked in front of each other – it's all a form of torture'. Two Iraqi faces that do appear in the photographs are those of dead men. There is the battered face of prisoner No.153399, and the bloodied body of another prisoner, wrapped in cellophane and packed in ice. There is a photograph of an empty room, splattered with blood. The 372nd's abuse of prisoners seemed almost routine, a fact of Army life that the soldiers felt no need to hide . . ."

When questioned about the humiliations, Lynndie England maintained that ". . . It was just fun and games. What was the Big Deal about it?" – a pretty one-sided dismissal of some pretty one-sided games, which were clearly no fun at all for the Iraqis.

The "Big Deal" was well encapsulated in Mahmood Jamal's poem, *'What's It All About?'*: ". . . It is about/ Baghdad/ Basra/ Fallujah/ Abu Ghraib/ Guantánamo// It is about/ Oil/ Money/ Contracts/ Power// It is about/ Ramallah/ Jerusalem/ Jenine/ Jericho// It is about Tanks/ Gunships/ Occupation// It is about/ 165,000 dead/ Cities Wasted// It is about/ Tiny coffins lined up/ An Afghan hillside/ It is about naked men piled up/ Like dead meat/ It is about hooded prisoners/ Chained to a wall// It is about/ Mothers, widows/ Limbless orphans/ Bombed from the sky/ Not knowing why./ It is about/ Wedding parties/ Torn to shreds by missiles// It is about collateral damage/ Running into thousands/ It is about/ War criminals/ Wielding death. // It is about/ Assassination/ Humiliation/ Exclusion/ Impotence// It's not about/ Our Way of Life// – *BUT THAT DOESN'T MAKE IT RIGHT* . . ."

See also the notes to *"Humiliation . . ."* on pages 351-366; *'The Abu Ghraib Files'* on *www.salon.com*; *www.torturecare.org.uk*; and *www.helenbamber.org/programmes.html*

Page 216

Photograph of Haifa Suicide Bus Bombing

The CNN report of the incident whose aftermath is depicted on these two photographs, compiled by Jerusalem Bureau chief Mike Hanna and correspondents Jerrold Kessel and Kelly Wallace, runs as follows:

"HAIFA SUICIDE BOMBER KILLS FIFTEEN – 11 March 2003.

"HAIFA, Israel (CNN) – A suicide bomber set off a powerful explosion that destroyed a suburban bus in the northern Israeli port city of Haifa on Wednesday, killing at least 15 Israelis and badly wounding at least 40, Israeli police said.

"At the time of the Haifa bombing, bus No. 37 was carrying many high school and college students on Mount Carmel in Haifa about 2 p.m. (7 a.m. ET), Assistant Police Commander Dani Kuffler said.

"Three of the 15 who died perished en route to the hospital. Many of the wounded were in serious condition, authorities said. The suicide bomber was killed in the blast.

"A spokesman for the Islamic fundamentalist group Hamas lauded the attack: '. . . We are sending the clear message that the will of resistance will continue until the elimination of the occupation', Mahmoud al-Zahar said. 'This is a message for the government that Israeli crimes, Israeli aggression, will be answered by a well-effective resistance from the Palestinian side'.

"Hamas has been labelled by the US State Department as a terrorist organisation. Izzedine al Qassam has admitted responsibility for terrorist attacks against Israeli civilians as well as attacks against the Israeli military.

"Witnesses to Wednesday's attack described a scene of horror. A witness quoted by Channel 2 said, 'The center of the bus lifted up into the air, the roof was torn. It looked like a blast inside the bus, and within seconds people began taking the wounded out of the bus'.

"The blast, which occurred on the city's main Moriah Boulevard near the Carmel Center as the bus was pulling out of a stop, also damaged stores in the area, said Police Chief Gil Kleiman.

"Wednesday's bombing was the first terror attack inside Israel in two months. The last such attack was January 5, when at least 23 people were killed and more than 100 wounded in a double-suicide bombing in Tel Aviv.

"The attack in Haifa 'is yet another Palestinian bloodletting of innocent Israeli civilians', David Baker, an official in Prime Minister Ariel Sharon's office, told the Israel daily Haaretz. 'Israel will not tolerate this terror, and will continue to take the necessary steps to eradicate it'.

"Israeli forces 'have conducted an extensive campaign in Palestinian territories to root out terrorists', Israeli officials say. Palestinian Minister of Information Yasser Abed Rabbo said that this campaign has killed 154 Palestinian civilians since the last suicide bombing: '. . . We condemn all attacks against civilians, including today's attack in Haifa', he said. 'The attack will only serve to distract attention from the more than 150 Palestinian civilians killed by Israel over the last two months'.

"While the officials waged a media war of accusations and counter-accusations, authorities in Haifa were still searching the charred ruins of the suburban bus. Part of its roof was gone and the back end of the bus – where police believe the explosion took place – was thrown over the top."

Page 217

"Palestinian family with the remains of their demolished home in Galilee, February 2004 . . .'

This photograph by Jonathan Cook shows a Palestinian family standing on the site of their former home in the Galilean village of Beaneh, demolished by the Israeli authorities in February 2004.

In *'The Other Side of Israel: My Journey Across the Jewish/Arab Divide'* (HarperCollins 2005) Susan Nathan, a British Zionist in her fifties who moved to Israel, revealed that 500 Arab homes had been destroyed in 2003, usually without warning.

Amazed by her Jewish compatriots' ignorance about their Arab neighbours Nathan decided to live among 25,000 Muslims in the all-Arab Israeli town of Tamra, a few miles from Nazareth.

She points out that ". . . The road to the other side of Israel is not signposted. It is a place you rarely read about in your newspapers or hear about from your television sets. It is all but invisible to most Israelis".

Jonathan Dimbleby found *'The Other Side of Israel'* –

". . . a deeply troubling book. It should be read by anyone who wants to understand the reality of life for the Arab citizens of Israel. Susan Nathan's story bears witness to the shameful discrimination routinely practised against them by the Israeli authorities. Her experience transforms her from an ardent Zionist into an eloquent but sorrowful critic of the state she had previously revered. Her account is the more telling because she writes with just as much warmth about her Jewish friends as she displays towards the Palestinians who befriend her."

Nathan's daily example bears witness to the practical possibility of Jews and Arabs living peacefully together in a single community, cemented by their common humanity. Where entrenched attitudes based on patriotism, propaganda, prejudice, ignorance and fear tend to lead only to more violence and bloodshed, Nathan's experience, and her firm stand against knee-jerk reactions and fossilised assumptions, suggest that determined in-depth exploration of this other side – the road still not taken by the warring powers that prevail – is the only option likely to ensure long-term mutual survival.

"(Palestinian) David and (Israeli-American) Goliath in the West Bank, 2002"

The photograph shows a Palestinian boy throwing a smidgen of rock at an Israeli tank (supplied by the USA) in the West Bank in 2002.

On 7 April 1997, Lea Rabin, widow of the assassinated Israeli Prime Minister Itzhak Rabin (1922-1995), said in a speech to the Los Angeles World Affairs Council (*'Rabin: Our Life, His Legacy'*):

"When in November 1947, by the vote of the United Nations, we were finally granted the Jewish State, we were standing alone . . . The newborn Jewish State was now facing a major threat: seven Arab nations refusing to accept a Jewish State into their area and determined to destroy it; seven Arab countries invading Israel on the day of the declaration of the State, 14 May 1948. David standing in front of Goliath. Few and weak against the many well-equipped armies.

". . . Almost a whole generation was killed. After the War of Independence in 1948 it became clear that if we want to survive in the area, we have to build an exceptionally strong army.

". . . When in 1967 Israel was invaded by three Arab countries (who were once again sure that they were going to wipe out the Jewish State and throw it into the sea) it turned into the most amazing victory.

". . . Years went by, and the conflict between Israel and its Palestinian neighbours continued. The Intifada focused on the urgent need to put an end to this conflict . . . Itzhak condemned any terrorist activity and said time and again – 'Let us sit and talk'.

"We, the established Jewish State, with our very strong and well-equipped armed forces, against a people who have lived under our occupation for 30 years since the Six Day War, who want their freedom and independence, who want to restore their dignity – bitter and frustrated.

"Now we are Goliath and they are David. How do we morally handle this situation? We Jews who for two thousand years suffered persecution, discrimination and offence, we who had no homeland and no power to resist, we who were as a nation almost annihilated by Nazi Germany when six million were exterminated.

"And now we confront a society which has no land and no strength. They work for us and they watch us, and the frustration is ever-mounting.

". . . The solution will not be found other than by getting together and trying to create a dialogue and find a way . . . As we approach the dialogue, we must have in mind: we are now Goliath.

"We can afford to take a certain risk, to be more generous, to be morally a David. This is what as Jews we wish to be – to use our power for our defence. *'Thou shalt not do to your neighbour what you would not like done to yourself'*. . ."

Itzhak Rabin declared after the Intifada: *'. . . I have learned something in the past two and a half months – that you can't rule by force over 1.5 million Palestinians'* (Time, 3 January 1994).

Yet all these wildly warfaring years later, President Bush and his confrères and poodles have kept paying lip-service to their religions which sanctify David – and also Samson – as the goodies.

And yet, as Lea Rabin's speech so eloquently pointed out, the current State of Israel and its armed forces (and its Transatlantic backers) continue to be the Goliath, repeatedly and often wilfully casting Arab and Islamic freedom fighters, suicide bombers, and diverse disciples of Hamas, Hezbollah, Al-Qaeda and their likes, into the roles of heroic Davids and Samsons.

Ten year-old girl on Northern Gaza beach weeping beside her dead father, June 2006

Ten year-old Palestinian Huda Ghalia's father, stepmother and siblings were quietly picnicking on their local beach in Beit Lahia, Northern Gaza on the afternoon of Friday 9 June 2006, when suddenly the area fell victim to a barrage of Israeli shells. Both parents and five siblings lost their lives immediately.

Six thousand shells had been fired pretty indiscriminately from inside Israel onto Gaza since April, with the aim of deterring rocket attacks. The beaches became raddled with craters from the shelling. More than two hundred Palestinians were killed in Gaza between early July and early September 2006.

On 17 July '06 Chris McGreal wrote in the Guardian that –

". . . Heartrending pictures of Huda Ghalia running wildly along a Gaza beach crying *'father, father, father'* and then falling weeping beside his body turned the distraught girl into an instant icon of the Palestinian struggle even before she fully grasped that much of her family was dead."

One of the survivors, Hani Asania, grabbed his daughters aged 4 and 7 when the shelling began and ran towards his car at the edge of the beach, where the Ghalia family were on the sand waiting for a taxi. Mr Asania said:

"There was an explosion maybe 500 metres away. Then there was a second, much closer, about two minutes later. People were running from the beach. Maybe two more minutes later there was a third shell. I could feel the pressure of the blast on my face, it was so strong. I saw pieces of people . . ."

Donald Macintyre reported (Independent, 11/6/06) that Huda's 15 year-old half-sister, Ilham

". . . was decapitated, and her 16 year-old half-brother Reham was so badly wounded that medics said both his arms had to be amputated.

"At the mourning tent for the family in Beit Lahia yesterday, Eyam Ghalia, 20, the only member of the beach party to escape uninjured, described how they heard two booms, apparently caused by shells or missiles.

"Mr Ghalia, quiet spoken and still looking dazed with shock and grief, said they had then used a mobile phone to call a taxi to take them home to safety. 'We started to walk to the place where the taxi would pick us up, and suddenly the missile landed in the middle of where we were', he said: '. . . My father was behind me and I saw his stomach cut open and the intestines hanging out'.

"Asked about the calls for revenge – chanted yesterday by some of the mourners at the funerals of his dead siblings – Mr Ghalia declared: '. . . I think it would be better if the Israelis and Palestinians came to peace and lived together. We have had enough'. . ."

Amen to that. Let each side heed the positive voices of their common people. To wind down and wipe out the decades of mutual fear and loathing, aggravation and weaponry. And on top of that, to recognise, embrace and sustain the other side's right to exist. To study war no more. To replenish and reap the earth's riches together, everyone on the same side, the side of continuous life over premature death.

Page 220

"A P M gives audience"

Just one month before the initial self-styled "Shock and Awe" bombardment of Baghdad, Tony Blair was received in the Vatican by Pope John Paul II, then one of the most outspoken opponents of a war to disarm Iraq.

In the Observer (23 February 2003, *'Blair in prickly meeting at the Vatican'*), Sophie Arie reported that –

"Blair and the 82-year-old leader of the world's one billion Roman Catholics have both used moral arguments to support their diametrically opposed positions on the need to attack Iraq. Analysts said Blair, under pressure this week from the Archbishops of Westminster and Canterbury calling for more time for weapons inspections in Iraq, saw the audience with the Pope as a chance to demonstrate his moral convictions.

"A Vatican statement after the meeting said the Pope *'reiterated the need for all parties to the Iraqi crisis to collaborate with the United Nations and use the resources offered by international law to avoid the tragedy of a war which according to many people is still avoidable'*. Blair made no official comment after the meeting. Downing Street's silence on the visit has outstripped even the Vatican, notorious for sealing its best secrets within the Vatican City."

Pages 226-227 *and* 229

"Should old assurances be forgot / – Nay, banished from your mind . . . . . . / / . . . . . . We'll take a cup of kindness yet / – and launch / Our Timeship Earth anew."

The italicised refrains in this Epilogue can be sung to the tune of Robert Burns's *'Auld Lang Syne'* (1788). This is a long established favourite 'all hands together' anthem reaffirming solidarity at the close of communal festivities across the UK, and is traditionally sung (along with *'The Red Flag'*) as the convivial farewell at Labour Party Conferences.

According to the *'Encyclopaedia Britannica'* (Vol 2, p663), Burns ". . . never claimed *'Auld Lang Syne'*, which he described simply as an old fragment he had discovered; but the song we have is almost certainly his, though the chorus, and probably the first stanza, are old . . ."

Page 227

"Letting each of us have what we need . . ."

When the (still) unelectable Karl Marx outlined his controversial Second Way (lately traduced by Free World guru Tony's vaguer, glossier, more saleable update), in *'Criticism of the Gotha Programme'* (1875), he made the (still) revolutionary proposition: *"From each according to his abilities, to each according to his needs".*

Marx adapted this from Michael Bakunin's declaration on behalf of 47 anarchists who were on trial in 1870 after the failure of their uprising at Lyons. Though the balanced phrasing could have been Blair's, the socially desirable sentiment could hardly be further from the practice, legislations and manifest mind-set of the once self-styled People's PM.

"One day you too will be down and out . . ."

"We'll fill our cups, running over yet . . ."

Cf Psalm 23 *('The Lord is my shepherd')*: "– thou anointest my head with oil; my cup runneth over".

Page 228

"Now Israelis and Arabs/ play music together/ like seeds in the pod / of their godliesst/ nature curled . . . "

See *'Parallels and Paradoxes: Explorations in Music and Society'* by Daniel Barenboim and the late Edward W Said (Blooomsbury 2003) – and listen to Barenboim's inspired and inspiring West-Eastern Divan Orchestra, as well as to the other supranational musical formations that abound. All power to their artistry.

Page 229

"You preached . . . // to sponsor/ and market/ world war . . ."

In the very first month of his first term as Prime Minister, Tony Blair made a speech declaring that: ". . . Mine is the first generation able to contemplate the possibility that *we may live our entire lives without going to war, or sending our children to war. That is a prize beyond value"*. Only six years later, he had ordered British troops into the service of no less than five wars, more than any previous Prime Minister since before World War II. Thousands and thousands of UK service personnel were in fact still fighting and dying daily in Iraq and Afghanistan an*other* four years on, and the consequence has been that on every one of those days still more terrorists and suicide bombers were born and made, and on every one of those days more and more innocent children, women and men were wounded and killed.

In Part 2 of his TV trilogy *'Blair: The Inside Story'*, broadcast on 27/2/2007, Michael Cockerell interviewed a number of Blair's sometime associates regarding this abrupt and extreme *volte face*, including Clare Short who remarked that ". . . Tony got the taste for war in Kosovo. It made him a heroic figure . . . It should never have been indicated that you won't go on the ground; that just prolongs the length of the resistance. It was Russia and France that brought it to an end. But Tony got lots of credibility and stature out of it".

The most troublesome of each of these deeply troublesome wars has been the one still raging in Iraq at the time of completing this book, for all that it had been officially declared Won by the Coalition only weeks after 'we' invaded. Britain's way into it reeked of bad faith from years before. For example, this is what Blair said many months before his sheeplike following of Bush on 20 March 2003 in bombing Baghdad with Shock and Awe: ". . . When I say that this is an issue that has to be dealt with, I mean it not because America thinks it's important. I think it's important. I think Britain thinks it's important, *or Britain SHOULD think it's important*, because it's a real issue. . ." – my italics, for you to note the sleight-of-mouth contradiction at the end there. – And to note how the robber-baron counterweight was about to commandeer its possible opponents' senses of what they might consider the more important of the two quite distinct, though would-be King Arthur Blair-blurred, alternatives.

As it turned out, on Saturday 15 February 2003, the biggest protest demonstrations the UK had ever known made it clear that two million-plus citizens thought it important *not* to invade Iraq. The Trevor McDonald Archive contains the remonstrations of a woman who pointed out to Blair at the time, ". . . You and Mr Bush are now going to bomb Iraq, and it's not dissimilar to what bin Laden and al-Qaeda did to America". Blair replied, ". . . Whenever you take military action, innocent people die as well as guilty ones. But sometimes you have to take that action if it's the only way of dealing with the threat that is there".

The trouble with this "Pre-emptive strike is the only way" was that several other ways *were* open, and indeed warranted to Blair, because virtually every available piece of evidence had proved by early 2003 that there was *no* threat of Weapons of Mass Destruction in the hands of Saddam Hussein. The multilateral failure to find any after such exhaustive trawling struck a chord with the late lamented Linda Smith, regarding her constant inability to find any scissors in her home. – But, as she trenchantly added, "I know that I do have some scissors there . . ."

Americans had been flying and spying all over Iraq for twelve years, and would have known full well that there could be precious little Iraqi resistance to invasion. It is unthinkable that the US – a world power more perpetually on security alert than perhaps any other in history – would have risked the extinction of 100,000 troops and such a vast array of weaponry at Saddam's palace gates, if they suspected that he might have had a single nuclear or other WMD to throw at them.

The Yanks deliberately dismantled Hans Blix's team of weapons inspectors in order to keep the smokescreen of possible WMDs as a would-be legal and pseudo-ideological cover for the US's own enterprise of massive destruction, occupation and control. Brits were offered the sop of ten-year contracts to drive lorries around Iraq soon after landing, so it was clearly never meant to be a quick operation. A divided and crippled Iraq suited the US neoconservative administration's oily ulterior motives to a toxic Texan tee.

What a pity this greed and superpower-mania blinded the so-called Coalition to the predictable resulting conversion of Iraq into the biggest homeland, breeding-ground and hunting-haven for terror on the planet.

In all of this, Blair stayed shoulder-to-shoulder with Dubbya, as both of them kept parroting. But if Blair had been truly convinced of the threat to Britain of WMDs from Iraq at 45 minutes' notice, was it not blatantly treasonable of him to offer up all those enlisted youngsters' probable instant collective slaughter, by so "passionately" consigning their bodies into the innermost jungle, lair and maw of the presumed most Massively Destructive beast on earth?

Let us hope that Tony Blair's successors in power take a leaf out of the not always so quoteworthy Jacques Chirac's book. Chirac told Blair, pre-Shock'n'Awe, that his personal experiences of serving in the Algerian war had taught him that war ". . . was a brutal thing, and that even though Saddam Hussein could be overthrown, *the subsequent consequences would be disastrous*: I believe that *war is always the worst solution* . . ." – As do a goodly quorum of those, worldwide, concerned about the survival of humanity.

Violence invariably breeds violence, and ordaining ever more and ever bigger weapons, and ever more and ever bigger arms deals, makes the inevitability of ever more lethal consequences ever more likely. Blair's mission, based on his assumption of unerring omniscience as to always knowing what is "The Right Thing To Do", has left him, and his interventionist war promotions, with countless entirely undeserved and premature deaths and destructions to answer for.

Whether he will in fact be called upon to do so is a sad but serious question, as regards what and how future generations may learn from all this – and one hopes, may understand things better, by and by. If so, that could indeed qualify as ". . . a prize beyond value".

See also *'Blair's Wars'* by John Kampfner (The Free Press 2003, updated paperback 2004).

". . . . For healing the nations . . ."

– cf the Revelation of St John (22,2): ". . . the leaves of the tree were for the healing of the nations"

Page 233

"THE ROAD FROM IRAQ ('Well Tone. You wanted to be like me')"

Gerald Scarfe conceived this vision of Bush leading Blair into an uncertain sunset after the suicide bombings that shattered London on 7 July 2005. Both men's backs are bloodied targets. It is the closing picture in Scarfe's *'Drawing Blood'* (Little, Brown 2005).

Blair's speech on 10 May 2007 at Trimdon Labour Club in his adopted County Durham constituency homeland was supposedly to announce the date of his eventual resignation as PM and Party Leader. It turned out to be as stage-managed, rhetorical and vainglorious as had become more and more the name of his game over the preceding decade. Its peroration coincided with the seemingly involuntary emergence of a solitary tear from one eye, though its perfect timing was a bit of a giveaway – and another nod perhaps, conscious or not, to Blur's abiding mentor Thatch, who had pulled the same would-be instant nostalgia-inducing trick at the most public moment of her long-deferred retirement. (See the note to *"Maggie/ quit her throne"* on page 311.)

The speech also made sure that its audience and media coverage would be comprehensively briefed with a re-run of Blair's Greatest Porkies, as the basis for his so long concocted "Legacy" bid. It's as though each Prime Ministerial decision and action had been planned, vetted and executed in terms of how well it would play in the annals of posterity.

The most scumbaggy-bogus boast of this corny blag was that Blair had ". . . *made Britain into a Leader, not a Follower".* As the Sedgwick goo-in was a one hundred percent *parti pris* party, there were no "WE VOTED BLAIR AND GOT DUBBYA"-type badges or banners on view to remind those who might have needed reminding that there have been few examples – if any – of more nonstop, abject, or fruitless subservience to a Leader in recorded history than the slavish Following, from 2001 to 2007, of President George W Bush by Prime Minister Anthony C L Blair.

Page 234

Civilian victims of 'War' in Haifa, July 2006

The London Israeli Embassy press office, who forwarded this photograph depicting a hospital in Haifa after one of the Hezbollah rocket attacks of late July '06, could not provide any further documentation on it. They advised me that if I emailed the Israeli Police the data would be emailed back – but unfortunately this organisation has not answered my query about it despite several requests and reminders.

Under the headline *'Hezbollah rocket attacks on Israel were war crimes'*, Patrick Cockburn reported from Beirut in the Independent (14 September 2006) that –

"Amnesty International has accused Lebanon's Hezbollah movement of committing war crimes by deliberately targeting Israeli civilians with its rockets. The 4,000 rockets it fired into Northern Israel during the recent war in Lebanon killed 43 civilians, seriously wounded 38 and forced hundreds of thousands of others to live in shelters. The Amnesty report is the latest review of the 34-day war, for which the winners and losers are still trying to justify their conduct and avoid blame. At least 1,000 Lebanese civilians died and whole villages were pulverised by Israeli bombs.

"The Israeli Prime Minister, Ehud Olmert, fighting for his political life after failing to eliminate Hezbollah, has played down Israeli losses. He bluntly told the Knesset foreign affairs and defence committee: *'Half Lebanon is destroyed. Is that a loss?'*

"Amnesty says Hezbollah fired 'some 900 inherently inaccurate Katyusha rockets into urban areas' and packed them with ball bearings lethal at 300 metres. This was out of a total of 3,970 rockets fired. Irene Khan, Amnesty International's Secretary General, said: 'The scale of Hezbollah's attacks on Israeli towns and villages, the indiscriminate nature of the weapons used, and statements from the leadership confirming their intent to target civilians, make it all too clear that Hezbollah violated the laws of war'.

"Hezbollah's leader, Hassan Nasrallah, said that shelling Northern Israel was in reprisal for the shelling of Lebanese civilians.

"In general terms Israel lost the war, which has left Hezbollah stronger and more confident. In Palestinian towns of the West Bank, Hezbollah DVDs showing Israeli tanks being destroyed are a hot seller."

Civilian victims of 'War' in Gaza, July 2006

This photograph depicts the bodies of a Palestinian mother, Asmaa Okal, aged 32, and her children Maria aged 5 months, and Shahed, 8 years old – all three killed by Israeli attacks on the evening of Wednesday 26 July 2006.

The Kuna News Details about the photograph were as follows:

"ISRAELI ATTACKS ON PALESTINIAN HOMES CONTINUE".

"GAZA, July 27 (KUNA) – Israeli attacks on Palestinian homes continued into the early hours of Thursday morning, killing civilians of ages ranging from 5 months to 70 years.

"Israeli tanks and F16 fighter jets have been firing at homes which, according to the Israeli military, are being used as weapon caches.

"A 70-year-old woman was killed Thursday in an attack by Israeli tanks on a Palestinian home that left several others of her family members wounded.

"The raids destroyed Jihad Al-Kahlout's home in Beit Lahiya, Northern Gaza. Medical sources said this attack left a number of Palestinians wounded. The casualties were taken to hospitals for treatment.

"Two air attacks targeted homes in Al-Shate camp in Gaza and another town in Beit Lahya. The two homes were empty at the time of the attack but were completely destroyed by the missiles.

"Last night, Asmaa Okal, 32, was killed when her home in Beit Lahya was destroyed. The attack also killed two of her children, Maria, 5 months, and Shahed, 8 years.

"A number of Palestinians reported during the past few days that they were being called by an anonymous number, claiming they are Israeli army personnel, telling them their home will be attacked within hours.

"An unspecified number of Israelis had been wounded by the missile attacks on Sderot. Medical sources have announced that 25 Palestinians have been killed during the past 24 hours in Gaza by Israeli fire. Over 70 people have been wounded in the attacks; some of them are in critical condition."

Page 235

Civilian victims of 'War' in Qana, Lebanon, April 1996

Jeff Huber, a retired US Navy Commander, posted on his weblog from Virginia Beach (*http://www.zenhuber.blogspot.com*) the following reminiscence of the disaster whose aftermath is depicted in this photograph:

"QANA: DEJA VU ALL OVER AGAIN

"By Benjamin Franklin's definition, '. . . *Insanity is doing the same thing over and over and expecting different results'.*

"Israeli shells hit a United Nations UNIFIL compound in the village of Qana, Lebanon, killing or wounding 230. Roughly 800 Lebanese civilians had taken refuge in the compound to escape the fighting between the Israeli Defence Force and Hezbollah. 106 of them were killed and roughly the same numbers injured. Robert Fisk was there, and wrote:

'It was a massacre . . . The Lebanese refugee women and children and men lay in heaps, their hands or arms or legs missing, beheaded or disemboweled. There were well over a hundred of them. A baby lay without a head. The Israeli shells had scythed through them as they lay in the United Nations shelter, believing that they were safe under the world's protection.

'. . . In front of a burning building of the UN's Fijian battalion headquarters, a girl held a corpse in her arms, the body of a grey-haired man whose eyes were staring at her, and she rocked the corpse back and forth in her arms, keening and weeping and crying the same words over and over: 'My father, my father'. A Fijian UN soldier stood amid a sea of bodies and, without saying a word, held aloft the body of a headless child. Israel's slaughter of civilians in this terrible ten-day offensive . . . has been so cavalier, so ferocious, that no Lebanese will forgive this massacre.'

"Israel immediately expressed regret for the incident, saying that Hezbollah rocket positions were the intended target, not the UN compound. Israel's Prime Minister said '– We did not know that several hundred people were concentrated in that camp. It came to us as a bitter surprise'.

"The IDF's chief of staff said, 'I don't see any mistake in judgment . . . We fought Hezbollah there [in Qana], and when they fire on us, we will fire at them to defend ourselves . . . I don't know any other rules of the game, either for the army or for civilians . . .' A U.S. State Department spokesman said, 'Hezbollah [is] using civilians as cover. That's a despicable thing to do, an evil thing'.

"Amnesty International later conducted an on-site investigation of the incident and concluded that '. . . The IDF intentionally attacked the UN compound, although the motives for doing so remain unclear. The IDF have failed to substantiate their claim that the attack was a mistake. Even if they were to do so they would still bear responsibility for killing so many civilians by taking the risk to launch an attack so close to the UN compound'.

"Human Rights Watch concurred: '. . . The decision of those who planned the attack to choose a mix of high-explosive artillery shells that included deadly anti-personnel shells designed to maximise injuries on the ground – and the sustained firing of such shells, without warning, in close proximity to a large concentration of civilians – violated a key principle of international humanitarian law'.

"Osama bin Laden, head of al-Qaeda, cited the Qana incident as a justification for his policy against the United States.

"This should all sound familiar to you, but not because it's something that happened last week. *What I've just described happened back in the spring of 1996.* And you should find it incredible that Olmert, Bush, Cheney, Bolton and the rest of the neocons think the results of a prolonged Israeli assault on Lebanon will turn out any better this time than they did a decade ago."

Civilian victims of 'War' in Qana, Lebanon, 30 July 2006

Sunday 30th July was the eighteenth day of Israel's summer 2006 campaign against Hezbollah in Lebanon. More than 750 Lebanese humans, mostly civilian, had been killed up to that day since Israel began its violent series of strikes in retaliation for Hezbollah's kidnapping of two soldiers. A total of 51 Israeli humans, 18 of them civilians, had been killed in Hezbollah counter-attacks over these seventeen days.

At about 1am on the Sunday a so-called precision-guided Israeli bomb smashed to smithereens an unremarkable residential building at the edge of Qana, a small village South-East of Tyre. Under the headline *'Fifty-six corpses were brought to hospital: thirty-four were children'*, Robert Fisk reported in the Independent (31/7/06 pp2-3) that –

". . . There was no doubt of the missile which killed all those children yesterday. It came from the United States, and upon a fragment of it was written: *'For use on MK-84 guided bomb BSU-37-B'*. No doubt the manufacturers can call it 'combat-proven' because it destroyed the entire three-storey house in which the Shalhoub and Hashim families lived. They had taken refuge in the basement from an enormous Israeli bombardment, and that is where most of them died."

This was the same kind of Israeli-American bomb, dropped from the air, that demolished a UN position in Khiyam just one week before and ended the lives of four UN observers. And Qana is the same village whose UN compound Israeli artillery had shelled indiscriminately ten years before – also in the name of confounding Hezbollah – killing more than 100 civilian Lebanese refugees sheltering there. And again more than half of these were children.

Fisk reported further:

". . . They wrote the names of the dead children on their plastic shrouds. 'Mehdi Hashemn, aged seven – Qana', was written in felt pen on the bag in which the little boy's body lay. 'Hussein al-Mohamed, aged 12 – Qana', 'Abbas al-Shalhoub, aged one – Qana'. And when the Lebanese soldier went to pick up Abbas's little body, it bounced on his shoulder as the boy might have done on his father's shoulder on Saturday. In all, there were 56 corpses brought to the Tyre government hospital and other surgeries, and 34 of them were children. When they ran out of plastic bags, they wrapped the small corpses in carpets. Their hair was matted with dust, most had blood running from their noses.

"You must have a heart of stone not to feel the outrage that those of us watching this experienced yesterday. This slaughter was an obscenity, an atrocity – yes, if the Israeli air force truly bombs with the 'pinpoint accuracy' it claims, this was also a war crime.

"Israel claimed that missiles had been fired by Hezbollah gunmen from the South Lebanese town of Qana – as if that justified this massacre. Israel's Prime Minister, Ehud Olmert, talked about 'Muslim terror' threatening 'Western Civilisation' – as if the Hezbollah had killed all these poor people.

"Israel later said it had no live-time pilotless photo-reconnaissance aircraft over the scene of that killing – a statement that turned out to be untrue when The Independent discovered videotape showing just such an aircraft over the burning camp. It was as if Qana – whose inhabitants claim that this was the village in which Jesus turned water into wine – has been damned by the world, doomed forever to receive tragedy."

Page 236

". . . it's a kinda plea/ What kinda world/ Dey going to leave fuh me?"
– from Grace Nichols's 'Baby-K Rap Rhyme' (– more of this poem is quoted on page 225)

Page 237

". . . mine in every land, / Mutual shall build Jerusalem, / Both heart in heart, and hand in hand . . ."
– from William Blake's 'Jerusalem' (1803-1820) I, 27

Back Cover Photograph of Camp Delta at Guantánamo Bay

Unaccountable US Military Prison receiving new inmates early in 2002. See the notes to *"Humiliation of unidentified political prisoners"* on pages 351-366.

Illustrations

Index of Artists' and Photographers' Works Reproduced

'THE SICK ROSE'

"O rose, thou art sick!
The invisible worm
That flies in the night
In the howling storm

Has found out thy bed
Of crimson joy,
And his dark secret love
Does thy life destroy."

— William Blake, from 'Songs of Experience' c. 1794

Acknowledgements

Excerpts from early drafts of this book appeared in *The Scotsman* (27/12/1997); *Gargoyle #39/40* (20th anniversary issue, London and Washington DC, 1997); the London *Evening Standard*; *The Independent* (13 March 1998); *'This is: The Poisoned Chalice'*, edited by Carol Cornish (1998); *The Jewish Quarterly #172* (Winter 1998/99); *Ape* ed Christian Pattison (Winter 1999); *'On a Camel to the Moon'* ed Valerie Bloom (Belitha Press/Chrysalis, 2001); *Connections: The Literary Scene in the South* (Autumn/Winter 2002, ed Jane Hardy); *The Rue Bella, Vol 9*, ed the Bird Brothers; *'Velocity: The Best Of Apples & Snakes'* ed Maja Prausnitz (Black Spring Press, 2003); *'Authors Take Sides on Iraq and The Gulf War'* ed Jean Moorcroft Wilson and Cecil Woolf (Cecil Woolf, 2004); *The Hill* (April 2005); *Tears in the Fence #41* (ed David Caddy, August 2005); *Saw #2* (ed Colin Shaddick, Autumn 2005); *CEN Magazine* (ed Korak Ghosh, June/July 2006); *Chimera #5* (ed Robert Cole and Susie Reynolds, Autumn 2006).

On 12 March 1998 I read a passage from the poem on BBC Radio 4's 'Today' programme; on 1 April 2000 another on Ned Sherrin's 'Loose Ends', on the same channel; plus yet another on 'Today' during an interview with John Humphrys about poetry and politics on 14 April 2005; and other excerpts on Radio 3's 'The Verb'.

I could not have completed this book without all sorts of help from many people and places, including: Simon Albury; Brian Aldiss; Tariq Ali; John Arden; Beryl Bainbridge; Jonathan Barker; Jeremy Barlow; Alfred and Selma Benjamin; Philip Black; Robin Blackburn and Verso Books; Terence Blacker; Margaret and Stephen Brearley; Pete Brown; Ellie Bruce; John Burrow; Robert Chalmers; Lis Charles; Tim Epps, Dudley Winterbottom, Penny Wools and others at Chelsea Arts Club; Tracy Chevalier; Jonathan Coe; the late William Cookson; Caroline Coon; Margaretta D'Arcy; Martin Davison; Robyn Denny; Sarah de Teliga; Polly Devlin; Jenny de Yong; Bea Deza; Tamara Dragadze; Drew & Co (Andrew Curtis, Charles Collier and Mark Johnson);

– also including: Carol Ann Duffy; Andrew Edmunds; Lydia Elias; Brian Eno; Jo Fairley; Karin Fernald; Miranda and Stephan Feuchtwang; Gerry Fialka; the late Alan Fletcher; the late Paul Foot; Peter Forbes; Juliette Foy; Camilla and Jonathan at Gallery 286, Earls Court Road; Brian Gascoigne; Juno Gemes; Mel and Rhiannon Gooding; Nestor and Robert Grace; David Graves; Linus Gruszewski; Marcelle Hanselaar; Michele Hanson; Pamela Hardyment; Colin and Sarah Harris; Henry and Tanya Harrod; Ronni and Spike Hawkins; Mark Haworth-Booth; John Hegley; Caroline Herbert; Sheila Hayman; Martin Horovitz; Patrick Hughes; Eve Jackson; Howard Jacobson; Zoë Jenny; Allen Jones; Tim Emlyn Jones; Alexandra Kent; Troy Kennedy-Martin; Michael Kustow; Inge Elsa Laird; Jean-Pierre Langellier; David Larcher; James LeFanu; Mike Leigh; Quentin Letts; Pauline Lisowska; Ann and Beric Livingstone; Dinah Livingstone;

– and also: Christopher Logue; John McEwen; Roger McGough; Hugh Mulseed and James Smith at the Book Trust; Lucinda Mellor; John Michell; Barry Miles; Adrian and Celia Mitchell; Jane Monson; all at the Movement for a Socialist Future; Gillie Mussett; Karyl Nairn; Greg Neale; Richard Neville; Helen Nicholson; Philip Norman; Michael Nyman; John O'Donnell; all at Ottolenghi, Ledbury Road; Eski Palmer; Molly Parkin;

– and also: Ian Patterson; Tom Payne; John Pilger; Harold Pinter; all at the Poetry Library, Royal Festival Hall; Valentina Polukhina; Helen Pyke; Andrew and Juliet Quicke; the late Kathleen Raine; Sheila Ramage and Notting Hill Books; Andrew Rawnsley; Jill Richards; Jeremy Robson; Su Rose; Sara-Jane Rossi; Julian Rothenstein, Hiang Kee and the Redstone Press; Geoffrey Roughton; John Rowley; Ron Rubin; Victor Schonfield; Diana Schumacher; Akiko and Henry Scott-Stokes; Brian and Elinore Shaffer;

– and also: Christine Shuttleworth; Jenny Skilbeck; Anthony Smith; Madeline Solomon; Ralph Steadman; Dave Stevens; Tom Stoppard; the late Joe Strummer; Bill Swainson; Susie Symes; Susannah Tarbush; Jenny Todd; Caryl Topolski; Jenny Towndrow; Lutz Unterseher; Ruth Vaughn; the late Ingrid von Essen; Daniel Weissbort; the late John Willett; Suzy Williams; Marcus Williamson; Barry Winkleman; Ann Wolff; Lucy Wright; Duncan Wu; Diana Wynne Jones; Emily Young, and Caroline Younger.

Apologies to anyone I've temporarily forgotten.

Special thanks are also due to Satpaul Bhamra; Tim Street, Chris Wrigley, and others at the Campaign Against Arms Trade; Nick Hiley, Jane Newton, and their Centre For The Study of Cartoons and Caricature at the University of Kent in Canterbury; Dave 'Toff' Holland; Adam and Auguste Horovitz; Michael Gillard, Hilary Lowinger, Adam Macqueen, Tim Minogue, Tony Rushton, Bridget Tisdall, Francis Wheen and others at Private Eye; Joe Paice; Dave Russell; Ian Smith; and James Wilkes.

And equally special thanks are extended to each artist, photographer, cartoonist and writer, living and dead, whose work is reproduced in this book – and to their editors, publishers, executors, managers and agents.

Specifically: –

to LEWIS ALLAN (Abel Meeropol), for the excerpt from *'Strange Fruit'*, © Warner Chappell Music Ltd (Edward B Marks Music), and Music Sales Ltd;

to MAYA ANGELOU, for the excerpt from *'The Heart of a Woman'* (Random House, USA 1981, Virago, UK 1986);

to W H AUDEN, for the lines from *'The Cave of Making (in memoriam Louis MacNeice)'*, from *'Collected Poems'*, edited by Edward Mendelson (Faber and Faber 1976);

to STEPHEN BAYLEY, for the excerpts from *'Labour Camp: The Failure of Style over Substance'* (Batsford, 1998);

to LAURENCE BINYON, for the quatrain from *'For the Fallen (September 1914)'* in *'Collected Poems'* (Macmillan & Co 1931);

to BILLY BRAGG, for the excerpt from his adaptation for contemporary Britain of Woody Guthrie's *'This Land is Your Land'*;

to BASIL BUNTING, for *'What the Chairman Told Tom'* in *'Collected Poems'* (Fulcrum Press 1968) and in *'The Complete Poems'* (Oxford University Press 1994);

to PAUL CELAN, for the excerpts from *'Death Fugue'*, translated by Michael Hamburger, in *'Poems of Paul Celan'* (Anvil Press Poetry 1988, and Penguin Books 1990);

to JENI COUZYN, for lines from *'The Message'*, in New Departures #15 (1983) and in *'Life by Drowning'* (Bloodaxe Books 1985); revised version in *'A Time to be Born'* (Firelizard 1999);

to W H DAVIES, for *'Leisure'*, in *'Songs of Joy and Others'* (Fifield 1911 – © Jonathan Cape);

to FELIX DENNIS, for *'Rules of Success'* and *'Craft'* in *'A Glass Half Full'*(Hutchinson 2003);

to BOB DYLAN, for the excerpts from *'With God On Our Side'*, recorded by Dylan on *'The Times They Are A-Changing'* (Columbia Records 1964), © M Witmark & Sons); and from *'It's All Right Ma (I'm only Bleeding)'*, © Warner Brothers Inc, in *'Lyrics 1962-1985'* (Jonathan Cape 1986), recorded by Dylan on *'Bringing it All Back Home'* (CBS 1965);

to T S ELIOT, for the excerpts from *'The Love Song of J Alfred Prufrock'*, *'The Waste Land'*, and Choruses from *'The Rock'*, in *'Collected Poems 1909-1935'* (Faber and Faber 1936);

to ALLEN GINSBERG, for the excerpts from *'Howl'* and *'Death to Van Gogh's Ear!'*, in *'Howl and Other Poems'* (City Lights 1956), and from *'Who Be Kind To'*, in *'Wholly Communion'* (– anthology, film, video and dvd, Lorrimer Films 1965, and Hathor Films 2006); in *'Planet News'* (City Lights 1968); and in *'Collected Poems 1947-1980'* (Viking 1985);

to WOODY GUTHRIE, for the excerpt from *'This Land is Your Land'* (originally *'God Blessed America'*), © Ludlow Music Inc and Woody Guthrie Publications Inc;

to SPIKE HAWKINS, for *'Dear Mr Bush'*, in *'The POT! (Poetry Olympics Twenty05) Anthology'* (New Departures 2005);

to GEOFFREY HILL, for the excerpt from *'The Triumph of Love'* (Penguin Books 1999);

to ADAM HOROVITZ, for *'They Sit in Darkness'*, in *'Next Year in Jerusalem'* (HooHah Press, 2004);

to FRANCES HOROVITZ, for *'London Summer'*, in *'The High Tower'* (New Departures #6, 1970) and in *'Collected Poems'* (Bloodaxe Books in association with the Enitharmon Press, edited by Roger Garfitt, 1985);

to MAHMOOD JAMAL, for some of *'What's It All About?'*, in *'Sugar-Coated Pill: Selected Poems'* (Word Power Books, Edinburgh 2006);

to RUDYARD KIPLING, for the closing verses of *'The Craftsman'* (1894), in *'Rudyard Kipling: The Complete Verse'* (Kyle Cathie 1990);

to D H LAWRENCE, for *'Poor Young Things'*, *'WHY – ?'*, and for the excerpts from *'All That We Have is Life'* and *'Work'*, in *'The Complete Poems of D H Lawrence'* (Penguin Books 1994);

to JOHN LENNON, for the excerpt from *'Imagine'*, in *'The Lyrics of John Lennon'* (Omnibus Press 1997) – recorded by him on Parlophone singles in 1968, and on the eponymous Apple Sapcor album released in 1971;

to PRIMO LEVI, for the lines from *'Shemà'*, in *'Collected Poems'*, translated by Ruth Feldman and Brian Swann (Faber and Faber 1988);

to EMANUEL LITVINOFF, for *'To T S Eliot'*, in *'Notes for a Survivor'* (Northern House 1973);

to STACY MAKISHI, for lines from *'SPAM'*, in *'The POT! (Poetry Olympics Twenty05) Anthology'* (New Departures 2005);

to ADRIAN MITCHELL, for the excerpt from *'Quite Apart from the Holy Ghost'* in *'Heart on the Left: Poems 1953-1984'* (Bloodaxe Books 1997);

to NIK MORGAN, for *'Cannon Fodder'* and *'Burial'*, in *'Grandchildren of Albion: Voices and Visions of Younger Poets in Britain'* (New Departures 1992);

to GRACE NICHOLS, for the excerpts from *'Baby-K Rap Rhyme'*, in *'No Hickory No Dickory No Dock'* (Viking 1991); in the anthology *'Grandchildren of Albion: Voices and Visions of Younger Poets in Britain'* (New Departures 1992); and – chanted by Grace herself, with audible baby participation – on *'Grandchildren of Albion Live'* (on cassette and CD – NDC 23, New Departures 1994, and NDCD 24, New Departures 1996);

to JOHN OSBORNE, for the excerpt from *'Look Back in Anger'* (Faber and Faber 1957);

to TOM PAULIN, for the excerpts from *'Marc Chagall,* Over the Town' in *'The Wind Dog'* (Faber and Faber 1999);

to EZRA POUND, for the excerpts from *'Hugh Selwyn Mauberley'* (Faber 1920); *'An ABC of Reading'* (Faber 1934); and *'The Pisan Cantos'* (Faber 1948);

to KAZUKO SHIRAISHI, for the lines from *'Little Planet Blues'*, translated by Allen Ginsberg, in *'Little Planet and other Poems'* (Shichigatsudo, Tokyo, 1994), and in *'The POW! (Poetry Olympics Weekend) Anthology'* (New Departures 1996);

to MURRAY LACHLAN YOUNG, for the excerpts from *'The Lover's Dream'*, *'Simply Everyone's Taking Cocaine'* and *'Designer Labels'*, in *'Casual Sex and Other Verses'* (Transworld Publishers 1997).

Michael Horovitz and New Departures have made every effort to trace copyright holders for all the texts quoted and images reproduced in this book, but in a few cases we may not have given complete details. We would be keen to rectify any such instance, should we manage a second or revised edition.

Andrew Jackson (US president 1829-1837) perceived that
"All wars are judged by the quality of the peace that they help to create"